The European Economy

Edited by
DAVID A DYKER

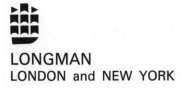

LONGMAN
LONDON and NEW YORK

Longman Group Limited,
Longman House, Burnt Mill,
Harlow, Essex CM20 2JE, England
and Associated Companies throughout the world.

Published in the United States of America
by Longman Publishing, New York.

© Longman Group UK Limited 1992.

First published 1992.
Third impression 1995

ISBN 0582-059194 CSD
ISBN 0582-05883X PPR

British Library Cataloguing-in-Publication Data

A catalogue record for this book is
available from the British Library.

Library of Congress Cataloging in Publication Data

The European economy / edited by David A. Dyker.
   p. cm.
  ISBN 0–582–05919–4 (v. 1: cased). – ISBN 0–582–05883–X (v. 1:
pbk.)
   1. European Economic Community. 2. Europe–Economic integration.
  3. European Economic Community countries–Economic conditions
HC241.2.E8573 1992
330.94–dc20   92–10139
                                       CIP

Set by 8 in 10/12.5 Times
Produced by Longman Singapore Publishers (Pte) Ltd.
Printed in Singapore

The European Economy

This book is to be returned on or before
the last date stamped below.

AUTHOR DYKER, David. Editor

TITLE The European Economy

330.94 DYK

RO4963

Date	Name
26/11/01	Daniele Reder UVI2
30/10/03	Delger Enkhbayar LVI

Contents

Preface

The origins of this work, and its companion volume *The National Economies of Europe*, go back to 1988 and a series of discussions between myself and Christopher Harrison of Longman and Professor Michael Sumner of the University of Sussex. That the works have come to fruition is at least as much a tribute to their vision and encouragement as to any efforts on my own part. Much has changed in Europe since 1988, and while this has highlighted the interest and importance of the subject matter, it has created its own species of editorial difficulty, as conscientious authors have sought to keep abreast of developments. To the extent that, in the end, events have still managed to get the better of us, we ask merely to be judged by the degree to which we have succeeded in catching the essence, and the issues, of a uniquely exciting time in European economic (and political) history.

The collective of authors of *The European Economy* and *The National Economies of Europe* is drawn largely from the University of Sussex – not just from the teaching staff of the Economics Subject Group, but also from the Geography Subject Group and from associated institutions – the Science Policy Research Unit and the Institute of Development Studies. Beyond that we have called on old friends, former colleagues and former students to make their own unique contributions. On the basis of these two volumes, then, the reader can judge the role of the University of Sussex, and of the 'Sussex connection', in the development of contemporary European studies. Finally I must thank Leila Burrell-Davis of the University of Sussex Computing Service, without whose skill in translating computer files of all shapes and sizes into a common format the task of editing would have been simply impossible.

David A Dyker
School of European Studies, University of Sussex
February, 1992

Acknowledgements

The publishers are grateful to the following for permission to reproduce copyright material:

The Financial Times for table 15.5; The National Institute of Economic and Social Research for table 12.13; The Organisation for Economic Cooperation and Development for figures 2.2–2.15c, 2.18b, 2.19 and tables 8.3, 11.1, 11.2, 12.2, 12.3 and 12.7; table 9.2, reproduced from Benko, G. and Dunford, M.: *Industrial Change and Regional Development*, Belhaven Press, London, 1991; tables 12.4, 12.5, 12.6, 12.8, 12.10 and 12.11 reproduced from Freeman, C., Sharp, M.L. and Walker, W.B: *Technology and the Future of Europe*, Pinter Publishers Ltd, London, 1991. All rights reserved.

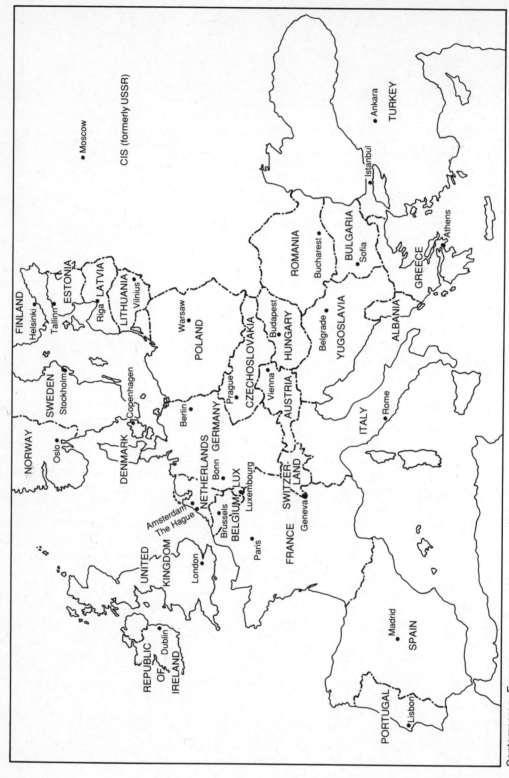

Contemporary Europe

CHAPTER 1

Introduction: the issues of European economic development

DAVID A DYKER*

Among all the high GNP per capita regions of the world, Europe is unique. In cultural and historical terms, it is extraordinarily hetergeneous, boasting some fifty major nationalities (not all of which enjoy separate statehood) and nearly as many major languages. European economic development has, therefore, proceeded in the face of, and as a constant challenge to, a whole range of cultural and linguistic barriers. It is a tribute to the strength of that developmental impetus, as well as to the small size of the typical European state and the comparative poverty of Europe in raw materials, that the economies of the continent characteristically trade a much higher proportion of their GNP than the countries of any comparable region. The contrast between all this and the richly endowed, super-state/melting-pot image of the United States is total. The point is still valid, if less comprehensively so, when we compare Europe with the countries of the Pacific Rim.

But Europe's heterogeneity does not stop there. For nearly half a century following the conclusion of the Second World War in 1945, Europe was cut in half by the bipolar politics of the East–West confrontation. While the term 'Iron Curtain' may seem now like a piece of quaint Cold War rhetoric, it is a fact that normal human and commercial intercourse between Western and Eastern Europe was for several decades severely hampered, if not totally excluded, by a bizarre collection of walls and barbed-wire fences. Behind the walls and barbed wire, East European countries, all under communist one-party rule and mostly under some degree of domination from Moscow, followed the model of the planned, socialist economy, which excluded large-scale private ownership of assets on principle, and excluded normal trading relations with other countries (including other socialist countries) in practice. Some of the socialist countries, notably Yugoslavia and Hungary, reintroduced substantial elements of the market into their socialist systems from an early date. But neither the centralised nor decentralised model of East European socialism was able to survive the economic and political challenges of the late 1980s and early 1990s; by 1992 there was hardly a state or proto-state in Eastern Europe that still referred to its (ideal) economic system as socialist.

* The author gratefully acknowledges the help of Peter Holmes and Michael Sumner in the writing of this introduction.

But the East European revolution of 1989 and its aftermath, in removing many of the artificial barriers and politically imposed differences that had separated East and West, served only to bring into sharper relief the deep-seated underlying contrasts between the two major regions of the continent. In systemic terms, the East European countries continue, willy-nilly, to display a markedly 'state capitalist' profile, with the public sector totally dominant within industry, and likely to remain so at least for the next five or ten years. 'Shock therapy' has proved effective enough in re-establishing short-term macroeconomic stability, but has at best (the case of Poland) left fundamental restructuring problems unresolved, even exacerbated, thus building but a weak foundation for the extension of macroeconomic stability into the medium term. In the worst case (that of Yugoslavia) it has been torpedoed by the outbreak of regional conflict escalating into civil war. In more immediate terms, the priorities and circumstances of restructuring have produced sharp falls in levels of national income and real personal incomes everywhere in Eastern Europe, greatly reinforcing an East–West gap which was already substantial before the collapse of communism in the region.

Of course variations in economic system and level of economic performance are equally, if less dramatically, visible within 'rich' Western Europe. Two of the twelve full members of the European Community – Portugal and Greece – have levels of GNP per head of much less than half the EC average; another two – Spain and Ireland – report levels of GNP per head only a little above half of that average. Differences in levels of development between major regions have been a persistent problem in a number of West European states, notably Italy and Spain. But it is on the systemic dimension that intra-West European contrasts have been most clearly marked. While nearly all the West European economies have state sectors which are large by North American or Japanese standards, there are deep and abiding differences in style and approach to economic policy-making, whether for private or public sector, among the major West European countries. It has in the past often been the politically more conservative governments of France, Italy and Spain that have emphasised most strongly the role of the 'state as entrepreneur'. In archetypally social-democratic Sweden, by contrast, the role of the state in relation to everything that affects the citizen directly – wages, welfare, etc – has been as dominant as its role in relation to the *running* of industry has been low-key. We can talk of a degree of Europe-wide Keynesian consensus on macroeconomic policy-making in the period up to 1974, but even here West Germany stands out as a country which has consistently performed best of all on macroeconomic stability, on the basis of a conservative and very simple approach to monetary policy. On both macro- and micro-levels British economic policy in the 1960s and 1970s seemed to go some way towards institutionalising that most pernicious of East European characteristics – the 'soft budget constraint'.

Yet while the differences within Western Europe are plain for all to see, the *tendency* to convergence is just as obvious. The dominant policy themes of the 1980s – the fight against inflation, deregulation, privatisation, etc. – have been equally the major preoccupations of nominally socialist governments in Paris as of Thatcherite ones in London. There has been a palpable tendency for all the EC countries to move towards the West German model of the social market economy and the West German style of macroeconomic management. Most important of all, the history of European integration, from the Treaty of Paris and the Treaty of Rome to the agreement in principle on the creation of the European Union in 1991, has, for all its hesitations and false steps, been a uniquely successful story of supranational economic policy co-ordination. The prospect that by the year 2000 the EC *may* encompass a single market, with a single currency and a single citizenship for some 400 million people, provides a counterpoint to the theme of heterogeneity, and a challenge to the great national economies of North America and the Far East, such as would have seemed quite inconceivable even a couple of decades ago.

While the theme of integration becomes ever more dominant in Western Europe, however, we find in the 'new' Eastern Europe an equally powerful theme of disintegration and fragmentation. In 1990 the CMEA (Council for Mutual Economic Assistance – Comecon) collapsed, ending a period of some thirty-five years of Soviet-dominated bilateralism in Eastern Europe. From now on settlements within the region would be on a hard-currency, multilateral basis. But while the principle of multilateralism seemed an irreproachable development, the practice that evolved through 1991 was full of disturbing features. A combination of lack of trust between the countries of Eastern Europe, fed partly by historical rivalries and conflicts, and an extreme shortage of hard currency intensified by debt service commitments to the West, was enough to send the volume of trade within the region plummeting at a time when the rigours of domestic restructuring were already having a big negative impact on production and welfare levels. The dramatic events of 1991 in Yugoslavia, culminating in the outbreak of a full-scale civil conflict, tended perhaps to divert attention from the underlying force of republic-level economic autarkism which had already taken deep root, particularly in Serbia. In the case of the Soviet Union, now a name of purely historical significance, the political drama of the break-up of the USSR was highlighted by the failure to achieve a workable agreement on economic union within Soviet economic space. In the meantime, against the background of the breakdown in the old union-level institutions and the collapse of the rouble, regional authorities, by late 1991 with the new status of 'independent states', were increasingly retreating into local fortress economies, mediated by a certain amount of crude barter.

Paradoxically, these themes of integration and disintegration had come by late 1991 to intertwine closely. As countries and republics freed themselves from the suffocating inheritance of Soviet communism, their integrationist aspirations, strong enough in themselves, focused sharply on the West, and in particular on the EC. Those aspirations were crowned in December 1991, for Poland, Czechoslovakia and Hungary, by the signing of a series of bilateral association agreements with the EC which laid out a path calculated to culminate in free trade within ten years. But these agreements highlighted the difficulties as well as the hopes engendered by this westwards integrationist orientation. In a Europe where countries have, in the post-war period, grown prosperous by trading with their neighbours, how will Poland, for example, fare if it trades only with Germany, and not with Lithuania, Byelorussia, Russia, the Ukraine and Czechoslovakia? The need for some kind of liquidity support mechanism to provide a minimal 'float' for intra-regional trade within Eastern Europe, in the context of an extreme shortage of hard currency throughout the region, seemed at least as urgent a consideration for the European Commission and West European governments at the end of 1991 as association *per se*. That urgency was not lessened by the knowledge that purely technical liquidity measures might in themselves be insufficient to break down the political and psychological barriers to the emergence of a new division of labour within Eastern Europe.

But the association agreements of December 1991 raised another complex of issues which take us well beyond the boundaries of Europe itself. The immediate value of the agreements to the three East-Central European countries was limited by the appending of special protocols covering the 'sensitive' areas of food, steel and textiles. Thus while the principle of free trade has been proclaimed, the governments in Warsaw, Prague and Budapest have been informed that that principle will not, at least for the time being, be put into practice in relation to precisely those sectors where the planned economies in transition (PETs) might be thought, on the basis of a consideration of the pattern of comparative advantage, to have a real chance of conquering hard-currency export markets. It is perhaps not surprising that West European governments, faced with chronic problems of long-term unemployment, should be anxious to protect employment in low-tech and traditional industries, especially when they are regionally highly concentrated, and should seek to do so through a complex of formal protectionist measures, 'voluntary' export restraints and murky customs procedures imposed, in some combination, on every region of the trading world. It is at the same time outrightly contradictory that a community dedicated to the development of free trade should take such an illiberal stance *vis-à-vis* the natural economic strengths of other regions.

The contradiction does, of course, go beyond the injury inflicted on non-EC trading partners or potential partners. Non-tariff barriers in particular are shown to be *particularly* injurious to the interests of the citizens *qua* consumers of the EC itself. Protection of essentially uncompetitive industries, whatever form it takes, deprives a country or region of the full benefit of its own economic strengths, distorting resource allocation and hindering the full exploitation of new technological possibilities. That is not to say that high-income countries are constrained to conform to a uniformly capital- and high-tech-intensive production profile if they are to maximise national income. On the contrary, as the examples of Italian textiles, leather goods, footwear and furniture demonstrate, there are plenty of opportunities for national economies to do well producing the 'wrong' things. The point is rather that free trade outside as well as inside the Community is the only sure way of ascertaining whether a particular sector is really as strong as it looks. The completion of the single market promises a narrowing of the scope for the imposition of non-tariff barriers. But it does not promise to get rid of them, and says very little at all about the Common Agricultural Policy (CAP). The issue of EC trade policy *vis-à-vis* the rest of Europe and the rest of the world will surely remain a burning one in the years after 1992.

The West European record on efficiency of resource allocation seems, then, to have been a mixed one. The EC has done perhaps surprising well on the internal market, but not so well in its global trading posture. Can we find further evidence from the detailed chapters of this volume and its companion volume *The National Economies of Europe* to flesh out this provisional assessment of the efficiency record, and to extend it into the dimension of dynamic efficiency?

It is perhaps useful to start the inquiry beyond the boundaries of the EC, in Eastern Europe. Up to the 1960s most of the countries of that region seemed to present striking confirmation of the effectiveness of central planning as an engine of growth. For all the manifold and much publicised weaknesses of central planning in relation to short-term microeconomic efficiency, the system appeared to work very well as a vehicle for *extensive development*, producing a powerful industrialisation impetus, in the main through mobilisation of cheap labour and energy resources. Productivity trends were mediocre and wastefulness widespread, but the system was at least effective in implementing the goals of communist governments in terms of the growth of output, *as measured by criteria which admittedly often bore but a tenuous relationship to any concept of human welfare*.

It was against the background of the changes in resource availability in Eastern Europe, as the scope for rural–urban migration narrowed and the female participation rate reached its upper limit, and as energy became more expensive in terms of extraction costs in the Soviet Union and subsequently in terms of the world price of oil, that the debate about economic reform as an instrument for implementing a gear-change to *intensive development* came to dominate the agenda of the communist governments of the region, not excluding the more conservative ones. Behind this debate lay a plausible generalisation not inconsistent with much of standard Western development theory – that processes of industrialisation quite naturally have two stages – an early stage of extensive development, as fallow resources are mobilised, and a second stage of intensive development, as technological change in the broadest sense comes to be the dominant source of economic growth. Socialist planning on the Soviet model had been able to speed up the first stage. It stood to reason in terms of Marxist-Leninist ideology that the political commitment to continued progress towards 'full communism' would require – and deliver – thoroughgoing systemic change as that first stage come to its logical conclusion.

It is clear, with the benefit of hindsight, that for all its economic and ideological plausibility this line was little more than a convenient political rationalisation. The communist systems of Eastern Europe, including the market socialist ones of Yugoslavia and Hungary, showed themselves to be totally incapable of evolving new institutions and practices such as might have given productivity trends a fresh impetus. Indeed the period of the great debate about intensive development was marked by deterioration rather than improvement in productivity trends. It became clear that Soviet-style planning, even in much modified forms, could *only* generate growth on an extensive basis, whether the conditions were appropriate or not. It became equally clear that much of the reported growth of the extensive development period represented growth in sectors which were either of purely military significance, or were hopelessly hostile to the environment and/or obsolete in their technologies. By the time the debate about the future of socialism had turned into a debate about the restoration of capitalism, it was obvious that the 'triumphs' of extensive development would in the main be obstacles rather than bridges to any intensification of the economies in question.

It is not possible to make direct comparisons between Eastern and Western Europe in this regard, because most of Western Europe was in 1945 already much more developed economically than most of Eastern Europe. There is, certainly, a sense in which the post-war economic miracle in Western Europe was based on cheap labour, including female and immigrant labour, and cheap oil. It is equally striking that post-war economic development in France, one of the least industrialised of the West

European countries with one the biggest shares of the working population still in agriculture in 1945, has been very largely based on productivity growth. Again, while the post-1974 period in the West has certainly been one of rapid technological and structural change, and of comparatively rapid productivity growth, it has also been marked by extremely high levels of unemployment. Thus the scope for extensive development in the West since the early 1970s has in fact been very considerable. The fact that that scope has not been fully exploited may to a degree be explicable in terms of policy errors on the part of governments. Beyond that, it seems to reflect, in particular, a pattern of technological change which makes few calls on unskilled labour. If the demand for labour comes through more and more in the form of demands for personnel with very specific skill and training profiles, then we may question how useful it is to seek to identify development patterns in terms of an aggregated L. If the answer to the question is negative, then the whole conceptual basis of the distinction betwen extensive and intensive sources of development is undermined.

What *is* clear from the West European record – and indeed from that of Eastern Europe as well in a negative sense – is that productivity trends are nearly always the best indicator of overall medium-to-long-term growth trends. To the extent that West Europe has done well since the Second World War it has done so through a sustained increase in total productivity. Countries like the UK which lagged behind systematically on growth in the period to 1975 also turn out to have poor productivity records over the same period. Equally significantly, the British revival in the 1980s was to a great extent based on a 'productivity miracle'. Patterns of productivity gain have in turn reflected a great diversity of factors, with technology in the narrow sense only one of the most important. Both British and Swedish cases testify, in their opposite ways, to the key role which socio-political factors can play in this regard. But if productivity is the key to sustained growth, then perhaps we should simply conclude that intensive development is the *only* kind of real development. We can make the point in a slightly different way if we observe that it was not the priority on industry *as such* that was wrong with the Soviet approach, it was rather the priority on the wrong kinds of industry. The Western experience demonstrates forcibly that, however much growth may have been concentrated in services sectors in recent decades, it is industry that remains the basis of international competitiveness, and of productivity dynamism, including in those services sectors. But the decisions that have formed the basis of that competitiveness, that productivity impetus, have been taken largely on the basis of an assessment of profitability, not obedience to some grand strategy of economic development imposed from above.

If the growth of the past has come largely from productivity gains, what about the growth of the future? We can read from the history of industrial front-runners, European and non-European alike, that strong productivity performance is nearly always reflected in a high level of competitiveness on international markets – indeed this is merely to reiterate, from a different angle, the point of the last paragraph. It is particularly noteworthy that of the three chapters of this book that concentrate on key industrial sectors accounting for large proportions of European output, with good prospects for the future in terms of the pattern of demand and built on significant European technological leads from the past – chemicals, electronics and motor vehicles – the latter two highlight key competitive weaknesses, including technological weaknesses, while the first stresses the critical importance of facing up to the competitive challenges to the European industry that the world economy will undoubtedly present in the 1990s. It is clear, to return to an earlier theme, that it will be difficult for Europe to concentrate on the reinforcement and development of comparative advantage if she continues to devote substantial resources and substantial attention to the preservation of declining sectors. Quite apart from matters of trade policy narrowly defined, the Commission of the European Communities will find itself after 1992 under increasing pressure to resolve highly sensitive issues – for example, should the EC extend the coverage of its technology-support initiatives, which feature particularly strongly in the electronics industry, to US and Japanese firms based within the EC? There must be many European policy-makers who scorn the notion of Fortress Europe, but who would nevertheless baulk at such a move.

To say that the European economy will still face serious problems after 1992 is, of course, simply to restate the implications of participation in a dynamic world system. The capacity of the EC to resolve these problems has, certainly, been enhanced by the refinement of its collective problem-solving apparatus, particularly in connection with the revival of the practice of majority voting on a range of important policy headings within the Council of Ministers. The developments of the 1980s have in particular highlighted the dimensions of *credibility* and *trust* within the dynamic of the integration process, and the increasing commitment to conduct calculated to consolidate rather than strain the system. To take one rather technical example, the essential rationale for membership of the ERM for any country apart from Germany must be understood in terms of the possibility thus afforded of drawing on the credibility of the Bundesbank, the German central bank, as a bulwark against inflation. But as Michael Sumner shows in his chapter in *The European Economy* on monetary integration, the accretion of credibility is a slow business, for the trust of others, and in particular of the money markets, does not come with the mere publication of a policy goal. The failure of early attempts to progress towards monetary union demonstrates, indeed, that the declaration of ambitious objectives, even in conjunction with the creation of new institutions like the Snake, can achieve nothing unless the participants behave consistently, that is in a way conducive to the development of mutual trust. The frequency of exchange rate realignments during the first few years of the ERM confirms how difficult it is to create a 'zone of monetary stability'. But from 1983, as exchange rate changes came increasingly to be viewed as a matter of *common* rather than national concern in the spirit of the Treaty of Rome, the ERM began to show results. What this meant in practice was that the frequency of significant realignments was substantially reduced. To take the case of The Netherlands, the country perhaps most heavily committed to the accretion of credibility, there has been no change in the bilateral guilder–deutschmark rate since 1983. In entering the ERM on the understanding that exchange-rate adjustments are permissible, then, a given country bent on extracting maximum benefit from membership in fact puts itself under the obligation largely to eschew such adjustments.

A similar story can be told in relation to the wider drama of the implementation of the Single European Act. As Peter Holmes shows in his chapter in *The European Economy* on the political economy of European integration, the adoption of the Single European Act and implementation of the 1992 programme would have been inconceivable without a degree of something akin to self-hypnosis. Had the signatories of the Single European Act not in effect committed themselves implicitly to a good deal more than they were committing themselves to explicitly, it is doubtful whether the dynamic policy impetus which is the essence of 1992 would ever have got going. The fact that the UK government, in particular, is manifestly unhappy about all this must surely reflect some basic lack of trust of the Commission, and indeed of the whole EC structure, on the part of that government. The fact that the other EC governments take a much more positive view surely reflects a sense of mutually reinforcing accretion of credibility at Commission *and* national government level.

It is instructive to extend this mode of analysis to the very different conditions of Eastern Europe. One of the most striking aspects of the Yugoslav civil war of 1991 was the total ineffectuality of one cease-fire after another. The reasons for this certainly lay partly in the fragmented nature of the war itself, with no single line of command on either side which could be relied upon to have the capacity to 'deliver' a cease-fire. There was also manifestly an element of bad faith. Military leaders seemed content repeatedly to promise much *more* than they were in reality prepared to deliver.

But the Yugoslav civil war, the reader may say, has nothing to do with the articulation of economic policy. In fact, perusal of the chapter on Yugoslavia in *The National Economies of Europe* will confirm that this same element of bad faith, this same practice of signing cheques knowing that they would 'bounce', was a key element in the degeneration of the economic policy mechanism which presaged the violent break-up of the old Yugoslavia. To bring the issue into sharper focus, however, let us try the same approach in relation to a process which was outwardly very similar to the processes of the Single European Act – namely the attempt by Mikhail Gorbachev, in his last months as Soviet president, to forge a new economic and political union out of the old Soviet Union. Many of the issues that were raised in the course of the negotiations on these matters in late 1991 were just the issues that were simultaneously exercising the Commission and the national governments of the EC in the West – the question of free movement of goods and people, the various monetary options open, the problem of fiscal balance. The difference between the two processes is that whereas in the West commitment was being built upon commitment, in the East successive deals or near-deals were being torpedoed by a volte-face, a crucial failure to sign a critical document, or a flat refusal to accept the implications of integration. (The reader may find it instructive to compare the pattern with the earlier stages of the development of the EC.) This process of *decretion of credibility*, to paraphrase Michael Sumner's telling phrase, reached its climax in December 1991 when the leaders of the three Slav republics of the old USSR – Russia, the Ukraine and Byelorussia – announced after a private meeting at which neither Mr Gorbachev nor any other republican leader was present, that they were abandoning the idea of a new confederation, the idea on which Mr Gorbachev had staked his political future. The meeting was held the day before a planned meeting between the three leaders and Mr Gorbachev to discuss precisely the issue of confederation.

All of this came a couple of months or so after the three Slav republics had initialled Gorbachev's Treaty of Economic Union. Does that mean that Presidents Yeltsin, Kravchuk and Shushkevich think that they can create a single market – in a region of the world where there has been no market at all for seventy years – while simultaneously abandoning the quest for political reintegration? Does it mean that they believe it will be possible to remove the colossal macroeconomic imbalances that plague all the regions of Soviet economic space, in a part of the world which knows nothing of fiscal and monetary policy as we define them in the West, without a large measure of political goodwill? In reality, it may mean simply that they see new economic union and new political union as equally infeasible under present circumstances. If those goals ever do come back on to the agenda in this most easterly part of Europe, possibly under the rubric of Yeltsin's, Kravchuk's and Shushkevich's 'Commonwealth of Independent States', the experience of the EC with the 1992 programme will surely provide many valuable lessons on the importance of credibility and trust in any programme of economic integration.

Returning to more technical matters, the notion of independent national monetary policies begins to look increasingly unreal in a European context. On a world level, as R K Eastwood shows in his chapter on macroeconomic co-ordination in *The European Economy*, it is not clear that national independence has much meaning in relation to *any* aspect of macroeconomic policy-making for countries with liberal regimes on trade and capital movements. By the same token it is not evident that we can meaningfully talk about national policies of capital transfer. The crisis in Eastern Europe has triggered an extensive discussion of the role that aid might play in the restructuring of the economies of the region, and there has been talk of a 'Marshall Plan' for Eastern Europe. The pros and cons of different proposed aid packages are discussed in the relevant chapters of *The National Economies of Europe*. The anxieties which the issue of capital transfer to Eastern Europe has understandably given rise to in the Third World are treated in Christopher Stevens' chapter in this volume. At this introductory stage we seek merely to emphasise that only countries with surpluses on balance of payments, current account, can be net exporters of capital. There is, of course, nothing in principle to stop Western Europe borrowing from the surplus countries (most of them in East Asia) in order to re-lend, or even grant, to Eastern Europe. But such an operation could put colossal strain on the West European economies unless it were done on a strictly commercial basis. Again, there is nothing to stop West European countries adopting policies (presumably deflationary) such as would tend to generate 'investible' surpluses on current account. But the likely impact of any such policies on the world economy hardly bear thinking about. It would be an oversimplification to say that as long as Japan and the other Pacific countries are the only major trading nations consistently running current account surpluses, they are the only countries that can really help Eastern Europe. It is nevertheless clear that the ongoing debate within the developed industrial world about the problem of structural surpluses and deficits on balance of payments may have an important bearing on the structural problems of Eastern Europe.

Both *The European Economy* and *The National Economies of Europe* may seem, at a first reading, to represent straightforward celebrations of the vigour of the market principle. The concept of the single market is lauded, the notion of Fortress Europe rejected, the collapse of the socialist 'alternatives' of communist Eastern Europe duly recorded. Yet the limitations of the price mechanism are as clearly highlighted as its strengths. Devaluation, for instance, is generally rejected as an instrument of international adjustment: it lays an economy open to inflationary pressures, and, more insidiously, it tends to weaken the essentially socio-political pressures for higher productivity which, as we have seen, may represent one of the most important sources of economic growth. And while the virtues of competition and the strength of private enterprise are plain for all to see, the chapters of both volumes pose many searching questions about the role of the *public sector*. One of the recurrent themes of the West European coverage of *The National Economies of Europe* is long-term unemployment. Once a man or a woman has been out of work for more than a year, it seems, he or she can be reabsorbed into the labour force only through a major effort of self-motivation and retraining. Some West European countries, notably Germany, have seriously addressed the problem. None has so far solved it. And this theme of the importance of the *structure of human capital* comes out again, in a much more dramatic form, when we turn to Eastern Europe. In a region where nearly everyone is highly literate, and a large proportion of the population is well trained in basic industrial skills, hardly anyone is trained to do the kinds of jobs that market economies demand. It is difficult to see how the economies of Eastern Europe can be transformed unless there is a massive, and inevitably costly, restructuring of the human capital stock, in addition to the more obviously necessary restructuring of the physical capital stock. But in a situation where budgetary stringency in the name of macroeconomic stabilisation has to be the watchword for East European governments, it is not easy to see how massive retraining programmes could be financed by those governments themselves. Once again, the ball comes back into the court of Western Europe, and of the advanced industrial world as a whole.

Finally, and continuing on the same theme, we return to Western Europe to review a policy area which will be critical for the implementation of the single market programme. With the amalgamation of the EC Regional Fund, Social Fund and Agricultural Guidance Fund under a new Structural Funds rubric, the prospects for a rationalised, integrated approach to the wider implications of Western Europe's own internal structural problems are brighter than they have been for some time. As the chapters of this book devoted to agriculture and regional problems make clear, this development has not come before time. It is clear, furthermore, that the implications of a steadfastly liberal approach to the question of the EC's economic relations with Eastern Europe and the rest of the world (not something that can be taken for granted!) could greatly increase the intensity of Western Europe's regional and socio-structural problems. If East European foodstuffs, Hong Kong textiles and South Korean consumer electronics were to be freed from existing EC importing restrictions, whole new areas of the West European economy could be threatened with massive contraction, with the attendant danger of another large increase in the pool of long-term unemployed people. In bringing the full benefits of the market mechanism, and of the international division of labour, to the consumers of Western Europe, national governments and European Commission alike would have to face up to the fact that in the conditions of the late twentieth century liberal economic policies may increase, rather than reduce, demands on the public sector, in quantitative terms and in terms of the quality and efficacy of programmes. Deficit financing will not be a medium-to-long-term option for the funding of such programmes, as witness the difficulties which so many European countries already have with their public sector borrowing requirements, not to mention the implicit fiscal requirements of EMU, so that there will inevitably be demands for increased tax revenue, at both EC and national level. It would almost certainly be impossible to accommodate such demands without a movement towards 'fiscal federalism', under which the European Community was empowered to levy its own taxes. Even in the context of the ambitious optimism of '1992' that would be an enormous undertaking. It is clear that the implementation of the Single European Act is but one more stage in a process, the end of which can only be guessed at.

Part I
The European integration movement

CHAPTER 2

The main trends of European economic history since the Second World War

NICK VON TUNZELMANN

Introduction

The interplay between politics and economics is one of the most fascinating aspects of the economy of Europe, and indeed of the world at large, in the post-war era. In the early post-war years, politics probably dominated economics in dictating the course of economic change *in individual countries*. However, from the 1970s onwards the balance was somewhat altered, and economics to a greater extent constrained politics, as well as the pattern of economic life itself. This argument presupposes, of course, that political and economic influences can be adequately distinguished at national level, which is a highly contestable proposition; but, with all due allowance for problems of identification, and for specific exceptions, the generalisation may help us to understand the broad course of events.

At the *international* level, it is even less easy to weight the relative influence of politics and economics. Both economic and political influences contributed to a rise in the significance of international (or supranational) factors in general, in comparison with purely national circumstances. To a considerable degree, indeed, the pattern noted in the first paragraph reflected the growing importance of the international economy.

To channel the discussion in this chapter, I have chosen to focus the analysis on the data available for most European countries covering some of the principal economic variables of interest. Generally I have drawn on official published data of the OECD, which relate predominantly to the richer countries from 1950 (the year of the creation of the OEEC as forerunner to the OECD). This is not always the best available source for particular series, but represents the most straightforwardly comparable set of data obtainable. Reliance on such data involves largely ignoring the immediate post-war recovery period (1945–50) and, more importantly, the East European countries, since the latter – apart from Yugoslavia – do not belong to the OECD. There are grounds for arguing that the condition of Eastern Europe after the ending of communism (from 1989) is similar in kind to that of the rest of Europe after the ending of the Second World War, but I shall make only passing reference to this theme. The theme is, however, developed in the relevant parts of *The National Economies of Europe*.

Extended discussion of individual countries would exceed my space constraints and is accordingly left to the chapters of *The National Economies of Europe*. It will thus be understood that there are many exceptions within individual countries to the broad characteristics portrayed in this chapter. Even with that caveat, Europe as a whole is too heterogeneous even in its broader trends to treat as a unit beyond the level of initial generalisation. Consequently I have divided Europe (excluding the USSR and Turkey) into four major sub-regions: West, North, South and East Europe.[1] (As already stated, data limitations mean that most of the discussion has to exclude East Europe.) This categorisation is obviously not always ideal: for example, in North Europe the picture is dominated by the UK, which contributes about three-quarters of the region's GDP, and this may tend to obscure the special characteristics of the Nordic countries. Similarly, within South Europe, Italy is the dominant country, although (and increasingly as time went on) Northern Italy often had more in common with West Europe than with the rest of South Europe. For such reasons, some consideration must be given even here to the underlying data at the level of individual countries.

The most natural measure of growth and fluctuation in economic prosperity is real national income per capita. Figure 2.1 presents World Bank data on real per capita GDP. These data have been prepared in such a way as to adjust as much as possible for differences in real purchasing power between countries, rather than by simply converting the monetary units of each country at official exchange rates, which sometimes bear little relationship to purchasing power (Summers and Heston 1984; 1988). This is most obviously true for East Europe, the countries of which have been included in this particular data set. It should be stressed that there are many problems of data deficiency and interpretation with these series.

The most extensively studied thesis regarding international differences in rates of growth of real incomes is the 'convergence' argument, namely that (with the exception of the very poor countries of Africa and Asia) levels of income per head across countries are becoming more alike. This thesis is especially popular among contemporary American scholars (Abramovitz 1986; Baumol 1986; Baumol et al 1989; De Long 1988; Dollar and Wolff 1988; Nelson and Wright 1991; cf Cornwall 1977 and earlier European scholars, eg Svennilson 1954), in their attempts to explain why US income levels are being steadily approached by those of other relatively wealthy countries, and why the growth rates of the USA have not been as fast as those of most of its rivals.

Figure 2.1a graphs the data by region on a linear scale, and suggests no obvious 'convergence' within Europe: the tracks of real GDP per head are approximately parallel. More precisely, West Europe overhauls North Europe, and South Europe overhauls East Europe in the mid-1960s. When the same data are charted on a logarithmic scale, as in Figure 2.1b, there is a slightly stronger indication of convergence. The data in this form can be regarded as indicating rates of income growth (a straight line on this scale represents a constant rate of growth – the steeper such a line, the faster the growth rate). Thus the gaps between richer and poorer regions of Europe remained roughly the same in absolute dimensions, although the poorer regions grew at slightly faster rates. Rather than convergence it might be better to adopt Abramovitz's 1986 title, 'Catching up, forging ahead, and falling behind' as a way of describing variations across the countries of post-war Europe.

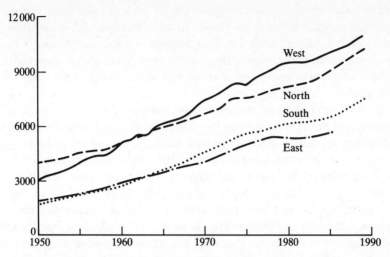

Figure 2.1a   Real GDP per capita by region, 1985 'international dollars'* (linear scale)
Source: Data from Summers and Heston 1984; 1988
Note*: International dollars are US dollars adjusted for the international rather
than the domestic US structure of prices and quantities

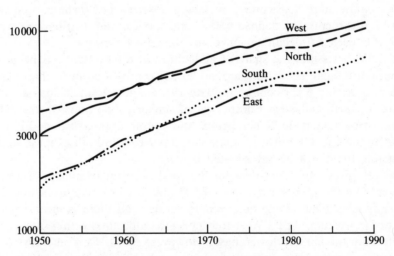

Figure 2.1b   Real GDP per capita by region, 1985 'international dollars'* (logarithmic scale)
Source: Data from Summers and Heston 1984; 1988
Note*: As for Fig. 2.1a

    Figure 2.1b can also be used as a basis for comparing the two periods into which the
post-war European experience is commonly considered to have fallen. Although
absolute income levels continued to rise in most years, rates of income growth after the
early 1970s seemed to be slower in most regions than before, and fluctuations
considerably more serious. The graph gives reasonable support to this widely held
belief. North Europe shows no clear-cut decline in rates of growth (bear in mind that
its trend rate of growth is relatively slow), although the recession of the early 1980s is

apparent. The other three regions do show slower growth rates from the early 1970s, with the slowdown delayed until the 1980s in East Europe. Although data from the World Bank are not yet available for East Europe for the late 1980s, it is clear that retardation continued in that region throughout the 1980s, and in this lay part of the causes of the overthrow of communism at the end of the decade. (See relevant chapters of *The National Economies of Europe*.)

Although the evidence from income levels and rates of growth gives a less stark contrast than might perhaps have been expected, there seems little doubt that much of the second half of the post-war period to date has been characterised by a greater sense of disquiet and insecurity than was present in the 1950s and 1960s. By the mid-1960s there was a widespread feeling in the advanced industrial countries that the major economic problems had been solved: people could look forward to more or less sustained improvements in their prosperity and living standards, and the chief remaining task was to diffuse that prosperity to the still underdeveloped nations of the earth. With hindsight it is obvious that such expectations were at least premature. But that makes it if anything rather more interesting to examine some of the factors that encouraged them. In the terminology of economics, it is appropriate to divide these into supply-side factors and demand-side factors.

The data on sectoral shares in total output in Figures 2.2 and 2.3 cast some light on the more significant factors involved on the supply side.[2] In Figure 2.2 the major sectors for study here (agriculture including forestry and fishing, mining, manu-facturing, 'infrastructure' as defined below, and services and distribution) are graphed separately for each European region other than East Europe.

Figure 2.2a shows that the share of agriculture in total output has been highest in South Europe, though it fell from around 23 per cent of output in that region in the early 1950s to around 6 per cent by the late 1980s. The rate of relative contraction of agriculture in North and West Europe was of similar proportions. In the early 1950s, the sector represented about 10 per cent of total output in the North and 15 per cent in the West; by the late 1980s it was only about 3 per cent in both of these regions. The causes of this trend will be investigated below.

Figure 2.2b gives equivalent data for the smaller sector of mining. These data are less reliable than for agriculture, since OECD data for several European countries do not distinguish between mining and manufacturing, and there is inconsistency in the treatment of petroleum. Again West Europe shows a decline, with a smaller decline in the South from an initially lower base. However, North Europe shows a different pattern, with a sharp relative increase from the early 1970s to the mid-1980s: this is the effect of North Sea oil and gas, especially on the UK, Norway and (to a lesser extent) Denmark. The most obvious explanation for the contrasting trends of West and North Europe in the 1970s and 1980s is thus the fact of new local fuel sources coming on stream. This has been less emphasised but was probably more significant than other causes, such as government policy (discussed on pp. 40–4; see also Feinstein and Matthews 1990). These contrasting trends came through most strongly in terms of aggregate growth rates. By the mid-1980s Norway was easily the richest country in Europe in terms of real GDP per capita, about 20 per cent above the next richest (Switzerland), according to World Bank data (from Summers and Heston 1988). However, the availability of new resources was no guarantee of economic growth: in

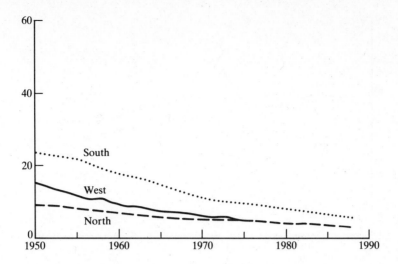

Figure 2.2a   Share of agriculture in total output (per cent)
Source: OECD data.

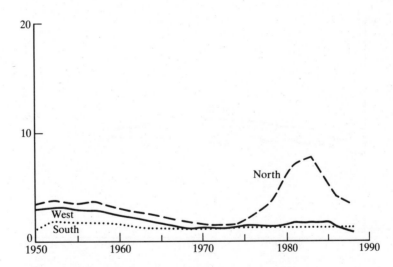

Figure 2.2b   Share of mining in total output (per cent)
Source: OECD data.

the Netherlands in the later 1970s, for example, the rapid expansion of production of natural gas led to stagnation, by crowding out expansion in other sectors of the economy – a severe case of what became known as the 'Dutch Disease' (van Wijnbergen 1984).

Of much greater quantitative importance were the changes in the contribution of the manufacturing sector, as shown in Figure 2.2c. In West Europe this share held up until *c* 1970, but then the trend was downwards; in North Europe (where the share was initially similar to that in West Europe), the relative decline set in about a decade

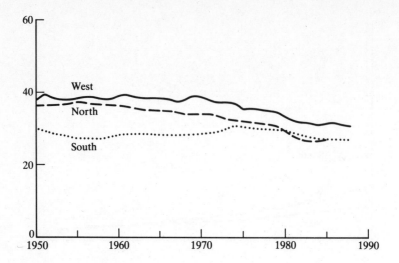

Figure 2.2c   Share of manufacturing in total output (per cent)
          Source: OECD data.

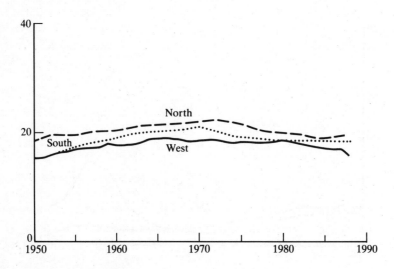

Figure 2.2d   Share of infrastructure in total output (per cent)
          Source: OECD data.

earlier and was more sustained, propelled by events in the UK. This phenomenon became known as 'deindustrialisation'. Public anxieties about deindustrialisation reflected not only possible loss of jobs, but also fears of a contracting base of 'wealth creation'. While economists have generally paid less regard to the unique importance of manufacturing implied by the 'wealth creation' argument, that argument receives some support from the finding that the overwhelming proportion of innovations and patents in the modern economy stem from manufacturing (95–97 per cent in the USA: see Scherer 1984). The economists are certainly correct to argue that a dollar or pound

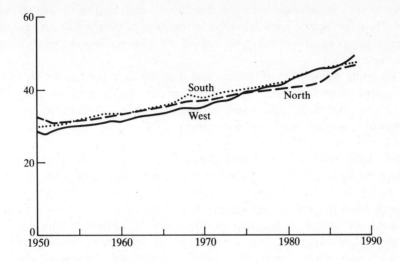

Figure 2.2e   Share of services in total output (per cent)
          Source: OECD data.

earned in manufacturing is no more valuable than the same earned in service activities. But manufacturing nevertheless acts as the hub of dynamism for most large economies, and consequently their ability to generate *future* dollars or pounds. (See Sharp, Chapter 12 in this volume, on changing industrial structures for a development of this argument.)

South Europe initially experienced the opposite phenomenon of 'industrialization'. Its early lag in manufacturing is reflected in a total output share for that sector about ten percentage points lower than for the North or West. But once it had caught up with the North in the mid-1970s, the South too witnessed stagnation in the share of manufacturing in total output.

For the purposes of this chapter, economic 'infrastructure' is defined as the sum of transportation and communications; gas, water and electricity supplies; and construction. These are some of the major overheads assumed to be necessary to the functioning of other sectors of the modern economy. Figure 2.2d shows that the European economies devoted a steady and approximately similar share of total output to the operation of this infrastructure. North Europe initially had a somewhat higher share than the West or South, but the differences had largely disappeared by the 1980s.

Finally, Figure 2.2e charts the rise of the remaining principal sector – services and distribution. The pattern is similar in all three regions, with a steady relative increase from under one-third of total output in the early 1950s to nearly one-half by the late 1980s. The rate of increase is fastest in the richest of the three regions (West Europe), but the most striking feature is this similarity of expansion path in all three. It should be pointed out that the sharp demarcation of services from other sectors implied in these diagrams and in the data from which they are derived may be less clear in practice, and arguably less and less clear over time. Activities such as communications, listed here under infrastructure, also have services characteristics which are increasingly difficult to separate from infrastructural. To put it into the language of information technology, the boundaries between 'hardware' and 'software' are in many cases obscure. How far income growth can be left to depend on the software (services) side, however, remains controversial (compare pp. 19–20 regarding the wealth creative role of manufacturing).

The generally rising share of services and distribution is seen as clearly in Figure 2.3, where sectoral shares of each major type of productive activity are graphed for each region in turn. The major differences between regions are thus in the trends exhibited by agriculture, mining, and manufacturing.

How are these patterns, and the change from a scenario of growth to one of fluctuation, to be accounted for? On the supply side, the main point is that economic growth and industrialisation could proceed in early post-war Europe with relatively little check from the side of resources: that is resources were available in relatively plentiful supply and at comparatively low cost, to permit twenty years or so of untrammelled growth. It is clear, in the light of subsequent developments, that the most important of such resources was *oil*: the period saw a sustained shift from older forms of fossil fuel, like coal, to petroleum, a fuel that was not only cleaner than coal but also for a time remarkably cheap, with extraction costs in the Middle East so low. But it was not just oil; other raw materials for industry remained cheap by longer-term standards, many of them mined or otherwise extracted from the less developed countries by means of cheap local labour. Not surprisingly, some critics saw the prosperity of the advanced industrial countries as being dependent on the continuing backwardness of the developing countries. Others, however, argued that in the fullness of time the effects of growth in the richer countries would spill over to the poorer: that it was better for the latter to have *something* to export to the former, even if the terms of trade on which these exports were based were not fully satisfactory. In the end, the terms of trade were to be dramatically altered by the events of 1973–4, though not in a way that had been predicted, nor with quite the kind of spillover effects on poorer countries that had been anticipated. Instead, the major oil exporters were able to form an effective cartel, called OPEC (Organisation of Petroleum Exporting Countries), which was able within a few months to quadruple the price of crude oil. This occurred not because of any considerable increase in the cost of pumping out the oil, which remained low for the largest producers,[3] but because Middle Eastern and other producers were able to cash in on the very geographically concentrated nature of cheap oil supplies, in a demand-side context in which production and transportation in all countries had become so highly dependent upon oil. The situation was exacerbated by a further round of price increases in 1979.

Europe was by no means the only region affected by the Oil Crises, and probably suffered less than the developing countries. It is true that Europe was not well endowed with supplies of cheap oil. But at the higher prices now prevailing, it became feasible to investigate higher-cost sources such as the North Sea. In the longer run there was a stimulus to the development of alternative energy sources, of which the major immediate beneficiary was nuclear power. (A major nuclear construction programme was already under way in France.) More fundamentally, there was an incentive to save on energy, the profligate use of which, for example in the gas-guzzling cars of the 1960s, now became more obvious. But each of these lines of advance entailed a period

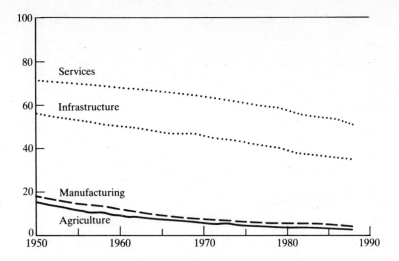

Figure 2.3a Percentage shares of sectors in total output: West Europe
Source: OECD data.
Note: The small sector between agriculture and manufacturing is mining.

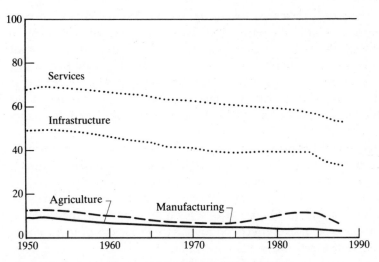

Figure 2.3b Percentage shares of sectors in total output: North Europe
Source: OECD data.
Note: as for Fig. 2.3a

of setback to growth, before any substantial alternative could be developed. Figures 2.2c, 2.3a, 2.3b and 2.3c show particularly clearly that the periods of most rapid deindustrialisation (decline of manufacturing) coincided with the two Oil Crises of the 1970s.

The Oil Crises, then, explain the sharpness of the break between sustained growth and spasmodic growth; but there are many who contend that they are not a sufficient explanation of that break, and not the most important explanation. As half-implied

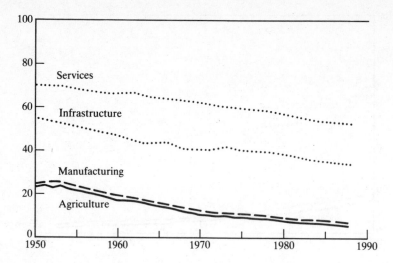

Figure 2.3c   Percentage shares of sectors in total output: South Europe
Source: OECD data.
Note: as for Fig. 2.3a.

above, the Oil Crises themselves were more a product of growth in both richer and poorer countries – that is, the outcome of demands for growth dependent on cheap fuel – than of any significant supply-side pressures such as increased costs. In that sense, the development of OPEC simply represented the chickens of oil-biased growth coming home to roost. But on this wider view some meatier chickens were also coming home to roost. It is noteworthy that the figures show a larger decline of manufacturing following the Second Oil Crisis, although it is generally regarded as having been of less potency than the first.

Even after the OPEC price increases, fuel continued to account for only a relatively small proportion of total costs in most industrial activities. By contrast, *labour* was everywhere (except in the oil industry!) a large proportion of total costs: over half of total costs in nearly all industries consisted of direct labour costs, and often the proportion was considerably higher. Consequently, changes in the supply conditions of labour could have pervasive effects on industry even if the proportionate increases in labour costs were much lower than for energy.

Two short but influential studies, published before the crisis broke, argued that Europe's post-war prosperity was built on its access to supplies of labour – moderately cheap but above all reasonably abundant labour. The basic view of Charles Kindleberger and the late Nicholas Kaldor was that rapid expansion of manufacturing required that the labour force be rapidly expanded, inasmuch as labour was quantitatively the most important factor of production. Countries or regions able to tap abundant labour sources thus had an advantage in respect of opportunities for sustained growth: they would be less likely to be brought to a halt by an inability to find the workers they needed to staff their factories. With one significant exception, namely the huge influx of refugees from East Europe into West Germany immediately after the Second World War, labour supplies in the 1950s were mainly dependent on local

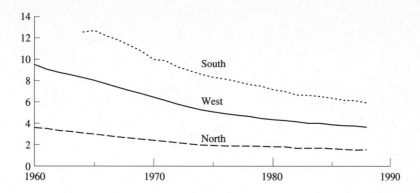

Figure 2.4a   Employment in agriculture (millions)
Source: OECD data.

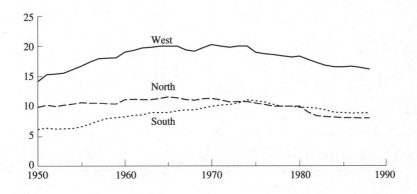

Figure 2.4b   Employment in manufacturing (millions)
Source: OECD data.

sources. A brief post-war baby boom enlarged the population, but would obviously take twenty years or so to enlarge the labour force. Meanwhile the factories of the 1950s had to rely for new entrants on the population growth of the 1930s, which had been stunted by the Depression, not to speak of the losses, principally of young men, in the Second World War itself. The labour thus had to come partly from other occupations, and here Kindleberger (1967) and Kaldor (1966) stressed the availability of surplus labour in the surrounding countryside, paralleling the situation in the underdeveloped countries. In particular, Kaldor argued that the UK was disadvantaged because of its lack of an agricultural labour surplus, and accordingly contended that

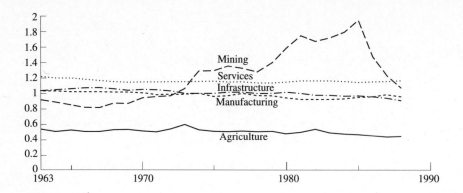

Figure 2.5a   Sectoral labour productivity (share in total output divided by share in total
employment): West Europe
Source: OECD data.

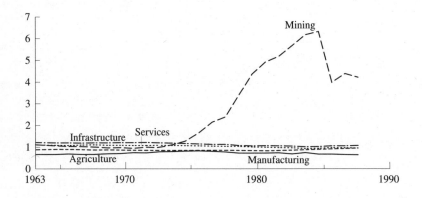

Figure 2.5b   Sectoral labour productivity (share in total output divided by share in total
employment): North Europe
Source: OECD data.

Britain's slow post-war rate of growth by comparison with Western Europe is attributable to a considerable degree to its lack of spare labour available for manufacturing.

Figure 2.4 displays data on employment in agriculture (Figure 2.4a) and manufacturing (Figure 2.4b) in each major region, measured in millions of employees. (These
figures differ from those published in the first edition, which excluded the self-
employed). The sectoral comparison does indeed give some indication of a negative
relationship between agricultural employment and manufacturing employment, with

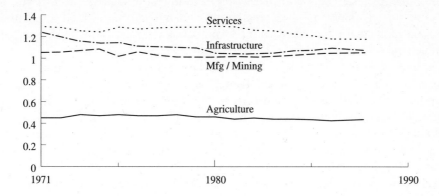

Figure 2.5c   Sectoral labour productivity (share in total output divided by share in total
employment): South Europe
Source: OECD data.

the flattening out of declines in the former corresponding in time with the beginnings
of decline in the latter. The chronology of the employment patterns also corresponds
with those for sectoral output patterns in Figure 2.2 above. The time pattern would
therefore appear to support a possible causal relationship. More important is the
pattern across regions, where it can be argued that the later onset of deindustrialization
in South Europe owed much to the far higher initial absolute level of agricultural
employment (and underemployment) in that region. The low levels of agricultural
employment in North Europe support Kaldor's notion of 'premature industrialization'.
However the rates of decline of agricultural employment were very similar in all three
regions, being 4 to 5 per cent p.a. in the 1960s and falling to about half of that in the
1980s. Moreover, North Europe (as well as the other regions) had an alternative labour
source in the other major primary product, namely mining employment.

Figure 2.5 combines the data on employment underlying Figure 2.4 with those on
output in Figures 2.2 and 2.3, to give estimates of comparative labour productivity
('comparative advantage' acording to Ricardo's original definition) by sector. Relative
productivity is lowest in agriculture in all three regions, but especially so in West and
South Europe. The finding that North Europe had a comparative advantage in
agriculture is unsurprising for the Kaldorian thesis although surprising for the more
orthodox Ricardian view about specialization. The other conclusions to be derived
from Figure 2.5 are less likely to have been foreseen. There is no upward trend in the
relative labour productivity of the main declining sector, agriculture, which one might
have expected from the transfer of labour out of underemployment. Mining, as the
other sector with steadily declining employment, does show a rapid rise in relative
productivity, mainly from the advent of North Sea hydrocarbons (though West Europe
shows a similar if more muted pattern). Services, which are often regarded as a sector

also characterised by heavy underemployment, in fact show high relative productivities in all three regions. The sector that was second lowest in relative productivity with an absolute disadvantage in each region was manufacturing, which thus limits the potential gains that might have accrued from labour transfer of the kind asserted in the Kindleberger-Kaldor model.

In any case, even those countries with larger local pools of surplus labour soon began to exhaust them. As local labour supplies started to dry up, countries like Germany and Switzerland turned further afield for their male factory labour. Italians began working in those countries on a short-term basis, often returning home at weekends. As this source became increasingly expensive, West Germany turned to Yugoslavia, Greece and (by the early 1960s) Turkey for supplies of factory labour. France drew labour from North Africa and other colonies. The male bias and ethnic mix, compounded with the frequent harshness of the so-called *gastarbeiter* system, which forbade permanent immigration or families, created considerable social problems, many of which remain with us today. Be that as it may, Germany became heavily dependent for unskilled factory labour on such casual sources. The UN estimates that continental Europe had received 11 million immigrants up to 1975, not counting another 3 million going to the UK (many from Commonwealth countries) (Bernabe 1982).

There was another prospective source, namely women. Female employment in industry had risen rapidly during both World Wars, but it is less often pointed out that it dropped away almost as rapidly after they ended. The 'Back to the Home' movement after the Second World War in women's magazines, for example, fostered an ethos favouring a return to the traditional nuclear family, with male head as bread-winner and the wife busily rearing the baby boom. As opportunities for unskilled and often menial labour began to fall vacant, however, this ethic began to be undermined by women returning to work. Across most of Europe, the major change in the indigenous work-force, in terms of participation rates, was the influx of married women. Because they were married, the work was frequently part-time (see OECD 1980). (A range of social changes followed in part from this trend, but there is no space to pursue these here.)

It is generally supposed that much of this female labour found employment in relatively inefficient service occupations. However, we have already seen that services were not particularly inefficient, even without allowing for differences in labour quality (Figure 2.5). The relationship between types of labour available and output trends clearly warrants more thoroughgoing investigation than can be undertaken here.

All in all, it is obvious that labour supplies are far from being the whole story. For one thing, the higher levels of unemployment that characterised the cyclical fluctuations after the early 1970s provided a potential labour supply that was locally available and not necessarily very costly; indeed, unemployment in the mid-1970s was concentrated among youths, who could have provided a flexible source of new entry. Again there were social implications that I have to leave aside, but the important point in the present context is that labour supply conditions by themselves are inadequate as an explanation of comparative trends: for labour surplus to produce growth there has to be a matching demand for labour from the side of industry. The situation of the less-developed countries (LDCs) shows this all too well, as indeed Kindleberger was the first to argue. Beyond that, the 1970s began to show up mismatches between the kinds of labour available, however cheaply, in the job market, and the kinds of labour industry really wanted – people with greater skills than usually possessed by youths, or part-time married women, or part-time immigrants from the poorer parts of Europe or the globe. Finally, even with the accessing of the various new sources of labour supply, the growth rate of the labour force in the post-1945 period was not so markedly different from that recorded in the depressed years before the Second World War; what was different was the greater rate of increase in *labour productivity*.

The thing that did grow very much faster than before the war on the inputs side was *capital*, and especially fixed capital (machinery, factories, power plants, etc.) (cf Maddison 1976). Since that rapid growth of plant and equipment allowed newer techniques to be installed all the faster, it is not too surprising to find such rapid productivity growth. Labour was working with much more up-to-date machinery, and the pace of rebuilding from war devastation in North-West Europe accentuated this phenomenon. So long as business savings remained high, or other sources of savings could be tapped through the banking system and financial institutions, investment in fixed capital could proceed at low cost (low rates of interest). Business savings in turn came largely from profits, so from another perspective the rapid expansion of capital is often seen not as the cause of rapid post-war growth, but as its consequence – high levels of consumption of goods and services by the public at large generated high profits for industry, which permitted the latter to renew expansion to meet further increases in consumer demand. In this way a virtuous circle of high growth and high profits seemed to have been established.

Figure 2.6 shows the post-1950 investment experience of the three major regions. The share of *gross domestic fixed capital formation* (GDFCF) in GDP is shown in Figure 2.6a. In West and South Europe, this ratio rose from about 17 per cent in 1950 to a peak of around 25 per cent in the early 1970s, before falling back to about 20 per cent by the end of the period. In North Europe the pattern is similar, but the share is about one point lower at the beginning and end of the period and about two points lower in the middle. Evidently the higher ratios for the West and South relate to the higher levels of growth performance shown in Figure 2.1, but the more surprising feature of Figure 2.6a is again the similarity across regions, in particular a comparable relative pattern for South and West Europe despite the much lower level of real GDP per capita of the former. Although cross-country data for GDFCF are much less reliable for the period before the Second World War, there seems little reason to doubt that all these ratios were considerably higher post-war than inter-war. Data on *net fixed capital formation* – that is, GDFCF minus depreciation and scrapping – are even weaker. But isolated evidence for individual countries such as the UK indicates that the pre-war/post-war contrast in net fixed capital formation would be very much greater than in GDFCF, reinforcing the argument of the previous paragraph about the role of new machinery and equipment after the war. Machinery and equipment (producer durables) generally make up about one-half of GDFCF, and Figure 2.6b shows the regional trends in that variable in the post-war period. Relative to GDP, the shares are somewhat more erratic than for GDFCF as a whole, but the general conclusions are similar. However, it will be noticed that the share of this element in GDP is much the same in North Europe as it is in West and South Europe, so that differences in investment in machinery and equipment alone do not seem to explain the slower growth of the North.

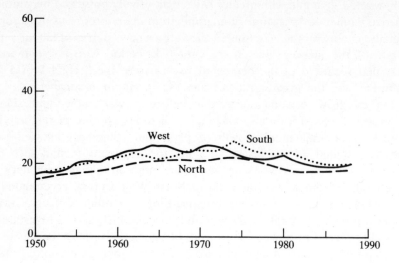

Figure 2.6a Share of gross domestic fixed capital formation in GDP (per cent)
Source: OECD data.

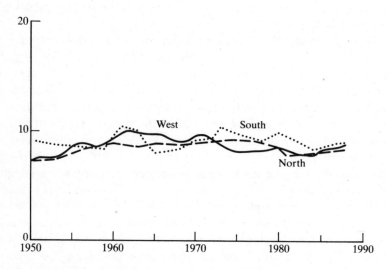

Figure 2.6b Share of output of producers durables in GDP (per cent)
Source: OECD data.

Figures on Research and Development (R&D), where available, provide some guidance on the extent to which productivity has been enhanced through technological advance. However, it has to be emphasised that the data are especially poor when one turns to R&D. Although attempts were made from the 1960s to standardise accountancy practices across countries in regard to R&D, most notably through the publication of the OECD's 'Frascati Manual', it is obvious that the data are still by no means consistent from country to country, or from period to period. The data graphed in Figure 2.7 should therefore be treated with extreme caution.

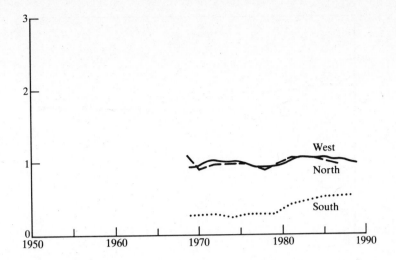

Figure 2.7a Government-funded R&D as percentage of GDP
Source: OECD data.

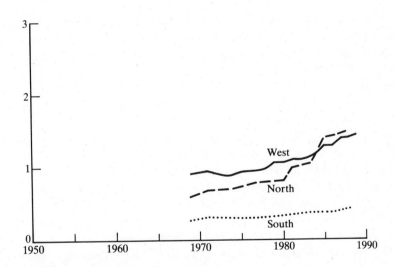

Figure 2.7b Business-funded R&D as percentage of GDP
Source: OECD data.

Data relating to *R&D conducted by governments*, given in Figure 2.7a, are marginally less unreliable than those for private-sector activity, though the importance of military R&D in a number of these countries undermines the accuracy of the governments' own figures, which may be distorted in the interests of secrecy and general obfuscation. In West and North Europe, government-funded R&D has represented about 1 per cent of GDP, rising slightly in the former and, in the longer term, stable in the latter. In South Europe the share was only about one-third of 1 per cent in the early 1970s, rising to about half of that recorded for the West and North by the end of the 1980s. However, the allocational pattern of government-funded R&D

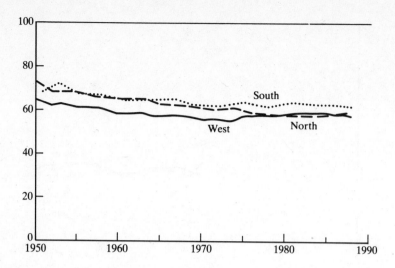

Figure 2.8   Share of consumers' expenditure in GDP (per cent)
Source: OECD data.

has been subjected to a certain amount of criticism, with particular regard again to the often large military share. Ergas (1987) convincingly stressed the excessive role of what he termed 'mission-oriented' programmes in countries like the UK and France (and also the USA), with grand objectives and often little domestic spillover or commercial success. By contrast, West Germany, Switzerland, Sweden and so on, have placed greater emphasis on 'diffusion-oriented' research, with more limited but more practical and probably more pervasive objectives.

It is therefore *business-funded R&D*, graphed in Figure 2.7b, which would appear to have the closer relationship to commercially oriented technological progress. The share of business-funded R&D in GDP is generally similar to that of government-funded, but the trends are the reverse of those in Figure 2.7a, with North Europe seemingly showing the greatest gain and South Europe the smallest. Again it is necessary to emphasise the data limitations, which because of widely varying commercial practice are at their greatest here. To the extent the figures can be believed, they appear to reflect above all the varying extent of shift into 'high-technology' sectors such as information technology, for the simple reason that R&D intensities (the shares of R&D in total sales) are so much greater in such sectors than in older and 'low-tech' sectors. The inverse relationship between public-funded and private-funded R&D would appear to give some support to the 'crowding-out' theory, which encouraged some governments in the 1980s to cut public expenditure on R&D in the avowed hope of fostering increases in privately funded R&D to fill the void. However, at the level of individual countries this argument commands less support; for example in North Europe the largest increases in business-funded shares were in the Nordic countries taken together, rather than in the UK, although the largest cuts in government-funded shares were in the latter.

The similarity of regional patterns in investment shares (Figure 2.6) and the ambivalence of those in R&D shares (Figure 2.7) may, indeed, suggest a type of

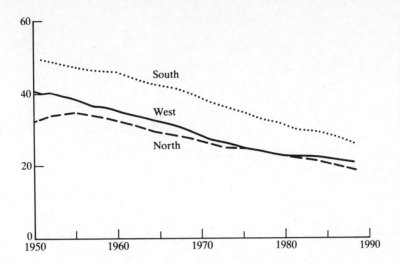

Figure 2.9a   Share of food, drink and tobacco in consumers' expenditure (per cent)
Source: OECD data.

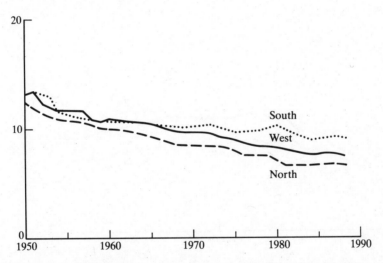

Figure 2.9b   Share of clothing and footwear in total consumers' expenditure (per cent)
Source: OECD data.

explanation rather different from the growth pushed by investments in fixed capital and R&D model. As we saw above, it can be argued that investment shares may be as much a result as a cause of growth. An analogous argument might be made for R&D, perhaps more strongly at the level of the individual sector or industry than at the macroeconomy level: larger profits from greater sales as well as lower costs permit higher investment in R&D, and thus foster newer products or further savings in unit costs. And the level of sales is, of course, a function of the level of sectoral *demand*. To interpret the data fully we must clearly add the dimension of demand–pull to that of supply–push (or supply–constraint). It is to the demand side that I next turn.

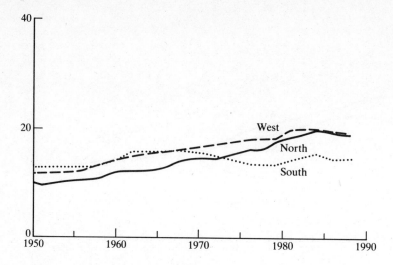

Figure 2.9c   Share of household rents and fuel in total consumers' expenditure (per cent)
Source: OECD data.

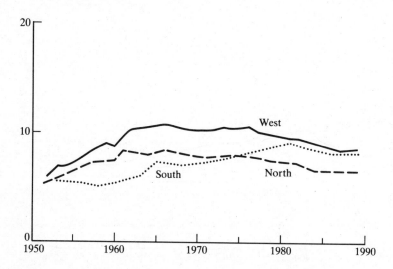

Figure 2.9d   Share of household durables in total consumers' expenditure (per cent)
Source: OECD data.

Quantitatively the largest element in aggregate demand is *consumers' expenditure*, graphed as a proportion of GDP in Figure 2.8. Although consumption is often regarded as competing with investment demand and other elements more conducive to economic growth, the decline in the share of consumers' expenditure has in fact been greatest in the most slow-growing region, North Europe. Some aspects of this apparent paradox will be studied below.

In the meantime Figures 2.9 and 2.10 disaggregate consumers' expenditure into six major categories: food (including drink and tobacco), clothing, household rents (including fuel and power), household durables, transport and communications (figures

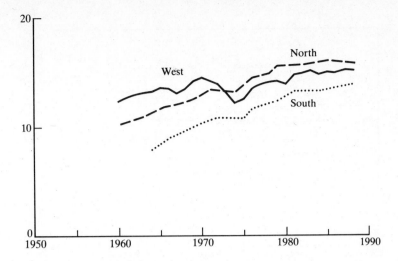

Figure 2.9e   Share of transport and communications in total consumers' expenditure (per cent)
Source: OECD data.

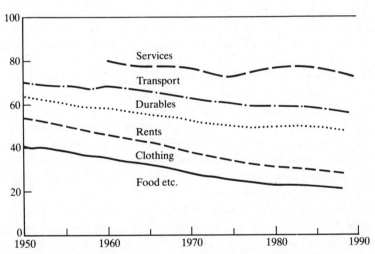

Figure 2.10a   Shares of consumption items in total consumers' expenditure: West Europe
Source: OECD data.

beginning in the 1960s), and a residual element of services. Although there are some evident similarities with the sectoral classifications of Figure 2.2, there are also some major differences. Food, for example, represents a considerably larger proportion of consumers' expenditure, and even of Gross National Expenditure, than does agriculture of the Gross National Product. This is partly because of its broader coverage (equally, of course, agriculture supplies needs other than just food), but mainly because of the increasing importance of manufacturing in the preparation of foodstuffs for final consumption. This latter development has weakened the impact over time of 'Engel's Law', which predicates that the proportion of expenditure on

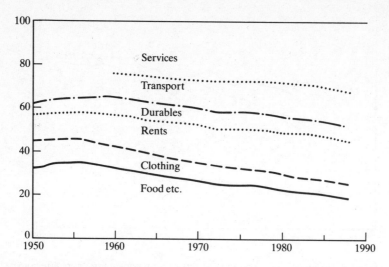

Figure 2.10b   Share of consumption items in total consumers' expenditure: North Europe
Source: OECD data.

food falls as incomes rise (cf Deaton 1975). (However, Figure 2.9a shows that food industry trends by no means fully offset the operation of that 'Law'.) As would be expected, the proportion of total consumption going on food is highest in the lowest-income region, namely South Europe. Clothing, as another 'necessity', also trends downwards as a proportion of total expenditure (Figure 2.9b). The shares here are initially very similar among the different regions, with the fall being least marked in South Europe, possibly because in countries like Italy (where the share is especially high) clothing is regarded as an important status symbol; that is, clothing is a 'decency' or even luxury as well as a necessity. Conversely, the proportion allocated to the remaining 'necessity' – household rents and fuel – hardly changes in South Europe after the early 1960s, though it rises up until the mid-1980s in North Europe, and even more strikingly in West Europe (Figure 2.9c).

Turning next to the articles normally regarded as decencies or luxuries, we find surprisingly little trace of the alleged consumer durables revolution in Figure 2.9d. Indeed the share trends slightly downwards in the richer regions of North and West Europe after about 1960. This parallels similar findings for the USA over the twentieth century as a whole (Vatter 1967). The issue here is partly (but not wholly) definitional, as one significant consumer durable, namely private motor vehicles, appears in the next graph, Figure 2.9e, covering transport and communications. The influence of the motor car factor does come through in terms of the effects of the Oil Crisis of the early 1970s on transport expenditure, though as Figure 2.9e shows, this was of consequence only in West Europe.

Services bulk less large within total consumers' expenditure than do distribution and services within total output as displayed in Figure 2.3, and the relative increase is less pronounced, despite the fact that consumers' expenditure represents only about two-thirds of the aggregate of total output (cf Figure 2.8). Part of the explanation would seem to lie in the growing service element within a broad range of products, including

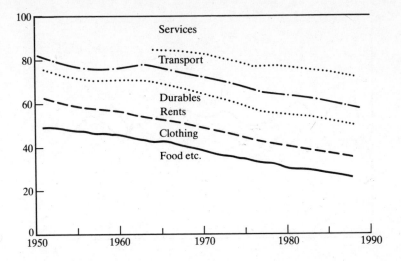

Figure 2.10c   Shares of consumption items in total consumers expenditure: South Europe
Source: OECD data.

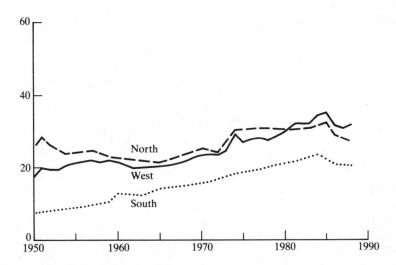

Figure 2.11   Visible exports as % of GDP
Source: OECD data.

manufactures, as noted earlier. Be that as it may, the upward trend in the share of services in total consumption is clear enough for all regions. This reflects in part a revolution in the nature of services. Traditionally services have been regarded as by definition consumed at the time and place at which they are produced. Technological advances have, however, conspired to break down this definition (Soete 1987). Increasingly, now, services can be stored for future consumption (eg musical recordings) and traded across national boundaries (eg trans-border data flows in telecommunications).

This brings us to international trade in goods and services as a second major element in aggregate demand. The post-war economies, whether European or non-European,

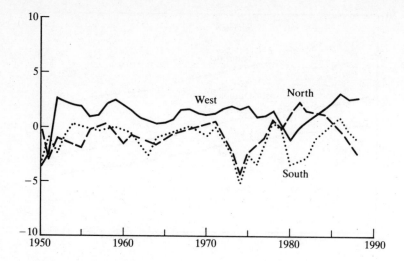

Figure 2.12a   Visible trade surplus (deficit) as % of GDP
Source: OECD data.

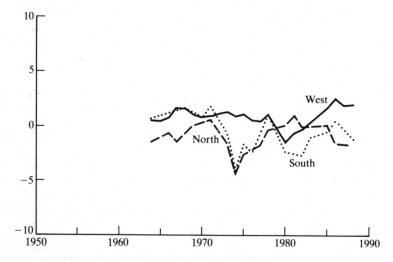

Figure 2.12b   Current account surplus (deficit) as % of GDP
Source: OECD data.

have frequently been regarded as increasingly trading economies, obtaining imports world-wide and competing globally for markets for their exports. Some of the characteristics of this pattern of globalisation will be dealt with below. Remaining for the moment at the level of aggregate statistical trends, we see from Figure 2.11 that the ratio of visible exports to GDP grew steadily until the mid-1980s in both West and South Europe, this indicating an increasing degree of openness on the part of the constituent economies of those regions. Of course, since the figures are weighted averages of individual countries, some part of this upward trend probably reflects growth in the intensity of intra-trade between the countries making up West or South

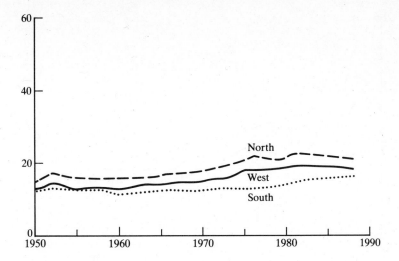

Figure 2.13 Government final consumption as % of GDP
Source: OECD data.

Europe. Just how much this is the case cannot be determined from these figures alone.

By contrast with West and South Europe, North Europe does not show any marked increase in the degree of openness to trade, except briefly at the time of the First Oil Crisis. As the North is dominated by the UK, this may be ascribed to the traditional weakness of the UK as a trading economy. The argument can to a degree be assessed from the data in Figure 2.12. Figure 2.12a shows trends in the *visible trade surplus* – that is, visible exports minus visible imports. West Europe is clearly the strongest of the three regions for the bulk of the period, once the immediate after-effects of the war and the dollar shortage had been overcome (through the Marshall Plan, etc.). However North Europe's visible surplus/deficit behaved very much like that of South Europe, both in trend and pattern of fluctuation, aside from the brief North Sea hydrocarbons era of the early 1980s when for a time North Europe was in the strongest trading position. Thus the balance between visible exports and imports does not account for the differing trends exhibited by North and South Europe in Figure 2.11.

Figures on the *current account surplus*, shown in Figure 2.12b, are available by macro-region only from the mid-1960s. It is here that we do, indeed, pick up a greater weakness of the North relative to both the other regions in the late 1960s, and this seems at first sight to fit with the conventional theories of unduly delayed British devaluation in the struggle to retain the pound sterling as a key currency, and so on. But it is less clear why these factors should have had so much greater an effect on the current account balance – which includes autonomous invisible items as well as the visible balance of Figure 2.12a – than on the visible balance itself. From about 1970 the current and visible balances of each region behave similarly.

The trade and payments figures do, then, provide a starting-point for further investigation rather than conclusive proof on the relationship between trade and growth. Nevertheless, propositions about virtuous and vicious circles in that relationship are well established (eg Beckerman 1962; Dosi et al 1990), for example in

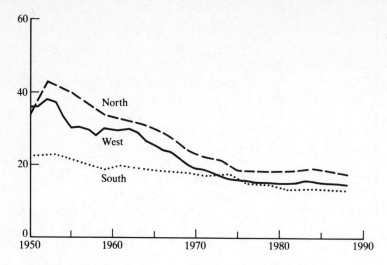

Figure 2.14a   Defence expenditure as % of government final consumption
Source: OECD data.

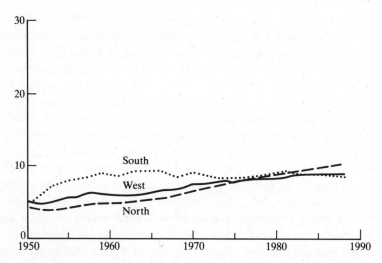

Figure 2.14b   Social security expenditures as % of government final consumption
Source: OECD data.

relation to the UK's notorious 'stop-go' policies of the 1950s and 1960s. In seeking to formulate useful generalisations on this key topic we should proceed with caution rather than scepticism.

Levels of *government final consumption* are examined in Figure 2.13. The share of government consumption in GDP did, indeed, show a marked rise from the early 1960s to the mid-1970s in both West and North Europe; moreover the share was throughout highest in the slower-growing North. However, in both cases the share trend flattened out in the period of slower and less stable growth from the mid-1970s. Ironically, the only other period of increase in the two regions was in the early 1980s, precisely the

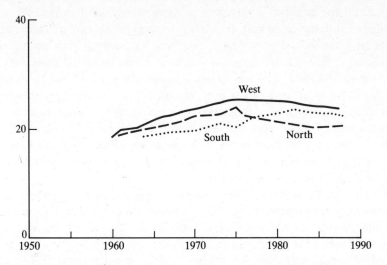

Figure 2.14c Education expenditure as % of government final consumption
Source: OECD data.

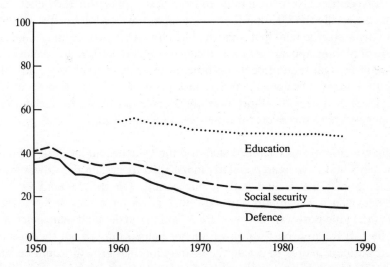

Figure 2.15a Shares of expenditure fields in government final consumption: West Europe
Source: OECD data.

time when governments like that of Mrs Thatcher in the UK were making their most strenuous efforts to cut public spending.

The panels of Figures 2.14 and 2.15 show, however, that *defence expenditure* – usually regarded (at least by economists) as the most wasteful form of public expenditure – declined as a proportion of the total in all regions after the brief Cold War increase of the early 1950s, and declined fastest in the North and West. By the late 1980s the share of defence in total public expenditure had converged in the three regions, being about 18 per cent in North Europe, 15 per cent in West Europe, and just under 14 per cent in South Europe (Figure 2.14a). The other item of public spending often singled out for criticism – though less unanimously so than defence – is *social security*. Figure 2.14b indicates that, in relation to total public expenditure, the element of social security has indeed grown most rapidly in the slowest-growing region, North Europe. However, that relative increase was from a smaller initial base, and again by the end of the period there was convergence among the regions: North Europe stood highest with a share of around 10 per cent, but the other two were committing about 9 per cent of their governmental expenditures to social security. (Note, however, that the figures are affected by differences between national systems – cf Sawyer 1982.) Again, attempts to cut back expenditure in this area, most prominent in North Europe, failed to reverse the trend, and in the UK the share continued to rise under Mrs Thatcher (partly because of high unemployment).

The shares of *health and education*, normally regarded as having an investment as well as a consumption element for society at large, showed modest increases in each region for the periods for which we have data. By the late 1980s, the share of public expenditure accounted for by education was about 24 per cent in West Europe, 23 per cent in South Europe, and just over 20 per cent in North Europe (Figure 2.14c). It needs to be emphasised that these figures relate purely to governmental expenditures. Non-governmental outlays on health and education, for example, are believed to vary widely across countries. Nevertheless there is modest support for the belief that North Europe, and especially the UK, has if anything under-invested in health and education. The widely advanced argument that countries like Great Britain have undertaken too little in the sphere of training appears very convincing (see eg Prais 1989; Steedman et al 1991). The imposition of legal requirements on firms to train their employees, notably in the former West Germany, has done the firms concerned (collectively) no obvious harm and probably a great deal of good. More recently, France has also introduced a minimum quota (proportionate to turnover) for firms' spending on training.

In the final section of this chapter I shall use the evidence adduced to appraise some of the arguments that have been popularly marshalled to explain the slower growth and greater instability of the second half of our period. On the demand side, there is considerable evidence to support the view that government economic management underpinned the long post-war recovery. By adopting the demand management policies advocated by J M Keynes, post-war governments helped smooth out the business cycle and induced business people to act on the assumption that growth would be sustained. Such government intervention went beyond fiscal and monetary policy, to include trade policies (including the active use of exchange rate variations), industrial policies to promote industry through direct intervention, and incomes policies to try to restrain the rate of rise of labour costs. There seems widespread agreement among economic economic historians that Keynesian policies, though not always applied in the best way possible, promoted growth up to the end of the 1960s, and may even have been the decisive factor on the demand side differentiating post-war growth from pre-war upheaval (see eg Boltho 1982a). However, there are also grounds for arguing that such Keynesian policies were increasingly inappropriate to the emerging world of the 1970s and after. First, expansion led by government demand, ie through cutting taxes or increasing public expenditure, worked best to expand output when resources were

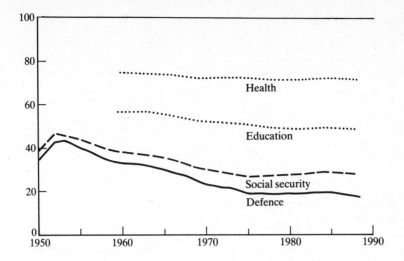

Figure 2.15b   Shares of expenditure fields in government final consumption: North Europe
Source: OECD data.

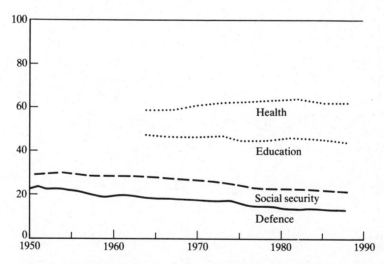

Figure 2.15c   Shares of expenditure fields in government final consumption: South Europe
Source: OECD data.

available in elastic supply. As I have already noted, the 1970s witnessed increasing constraints to the supply of raw materials (like oil), labour and so on. Second, Keynesian policies assumed the effective sovereignty of the nation-state. In practice, political sovereignty was becoming increasingly less relevant to economics; as the pattern of economic relationships became more and more international, the nation-state had less and less power to act independently to determine its own economic fate (van der Wee 1986: ch. 8; see also Eastwood, Chapter 7 in this volume).

The consequence was a reaction by the state against Keynesian economic management that reached its political fruition in the 1980s. In part this was based on a

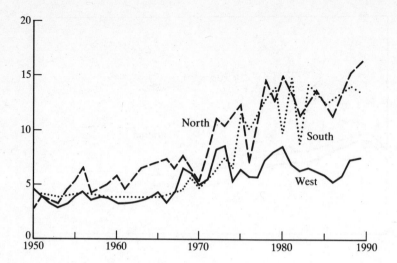

Figure 2.16a Nominal interest rates (per cent)
Source: Central Bank data.

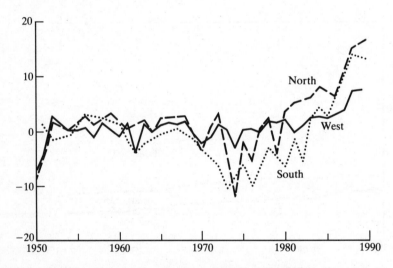

Figure 2.16b Real interest rates (nominal rates less rate of inflation) (per cent)
Source: OECD data, Central Bank data.

crude fundamentalist belief that the economy should be run like a corner-store; but there was a more serious argument to the effect that government expenditure was 'crowding out' private investment, and forcing interest rates up to levels higher than was good for business or indeed the country at large. There is, it must be said, little quantitative support for the direct crowding-out argument, in that government expenditure (Figure 2.13) more often moves in the same direction relative to national income as investment (Figure 2.6) than in the opposite direction. Where exceptions occur, as in North Europe in the 1980s and South Europe from the 1970s, the break in the relationship appears to come from the investment side rather than from increased

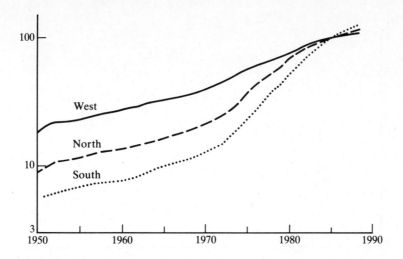

Figure 2.17   Price inflation by region (GDP deflators on logarithmic scale 1985 = 100)
Source: OECD data.

public spending. The indirect crowding-out that might have occurred via pressure on interest rates (assuming an inelastic supply of savings) can be gauged from Figure 2.16. It must be emphasised that there is no unique measure of the interest rate; rather there is a spectrum reflecting differing assessments of risks and returns to each type of asset. Figure 2.16 uses mainly central bank rates of discount as its measure. Consideration of other rates would undoubtedly affect the absolute levels calculated, but it is unlikely that it would greatly alter the time pattern. The much higher nominal rates of interest in the second half of the period, especially in North and South Europe, are evident from Figure 2.16a.

However, some part of this shift simply reflects the higher rate of price inflation of the second half of the period. Figure 2.16b adjusts the nominal rates of Figure 2.16a by the rate of inflation in the immediately preceding period, to give a measure (even rougher than the nominal one) of the 'real' rate of interest. The 1970s then emerge as a period of very low real interest rates; indeed substantially negative rates according to these particular measures in both North and South Europe. It is rather the 1980s which saw high real rates (paradoxically, particularly in the Britain of Mrs Thatcher, who was most strident in her concern to reduce 'crowding-out'). Again, there is little evident inverse relationship with aggregate GDFCF, as plotted in Figure 2.6a, although the data on producer durables in Figure 2.6b suggest that fixed investment of other types (factories and dwellings, etc) may indeed have been restricted by high real rates of interest in North and South Europe from the late 1970s onwards. In West Europe, by contrast, such forms of investment expanded.

A second popular explanation for slowdown, often advanced by the same theorists and politicians, was that excessive inflation itself was curbing expansion, with the advent of 'stagflation' in the 1970s. Figure 2.17 charts the implicit GDP deflators from the above calculations, using a logarithmic scale to reflect rates of growth in the price level (rates of inflation). West Europe certainly had the slowest annual rate of inflation,

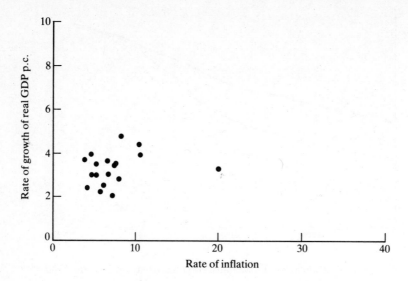

Figure 2.18a   Growth rates of price level and real output per head, 1950–85
Source: World Bank output data, OECD price data.

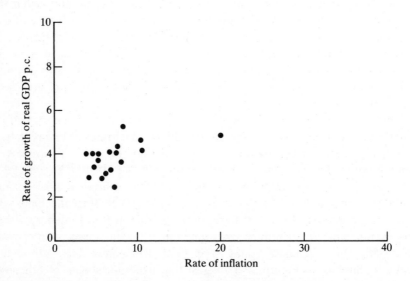

Figure 2.18b   Growth rates of prices level and real output per head, 1950–88
Source: OECD output data, OECD price data.

but South Europe, which had marginally the highest real rate of growth, also had the highest rate of inflation. North Europe, with its slower rate of growth, stood about halfway between the other two regions in terms of inflation rates.

As other factors may be surmised to have distorted this inter-regional relationship, Figure 2.18 has been drawn as a scattergram of rates of inflation (the implicit GDP

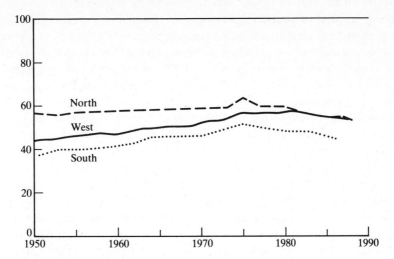

Figure 2.19   Labour share in GDP (per cent)
Source: OECD data.

deflators) against rates of economic growth (real GDP), in this case at the level of individual European countries. Figure 2.18a uses the World Bank data on the latter variable to show the relationship by country for the period 1950–85. Even if Iceland, with its 20 per cent-plus annual rate of inflation, is excluded, there is no statistically significant relationship between the two variables, and whatever relationship there is is positive rather than negative as required by the hypothesis. Use of the somewhat less reliable OECD data for real GDP growth for the period 1950–88 (Figure 2.18b) produces the same result. This is not to imply that inflation was unimportant. Rather it indicates that governments which chose to try to cure the slowdown through single-minded reliance on bringing down inflation ran the risk of making the patient far worse, especially in the context of the painful measures that were sometimes adopted to this effect.

A third possible explanation, related to the above, was that labour was demanding 'excessive' wage increases, which limited investment through cutting profits, and also priced the products labour was employed to produce out of increasingly competitive markets. Such arguments have been put forward by left-wing as well as right-wing critics (eg Mazier 1982). The argument at the European level runs as follows: in the course of the 1960s, the steady tightening of the labour market pushed unions towards making larger and larger wage claims, to the point where by the end of that decade they were going well beyond what could be justified by the growth rate of productivity. On top of this, labour unions were cultivating restrictive practices, especially with a view to raising the degree of job security of their members. It is easy to understand why they should have wanted to do so, but, according to the argument under review, the effect was to make the labour market less and less free and more and more immune from the realities of economic circumstances. Labour was seen as pricing itself out of the job market. General support for this argument was visible by the end of the 1970s in the form of a widespread feeling that radical labour reform was required.

The focus on the role of labour was by no means limited to the UK (although the exceptionally restrictive practices prevalent in that country, leading to closed shops, demarcation disputes, and so on, may help account for why the UK prospered so much less than continental Europe). Indeed the most spectacular episode in the evolution of that role were the *événements* in France in 1968, which produced an explosion of wage claims and restrictive practices, to which the threatened French government was only too happy to concede.

The left-wing approach to the possible role of labour in the slowdown has not been so much to deny it, as to see it as only one aspect of a story which featured business as well as labour continually claiming too much of the cake. It must be granted, however, that, according to the available statistical evidence, labour was more successful than business in fighting for shares in the national cake, at least in the short term. The evidence is set out in Figure 2.19. Labour's share rose up to the mid-1970s, and only in the 1980s was there any appreciable decline. However, the increases in the faster-growing macro-regions of West and South Europe were much greater than in North Europe, where the issue probably drew greater attention. Moreover, the rising wage share of the earlier years went with a rising investment share, and conversely the declining wage share of the later years was associated with lower rates of investment, so that there was no one-to-one correspondence between rising wages on the one side and falling profit shares leading to falling investment shares on the other. The answer to this apparent paradox is to be found in the decline in the share of consumption in GDP (Figure 2.8), which was actually at its most precipitate over the period in which the wage share rose. In the end, then, the 'role of labour' argument also lacks conviction.

Summary

This chapter has examined macroeconomic data for Europe with two major contrasts in mind – that between the major regions within Europe and that between the more sustained growth trend of the earlier half of our period and the more erratic one thereafter. In the final section of the chapter, various theories about the causes of relative decline were assessed on the basis of the available data. In general, the theories appeared to merit rejection on one dimension of comparison or the other. It hardly needs to be added that most of the tests used are rather elementary, and each issue merits much more sophisticated analysis.

But if these theories do not suffice, how else should one seek to account for the contrasts observed? The earlier part of this chapter develops the common view that there was a shift around the middle of our period from extensive growth based on elastic supplies of resources, including labour, to more intensive growth based on better utilisation of less elastically supplied resources (cf Rostow 1978; van der Wee 1986: chs 4–5). The countries which fared best were those that best handled this shift from extensive growth to intensive growth. My personal view is that overall too much attention was devoted to getting things like prices or government expenditure or wages down, and not enough to getting productivity up. This was particularly so in the less successful countries (cf also OECD 1986). While excessive bureaucracy could snarl up growth, to an extreme extent exemplified in Eastern Europe, the opposite extreme of hands-off free marketeering was not necessarily the best way of achieving productivity dynamism. The countries and regions in Europe that were more successful appear to have devoted much greater attention to the micro level – to the individual employees, firms and industries that make up the macro-economy. Space precludes a full microeconomic analysis, which in justice would have to be at least as detailed as the above macro study. Suffice to point out at this stage that the rising competitive threat of Japan and the newly industrialising countries (NICs) seems to have been much more obviously based on getting the microeconomics right – in areas like industrial organisation, technology, training, and so on – than on contractionist macro management. The micro theme will, of course, form one of the leitmotifs of the chapters which follow.

Notes

1   The countries included under West Europe are Austria, Belgium, France, the former West Germany, Luxembourg, the Netherlands and Switzerland. North Europe comprises Denmark, Finland, Iceland, Ireland, Norway, Sweden and the United Kingdom. South Europe is made up of Greece, Italy, Portugal and Spain. Where figures on one or more of these member countries are missing for particular years, they are estimated in a variety of ways, usually by comparison with other countries of the particular region. The most onerous task was to make the data time-consistent, which was done by overlapping series backwards from the final year for which data in each case were available.

2   Total output is defined as what is termed 'all industries' by the OECD; it differs from GDP mainly in excluding the government sector.

3   As with North Sea oil, the opening up of high-capital-cost Siberian oil deposits in the 1970s was, if anything, a *response* to the increases in the price of Middle Eastern crude. In the face of a sharply rising long-run marginal cost curve for oil production, the Soviet Union remained largely a price-taker on international oil markets.

References

Abramovitz M (1986) Catching up, forging ahead, and falling behind. *Journal of Economic History* **46**(2): 386–406

Baumol W (1986) Productivity growth, convergence, and welfare. *American Economic Review* **76**(4): 1072–85

Baumol W, Blackman S A B, Wolff E N (1989) *Productivity and American Leadership*. MIT Press, Cambridge, Mass.

Beckerman W (1962) Projecting Europe's growth. *Economic Journal* **72**(4): 912–25

Bernabe F (1982) The Labour Market and Unemployment. In Boltho (ed) 1982a

Boltho A (ed) (1982a) *The European Economy: Growth and Crisis*. Oxford University Press

Boltho A (1982b) Growth. In Boltho (ed) 1982a

Cornwall J (1977) *Modern Capitalism: Its Growth and Transformation*. Martin Robertson

Deaton A S (1975) The structure of demand 1920–1970. *Fontana Economic History of Europe* vol 5(2). Fontana

De Long J B (1988) Productivity growth, convergence, and welfare: comment. *American Economic Review* **78**(4): 1138–59

Dollar D, Wolff E N (1988) Convergence of industry labor productivity among advanced economies, 1963–1982. *Review of Economics and Statistics* **70**(4): 549–58

Dosi G, Pavitt K, Soete L (1990) *The Economics of Technical Change and International Trade.* Harvester/Wheatsheaf

Ergas H (1987) The importance of technology policy. In Dasgupta P, Stoneman P (eds) *Economic Policy and Technological Performance.* Cambridge University Press

Feinstein C H, Matthews R (1990) The growth of output and productivity in the UK: the 1980s as a phase of postwar development. *National Institute Economic Review* 133: 78–90

Kaldor N (1966) Causes of the slow rate of economic growth of the United Kingdom (inaugural lecture). Cambridge University Press

Kindleberger C P (1967) *Europe's Postwar Growth: The Role of Labor Supply.* Harvard University Press, Cambridge, Mass.

Maddison A (1976) Economic policy and performance in Europe, 1913–1970. *Fontana Economic History of Europe* vol 5(2). Fontana

Mazier J (1982) Growth and crisis – a Marxist interpretation. In Boltho (ed) 1982a

Nelson R R, Wright G (1991) The rise and fall of American technological leadership: the postwar era in historical perspective. Forthcoming in *Journal of Economic Literature*

OECD (1980) *Women and Employment: Policies for Equal Opportunities.* Paris

OECD (1986) *Productivity in Industry: Prospects and Policies.* Paris

Prais S J (1989) Qualified manpower in engineering: Britain and other industrially advanced countries. *National Institute Economic Review* 127: 76–83

Rostow W W (1978) *The World Economy: History and Prospect.* Macmillan

Sawyer M (1982) Income distribution and the welfare state. In Boltho (ed) 1982a

Scherer F M (1984) *Innovation and Growth: Schumpeterian Perspectives.* MIT Press, Cambridge, Mass.

Soete L (1987) The newly emerging information technology sector. In Freeman C, Soete L (eds) *Technical Change and Full Employment.* Basil Blackwell

Steedman H, Mason G, Wagner K (1991) Intermediate skills and the workplace: deployment, standards and supply in Britain, France and Germany. *National Institute Economic Review* 136: 60–76

Summers R, Heston A (1984) Improved international comparisons of real product and its composition. *Review of Income and Wealth* **30**

Summers R, Heston A (1988) A new set of international comparisons of real product and price levels: estimates for 130 countries, 1950–1985. *Review of Income and Wealth* **34**

Svennilson I (1954) *Growth and Stagnation in the European Economy.* UN Economic Commission for Europe, Geneva

Van der Wee H (1986) *Prosperity and Upheaval: The World Economy, 1945–1980, Pelican Economic History of World Economy Series.* Penguin

Van Wijnbergen S (1984) Inflation, employment and the Dutch Disease in oil-exporting countries: a short-run disequilibrium analysis. *Quarterly Journal of Economics* **99**(2): 233–50

Vatter H G (1967) Has there been a twentieth-century consumer durables revolution? *Journal of Economic History* **27**(1): 1–16

CHAPTER 3

The political economy of the European integration process

PETER HOLMES

Introduction: the political roots of European integration

Before proceeding to an examination of the process of economic integration, it is necessary to look at the political basis of European integration. The reader will need no reminder that the agreement to establish the EEC was signed barely a decade after a savage war between Germany and its neighbours, following a century of invasion, humiliation and renewed fighting. In the late 1940s, as Europe faced the twin problems of reconstruction and the apparent threat from the East, it seemed quite likely that within twenty years of the end of the Second World War history might repeat itself. Drastic plans were envisaged to put an end to this threat. The Morgenthau Plan, seriously contemplated by the Allies for a while, envisaged the physical removal of all German industrial strength. Common sense, and the feeling that West Germany was needed as an ally against the East, ruled this out. Consequently an alternative had to be found that would both allow German recovery and remove French fears of a new war. A federal union of European states was actively discussed, and the Council of Europe in Strasbourg was seen as a possible core for it. Such ideas foundered largely on British opposition. The UK saw itself as a great imperial power, with Atlantic and Empire links that could not be sacrificed to purely regional interests.

The other West European states conceived of their own interests as being best served by progress towards some form of union. Within Western Europe, as elsewhere in the world, many analysts (see, for example, Kindleberger 1987) saw the Second World War as the result of economic conflicts that had got out of control as a result of inadequate international co-operation. The slump of the 1930s, and the ensuing 6 million unemployed, were seen as having been a direct cause of Hitler's rise to power. The closure of the national markets of the European states to each other's goods through the 'beggar-thy-neighbour' protectionist policies of the 1930s had, arguably, been one of the principal causes of Germany's drive for eastwards expansion. With the post-1945 closing off of eastern markets and raw material supplies by the Cold War, Germany's need for secure economic ties with the West now became critical. It was clear that these economic ties could be built only on the basis of secure political links.

With this in view, and bearing in mind the failure of the Council of Europe to create any real integrationist momentum, Jean Monnet proposed the setting up of a European Coal and Steel Community (see Anne Stevens, Chapter 4 in this volume), an essentially economic arrangement, but one which was intended to deal with crucial political problems. The impetus behind the initiative did, indeed, run largely along the Franco-German axis. The French were anxious to secure an arrangement with Germany that would eliminate the risks of another war. It is clear that in the immediate post-war period the West Germans had little to lose from this. They were constrained in their military role, and felt the need for political arrangements to guarantee access to markets.

The 1950s saw a series of proposals for further moves towards union, resisted by the British, accepted by the Germans, and viewed with considerable equivocation by France. Thus, for example, the project for a European Defence Community as a framework within which Germany could be allowed to re-arm was rejected by the French parliament. This underlined the extent to which France viewed the cause of European unity as essentially a basis for safeguarding French national interests, a theme that would recur subsequently.

Thus by the mid-1950s the member states of the Organisation for European Economic Cooperation (see Chapter 4) found that the most obvious political routes to union had been foreclosed by the Council of Europe's failure to develop beyond the level of discussion forum, and by the collapse of the European Defence Community initiative. But the success of the European Coal and Steel Community, and of earlier economic co-operation arrangements such as the European Payments Union, confirmed policy-makers in the conviction that the correct path was to seek some form of economic link that would bring with it the need for enhanced political co-operation. The enhanced political co-operation – if indeed it could be realised – would in turn promote political stability. This stability should produce further economic benefits, creating a virtuous circle. The process was not predestined from the start to succeed, and there was ample scope for dispute as to the form of economic integration to be adopted. This truth was brought home sharply by the bitter row between the British on the one hand, and the major continental powers on the other, over whether the goal should be a minimalist 'free trade area' or something more ambitious. But before continuing with the story we must pause to clarify our terms.

Concepts of integration

It is traditional to distinguish a number of alternative forms of economic integration. In a *preferential trading area* members agree to lower (not eliminate) trade barriers against goods coming from each other; but they leave barriers against third countries in place. In 1982 Nicholas Kaldor described the EEC as such an area, on the basis that, although all tariff barriers had been removed, only some of the non-tariff barriers were down. In a *free trade area all* barriers against partners are removed. Both these arrangements presuppose the continued existence of some form of economic frontier; even the free trade area does not allow free circulation of third-country goods, which are liable to the duty levied by the final importer. A *customs union* goes further, involving as it does a *common* external regime against third-country goods, so that in principle all internal barriers against the free movement of goods can be removed. The original Treaty of Rome committed the signatories to establish, by 1969, a *common market*. A common market takes us outside the limits of a customs union in implying the free movement of *factors of production* as well as of goods and services. (This principle was accepted by the six states that signed the treaty at the time, though as we shall see in Chapter 4 General de Gaulle did not wish to go beyond the narrowest interpretation of the concept of common market.) An *economic and monetary union*, finally, would go one step further still, with full integration of fiscal policy and a common currency (though there is debate about how much fiscal integration is required once a monetary union is in place).

The concepts in action

The British were always against the broader goals. Even after the signing of the Treaty of Rome by the original Six, the British continued to try to convince the rest of Europe of the virtues of the free trade area as opposed to the common market. Under the former arrangement, each country would still be able to have its own individual trade policy with respect to third countries. This would have the advantage for Britain that its membership of the free trade area would not affect its relations with the USA or the Commonwealth. Indeed, at the same time as the EEC was set up by the Treaty of Rome, the British persuaded six other smaller European countries (Sweden, Norway, Denmark, Switzerland, Austria and Portugal) to join it in EFTA (European Free Trade Area). These countries had in common either a history of close economic links with the UK or a commitment to neutrality and hence a reluctance to cede sovereignty. EFTA promised free trade in industrial goods, but no common external tariff and no common agricultural policy. (In fact EFTA states each continued to pursue rather costly national protection regimes for agriculture.) In the first few years after the signing of the Treaty of Rome the British tried to persuade the continental European partners to give up on the more ambitious EEC project and create a wider EFTA. However, from about 1963 the British realised that not even de Gaulle's hostility to certain aspects of the EEC could prevent its growth. So the UK began the long and painful process of applying for membership of the Common Market.

Although the Treaty of Rome did not explicitly define the term Common Market, its articles called for free internal trade, a common external tariff, and the free movement of services, workers and capital within the European Economic Community. As we shall see in more detail, the signing of the Single European Act (SEA) in 1986 reaffirmed a solemn commitment to these original goals of the Common Market by defining the 'internal market', to be created by 31 December 1992, as 'an area without frontiers in which the free circulation of goods, services, persons and capital is ensured'. The preamble to the SEA spoke af a general commitment to a complete 'European Union'. But the amendments to the Rome Treaty brought in by the SEA permitted, rather than required, the member states to go further and establish a fuller economic and monetary union. The preamble to the Single European Act appears to commit those states to the creation of a 'European Union': in effect a United States of

Europe. The UK government has, however, argued that this is not a legal commitment, but merely a pious hope. Nevertheless the draft treaty on union under discussion during 1991 explicitly proposes the creation of a 'European Union'. We shall argue that the political dynamics of this situation are such that the nature of the general political undertakings are just as important as any concrete proposals.

The putative *economic benefits of economic integration* are customarily thought of as based on the proposition that a customs union (CU) is a first step towards universal free trade, itself a good thing. But such a union involves discrimination against non-members, and this has raised doubts in some minds about that basic proposition itself. The GATT (General Agreement on Trade and Tariffs) agreement of 1947 enshrined as its cornerstone the principle of 'most favoured nation' (MFN), which posits that any trade preference extended to one trading partner must be extended to all. This was intended to stop the world descending into a sub-zero game of exclusive trading blocs. However Article 24 of GATT made a special exception for trade groups that were abolishing tariffs and other trade barriers to create fully fledged FTAs or CUs; these were permitted, on the grounds that they represented genuine steps towards world-wide free trade as opposed to ways of introducing new elements of discrimination. But it is not quite as simple as that.

Trade creation and trade diversion

Needless to say, Adam Smith had in the *Wealth of Nations* (Bk IV, ch. 6) identified the problem as early as 1776. It was subsequently rediscovered in the 1950s. Suppose a country opens up trade exclusively with one other country, while maintaining barriers against third-party countries; then the partner's 'merchants and manufacturers enjoy a sort of monopoly in the country which is so indulgent to them'. This must be the earliest reference to what has been called 'trade diversion'. In the 1950s a new literature on the theory of customs unions began to formalise the idea that partial liberalisation of trade might actually make things worse. The 'theory of second best' argued that if there were a wide range of trade barriers in place covering all goods and all partners, there could be a worsening of economic efficiency if some, but not all, of the barriers were removed. Writers such as Viner (1950) and Lipsey (1960) made a distinction between *trade creation* and *trade diversion*.

These terms have been used in numerous subtly distinct ways, but the broad idea is to distinguish newly created trade flows (trade creation) from those which simply displace pre-existing trade flows (trade diversion). In essence, trade creation occurs when liberalising imports from the union causes a country to import something that it had previously been making at higher cost at home. Trade diversion occurs when the special discriminatory privileges accorded to the union members allows them to capture markets previously supplied by non-member states. From the point of view of the importing country, this leads, of course, to economic losses. The outsiders had been able to take the market even in the face of the tariff that is abolished (for union members) when the union is established. This must mean that they are the most competitive source of supply in the world, and transferring the demand of the given country to a union supplier means paying a higher price. This does not mean that a customs union is always a wholly bad thing if it leads to trade diversion. If the trade liberalisation leads through lower consumer prices to a higher total volume of sales of the imported item, there may still be net benefits even if the sales come from the 'wrong source'. As Smith put it, 'even the favouring country, therefore, may still gain by the trade, though less than if there was free competition' (Bk IV, ch. 6). For example, if we have tight rules on Japanese car imports but import cars freely from Germany, there is trade diversion. But if German cars are better value than our own and nearly as good as Japanese cars, then there can be a net gain. (Better value in this context means that British workers have to work less hard to produce exportable goods that can be sold to pay for German imports than if they had to make the cars at home.) We can argue about whether the new trade flows should be called diversion or creation of trade; probably, we should say that a given change in trade flows can simultaneously involve both diversion and creation.

These distinctions help us to understand how modern trade theory is able to specify the conditions under which customs unions will be a step towards general free trade. It can be shown that if the right level of tariffs and taxes/subsidies is set, any union can be made efficient for all partners. But with the wrong policies unions are not always advantageous, which helps explain why so many free trade arrangements among LDCs have broken down (see Vousden 1990: ch. 10; for a full non-technical survey of the theory of economic integration as applied to the EC, see Krugman 1987). In brief, when the new union has low external tariffs, there is likely to be a gain. Little trade diversion will occur, and such trade diversion as there is will bear a small unit cost. More specifically, recent analysis has demonstrated that for any potential customs union there is always *some* external tariff that will make the union a beneficial one. If the level of external protection is low enough, we can be sure that trade creation gains will exceed trade diversion losses.

The most obvious example of trade diversion in Europe is the EC's Common Agricultural Policy (see Howe, Chapter 16 in this volume, on agriculture). This was set up in the mid-1960s under French pressure. The French feared that they would be flooded with imports of manufactures from Germany under Common Market liberalisation, and wanted in return to have a large part of the German foodstuffs market reserved for them. The conception is mercantilist, but it highlights the fact that simple calculations of gains from trade may be politically irrelevant if some important sectional economic interest thinks it will lose from a given trade liberalisation measure. Economists will query the need to buy off farmers, but it was clearly considered politically necessary at the time. (Sectional-interest politics, it may nevertheless be noted, can breed strategies that are downright mistaken, rather than merely misconceived. There is some irony in the fact that French farmers have actually always been more competitive than German farmers, and it is really the part-time farmers of Germany who most need protection.)

Another idea that is somewhat surprising at first sight, but critical to an understanding of integration processes, is that countries will gain from a union if they are currently producing similar goods, but potentially suited to producing different goods. This is because in the free trade comparative advantage perspective, the benefits of a union accrue through the lower cost of imports, and the transfer of resources out of industries in which the given country does not have a comparative advantage. The gains from trade arise because as one activity shuts down, the resources employed in it can transfer to an activity in which their marginal product is higher. In the simplest textbook 'Ricardian' model, producers are assumed to be homogeneous so that they can adapt easily to any new activity. (The stress is worth placing on 'activity' rather than sector, because typically a firm faced with new competition will modify its production line within an industry, rather than change industries altogether.) More complex models acknowledge that factors of production tend to be better suited to some activities than others. But in general the trade theory used by economists assumes that resources leaving one activity will find employment in another. This is, of course, unrealistic, but as a first approximation it is no more unrealistic than the alternative extreme view, which is that they will never find re-employment. What certainly can be said with confidence is that the ending of trade barriers will mean that investors are no longer given false signals about the relative profitability of alternative uses of capital.

We can illustrate this last idea by looking at the case of relatively inefficient countries joining the EC. Consider the cases of Spain and East Germany. Under Franco in Spain and the communists in the GDR, these countries had built up industrial sectors not exposed to international competition. A lot of what they were producing would never have justified the investments made if they had had to satisfy the test of profitability in a free market. If Spain and East Germany had had free trade, the workers in those activities/sectors would have been employed in something else. Once in place, and then exposed to competition after EC entry, the activities/sectors cannot survive. Is this bad for the countries concerned? The specialisation argument runs as follows: on the contrary, freer trade is a golden opportunity to abandon unprofitable activities that are a burden on the rest of the economy, and which condemn their employees to low productivity, and therefore ultimately low real wages. Tariffs and state regulation preserve such activities. Thus, from a free trade point of view, the benefits of Spanish entry into the EC should primarily accrue to Spain. Spain had higher tariffs before it entered the EC. It agreed to remove more barriers on entry than the rest of the EC did, and therefore stood to benefit from a greater reallocation of resources from uncompetitive to competitive activities, and hence to make the greater gain. By analogy, it should in the long run be East Germany that has more to gain than West Germany from the restructuring consequential on German unification. But what about the short run?

It is clear that lowering tariffs can cause a country immediate balance of payments difficulties. Hence it has long been argued that exchange rate flexibility is needed during the transition period when a customs union is established, so that a generalised boost can be given to the exporting industries to offset the loss of activity in import-competing industries. The argument has been adapted in recent years. Many writers hold that once a customs union has been formed, fixed exchange rates and a common currency are desirable. (This issue is dealt with in Chapter 8 of this volume.) Here we shall just focus on one aspect of the relationship between trade and exchange rate policy. Suppose that some event has taken place which worsens the competitive position of a country – either a burst of inflation or a lowering of tariffs. Then a subsequent devaluation can correct this situation. However, the correction would only be temporary if the devaluation itself stimulated a new offsetting response which wiped out the gain from the devaluation. That might take the form of a burst of inflation, or a relaxation in the pursuit of productivity growth as competitive constraints are eased. Even worse would be a situation in which every time firms experienced an intensification of competition they expected the government to help them out through devaluation. Now it is by no means clear that the risk of devaluation does modify expectations in this way, but there is a widespread perception that it may do, and a corresponding desire on the part of governments to restrict their own freedom to use this instrument.

Economies of scale and X-efficiency effects

Economies of scale have been pinpointed as a major additional source of gains from customs unions, in addition to the basic trade-creation benefits. The scope for improving efficiency is greater where there is scope for economies of scale for the following reason. Conventional 'gains from trade' involve shifting resources from one sector to another, with the productivity improvement affecting only the resources which actually move. Resources which stay put have unaltered productivity. However, certain types of economy of scale are capable of enhancing the productivity of non-marginal, ie non-mobile resources. If costs in a given industry depend on the scale of output, then by shifting additional resources from declining industries to expanding ones we can lower costs and raise unit output, not only on the new production but also on the pre-existing volume of activity. This may arise for a number of reasons, most obviously where fixed costs can be spread over a greater volume of output. If the declining activity disappears altogether, then we do not have to worry about loss of economies of scale in that sector caused by its contraction (Corden 1972).

Most early analyses of customs unions considered that the scale economy effects would be very hard to measure, but the more recent work of Owen (1983) has sought to demonstrate that a very large part of the gains from the initial formation of the EEC came from the exploitation of scale economies. Opening up an economy to trade can, of course, alter the efficiency of the entire traded good sector, and not merely the resources directly affected by the adjustment process. Exposure to more intense competition may cause all firms to improve their efficiency across the board. The early writers on European integration (eg Scitovsky 1958; Balassa 1961) argued that European business people before the formation of the EEC simply did not avail themselves of the best practice techniques that were available in *Europe*, let alone across the whole world, that is their levels of *X-efficiency* were low. This could have been due to limited knowledge and limited horizons of comparison. Exposing the firms to more local competition would force them to rethink their activities. Pelkmans (1984) has warned that this 'cold shower' effect is not a logical inevitability. A 'warm sun' effect might make firms more willing to innovate if they knew they had a secure market, and one may ask what is so special about competition within the Common Market as opposed to the generalised benefits from free trade. The case for the EC can be supported by the recent research of Porter (1990), who argues that competitive rivalry leads to a desire to emulate and that geographical closeness is more likely to ensure that rivalry leads to imitation.

It must be stressed in all this that the X-inefficiency idea is somewhat at odds with the neo-classical idea that firms instinctively know how to maximise profits. But if X-inefficiency is widespread, and can in principle be eliminated, there is very large potential scope indeed for efficiency gains. Moving a small fraction of the nation's work-force from declining to strong industries is costly and painful; it is obviously more effective to discover ways in which entrepreneurs can learn how to raise the productivity of existing resources in *all* existing uses. What remains unclear, however, is why forming a customs union such as the EC should *by itself* force firms to exploit such gains, if they had not been exploited already.

Let us try to generalise this point. The problem with most analysis of scale economies and competition effects is that if there are very big gains to be had from their exploitation, one does not need to form a customs union in order to secure the gains. It is easy to illlustrate the argument by supposing that doubling the size of a plant can reduce unit costs by 10 per cent. If there are only two options, a smaller plant to serve just the national market and one twice as big capable of meeting European demand as well, then the investor has an interest in building the larger plant under the pre-Common Market regime as long as foreign tariffs do not outweigh the cost savings. It was pointed out in the 1960s (Lundgren 1969) that if you could lower costs by 10 per cent through having the Euro-size plant, a 10 per cent tariff would not discourage you from building one. (And if you did not choose to have such a plant with the tariffs in place, you would not build one when the tariffs were removed on economic grounds alone.) By lowering average costs by 10 per cent when the bigger plant is built, not only do we produce the extra output at lower cost, but we also save 10 per cent on what we are already producing for the domestic market. It is a fact that in the 1960s the typical industrial tariffs that were being removed were of the order of 10 per cent. The same line of reasoning leads one to ask why removal of tariff barriers should have so great an effect on the intensity of competition. Here, as in the case of economies of scale, modest tariffs can only protect and permit the survival of firms that are *slightly* less efficient than their foreign rivals. The implication is that the clinching arguments in favour of integration may indeed relate to the vaguer end of the X-efficiency spectrum. We take up this point again later.

The argument presented so far suggests that the bigger the potential economies of scale, the greater the gains from specialisation and trade integration, *particularly* for a small country. As pointed out in a recent OECD report (1987), many of the fastest growing countries in the post-war world have been small or 'dependent' states with a limited home market, able to exploit access to world markets following liberalisation of trade. In addition, free trade for imports as well as exports is the only way for such economies to reconcile the twin aims of a high degree of specialisation and concentration of production on a smaller range of items and the preservation of competition, which is needed as a spur to innovation. Thus the majority view among economists would be that the presence of scale economies makes the integration of economies desirable even for relatively small and/or weak countries, who can in this way at least concentrate on what they are best (or least bad) at.

There is, however, another school of thought, associated with the concept of 'cumulative causation' (Marquez Mendez 1987; see also Dunford, Chapter 9 in this volume), which argues to the contrary. Critics of orthodox trade theory maintain that international trade does not contain self-equilibrating mechanisms to ensure a convergence of economies. Economies of scale, they say, will lead to concentration of economic power in existing poles of development and a further accumulation of capital, expertise and purchasing power in the richest countries, as strength breeds strength. From this point of view Germany has the most to gain from any integration process. Such views are widely held by those sceptical of the invisible hand.

Clearly the argument cannot be dismissed out of hand. Equally it is difficult to demonstrate it conclusively from the empirical record. Historical evidence does *not* show a continuous process of impoverishment of Southern Europe since it began integrating with the North. It is indeed true that successful high-growth regions in a given period attract investment and continue to experience relatively rapid growth in succeeeding periods. But durability of success does not mean permanence of cumulative advantage, and we have many examples of regions which see a turn-around in their fate quite rapidly from one decade to the next. This is probably most marked in the USA, as one sees, for example, the rise of the South as a manufacturing region and the successive ups and downs of the North-East and North-West. In Europe, the 1970s witnessed much faster growth in the South than in the North. France, in particular, has seen a remarkable transfer of economic activity away from its old industrial regions. West Germany itself did not display patterns of regional concentration *within* its boundaries. Reunification has, of course, retrospectively changed all that.

One reason for optimism in the face of the renewed strength of the integration process in Europe is that economies of scale do usually induce countries and firms to specialise, not in whole industries, but in narrower product bands. The dominant pattern of specialisation in European industry now is what is known as *intra-industry* trade. This means that countries export and import more or less the same things. Many national industries that have a high share of import penetration also have a high share of exports in total output. Clearly micro-specialisation raises far fewer problems in terms of the possibility of structural unemployment than macro-specialisation. Britain's problem is that, compared to its EC partners, the higher import shares are higher still than the higher export shares. For Germany it is the other way round.

It is ironic, but fully in concordance with the arguments we have put forward, that weakness often arises from failure to specialise sufficiently. The British car industry, for example, might well have been far more successful in its attempts to restructure from the 1960s onwards, if it had concentrated its resources on the segments it was good at, and abandoned low-value-added mass production as did the Germans in the 1960s. That was how Germany profited from intra-industry trade in this particular sector.

Some people have argued that the scope for economies of scale must be constrained by limits on the scope for specialisation itself, since the same number of industries seem to survive in each country. But it is more common to suppose that specialisation within industries is due to economies of scale in particular *production processes*, rather than being associated with the overall size of the given sector. This serves to reinforce our key conclusion that the pattern of specialisation that has developed under the aegis of the EC has had very few direct implications for the balance of the main sectors of the different national economies.

There does remain considerable room for controversy, however, about the directionality of the causal relationship between economies of scale and specialisation. Clearly, economies of scale promote specialisation and specialisation permits their realisation. There is some debate at present about whether new technology is increasing or decreasing the role of economies of scale. Computerised 'flexible manufacturing systems' permit small production units to gain access to the latest technology. This devolution to smaller *production units* does not, however, necessarily mean that the *firms* they belong to will always be smaller. We are at the same time currently witnessing the phenomenon of 'globalisation' of industry, whereby investment flows across borders, inside and outside the EC, are becoming as important as, or more important than, traditional trade flows. Many of the small production units just referred to form part of large multinational firms. Julius (1990) has estimated that US firms sell far more in Europe from their locally owned production units (often operating on a small-to-medium scale) than they do in the form of imports from the USA. The two interpretations of the process converge in the idea of the global corporation seen as a network of small flexible sites close to their markets.

Thus the process of European integration is taking the form, not so much of concentration of production of individual products in 'metropolitan' factories to gain economies of scale, as the expansion of firms across borders through investment. This has positive and negative aspects. The theory of multinational firms (Caves 1982) tells us that firms invest abroad to capitalise on a firm-specific asset that they can exploit only within the firm, and where there are not enough economies of scale to justify production for the whole world in one place. The easiest way to set up a production base in a neighbouring country is to buy an existing firm. This is good if it means Europe-wide exploitation of hitherto localised know-how. But as we shall see later, it also poses problems for competition policy.

Quantifying the impact of the original Common Market and the role of invisible barriers

Alasdair Smith (Chapter 5 in this volume) explains the detailed calculations that have been done to quantify the '1992' plan. Before looking briefly at this issue, it is worth trying to assess the quantitative significance of the arguments we have detailed in relation to the *initial* stages of integration. If we are to do this properly, it is not enough just to look at economic circumstances before and after the removal of tariffs. British entry into the EC in 1973, for example, coincided with so many other shocks that 'before and after' will not do. So any serious calculation has to compare actual events with what would have happened if the EC had never been created, or if a given country had never joined it. Or to compare predictions of the EC economy in the 1990s on the basis of 'existing policies' with other predictions that assume the 1992 plan has already been articulated. It is relatively straightforward to look at one industry and predict what might happen to it if tariffs altered and nothing else changed, but it is harder to picture the effects on a continental economy of the creation of the Common Market or the Single Market, including the inevitable consequential effects. What we *will* find is that when we restrict our attention to the easily measurable we obtain modest figures. When we try to incorporate all the factors that may change, we simply cannot avoid speculation.

It is perhaps only superficially surprising, therefore, that while European economic integration seems to have been of major historic importance, no study before the 1980s estimated the benefits of the creation of the original Common Market as adding up to more than about 1 per cent of GNP. Behind this lies the fact that even in the 1960s the tariff barriers that were abolished were already very low – typically under 10 per cent. Lipsey (1960) put the figure for the benefits of initial integration at just about 1 per cent of GNP. This figure is based on calculations of increases in consumer surplus resulting from cheaper imports (Lipsey 1960). In a curious footnote appended several years later to a reprint of the same article, he gives an intuitive argument to support the 1 per cent figure. He observes that the only improvement in efficiency attributable to trade creation stems from the shift of a proportion of the resources in the tradeable sector of the economy to higher productivity activities. Only a small amount of the economy is in activities protected by tariffs, the argument continues. (None of the service sector is, for example.) Tariffs are typically quite low, and the productivity differences between protected activities critically dependent on protection and the rest of the economy cannot be more than the height of the tariff. So if 10 per cent of the resources in the economy move to uses 10 per cent more productive, then the net effect is 1 per cent.

In the same footnote Lipsey argues that he does not believe these so-called *static effects* would be significantly augmented by *dynamic effects*. Static effects accrue when we remove tariffs and keep other things equal, notably all the elasticities of the system and the general level of productivity *within* sectors. The dynamic effects are what we get if we allow these other factors to vary as well. Those dynamic effects essentially boil down to the fuller exploitation of economies of scale and of the beneficial impact of greater competition, as discussed above. However, modest tariffs of about 10 per cent could frustrate only the realisation of modest scale economies. Owen (1983) argued forcefully that indeed there could have been economies of scale that were accessed as a result of the creation of the EC, but which would otherwise have stayed unexploited. He suggests that having guaranteed access to neighbours' markets would make it worthwhile investing in large-scale plants: the size of plant you would choose would depend on the number of competitors you could 'knock out'. He estimates on this basis that over a twenty-year period the establishment of the original Common Market must have generated not 1 per cent, but 3 per cent extra GNP. However, detailed inspection of the calculations in Owen's book shows that many of the gains from scale economies he attributes to the EC would have been reaped even if the kind of tariff barriers actually in place in the 1960s had not been removed. Owen notes that the removal of the tariff barriers combined with an increase in 'animal spirits' could have had quite a major impact. However, such an increase in entrepreneurial enthusiasm represents a factor not remaining equal, and we do need to explain it.

The most natural explanation is that the removal of tariff barriers altered expectations in a substantial way. It is obvious that when investment is being planned it is not so much the existing level of tariffs that matters as the level of tariffs that is expected to prevail at the time the investment comes on stream. A government determined to reduce the incidence of protection but unable to guarantee the policies of its successors and its trading partners may well find itself caught in a trap: it is all very well for it to tell firms suffering from import competition that they should invest in another activity; the import competition is here now and the prospective markets are uncertain. What should an import competing firm do? Its best bet may well be to stay in the industry for the time being, hoping to persuade a new government to reverse its policies and give protection or some kind of 'temporary' subsidy. If the firms stick to their decisions, the government may be impelled by popular outcry to provide the protection. This outcome is all the more likely if there is no way access to foreign markets can be guaranteed.

But in the case of the EC, the governments *had* made a binding political commitment to each other that they would remove, *and never restore*, tariff protection. This offered firms a carrot and a stick – the certainty of incoming duty-free imports, but an equal certainty of free access to others' markets if they specialised. To place the matter in perspective, let us look at another major vehicle of trade liberalisation. The GATT establishes a high degree of certainty that tariffs 'bound' by the agreement will never be increased. But it has no institutional mechanism for penalising backsliders. The EC, by contrast, contains both legal and political remedies. The European Court of Justice was set up expressly to ensure that EC law prevails over national law, while within the decision-making system violations of EC rules of the game by one member state (unless formally or informally agreed) are likely to lead to subtle retaliation by others. (This explains British government willingness to accede to many proposals that are in themselves unpalatable to that government; it is in order to secure other benefits.) It is thus the impetus to change in the *policy process* that induces changes in expectations capable of having big leverage effects following an initial tariff change.

It follows from all this that we cannot sensibly ever ask what the effects would be of just removing certain tariffs and leaving other things unaltered. In that event very little indeed would alter: what we really want to do, rather, is to quantify the effects of removing tariff or non-tariff barriers, and of all the political changes that would be needed to bring this about, and that would in turn be entailed by the initial move. Thus if we built a 'counterfactual' or *anti-monde* in which the Treaty of Rome did not exist *but everything else were the same*, we should be creating a nonsensical scenario. On the other hand, if we started trying to estimate what the German defence budget would be if there were no EC, we would be in the realms of science fiction. And yet there is no other way properly to evaluate the impact of the EC. How prescient of John Stuart Mill (quoted by McCloskey 1987) to observe that 'two countries that agreed on all but their commercial policy would agree on that as well'.

If we are to assess the economic effects of the creation of the EC and the Single Market, then, we must compare the existing situation with one in which the institutions and policies of the Common Market are totally absent. If we consider the question of the quantification of the impact of the Single Market, we must compare some form of status quo with both the measures directly associated with the 1992 package and the underlying political changes that will be necessary to bring them about. The Cecchini analysis estimated that a gain of 6 per cent of EC GDP could result from the creation of the Single Market. Of this, only a tiny fraction is attributable to the direct cost savings conditional on '1992'. The rest is based on the assumption that the political changes needed actually to implement the 1992 plan would necessarily generate a more intensely competitive environment in the EC. Nothing better illustrates the fundamental proposition that the politics and economics of European integration can never be separated.

The enlargement to the South

One of the least appreciated factors in the renewal of the impetus of the EC integration process was the decision to admit as new members Greece (1980), Spain (1986) and Portugal (1986). The prospective presence of these new members focused the minds of decision-makers on the problems of the existing Community. Chief among these was the Common Agricultural Policy (CAP) – a trade-diverting nightmare that addressed political problems that have long since been transformed out of all recognition. The CAP was imposing severe burdens on many of the existing EC states, and pre-empting 70 per cent of the EC budget for purposes that brought in no political benefit to the EC institutions. Calculations done in the 1970s suggested that the Southern European states stood to gain very little from the CAP. Portugal is a very poor agricultural performer, and a major importer of temperate products, the prices of which are artificially inflated by the CAP. Spain's strengths in fruit and vegetables are in a sector to which the CAP gives very little support, and it is also a major importer of cereals. The Northern members of the Community were reluctant to tackle this imbalance by extending the wastages of the CAP across the whole range of Mediterranean products. They therefore agreed to Greece's request that the role of regional policy be enhanced in any restructuring of the EC, and this was subsequently introduced as an important side-condition to the agreement on the main 1992 plan.

The role of regional funding, and the impact of the Common Market on the Southern members is, as we have noted, a matter of some controversy. Opinion is split between those who fear polarisation and those who argue that market discipline will help rationalise Southern European industry. Sceptics fear that the goals of regional policy are too soft and that further inefficiencies could be introduced into Southern industries through encouragement of the expectation that subsidies will be forthcoming from Brussels for bail-outs. The argument is advanced that, in Spain and Greece in particular, state-sponsored industrialisation in the 1960s and early 1970s led to the creation of a bureaucratised and politicised industrial structure. EC membership can have the same effects on Spanish and Greek industry as it did on French if firms are convinced that governments are credibly committed to conforming to EC rules (Bliss 1990). The EC can perform a very useful role here in stiffening governments' resolve, since if firms do not believe the state's claims that it cannot afford to subsidise them they will arguably not restructure by themselves. The willingness of the Spanish government to take tough economic measures, and the recent conditionality of EC loans to Greece, suggest that the logic of the EC system is being increasingly appreciated in Southern Europe. The aim of EC policy-makers is to use competitive forces, including free trade for labour-intensive goods from LDCs, to drive Southern European states towards a pattern of more sophisticated 'intra-industry specialisation', as an alternative to concentrating on labour-intensive goods. The logic of this approach is spelled out in a number of recent Commission analyses (EC 1990a; 1990b).

The success of this approach depended, of course, on political as well as economic factors. For the 'external discipline' strategy to work, there needed to be some guarantee that the organisational paralysis afflicting the EC since the late 1960s could be overcome. Enlargement thus focused attention, not only on the imbalances in spending priorities in the EC, but also on institutional reform. If every member state including Greece and Portugal had a veto on everything, progress risked becoming impossible. This was yet another factor militating in favour of a rethink of objectives and methods in the mid-1980s.

The political-economic logic of the 1992 plan

As we saw, the original goal of the Treaty of Rome was to create a common market by 1969. The job was left only half complete, however. Tariff barriers were removed, but the political consensus to act to eliminate the national policies that sustained the remaining barriers was absent. We can trace the failure to remove non-tariff barriers (NTBs) largely to the vision of General de Gaulle, French president 1958–69. It would be quite wrong to say that he was hostile to European integration, since he saw to it that France removed all its tariff barriers. But he was concerned not to give the EC institutions a blank cheque. He had agreed to remove tariffs and did so. He wanted, however, to retain the right to carry out whatever national industrial policies seemed appropriate to him. France was not willing to constrain its freedom to use other national policy instruments indefinitely by agreeing that economic policy be subject to majority voting in the Council of Ministers. There thus emerged a tacit understanding that many aspects the Treaty of Rome were to be treated as ambitions rather than obligations (see Chapter 4 for the details of the Luxembourg Compromise).

One result of all this was that while Article 113 of the Treaty of Rome said that there should be a common external trade policy for all member states, no agreement on what it should be was ever reached. Some states were more liberal and open than others. So a variety of non-tariff barriers against external imports were erected by less liberally inclined governments. Since these differed from country to country, the EC was forced to develop a panoply of devices to stop outside goods spilling into specific countries via EC neighbours. These ranged from measures authorised by the EC Commission under Article 115 specifically directed at 'third country' goods, to an array of very dubious non-tariff barriers.

The non-tariff barriers that survived the initial round of integration fall into a number of categories. *Public policies* may directly segment markets, as for example when mandatory standards are set or public procurement rules used to exclude foreign firms. All too often, however, it was *private firms' behaviour* that segmented markets, with public policies merely reinforcing this. For example most standards are set by industry itself on a voluntary basis. It may suit multinational firms to be able to produce slightly different goods in different markets, in order to create scope for price discrimination. The technical rules that allow car firms to set higher prices in the UK than in Belgium, for instance, are set by firms to stop retailers and wholesalers taking advantage of such differentials. This kind of fragmentation is *not* imposed by governments on firms. The rules of the EEC as originally constituted did make it difficult for governments to harmonise standards. The Treaty of Rome called for unanimity among member states in matters of 'harmonisation of laws'. So any one state could veto changes. But of course firms were free to press for Europe-wide norms if they wished.

Even in the field of public procurement, it is clear that in many sectors the same multinational firms operate in each separate national market and *choose* to compete only from their local base. The EC Council of Ministers decided in 1962 not to draw up the legislation on free trade in the domain of public procurement that the Treaty of Rome strictly obliged it to draw up. This no doubt imposed costs on firms, in the form of higher costs from non-unified standards, but these could, of course, be passed on to the consumer. So many firms gained more from weakened competition than they lost from higher costs consequent on the failure to realise a true common market.

Other forms of industrial policy were also able to flourish at the national level within the incomplete single market. National governments had a tendency to use subsidies as well as standards and procurement rules to protect 'national champions', with the French acquiring a reputation as masters of this particular game. However, by the early 1980s severe disillusionment had set in with the meagre results and even more meagre prospects for national champion policies in an increasingly globalised world market economy (see Sharp, Chapter 12 in this volume, on changing industrial structures), in which the micro- and macro-roles of national government spending were less and less important. Geroski and Jacquemin argued in a contemporary study that 'the root cause of the current industrial crisis in Europe is not the small scale of European firms but rather that they have been too slow in initiating and responding to change' (Geroski and Jacquemin 1985).

The European economy was in severe difficulties in the early 1980s. The US seemed to be on the verge of a new take-off. Japan and the NICs appeared to pose a threat to high-tech and traditional industries alike. The external political environment looked threatening. And yet the EC had never been less unified than it was in the early 1980s. Germany was showing signs of neutralism, while the UK was betraying an inclination to leave altogether. Had the Labour Party won the 1979 general election in Britain, national protectionist forces would have come through very powerfully. The benefits from the impetus of trade creation were being masked in the UK and elsewhere by recessionary forces. Moreover, given that non-tariff barriers were unaffected by the EC, legitimate doubts could be expressed, in a world where most industrial tariffs were very low, about whether the gains from having the Common Market really covered the costs of the CAP (see, for example, Kaldor 1982).

Indeed with Mrs Thatcher as its best friend, UK participation in EC integration did not, arguably, need enemies. But if the UK had left or paralysed the EC, the structure of alliances on the Continent would have been threatened. This very perception of crisis provoked a reaction. In 1984 the newly nominated EC President Jacques Delors drew up a series of plans for reviving the European Union process referred to in the Treaty of Rome. He proposed a new Defence Community, or Monetary Union, or a form of political union. His idea was that *any* of these policy measures would be both desirable in its own right, and would also act as a spur to further moves in the direction of integration. An analogy is often drawn between the EC integration process and a bicycle which must move at a certain minimal speed if it is not to collapse. In these terms, the EC in the early 1980s was engaged in a precarious balancing act which might have led to total disillusionment at any time. The need for some pressure on the pedals was plain for all to see.

Unfortunately for M Delors, however, none of his plans proved universally acceptable in 1985. The British government seems to have proposed the *Single Market* notion as an alternative idea. This is, of course, the same as the original *Common Market*. The usual interpretation of British policy at this juncture is along the lines that this was seen by the Thatcher government as a way to demonstrate that the EC really meant business, and to achieve the British aims of freer markets, but without getting involved in any of the political ambitions nurtured by the others. The flaw in the Thatcherite vision lay in the failure to see that, in order to achieve even the limited economic goals in question, an unprecedented degree of political co-operation would be needed: in order to realise the Single Market, one would have to do away with all the political barriers that had frustrated the emergence of the Common Market in the first place. The Single European Act was bound either to fail totally or to set in train a new political movement that would probably go further than the declared aims of the SEA itself.

The Single European Act provided for the use of qualified majority voting for new EC regulations and directives aimed at promoting the Single Market. But it would have had no impact at all unless the member states had not come to an agreement actually to use and accept the results of the majority voting process without reserving a de Gaulle-style right to opt out, in the style of the Luxembourg Compromise. In the event, a little publicised decision was taken in 1987 to take formal votes in the EC Council of Ministers. It was this step, not the Single European Act *per se*, that really transformed the EC (see Chapter 4).

Let us try to characterise the situation in more theoretical terms. Joint action by member states of the EC can be seen as a game. Game theorists distinguish 'co-operative' and 'non-co-operative' games. In the latter, players may act in such a way as to maximise the common good, but they do so only because of perceived self-interest. Firms in an oligopoly situation agree not to cut price because they know it might trigger off a price war; but they cannot be obliged to act in concert. This particular game is accordingly said to be non-co-operative. In the same way, sovereign states often sign voluntary agreements which they comply with in the expectation that others will comply too. The GATT agreement is of this kind, and so was the original Common Market. However, in such a non-co-operative game players (states) cannot bind themselves in advance to comply with the agreed strategy. After all, a new government may be elected and states are sovereign. What they can do, however, is to make agreements such that unfavourable consequences become highly probable if they renege on promises. If these penalties are sufficiently serious, it is almost as if the states are bound to comply with their earlier promises.

We thus transform the non-co-operative game into a co-operative game, in which agreements, once made, must be kept. The scope for mutually profitable agreement is now much wider, as all states can be sure that they will get what the others have promised. It is still, of course, necessary, when policies are agreed between member states, that no one expects to lose more from overall compliance than from defection. But the possibility of binding agreements makes it much easier to get through plans which raise overall efficiency but which hurt some interests. The Single European Act and the related decisions set up precisely such a possibility. We can now set up a package deal and arrange, say, for compensation to areas that might lose out from the Single Market, to be funded from the gains arising in the beneficiary areas.

It was, in fact, politically necessary in this context that when the agreement was made to create a genuine single market, a certain 'veil of ignorance' should obscure the exact details of who would be winners and who losers in the process, so that no one would get cold feet. Thus the Cecchini Report (1988) stressed the overall net gains from the 1992 process, but not who the winners and losers (if any) might be. The original title of that research project was 'The costs of non-Europe'. Its commissioning was viewed by top EC officials as part of the 'game' as described above. Creating strong expectations about growth from the internal market was seen as a way of forcing member states not to go back on the promises they had made to each other.

But as Alasdair Smith (Chapter 5 in this volume) shows, the main gains from the 1992 programme actually come from an intensification of intra-EC competition. The initial impact of this will be that profit margins will be cut and jobs shed. If optimistic expectations prevail, firms can be induced to invest and thus preserve overall profitability on the basis of bigger sales. The 1990–1 recession certainly did come at an awkward time!

The curious conjuncture of political and economic circumstances that made the Single Market programme universally popular has thus come under strain, both from the recession, and from the need to face up to the choices that were obscured in 1986 when the SEA was signed. The Single Market plan logically requires that the EC finally create a single external trade policy, but the 1985 Cockfield White Paper on *Completing the Internal Market* said nothing about the content of such a policy. The French commitment to the benefits of liberalisation is strong, but the appointment of Mme Cresson as prime minister shows the strength of political forces opposed to free trade. So far, the Community has been able to profit in a paradoxical way from Thatcherism. The UK deregulatory approached provided the Commission with an ideal excuse for demanding the dismantling of all protectionist national regulatory regimes. This was most striking in telecommunications, where the EC exercised no effective competence at all until 1987. But once national regulations are removed we are faced with the need for some kind of supranational re-regulation, since many aspects of telecommunications still retain features of natural monopoly. Exactly the same issues have been raised by the deregulation, at national level, of airlines. The Commission is, of course, the obvious supranational re-regulator.

It seems quite likely that a regulatory cycle will follow in which total deregulation will be replaced by a more market-oriented, but not totally *laissez-faire* approach. The choices still have to be made *explicitly*, however. Following the same line of analysis, we can see problems ahead in the fields of competition, trade and technology policy too. The SEA calls for a unified approach to these issues, and policy statements of November 1990 and April 1991 show the Commission grappling with the problems posed by the globalisation of industry. Competition is seen as the most effective stimulus to efficiency, and the work of Harvard Business School guru Michael Porter (1990) is favourably referred to. The new regulations on mergers of 1989 is designed to curb the tendency of big firms to get round the pro-competitive aspects of the 1992 plan by cross-border mergers and acquisitions. The EC is well aware that the past record shows mergers as rarely living up to expectations. And yet the key high-tech industries of the future display pronounced market imperfections, technological spillovers and economies of scale, the implications of which could leave the EC with no producers in certain fields. Moreover, the producers who were previously the importers to be feared, are now the inward investors to be courted. It is being increasingly acknowledged that restrictions on production by Japanese car and electronics firms within the EC pose an even more serious threat to the integrity of EC competition policy than did the old 'industry-to-industry' agreements to limit imports. (See Hobday, Chapter 14 in this volume, on the electronics industry.)

Conclusion

The European integration process was on ice for twenty years from the mid-1960s to the mid-1980s. In the 1990s it has now been dramatically unfrozen. The new dynamic is driven by two forces. First, the overall economic benefits from increased integration are clear. But beyond this, there is a political perception that certain global problems can only be solved collectively by the EC, and that the Single Market is an instrument to promote unity on a dimension hitherto undreamt of. Yet the economic consensus retains a certain fragility. There is a real danger that some actors will suspect that localised problems are due to the integration process. It is partly with this in mind that France and Germany, along with most of the other continental states, are anxious to proceed faster with other aspects of political and monetary integration than may seem sensible from a UK point of view. The analogy with the bicycle still grips many; if EC integration does not move forward decisively, it risks collapse.

Acknowledgement

I am extremely grateful to Professor François Duchêne for his help and advice in relation to this project. I remain solely responsible for the interpretation (and any misinterpretation) of his comments on an earlier version of this chapter.

References

Balassa B (1961) *The Theory of Economic Integration*. Allen & Unwin

Bliss C J (1990) Adjustment compensation and factor mobility in integrated factor markets. In Bliss C J, Braga de Macedo J (eds) *Unity and Diversity*. Cambridge University Press

Caves R (1982) *Multinational Enterprise and Economic Analysis*. Cambridge University Press

Cecchini P, Catinat M, Jacquemin A (1988) *The European Challenge*. Gower

Corden M (1972) Economies of scale and customs union theory. *Journal of Political Economy* **80**(1): 465–75

Duchêne F (1990) Less or more than Europe? European integration in retrospect. In Crouch C, Marquand D (eds) *The Politics of 1992*. Basil Blackwell

EC Commission (1985) *Completing the Internal Market*, White paper from the EC Commission to the European Council, June

EC Commission (1990a) The impact of the internal market by industrial sector. *European Economy/Social Europe* special edition

EC Commission (1990b) Industrial policy in an open and competitive environment. *Communication to Council* October

El-Agraa A (ed) (1990) *The Economics of the European Community*. Philip Allan

Emerson M, Aujean M, Catinat M, Goybit P, Jacquemin A (1988) *The Economics of 1992*. Oxford University Press

Geroski P, Jacquemin A (1985) Industrial change, barriers to mobility and European industrial policy. *Economic Policy* (1). Reprinted in Jacquemin and Sapir (eds) 1989

Jacquemin A, Sapir A (eds) (1989) *The European Internal Market*. Oxford University Press

Julius D (1990) *Global Companies and Public Policy*. F. Pinter/RIIA

Kaldor N (1982) Speech to House of Lords on EC internal market. Monday 13 December. Hansard **437**(21)

Kindleberger C P (1987) *The World in Depression 1929–39*. Penguin

Krugman P (1987) Economic integration in Europe: some conceptual issues. Appendix to Padoa-Schioppa T *Efficiency Stability Equity: a Strategy for the Evolution of the Economic System of the European Community*. Oxford University Press. Also reprinted as ch. 16 of Jacquemin and Sapir (eds) 1989

Lipsey R G (1960) The theory of customs unions: a general survey. *Economic Journal* **70**:496–513. Reprinted in Bhagwati J (ed) (1969) *Readings in International Economics*. 1st edn, Penguin

Lundgren N (1969) Customs unions of industrialised West European countries. In Denton G (ed) *Economic Integration in Europe*. Weidenfeld & Nicolson

McCloskey D N (1987) Counterfactuals. In Eatwell J, Milgate N, Newman P (eds) *New Palgrave Dictionary of Economics*. Macmillan

Marquez Mendez A J (1987) *Economic Integration and Growth in Europe*. Croom Helm

Molle W (1990) *The Economics of European Integration*. Dartmouth

OECD (1987) *Structural Adjustment and Economic Performance*. Paris

Owen N (1983) *Economies of Scale, Competitiveness and Trade Patterns Within the EC*. Oxford University Press

Pelkmans J (1984) *Market Integration in the EC*. Nijhoff, The Hague

Porter M (1990) *The Competitive Advantage of Nations*. Macmillan

Scitovsky T (1958) *Economic Theory and Western European Integration*. Allen & Unwin

Viner J (1950) *The Customs Union Issue*. Carnegie Endowment for International Peace, New York

Vousden N (1990) *The Economics of Trade Protection*. Cambridge University Press

CHAPTER 4

The institutions of the European Community: to 1992 and beyond

ANNE STEVENS

Introduction

At the beginning of the 1990s the impact of the European Community (EC) upon the domestic politics of its member states was exemplified by a number of notable events. In the autumn of 1990 the future of the EC and the nature of Britain's role within it lay at the heart of the dissensions within the British Conservative Party. Sir Geoffrey Howe's dramatic and bitter resignation speech in the House of Commons, which articulated a sharp criticism of Mrs Thatcher's style and stance towards the development of the EC, helped to initiate the chain of events which led to her relinquishing the office of prime minister which she had held since 1979. In France in May 1991, Edith Cresson became prime minister in succession to Michel Rocard with the firmly stated purpose of strengthening France in preparation for the coming of the Single European Market.

Underlying these striking events was one dominant fact. The salience of the European Community within domestic politics was increasing as a result of the growing role of the EC in setting the economic agenda for national economies and for different industrial sectors throughout Europe. The revolutionary changes in Eastern Europe that marked the beginning of the 1990s, and the striking changes in international political and economic relationships within Europe as a whole consequent upon them, increased the intensity of an ongoing debate about the widening and the deepening of the Community, and about the order of priority for the various possible developments. The Single European Act, which came into force on 1 July 1987, predicated a number of institutional changes which were seen as being essential to the introduction and operation of a single European market. But it was widely, though not universally, recognised that development could not be expected to come a halt at that point. From December 1990 two intergovernmental conferences (IGCs) – the mechanism for producing new treaties or treaty amendments – were in continual session. One had been detailed to draft a treaty of economic and monetary union, and the other a treaty on political union. When it transpired, in June 1991, that one of the proposed drafts for the latter treaty referred to the creation of a federal Europe, a notion that had hitherto never been articulated in any community document, there was a predictable furore, not least in Britain. The IGCs conclude their work in December 1991; at time of writing the precise outcome of the conferences was still unknown. What was already clear was that the European economy would, in the coming decades, increasingly be operating within a policy framework set by the institutions and methods of the EC. This chapter describes that framework as it has developed, and attempts to assess a number of institutional issues that remain on the agenda for the coming decades.

The origins of the European Community

In the first half of the twentieth century Europe suffered two devastating wars, both of which expanded into global conflicts, having originated as 'European civil wars'. The reconstruction of Europe which followed the second of these – the Second World War – was marked by a number of important features which provided key signposts for the future.

The first of these was the growing ideological and political division between East and West. In the countries under Soviet military occupation, including the eastern part of Germany, and in Yugoslavia and Albania, communist parties consolidated and finally monopolised power, and, except in Yugoslavia, the Stalinist system became entrenched. The division took a violent military form in Greece with the outbreak of civil war. It was dramatised through the blockade of Berlin in 1948. A second feature was the recognition of the dire political, economic and social consequences of the depression of the 1930s, and a determination, on the part of the peoples of Western Europe and of the governments they elected, that such conditions should not recur. In all the West European countries the late 1940s and 1950s saw the emergence of the welfare state, albeit in varied forms, and a commitment by governments to the principles (again varied in practice) of a mixed, managed economy.

A third feature of the period was the rejection of the notion of competitive and assertive nationalism as a basis for relationships between states. The war had fashioned a web of people and groups in many of the continental Western European countries committed to a common cause – resistance to Nazi occupation. After the war, the Christian Democratic parties which developed or emerged in a number of these countries stood out as particularly firm adherents of the notion that future conflict could and should be prevented within Europe through the building of institutions capable of integrating the nation-states and regulating potential conflict. These notions found their first institutional embodiment in the Council of Europe, founded in 1949 as a vehicle for intergovernmental co-operation. Although it was one of the founder members of the Council of Europe, the United Kingdom, sharing neither the experience of defeat and occupation nor the emergence of a Christian Democratic strand of politics, stood somewhat aloof from the developments. Attachment to the relationship with the United States and the Empire were stronger than any sense of a common European purpose. Winston Churchill's celebrated reference to a United States of Europe, in a speech in Zurich in 1946, was not intended to embrace the United Kingdom.

It was against this background that the early moves in Western Europe towards the creation of 'European' institutions were made. Defence relationships, initially directed against the threat of the re-emergence of a dangerously powerful Germany, rapidly adjusted to the conditions of the Cold War and what was perceived as the communist threat. NATO was founded in 1949. West European countries struggled to reconstruct their economies, in conditions which brought continued austerity and hardship to many. The United States, aware that economic growth and prosperity were required if Europe was to be a buoyant trading partner, and that prosperity was likely to be an important defence against the further development of burgeoning communist parties in countries like France and Italy, offered a large programme of financial assistance (Marshall Aid) but made the offer conditional upon co-operation between recipients. The consequence was the formation of an intergovernmental body, the Organisation for European Economic Co-operation (OEEC), with the aims of managing the aid, encouraging economic co-operation, and discouraging barriers to trade. In 1961 the OEEC became the Organisation for Economic Co-operation and Development (OECD).

At the beginning of the 1950s a number of Western European countries were faced with a quite specific economic and political problem – the future of the coal and steel industries. These industries were highly interdependent, of major strategic importance, and dependent upon natural resources whose geographical distribution did not fit neatly within political boundaries. The victorious allies, especially the French, were nervous of allowing the reconstruction and development of the West German coal and steel industries unless they were locked into some external system of oversight and control. Jean Monnet, the then head of the French government's economic planning agency, had devoted much of his rich and eventful life to the work of promoting international co-operation. He was deeply convinced of the need for international integration. He also believed that groups of rational people, if brought together and confronted with a specific problem, could and would find rational answers that would serve the interests of all. He saw the solution of the immediate problem as the first step in a long process whereby the merits of solving difficulties in this way would be borne in upon governments and their peoples. Union would result, and conflict, particularly Franco-German conflict, would become a thing of the past. Monnet enlisted the political enthusiasm of the French Foreign Minister Robert Schuman, and the consequence was the Treaty of Paris, signed in 1951 (to come into force in July 1952) between Belgium, France, Italy, Luxembourg, The Netherlands and West Germany. This was the accord that established the European Coal and Steel Community (ECSC). The ECSC differed from previous international organisations in one vital respect; the parties to the treaty agreed to be bound by the decisions reached within the ECSC framework even if they did not explicitly consent to them. They also agreed that the ECSC institutions – a decision-making High Authority (equivalent to the Commission of the later EEC), a supervisory Council of Ministers and a consultative Parliamentary Assembly – should be able to exercise their powers within the member states without requiring any further processes, such as, for example, national legislation.

It did not prove possible, during the 1950s, to extend this supranational principle into the field of defence, for a proposed European Defence Community foundered on the resistance, in France, of an unlikely alliance of Left and Right. By the end of the decade, however, the six member states were able to move forward in two areas – the economic field, where the particular emphasis was upon creation of a common market, and atomic energy, which was at that time seen as perhaps the key area for future technological and economic advance. The treaties establishing a European Economic Community and a European Atomic Energy Community were signed in Rome in 1956 and came into force in 1958. There were significant differences between these treaties and the ECSC treaty, but they all incorporated a broadly similar institutional framework. In 1967 the so-called Merger Treaty, which established a single set of institutions for the EC, came into force.

The nature and balance of the institutions: the 1960s

The EC is a set of bodies with a written constitution, consisting of the Treaties of Paris and Rome and the further treaties that have subsequently amended them, including the Single European Act (SEA). The policies of the EC are largely embodied in legal Acts which derive their legitimacy from that constitution, and their force from the political will of the peoples and governments of the member states. Policies may also be expressed, through, for example, international agreements with non-member states or groups of states. The role of the EC institutions is to formulate policy, to express it in legislation, and to oversee the implementation of the legislation and the identification, and where necessary punishment, of breaches of the law. The main institutions are the *Commission*, the *European Parliament*, the *Council of Ministers* and the *European Court of Justice*. The Commission elaborates policy and proposes the necessary legislation, and in some fields, such as agriculture and coal and steel, has important powers of secondary legislation and implementation. The Parliament debates, considers and advises, and the Council of Ministers decides. The Court of Justice, along with the Court of Auditors, has an essentially supervisory role. Through its interpretation of legislation, the Court of Justice has at times played a major role in the development of the EC's scope and powers and the balance of its institutions. The *Economic and Social Committee* has a purely advisory role.

As first the ECSC and then the EEC developed, the main initial fields of activity of the Communities were in rather specific sectoral areas where quite detailed parameters were (as in the case of coal and steel and of the customs union, for example, though not in that of agriculture) laid down in the treaties. Moreover, it was easy for the ECSC and the EEC to develop successfully in the generally thriving economic context of the 1950s and 1960s. Consequently the Commission found plenty of scope to be active and successful in proposing and administering policies. Walter Hallstein, the first president of the EEC Commission, was ambitious for the EC as a precursor of European union, and for the Commission as a key actor within the movement towards supranationalism.

During the early 1960s, accordingly, the Commission acquired a prominent role in the building up of the EC. In 1965, however, a serious political crisis shook the Community, and the consequences of that crisis shaped the balance of the Community institutions for nearly two decades. In 1958 General de Gaulle had come to power in France. He was firmly opposed to any developments that would diminish French status or influence. On the other hand, he was happy to work through the Community framework if the outcome would serve French interests, and would assist him in building up the prestige, indeed hegemony, of France within Europe. In so far as the Community was concerned with matters such as customs unification or agricultural policy, he was happy to view it as a useful mechanism for solving technical problems of economic management. But he did not see it as in any sense a precursor to a European union in which France would surrender or merge its position. He attempted to mould the EC more closely to his design by proposing the development of an essentially intergovernmental union leading to a Western European bloc in the fields of foreign policy and world affairs – areas in which France was undoubtedly already a leader – such as might produce a counterweight to the influence of both the USA and the USSR. These proposals, known collectively as the Fouchet plan, eventually foundered on the resistance of other members of the Community, especially The Netherlands (Collard 1990).

De Gaulle's unwillingness to allow France's influence within the Community to be rivalled by that of any other major member state certainly helps to explain his 1963 veto on United Kingdom membership, a veto which was fully within France's constitutional rights, for enlargement of the Community has always required the consent of all the member states. Thus when it became apparent that the Community could not be reshaped in accordance with his vision, de Gaulle sought to ensure that it would at least not develop along lines that he found distasteful. A summer 1965 deadlock over the extension of the powers of both Commission and Parliament led to France withdrawing from most of the operations of the Community for some six months. The crisis was finally settled by an agreement of January 1966 known as the Luxembourg Compromise. Most importantly under the Compromise, the Council of Ministers noted that France took the view that, where important national interests were at stake, the discussion of these interests should continue until unanimity had been achieved, even on those issues where the Treaties of Paris and Rome allowed decisions to be reached by majority voting. The Council sought at the same time to deflate the Commission's pretensions, for example by seeking to extend control over the information and public relations activities of the Commission which had been singing the praises of European integration and the Commission's role within it, and by insisting that the Commission should not receive ambassadors as though it were the government of a sovereign state. The effect of these events was to diminish the political role of the Commission. The Luxembourg Compromise took the form of an official communiqué of the Council of Ministers. It was a major political statement, but had no legal force.

The roles of the Commission and the Council

The Commission, which has since 1986 consisted of seventeen members appointed by the governments of the member states, acts as a collective body, and its members are required to be independent of the influence of their home country. It, and it alone, has the right formally to propose legislation to the Council of Ministers. (It may, and often does, make such proposals in response to a request from the Council of Ministers or Parliament). The Commission has a special remit to see that all the EC Treaties are observed, and it takes responsibility for implementing Community policy, extending to a number of delegated powers to make secondary legislation or to take action itself. In areas where common Community policies exist, it acts as the negotiator between the EC and non-member states, though it does so on the basis of policies agreed by the Council.

While the Commission continued after 1966 to make full use of its powers, it did so in an environment in which the 'momentum for European unity', which the Commission had previously done so much to stimulate, 'slowed to a virtual halt' (Palmer 1989: 12). A more concrete consequence of the Luxembourg Compromise was to tip the balance of the institutions within the Community much more strongly in favour of the Council of Ministers. The Council of Ministers consists of representatives of the member states' governments. It meets either as the 'general affairs council' attended by foreign affairs ministers, or as a specialised council attended by the ministers concerned with the matter under discussion – for example, agriculture or transport. The meetings all have equal status, and the decisions of all meetings are binding. The Council is the main Community legislator; it makes European Community laws, based upon proposals from the Commission, and following consultation, and in some cases a complex co-operation procedure, with the European Parliament.

The member states take it in turns, in alphabetical order, to chair the meetings for six months at a time, and this period of 'presidency' is usually regarded as an opportunity for the state concerned to give particular emphasis to matters which it regards as being especially important. The Council is supported by a complex structure of committees of officials from the member states, at the apex of which is the Committee of Permanent Representatives (COREPER). Most of the detailed work of agreeing upon the exact nature and wording of Community law is done in these Committees. In reaching its final decisions the Council of Ministers is, on some subjects, required by the Treaties of Paris and Rome to act unanimously. In general, unanimity is so required where the powers of the Community are being extended or a broadly new policy introduced, and in some other major areas such as the harmonisation of taxes. Otherwise the Council is in principle allowed to act by a qualified majority vote, which gives the member states different weights, determined largely by the size of their populations.

After the Luxembourg Compromise the practice of majority voting largely disappeared for a decade and a half, 'so much so that that voting had become almost a thing of the past in the Council, except for the annual adoption of the budget' (Louis 1990: 32). It became difficult for measures to be passed except as the result of complex agreements between the Commission and most (but not necessarily all) the member states. This diminished the political stature of the Commission, which had already suffered a blow to its ambitions from the implicit criticisms of its high profile stance contained in the Luxembourg communiqué. In an attempt to ensure some continued impetus to the activities of the Community, the practice of convening summit meetings of the heads of state or government of the member states developed. An example is the summit at The Hague in 1969 which helped to clear the way for the first enlargement of the EC. In 1974, the summit meetings were put on an organised and regular basis under the title of the *European Council*, which now meets at least twice a year. The European Council had no constitutional status until the Single European Act came into force in 1987.

During the 1970s the EC seemed effectively to abandon concepts of supranationalism and to revert to procedures which more closely resembled the intergovernmental methods of other international institutions which require all those affected to consent to legislation. Many commentators have seen the Single European Act, negotiated at the end of 1985 and brought into effect on 1 July 1987, as a declaration by the Community that it intended to return to the original ideals of the founders. The member states, accustomed since 1966 to fashion relations within the EC on the basis of political calculation and pragmatism, now seemed more prepared to abide by the letter of the Treaties. One of the most important goals of the Act was to erect a framework which would make smooth and easy the mass of complex decisions required in order to implement the plans for a European single market set out in the Cockfield White Paper of 1985. The Act contains provision for the extension of the qualified majority voting procedure to the measures needed for this purpose – the new Article 100A which was added to the Treaty of Rome. The logic of this provision is consistent with the principle embodied in that Treaty – that majority voting should normally be used for the implementation of a programme where the framework is already agreed. However, the institutional impact of the provision was greater than that statement implies, for it symbolised a willingness to return to the original intention on majority voting in general, which had been so largely abandoned. In the event, the majority voting procedure has been used to an increasing extent since 1985.

At the time of the signing of the Single European Act some member states sought to assert a continuing *de facto* right of veto where vital national interests were concerned. However, in 1987 the Council adopted rules of procedure which make it in principle impossible for a member state to insist automatically on continuing the discussion until unanimity has been reached, which is the form that the veto has taken in the past. If a member state requests that a vote be taken and a majority of the Council agrees, then the President of the Council must now put the matter to the vote.

The role of the European Parliament

The European Parliament (EP) was created as the European Assembly, and in 1962 voted to call itself the European Parliament, a name that was constitutionally recognised in the Single European Act. Initially it consisted of delegated members from the national Parliaments. In 1979 the in-coming members of the Parliament, now numbering 518, were for the first time directly elected within each member state. The EP, which is still an essentially consultative body, is organised along lines that are closer to those of the Parliaments of many of the other EC member states than to the Westminster model. Members sit in a semicircle, according to party group affiliation, rather than national origin. Recognised party groups acquire a privileged status. To achieve recognition they must have at least twenty-one members if those are all from one nationality, fifteen members if they are from two, and thirteen if they are from three or more. This allows party groups to be involved in the planning of the

Parliament's agenda. The Parliament has some eighteen standing committees, in which much of the initial discussion on any given issue takes place.

The Council of Ministers is required by the Treaty of Rome to consult the Parliament before it legislates. The EP has also always had the right to dismiss the entire Commission. In practice these two rights provide but an ineffectual basis for the articulation of the voice of the Parliament in the Community's affairs. The right to dismiss the whole Commission (with no counterpart prerogatives in relation to the appointment of a replacement) is too blunt a weapon, and has never been used. The right to be consulted carries little force when not backed up by any means of insisting upon the adoption of the views expressed.

The Parliament has nevertheless managed steadily to extend its powers. The first extension was into budgetary control, through Treaty amendments in 1970 and 1975 by which it gained the right to have a final say over some one-third of the total expenditure of the Community, and to exercise a veto over the entire budget. But this has also proved a limited and rather frustrating prerogative, producing conflict and difficulty between the institutions with very small offsetting gains. The direct election of the Parliament of 1979 was expected to increase the body's moral authority, since it could thereafter claim a legitimacy based upon the votes of individual citizens. Development was in the event slow, despite continued insistence on the need for democratic accountability within the Community. After 1979 the Parliament did, however, manage to increase the effectiveness with which it used the powers it already enjoyed. It also began to campaign, for example by drawing up its own draft treaty on European Union, for forward movement towards increased European integration. It sought to achieve through this a better balance between the institutions, and to acquire a genuinely legislative role. The Parliament's campaign probably facilitated the acceptance on the part of governments of member states of the idea that the measures required to achieve a single European market would have to be accompanied by an element of institutional reform.

The Single European Act enhanced the position of the European Parliament particularly in relation to the measures that would be needed to complete the single market, by instituting a co-operation procedure that applied to Acts based on ten key articles of the Treaty of Rome specifically related to areas of particular importance to the implementation of the single European market. Legislation promulgated under powers conferred on the EC by these ten articles must since 1987 be made not 'in consultation with' but 'in co-operation with' the Parliament. The somewhat complicated co-operation procedure requires the Council to refer back to the Parliament the measures it proposes to adopt, in the form in which it wishes to pass them, for a 'second reading'. If the Parliament rejects the legislation it can subsequently be passed by the Council only by a unanimous vote. If it wishes to amend it, and if the Commission is willing to endorse the amendments, then the Council must act unanimously if it wishes to alter them, whereas approval requires only a qualified majority. If the Commission is not willing to endorse the EP's amendments, then the Council must act unanimously to accept them; otherwise they are automatically rejected. The effect of this has not been to give the Parliament a decisive say in the final form of legislation, even when based on the ten key articles, for it can still be overruled. But it has undoubtedly given the EP a larger voice in law-making. Both the

Commission and the Council have become more attentive to its likely reactions (Nugent 1989: 296–80). The Council has used the right to overrule very sparingly, doing so only once (in relation to a directive on protection for workers) during the first two years of the arrangement (Lodge 1990: 19).

The Treaty also requires consultation on legislation in a number of fields with the Economic and Social Committee. The SEA has extended the range within which such consultation is required. Members of the Committee are nominated by member states' governments. Three main groups are represented: employers, workers, and 'other interests' such as farmers, small businesses and consumers. The purely consultative role of the Economic and Social Committee means that its influence is very limited. Most of the interests that it represents find other channels, leading more directly to national governments and the Commission, more effective.

The Court of Justice

European Community law takes two main forms: *regulations*, which apply immediately and directly, and *directives*, which set out what is to be done, but leave to the member states the choice of the exact legislative measures required. (Note, however, that directives can confer rights directly on individuals.) In addition, the Community authorities may take *decisions* – legal measures applied to a single entity – a firm, for example. The task of enforcing Community law falls mainly upon the courts of the member states themselves. The European Court of Justice can, however, hear cases brought by the Commission or member states against member states which have failed to comply with Community law, or brought by the Community institutions, member states or individuals which allege that a Community institution has acted illegally. The most important part of the Court's work is in giving preliminary rulings to advise and assist national courts which seek help in interpreting and applying Community law. These rulings are important because they have often allowed the European Court of Justice to clarify and develop the meaning of Community law, and to do so in ways that help to ensure that the law is applied uniformly in all member states. As a result, an increasingly homogeneous legal framework is being developed and applied throughout the area of the EC to an ever-widening range of economic activities.

The rulings of the Court in relation to equal pay, for example, have had important repercussions upon the provision of both public and private pensions (ECJ Case 262/88). The famous *Cassis de Dijon* case enlarged the scope of the free circulation of goods within the Community. The increasing amount of business coming before the Court, with the recognition of the major role that the application and interpretation of Community law is playing in the shaping of the Community, led to provision being made in the Single European Act for a *Court of First Instance*, which came into existence in 1989. It is particularly concerned with the competition cases which are likely to proliferate under all the new legislation implementing the single European market.

As the scale and scope of the Community budget grew, it became clear that tighter control was needed over the expenditure of EC funds if frauds and diversions of funds were to be countered. The 1975 treaty on Community financial procedures transformed the former Audit Board into a fully fledged Court of Auditors whose task it is to check that Community funds have been properly disbursed.

The working of the European Community and 1992

For nearly two decades after the 1965 crisis in the European Community institutions the development of the Community appeared to many observers to be proceeding in a slow and unspectacular way. The momentum of rapid early success in creating a customs union and a major common policy – the Common Agricultural Policy – was not sustained. A genuine internal market had not emerged, and the extent of non-tariff barriers became increasingly obvious. The CAP seemed less admirable when it was viewed, not as an example of the benefits of a common policy, but as a flagrantly extravagant device which did little to obstruct the perpetration of fraud or the wasteful accumulation of surpluses. As the international system of fixed exchange rates foundered and disappeared in the early 1970s, the development of economic and monetary union for the Community was first envisaged, but the immediate results were disheartening. Any impetus towards integration seemed to derive largely from essentially intergovernmental agreements, reached, for example, in the European Council, rather than from the supranational institutions of the EC (Urwin 1991: 165–72).

The EC did, however, continue to evolve during this period. The two decades after 1965 witnessed the first and second enlargements of the Community, and commitment to a third enlargement which in the event occurred in 1986. Although genuine economic and monetary union still seemed a distant prospect, the European monetary system was established, by political agreement, in 1979. The European political co-operation machinery (concerned with foreign policy) developed, albeit outside the framework, until 1987, of any treaty. The Regional and Social Funds were launched. Some of the judgments of the European Court of Justice made an impact upon the member states, for example the afore-mentioned 1979 *Cassis de Dijon* judgment, which subordinated to EC law the rights of member states to exclude from their own markets products which could legally be sold elsewhere.

By the mid-1980s a number of essentially institutional issues which had proved to be major obstacles to policy development within the EC had been removed. The Mediterranean enlargement had been agreed. A solution had been found, at the Fontainebleau summit of 1984, to the long-running dispute over the size of the British contribution to the EC budget. But the recognition that the EC was still a long way from fulfilling the original goals of the Treaty of Rome was conspiring with a certain frustration *vis-à-vis* the institutional patterns that seemed to have thwarted progress. The European Council at Fontainebleau accordingly set up an *ad hoc* committee for institutional affairs, stating that it should be guided in its work by the spirit of the draft Treaty of European Union that the European Parliament had endorsed. This committee looked back to the original aspirations of the Treaty, and sought to link institutional reforms with the creation of a 'homogeneous economic area'.

Very shortly after taking office as President of the Commission, Jacques Delors picked up this latter theme, and in his statement to the European Parliament in

January 1985 called for the elimination of all frontiers within the Community, with 1992 as a possible target date for the achievement of that objective. The Commission embodied its proposal in its *White Paper on the Completion of the Internal Market* drafted by Lord Cockfield. By the Milan European Council meeting of June 1985 the two strands had come together. The White Paper was approved, and agreement was reached on the calling of an intergovernmental conference to draft a treaty that would amend the institutional framework. The outcome of the negotiations within the intergovernmental conference was the Single European Act – a treaty that was a single Act both in the sense that it amended all the three founding treaties that formed the bases of the ECSC, the EEC and Euratom, and in that it brought into the treaty framework the political co-operation machinery.

The motivation and intentions of the Single European Act can be read in two ways. On one perspective, the SEA can be seen as resulting from a determination on the part of the member states to increase the scope and pace of integration. This would be achieved in part by returning to the intentions of the founding fathers, with the creation of a genuine internal market and the reinforcement of the initial institutional balance, including a return to majority voting in the Council of Ministers. That in turn would serve to move the whole process of integration up a gear. From a rather different angle it is possible to see the SEA as little more than the necessary framework for the achievement of the main goal, which was the creation of an open, competitive, liberalised and deregulated European market, providing for greater freedom of movement of goods and capital, and the extension of the competitive disciplines which alone would permit European enterprises to compete globally with the Japanese and others. In this latter, minimalist view, the passing of the SEA certainly did not mean the ending of the Luxembourg accord (Taylor 1989: 11), nor indeed, despite the 'further range of interdependencies' that would certainly emerge if businesses really did begin to treat the whole of Europe as one domestic market, were there major implications for the power of the central institutions of the EC (Taylor 1989: 23). As Urwin points out, 'the difference [between the two views] was that one was looking beyond 1992 to some kind of political union, while the other would be content with the internal market flanked by heightened cooperation among the member states on a host of other issues' (Urwin 1991: 240).

The Single European Act was the outcome of compromises, and this certainly shows in the diversity of ways in which it can be interpreted. However, its majority voting provisions *have* encouraged the revival of the almost defunct practice of voting within the Council of Ministers, and *have* speeded up the decisions required for the implementation of the single market. (It is clear that much will still remain to be done after 1992, especially in relation to the incorporation of EC measures into national legislative systems.) The SEA's introduction of a co-operation procedure involving the European Parliament *has* strengthened the Parliament's role. Finally, and perhaps most importantly, the impact of the single market (1992) programme has been such that many people now believe and expect that Europe *will* change. It has been possible for the Commission, and others, to argue that the implementation of the programme must inevitably result in change in a great many related areas. Those who, like John Palmer, think that 'as a direct consequence of 1992 a new European political agenda, or more accurately a series of different and to some degree competing agendas, is being created' may go on to agree that 'the Single European Act committed the Community to a great deal more than just the creation of a single market' (Palmer 1989: 47).

Issues for the 1990s

By the early 1990s questions relating to future patterns of political and economic decision-making in Europe were among the most important considerations bearing on the long-term development of the European economy. Four major issues seemed particularly crucial. They were first, the question of the cohesion and solidarity of Europe; second, the possibility of the emergence of a 'Fortress Europe' in the aftermath of the completion of the single market; third, the problem of the 'democratic deficit'; and finally, the debate around the 'widening' and 'deepening' options for Europe. We now look at these in turn.

Social and economic cohesion

The development of a single market will in the short to medium term have the effect of merging twelve economies with quite widely differing economic structures, levels of unemployment and burdens of and expectations about social provision. It will, indeed it is intended to, induce fundamental adaptation and restructuring of both manufacturing and services. Companies are likely to find themselves faced with new competitors in what may have been traditional and protected markets. The single market should – again, is intended to – produce an increase in the mobility of both capital and people. It is widely expected that settled patterns will be dislocated, and that if there are no accompanying measures to ease the process and induce acceptance of change, the perceived threat of these dislocations might make political programmes rejecting integration attractive to both parties and electorates (Palmer 1989: 47). The Single European Act explicitly contains the provision that 'to promote its overall harmonious development the Community shall develop and pursue its actions leading to the strengthening of its economic and social cohesion' (Article 130A). The mainspring of the action that the EC takes to achieve these objectives is the provision of funds to assist areas and groups of people that are especially disadvantaged. The SEA brought the Regional Development Fund, the Social Fund, and the Agricultural Guidance Fund together under the rubric of the European Structural Funds, and agreed, in 1988, that by 1993 expenditure on the Structural Funds should amount to 25 per cent of the EC budget. While this is a shift in the balance of expenditure within the EC, the sum involved is still very small indeed in relation to the total resources of the member states, for in 1988 the total EC budget amounted to only 1.15 per cent of the aggregate of the member states' gross domestic product. The Structural Funds were assigned five specific objectives:

1 the development of the less prosperous regions (defined as those whose per capita GDP is less than 75 per cent of the EC average)
2 the development of those regions affected by industrial decline
3 combating long-term unemployment

4 improving employment prospects for young people
5 facilitating agricultural restructuring and the development of rural areas.

The Commission has taken the view that the advent of the single market must be seen to bring with it improvements in living and working conditions for the EC population. The Social Charter, endorsed by eleven out of the twelve member states in December 1989 and backed by an Action Programme issued by the Commission at the same time, is the result. The Action Programme commits the Commission to bring forward measures in thirteen areas, covering employment, working conditions, equal treatment and social protection, though without imposing a timetable. Many of the proposals are likely to prove controversial, and some governments and employers are likely to argue that, if implemented, they would increase labour costs and decrease flexibility. The 1990s are likely, nevertheless, to see increasing social regulation of economic activity at Community level.

Fortress Europe?

The creation of a customs union and the installation of a common external tariff were among the earliest achievements of the EEC. A common Community trade policy was a necessary consequence, and the Community began to speak with a single voice in the negotiations that determine the framework for world trade, especially those under the rubric of the General Agreement on Tariffs and Trade. In this context the Commission acts as negotiator, through officials of the appropriate directorate-general, usually DG I (External Relations), on the basis of instructions approved by the Council of Ministers. In general terms the EC is committed to a liberal approach to world trade. In the words of the then Commissioner for external trade in 1988, 'The Community is already the world's largest trading partner. . . . As a result, we have a vital interest in the maintenance of a world-wide liberal trading system' (Owen and Dynes 1990: 200).

Nevertheless, the emphasis during the second half of the 1980s on the completion of the internal market led many to fear that the EC was concentrating upon the development of its domestic market, perhaps to the detriment of the interests of other trading nations. Much publicised conflict with the United States centred around the question of subsidies to agricultural products, in the context of the Uruguay Round of GATT negotiations, did little to dispel these fears. The situation is complex. There has been a good deal of concern about 'dumping' in the EC, especially by countries such as Korea and China, and the Commission has been urged by member states to be active in utilising the EC's anti-dumping provisions (see Smith and Holmes, Chapter 10, and Stevens, Chapter 11, in this volume, on relations with the USA, Japan and the Third World). There are fears that the countries of Eastern Europe, as they seek to move rapidly towards the market, might also be tempted to flood the EC with cheap goods. The opening up of the internal market seemed likely to expose companies in a number of areas that had been well-protected by non-tariff barriers such as public procurement policies to full-blooded intra-EC competition, and those companies might reasonably wish for an environment in which they could restructure and readjust without the pressure of additional competition from countries such as Japan. Precedents for direct EC action on such matters can be cited. The 1974 Multi-Fibre Agreement limiting textile imports into the Community, and the 1983 voluntary export restraint negotiated between the Community and Japan to limit the export of video cassette recorders by the latter to the former, are among them. A number of voices within the Community have called for the development of a Community industrial policy with the aim of at least strengthening Community companies against these challenges.

On another dimension, EC countries have differed in the degree of enthusiasm with which they have welcomed direct inward investment by non-EC enterprises. Some countries fear the opening-up of their national markets to the products of factories set up on EC territory by non-EC companies. Consumer electronics and car production are two sectors in which such factories are already firmly established. This forms the background to the tension between Britain and France in relation to the export to France of the products of the Nissan factory in the North of England. Even if such tensions are resolved within the single market and non-tariff barriers are abolished within the EC single market, such barriers, for example those raised by technical standards, could at the same time be reinforced against manufacturers outside the EC (Palmer 1989: 70–3).

Nor are concerns about the 'Fortress Europe' scenario confined to the major trading nations. Newly industrialising and Third World countries also worry about the creation of a more inward-looking Europe. The problems for the poorer part of the world may not be confined to the dimension of the movement of goods. The abolition of internal frontiers is likely to go hand in hand with tighter border controls at the point of entry to the EC for non-EC nationals, and there are strong pressures for the harmonisation of policies on immigration, visas and political asylum. The views of the most liberal member states may well not prevail. The 1990 Schengen agreement between the original six EC member states provided for the eventual removal of all border controls between them, but also for tighter joint visa controls around them.

All these issues – the possible articulation of an industrial policy for the EC, the degree of protection to be afforded to enterprises within the internal market against external competition, and the question of control over the movement of people – remain as major issues which the advent of the single market as such will do little to resolve.

The democratic deficit

The creation of a single market was the initial goal of the founders of the EEC when the Treaty of Rome was signed in 1956. The preamble to that Treaty suggests, however, a much wider set of aspirations, and now, as then, the creation of the single market is seen by many as a first step on the road to implementation of a much more extensive programme. There is widespread agreement that EC decision-making processes require reform if they are to develop the resilience to cope with whatever the future may bring. A particular concern is the 'democratic deficit'. There are two facets to the problem. First, there is the position of the Council of Ministers within the legislative process. In contrast to what happens in many member states, the initial formulation of EC legislation is a relatively public process, usually involving discussion between the Commission and the various interests and groups concerned, and, of course, consultation with the Economic and Social Committee and the EP. However, the final form in which the legislation emerges is the product of a theoretically confidential, though actually very leaky, process of negotiation within the machinery of the Council of Ministers. The only bodies who can hold the members of the Council to account for what they do are the national Parliaments, and their capacities to control such action are very limited. Denmark, Ireland and the United Kingdom have long had special parliamentary committees to keep an eye on EC activity, and the French Parliament has recently also begun to establish such a mechanism. Even so, ministers are subject to very little control over what they agree to, perhaps as the result of a compromise or package deal, or over how they vote.

The other facet of the 'democratic deficit' is the inability of the European Parliament to contribute in a major way to the processes of legislation, or to hold the other institutions of the EC to account. In her Bruges speech in September 1988 Mrs Thatcher rejected the notion of decisions being taken by an appointed bureaucracy. That was an over-simplification of the problem, but it reflected a real concern. The accountability of the EC's decision-makers to any group of electors would wane if influence shifted back from the Council of Ministers, whose members are at least answerable to their domestic Parliaments, to the Commission, over whom the European Parliament's control is clumsy and uncertain.

The establishment of democratic control would be especially important if, as Jacques Delors proposed in the plan which he advanced in April 1989, the EC were to move towards a monetary union. The European Council has now approved the Delors plan, and although the timetable, and the precise mechanisms, remain to be decided, the possibility of a European Central Bank, and even eventually a common currency, now seem much more real than it did in the mid-1980s (see Sumner, Chapter 8 in this volume, on European monetary integration).

A mechanism to ensure accountability for policies, including economic and monetary policies, will clearly be needed. The answer might well be a greater degree of involvement on the part of the European Parliament. The co-operation procedure has endowed the EP with some new powers, but those powers are still very circumscribed. The Treaty of Political Union which should emerge around the end of 1991 (see p. 86) will certainly include measures to reinforce the powers and capacities of the EP.

The shape of the European Community of the future

Another major issue for the 1990s is the future profile of the European Community. At the end of the 1980s two strands of thought were evident. There were those who saw the main work of constructing the European Community as having been broadly completed. The single market initiative and the Single European Act had pushed the EC back on course and given it the necessary impetus to carry out what had always been its primary task – the creation of a large, single free market. If there were to be further development, it should be in the direction of extending the benefits of this degree of free trade to an increasing number of countries. In this vein, negotiations were begun with the member countries of the European Free Trade Association on the creation of a European Economic Area which would embrace both the EC and EFTA. For some EFTA members this was likely to prove a second best, and applications for EC membership had been lodged by Austria and Sweden, as also by Cyprus and Malta (who are not EFTA members), to join the long-standing request for membership by Turkey. Norway is expected to renew negotiations for the membership which it rejected in 1972.

The revolutionary changes in Eastern Europe in 1989 seemed to open up even more possibilities. East Germany was automatically incorporated into the EC when German reunification occurred. This eventuality had been foreseen in the Treaty of Rome, however improbable such an occurrence then appeared. Czechoslovakia, Hungary and Poland all signed association agreements with the EC at the end of 1991, with a view to the establishment of free trade within ten years.

There are some, most notably within the European Commission, however, who have been less enthusiastic about rapid and massive enlargement. For them the goals of the EC are still far from being achieved. Movement towards a much deeper political and economic union seemed from this point of view the inevitable and desirable outcome of the advent of the single market. During late 1989 and 1990 Delors seemed to be trying to force the pace of discussion, clearly fearing that Germany's preoccupation with the incorporation into the single state of the five new *Länder* and pressures from aspirant members would distract attention and commitment from the achievement of 'an ever-closer' union. During 1991 there was intense discussion of drafts of a possible Treaty of Political Union. Drafts were produced by the Luxembourg government during the summer, and by the Netherlands government, which had taken over the presidency of the Council of Ministers in the early autumn. Debate raged over whether co-operation in matters of defence and security, foreign policy and home affairs (immigration policy, for instance) should be brought within the scope of the treaty. Their incorporation within the EC policy framework would, of course, give the Commission a role in policy formulation in these areas. Those who wish to move forward in this way towards the long-term goal of some type of European federalism acknowledge that such a giant step will be hard to achieve within a widening Community and an increasing membership. At the beginning of the 1990s, then, many questions remain to be answered about the shape and nature of the European Community into the next millennium. What is clear is that the Community, its institutions and its policy-making will continue to constitute a crucial factor in all economic activity within Europe.

Postscript: ever closer union

The draft treaty amending the legal basis of the European Community, agreed by the heads of government of the member states of the EC meeting in Maastricht in December 1991, establishes, in the words of the preamble, 'a European Union . . . an ever closer Union among the peoples of Europe, where decisions are taken as closely as possible to the citizens'.

The Maastricht decision lays down a timetable for movement towards economic and monetary union that could, by the end of the twentieth century, create a single currency for those member states meeting quite stringent conditions in terms of budget deficits, rates of inflation, and so on. The United Kingdom would not be bound by the outcome of a majority vote to move towards a single currency unless its government had made a specific decision to join in.

The treaty extends the European Community's commitment to joint policies in the fields of defence and security, stipulating unanimity in the Council of Ministers for the adoption of policies, but allowing for qualified majority voting on the actions required to implement them. The text includes a commitment to NATO as the basis for European defence, and associates the Western European Union – the European alliance linked to NATO – closely with the elaboration and implementation of defence policy.

The European Community's scope for action will broaden out in a number of fields, including consumer protection, training and education, public health, and cross-border networks of transport and communications. In many of these areas decisions will be made by majority vote. The European Parliament gains additional powers in certain areas, in the form of a right of final veto. It may be that the threat of such a veto will increase Parliament's influence over legislative outcomes.

A bizarre detail of the negotiations was the appending to the treaty of a protocol that incorporated what would otherwise have been its Social Chapter, allowing for EC legislation on working conditions and workers' rights. The United Kingdom was not prepared to assent to that chapter, so the other eleven member states agreed a protocol that will permit them to proceed without the UK if they wish. This is a remarkable departure from the established view that it is of the essence of the EC that all the member states should move together. It may be that it will provide a model for the future. Equally, as matters evolve, the United Kingdom may find that it wishes after all to move with the other states, on both monetary and social policy, and to avoid setting precedents for fragmentation that could hinder co-operation and strain trust, especially after the further enlargements expected before the end of the century.

References

Collard S (1990) The French presidency and the European Community. Unpublished paper for the annual conference of the *Association for the Study of Modern and Contemporary France*

Lodge J (1990) Ten years of an elected European Parliament. In Lodge J (ed) *The 1989 Election of the European Parliament*. Macmillan

Louis J-V (1990) *The Community Legal Order*. Commission of the European Communities, Brussels

Nugent N (1991) *The Government and Politics of the European Community*, 2nd edn. Macmillan

Owen R, Dynes M (1990) *The Times Guide to 1992*. Times Books

Palmer J (1989) *1992 and Beyond*. Office for Official Publications of the European Communities, Luxembourg

Taylor P (1989) The new dynamics of European integration. In Lodge J (ed) *The European Community and the Challenge of the Future*. Frances Pinter

Urwin D (1991) *The Community of Europe*. Longman

CHAPTER 5

Measuring the effects of '1992'

ALASDAIR SMITH

Traditional measures of the effects of European integration

In this chapter I shall focus on the quantification of the effects of the European Community's '1992' programme (and its possible extension across Europe as a whole). Before turning to the details of the programme, we have first to consider the general issues involved in measuring the effects of integration, and briefly to survey the studies that have been done of earlier episodes of European economic integration.

The traditional analytical basis for the measurement of the impact of economic integration is provided by the concepts of *trade creation* and *trade diversion*, as developed by Jacob Viner. When trade barriers are reduced between partner countries, trade between them will increase, with the increase normally attributable partly to diversion, partly to creation: trade diversion means the replacement of trade with other countries by trade with partners, while trade creation covers trade replacing home production or associated with increased consumption. There can also be 'external trade creation' if the integration process leads to a reduction in trade barriers with the rest of the world. Trade creation increases economic welfare, as higher-cost local production is replaced by lower-cost partner imports, while trade diversion reduces welfare, as lower-cost imports (subject to tariffs) from third countries are replaced by higher cost (but tariff-free) partner imports. (See Chapter 3 by Peter Holmes in this volume.)

In the case of the European Community, an initial glance at changes in trade flows suggests that much of the growth of intra-EC trade in *manufactures* since 1956 represents trade creation, since the growth of intra-EC trade in manufactures has been accompanied by rapid growth in external trade; while patterns of *agricultural trade* seem to involve a high degree of trade diversion.

But we have to do our accounting more carefully than this. It is not legitimate to compare the 1956 trade pattern with the 1990 trade pattern and simply attribute all changes between the two dates to the effects of European union. Rather what has to be done is to isolate the effects of integration from all the other effects associated with the passing of time, the natural development of trade flows, the growth of income, global trade liberalisation, and 'happenstance'. Mayes (1978) provides a useful survey of methodology and of estimates of the overall results of European integration; while the more recent survey of Winters (1987) focuses on the narrower issue of the effects of UK accession to the Community on trade in manufactures. The studies which they survey cover a wide range of methods, differing considerably in the degree of sophistication with which the non-integration effects are filtered out of the calculation, and producing a wide range of numerical estimates of the effects of integration. However, almost all of the estimates surveyed by Mayes suggest that the formation of the European Economic Community generated substantial trade creation and much less trade diversion.

The nature of intra-EC trade

Much intra-EC trade (as indeed much trade between developed countries) is intra-industry trade, with the German car industry, for example, exporting to France and the French car industry exporting to Germany. The very existence of intra-industry trade is hard to explain in terms of the standard textbook treatment of comparative advantage. If a country has comparative advantage in production of a particular good, whether arising from technological or factor endowment differences, that should come through as a price advantage in world markets which will enable the country to export the given good. Intra-industry trade between France and Germany seems to imply that France has a cost advantage over Germany and Germany a similar advantage over France in relation to the same product, and that simply does not make sense.

Some intra-industry trade is, of course, a purely statistical phenomenon, as the collectors of statistics allocate to the same category of goods, goods that are in reality quite different; and the finer the goods classification used to report trade flows the lower is the proportion of intra-industry trade. But even at the highest level of disaggregation there is still much intra-industry trade.

The most plausible explanation of the phenomenon of intra-industry trade is the existence of product differentiation. Some French consumers buy Volkswagens and some German consumers Renaults because there is a perceived difference between the different brands of cars. This explanation has to be supplemented by reference to the existence of 'economies of scope': Volkswagen cannot produce varieties of cars to satisfy every segment of the market, because there would be cost disadvantages to the production of so many models. At the same time product differentiation almost certainly implies imperfect competition: if a Renault 5 is seen by consumers as different from a VW Golf, then there is a downward sloping demand curve for the Renault 5, and Renault has market power which it can exploit.

The study of Balassa and Bauwens (1988) of intra-European trade flows in manufactured goods confirms that product differentiation is a significant influence on intra-industry trade. There is more intra-industry trade in industries where there seems to be a higher degree of product differentiation. Equally clearly, much intra-European trade is in the products of oligopolistic industries in which firms have large market shares. For example, almost 80 per cent of the cars sold in the European Community in 1988 were produced by six firms; while in Italy and France, over 60 per cent of the cars sold were produced by one and two firms, respectively. Dominant firms like these must have a considerable degree of market power, quite apart from any product differentiation. Further, the existence and survival of large firms suggests that economies of scale matter. (Economies of scale, as opposed to economies of scope, will, of course, tend to have a negative influence on intra-industry trade, since they will encourage rationalisation of production in a small number of firms. This is confirmed by Balassa and Bauwens.)

These facts suggest that the traditional theory of customs unions, based on the concepts of trade creation and trade diversion, is not a satisfactory approach to the analysis of the effects of European economic integration. It is often said in this connection that the traditional theory is 'static' and that we need also to consider 'dynamic' effects. But 'dynamic' is an imprecise term, and it is better to say that when we are considering industries in which product differentiation, imperfect competition, economies of scale and economies of scope matter, these features of the market should be incorporated into our analysis of the economics of integration.

Concentration is obviously encouraged by the existence of economies of scale internal to firms. There may also be scale effects external to firms but internal to industries, as firms benefit from being part of a larger complex. Perhaps the most persuasive single piece of evidence confirming the importance of external economies is the tendency for particular lines of production to concentrate in particular locations. This dimension, too, needs to be incorporated into the analysis of the effects of integration.

Finally, we need to consider the specific nature of the '1992' programme. Studies of previous stages of European integration have looked at the effects of the removal of intra-EC tariff barriers (and the harmonisation of external tariffs). The motivation for the single market programme stemmed from the realisation that there are non-tariff barriers to intra-EC trade; and the objective of the programme is the reduction of these barriers. There are two implications here that complicate the measurement of the effects of '1992'. First, the nature and quantitative importance of non-tariff barriers varies from sector to sector. The opening up of telecommunications procurement to all EC producers, the harmonisation of technical regulations on the safety of toys, the reduction of road transport delays at border posts, will each have distinctive effects which will not be the same as the effects of a simple, across-the-board tariff reduction. Secondly, many of the border barriers being reduced involve real cost effects (as opposed to tariffs, where the cost is a financial transfer to the government, or quotas, where there is a financial transfer to the holder of the quota licence). Thus a switch in imports from foreign to partner sources as the real costs of buying from a partner are reduced is not a welfare-reducing trade diversion, but a welfare-improving cost reduction. Further, some of the cost reduction may apply to external trade as well as internal trade – if, for example, non-European suppliers as well as European producers benefit from the harmonisation of regulations.

Integration with returns to scale and imperfect competition

An early approach to the incorporation of economies of scale into the study of economic integration comes from Corden (1972). Corden's analysis is of the effects of the integration of the market for a homogeneous good in which each country has at most a single producer before integration, and of which supplies are available from the rest of the world at a given price, and the analysis is confined to cases where it is reasonable to assume that price is determined by the world market price plus transport cost and tariff. This analysis identifies new possible effects of integration – cost reduction as a firm previously confined to its home market expands to supply the partner market also, and trade suppression as imports are replaced by home production which has become economic as a result of integration. Corden's methodology, although based on strong simplifying assumptions, provided the basis for the studies of North American integration by Wonnacott and Wonnacott (1967) and of European integration by Williamson (1971).

A different approach was taken by Owen (1983). The core of his analysis is a somewhat informal argument to the effect that integration will make efficient firms more willing to invest and drive out the inefficient by increasing the size of the market that can be wrested from the inefficient. Owen finds evidence for his hypothesis in the development of several major European industries and suggests, for example, that the gains from Italian exports of washing machines to Germany, Britain, and France were in the order of 54 per cent of the value of the trade, or 16 per cent of the value of Italian production. These are larger numbers than would typically be found in an assessment of the gains from trade that ignored economies of scale.

Smith and Venables (1988) offer an approach that is more general than Corden's and more formal than Owen's. Firms enjoy economies of scale and sell differentiated products. In applying their model to data on particular industries, Smith and Venables deduce the extent of product differentiation in each industry from information about the extent of economies of scale and the degree of concentration in that industry. For example, if an industry in which potential economies of scale are substantial remains relatively unconcentrated, the failure of firms fully to exploit the potential scale economies is explained in terms of inelastic perceived demand curves, and therefore a high degree of product differentiation. The model is used to analyse the implications of two interpretations of the primary impact of the '1992' policy change:

1   a simple reduction in the costs of intra-EC trade of 2.5 per cent of the value of trade;
2   the same cost reduction, coupled with an assumption that the EC becomes a single market in the sense that firms will be unable to set different prices in different national markets.

The size of the results obtained depends not only on the assumption made about primary policy outcome. Results under both policy impact variants vary from industry to industry, and depend both on the assumptions made about the precise way that firms form their hypotheses about their rivals' competitive behaviour, and also on whether firms are allowed to change the number of product varieties they produce and to enter and exit the industry.

The effect of the first primary policy impact variant on this model is to generate an increase in intra-EC trade, as trade costs, and therefore prices, fall. There is a further price-lowering effect from increased competition, and this also lowers profits. If firms leave the industry in response to the lower profits, the reduction in consumer prices is moderated, but there are still positive consumer gains. The welfare gains are greatest in those industries with the greatest economies of scale and with high intensities of intra-EC trade. Since Smith and Venables do not explicitly model external trade barriers, the welfare effect cannot be broken down into trade creation, trade diversion and other effects.

The alternative primary policy outcome variant generates substantially larger effects: firms that used to make their pricing decisions on the basis of their market shares in individual national markets are now looking at their shares of the whole European market. Since sales patterns in virtually all goods currently display substantial home-country bias, with firms having much larger shares of their home markets than of other European markets, the alternative policy outcome variant implies a shift to a more competitive market environment. Smith and Venables find that this latter policy outcome variant gives rise in the more concentrated industries to welfare gains that are several times larger than those associated with the first policy outcome variant.

It is important to realise that the second policy outcome variant does not strictly confine itself to the range of *primary* impact. Rather an initial policy outcome is accompanied by an assumed, but essentially unexplained, change in firms' behaviour. There seems to be considerable variation in prices across national markets in Europe, but the root causes of this variation are not well understood, and it is therefore not obvious that the '1992' programme will remove those unidentified root causes. If middlemen are prevented by differences in national regulations from buying goods in markets where prices are low in order to sell them in markets where prices are high, then '1992' will make a difference, since it will certainly remove this barrier to convergence of prices. On the other hand, in so far as the price variation is the consequence of different national currencies limiting cross-border competition, the additional gains of the second policy variant may have to wait for European monetary union. These gains are therefore best thought of as gains that would result *if* the single market programme were to have a substantial effect on market structure as well as on trade costs, rather than as gains that will necessarily flow from the programme *per se*. It must be added that some empirical support for the stronger assumption is given by Sleuwaegen and Yamawaki (1988), who found that 'EC-wide concentration rather than national market concentration is becoming important in determining the national price-cost margin in industries where the market is geographically integrated and the importance of intra-Community trade has been increasing' (p. 1472).

The most comprehensive study of the quantitative effects of the '1992' programme is Emerson et al (1988). In it a large volume of information is assembled on the nature of the barriers to be reduced by integration, on the characteristics of key industries and the different ways they are likely to be affected, on economies of scale, price dispersion across markets, and business perceptions of the potential effects of the single market. These disparate streams of factual material are drawn together into an overall assessment of the effects of '1992'. First, sector-by-sector information is assembled on the direct effects of the single market programme on the costs of both production and trade. Some of this data is based on detailed studies of particular issues or sectors, some inferred by extrapolation, with the results checked against the results of surveys of business opinion. Perhaps the most striking result to emerge from all this is that the

estimated effects on production costs are much greater than the effects on trade costs –
2.0 to 2.4 per cent of GDP for production costs as opposed to 0.2 to 0.3 per cent for
trade costs. This emphatically reinforces the point that the single market programme is
not to be thought of just in terms of trade barrier reduction, but rather as a general
programme of deregulation and encouragement of competition.

The next stage is to add to these direct cost reductions the savings resulting from
increased exploitation of scale economies. The description of this calculation (Emerson
et al 1989: 183) is a little opaque. The studies described earlier in this section took
explicit account of the need to explain what it was in the pre-integration situation that
prevented firms from exploiting scale economies; it is not clear how this has been done
in the Emerson study. The gains from exploitation of economies of scale are estimated
to be roughly equal to the gains from direct cost savings, and this contrasts with Smith
and Venables' finding that the effects of 'restructuring and increased production' are
typically a more modest multiple of the direct cost saving.

The final stage of the Emerson calculation is to add in 'competition effects on X-
inefficiency and monopoly rents'. Here the results of Smith and Venables (1988) are
used, supplemented by the results of the investigation of price dispersion included in
the Emerson study itself. The version of the Smith-Venables model with full market
integration gave, for the ten sectors to which the model was applied, a ratio between
the direct cost saving assumed and the final effect on economic welfare. Ratios were
inferred by the Emerson team on this basis for other sectors, according to their
characteristics, and 'final stage' estimates derived for all sectors.

This last step seems not quite correct, or at least not quite correctly labelled. In the
Smith-Venables model, there is no treatment of X-efficiency, and rents are treated as
transfers. One could interpret the formal model, in which scale economies are the only
source of 'restructuring' cost reduction, as standing proxy for a more general model in
which cost reductions are also available through the reduction of production
inefficiencies. But then one must ask the same hard question about X-inefficiency that
we asked about returns to scale: what is it about the integration process that leads
producers to do what they could have done before to reduce their costs but chose not
to do? On this interpretation, X-inefficiency is properly included in the second stage
(as, indeed, part of 'restructuring') rather than the third stage of the calculations.

Owen, Smith and Venables, and Emerson are all attempting to quantify the effects
of European integration in the context of economies of scale and imperfect
competition. It should be clear from our exegeses of the studies that they are all of a
somewhat speculative nature. We simply do not know enough about competition in the
real world to be able to develop empirically applicable models in which we can have a
high degree of confidence. But the same can be said about the traditional models,
based on perfect competition. While the models based on imperfect competition differ
quite substantially from each other both in assumptions and in results, they do agree in
attributing large pro-competitive effects to the integration process.

But what if the integration process falters? Taking the three stages of the Emerson
calculation in turn, doubts of different kinds can be raised about each. We can question
whether the '1992' programme will actually achieve the direct cost savings envisaged.
The Community may seem to have implemented a reasonable proportion of the famous
list of three hundred regulatory changes that were to be made by the end of 1992, but

the programme has not run smoothly. As difficulties have arisen, modifications have been made to important proposals, most notably in the area of tax harmonisation, and these modifications may weaken the integrationist impetus of the programme.

Consider the example of duty-free shopping, apparently not in itself of great significance. The UK government has obtained the 'concession' that duty-free shops be allowed to survive for several years after 1992. (It is not clear whether the UK government sought the concession as a symbol of the limited nature of its enthusiasm for the single market project or to protect the funding of airports – it is a concession that is certainly difficult to justify in strictly economic terms.) The implication must be that intra-EC travellers who might have had access to duty-free shops will have to be subject to customs checks in order to ensure that they have not 'abused' the privilege. The UK government also apparently intends to retain immigration checks on intra-EC travellers. If we still have border checks for these purposes for travellers by air and sea (checks which will have to extend in principle to commercial traffic as well as individual travellers), we will not have eliminated frontier and controls as the 1985 White Paper proposed, and this must raise a question mark over whether the savings assumed by Emerson will be fully taken up.

A second, much more important, problem is raised by the case of the car market, discussed in some detail in Chapter 10. The agreement that has been reached on Japanese car imports effectively requires the Japanese car producers to limit their imports into France, Spain, Italy and the UK specifically, as well as into the Community as a whole. If these national limits are to have any real significance, they will have to be supported by mechanisms which discourage cross-border trade in cars.

Thirdly, it has to be recognised that the true extent of many of the barrier reductions remains to be determined in practice. Whether intra-EC public procurement is really liberalised will depend on the wishes and behaviour of a large number of public bodies, both small and large, rather than on the rules hammered out in Brussels. If there is no great political commitment at the grass-roots level to open public procurement, it will not happen.

The second stage of the Emerson estimates also gives some grounds for scepticism – though here the error factor could go in either direction. It is notoriously difficult to produce reliable estimates of economies of scale. Further, many of the estimates used by Emerson are based on old studies, and the extent of economies of scale may well have changed as technology has changed. Increased computerisation may make technology more flexible and reduce the cost advantages of long production runs. More important, industrial studies typically show that the range of cost variations between firms of similar scale is much greater than the cost variations associated with scale – for example, the very great cost advantages that Japanese firms seem to enjoy over European firms in the car and electronics industries are *not* primarily based on advantages of scale. If 'restructuring' is to be taken to include the search for all conceivable cost reductions made possible by the enlargement of the market, we may be contemplating cost reductions that are larger than those assumed by Emerson, but whose implementation is somewhat more speculative.

The grounds for caution about Emerson's third-stage calculation have already been set out in the discussion of the work of Smith and Venables. To reiterate our earlier conclusion, we are looking here at the expectation that a change in the behaviour of firms will be induced by the '1992' programme. It is in practice simply not clear whether the institutional changes programmed will be sufficient to remove or reduce firms' ability to discriminate by price among national markets.

The general view of the Emerson study authors seems to be that they have sought to provide a maximalist estimate of the gains from the single market; the study itself notes (p. 151) that its 'ranges [of estimates] assume effective implementation of the programme set out in the White Paper and a positive attitude of firms in their strategic response to the new environment'. Baldwin (1989) argues, however, that the Emerson approach is too conservative. Increased output will, he posits, generate additional saving and investment which will contribute further to output growth. Increasing returns to scale or effects feeding through R&D could produce a permanent increase, not just in income, but in the growth rate of income. Baldwin suggests that these effects might double the Emerson numbers and add significantly to the rate of growth of GNP. Both his theory and his numerical estimates are speculative, even by the standards of the trade; but at the very least they serve to make the point that there is still much to explore in the area of the 'dynamic' effects of trade liberalisation.

In concentrating on the effects of '1992' on competition, we should not wholly lose sight of more traditional trade analysis. Neven (1990) suggests that although the pattern of trade among the Northern EC countries shows no clear pattern of comparative advantage, there is a pattern to North–South trade within the Community, so that the South may gain from the greater opening of Northern markets to labour-intensive Southern products. Buigues and Ilzkovitz (1991) attempt to identify which sectors will be most affected by '1992', and argue that the distribution of those sectors across countries and by factor-intensity is such that '1992' is unlikely to cause substantial comparative-advantage-induced changes to the actual pattern of trade within the EC. Gasiorek, Smith and Venables (1991) extend the Smith and Venables (1988) work into a general equilibrium model, but find relatively minor changes in factor markets flowing from integration, which suggests that the comparative advantage effects of '1992' are unlikely to give rise to substantial disruption.

One interesting recent piece of research casts light on the possible effects of European economic integration on regional disparities. Ben-David (1991) finds that the dispersion of income in the six original members of the Community was large and persistent before the Second World War, but decreased with post-war trade liberalisation. Ben-David finds further that the decrease in the dispersion seems closely linked to the growth of intra-EC trade. Income dispersion across a control group of countries that experienced limited trade liberalisation, but without the complete elimination of tariff barriers on the EC pattern, showed no tendency to diminish. These observations give some grounds for optimism on the effects of the single market programme on income dispersion in Europe.

The European Economic Area

Even before the '1992' programme had been implemented for the existing members of the Community, its extension to the wider Europe was under discussion. The agreements signed in December 1991 with Poland, Hungary and Czechoslovakia fall well short of incorporating these new associate members as full participants in the single market. However, the agreement reached in October 1991 between the Community and EFTA on the creation of a 19-member European Economic Area (EEA) goes some way towards incorporating the EFTA countries into the single market. The EEA will be a free-trade zone rather than a customs union, as the EFTA countries will not adopt the common external tariff of the EC; so border checks will continue between the EC and EFTA. Nevertheless, there will be free movement of EEA goods within the area, EFTA will adopt EC rules on competition and in other important areas such as consumer protection, and there will be free movement of labour and freer movement of capital. Further, several EFTA members are applying for EC membership, so the EEA agreement may turn out in practice to provide simply a channel for the transition to full membership.

The economic issues raised by the creation of the EEA are analysed in some detail, albeit in general terms, by Pintado et al (1988), and a numerical assessment of the implications, based on the Smith-Venables approach, is provided by Norman (1989). Unsurprisingly, Norman's results on the effects of EFTA joining the EC are analogous to the Smith-Venables results, but the estimated gains are somewhat greater, this reflecting the fact that trade liberalisation in the smaller EFTA countries would have larger pro-competitive effects.

1992 and the rest of the world

Naturally, non-EC countries are concerned about the likely effect of the '1992' programme on the EC's external trade. The reader will find in Chapter 10 of this volume a discussion of whether '1992' is likely to change the EC's *policy stance* on external trade; here we focus on the issue of what are likely to be the external trade effects of the single market programme *itself*. The EC Commission's own study of the economics of the single market (Emerson et al 1988) paid surprisingly little attention to this matter. It derived negative effects on extra-EC imports in stages 1 and 2 of the calculations, but not in stage 3; and the changes forecast are almost all of modest proportions – well below 10 per cent, and therefore likely, as Winters (1992) points out, to be offset by the positive effects of 1992-induced income growth on imports. Page (1991) reports estimates for the impact on the developing countries, based on Davenport and Page (1991). The additional exports to the EC induced by growth in the EC are estimated to exceed the loss of exports due to trade diversion for the developing countries as a whole, but there is a net loss for 'Four Asian NICs', as a result of there being the greatest degree of trade diversion in 'low-value, highly price-elastic goods such as textiles, clothing, footwear, leather goods, electronic components, metals, chemicals'.

Further direct effects on the rest of the world will arise from trade policy changes directly associated with '1992' and from changes in flows of foreign direct investment. There *have* to be changes in trade policy in those areas where there were, before 1992, national trade policies incompatible with the single market. The most notable product groups affected are cars, bananas, and textiles and clothing. A natural assumption to make is that national barriers will be replaced by an EC-wide barrier with 'equivalent' effect. Estimates of the effects of a policy change of this kind in the car market are provided by Smith (1990). There are varying effects on different consumer and producer groups within the EC, as the impact of EC-wide protection will be greater than that of the old national protection in some markets, less than in others; but the effects on the rest of the world (the Japanese suppliers) is positive, as restrictions on the intra-EC distribution of their products are removed, and they can redirect sales from low-price to high-price markets within the EC. The replacement of national MFA quotas on clothing and textiles will have a similarly positive, but modest, effect on the foreign suppliers, as the amalgamation of national quotas gives scope for fuller utilisation of quotas.

There is now an extensive literature on the possible effects of '1992' on the rest of the world (including Hufbauer 1990, Anderson 1991, Page 1991, Arndt and Willett 1991). It is striking to what extent this literature focuses much more on possible changes in the EC's external trade policy indirectly induced by the '1992' programme than on the direct effects of the programme itself. The question of whether '1992' will make the EC more protectionist (see Chapter 10, in this volume) is seen by the rest of the world, probably rightly, as much more important for them than the direct effects of the '1992' policy changes as such.

Conclusion

All economic quantification involves guesses and judgements, and the results are always subject to margins of error. The margins of error associated with the quantification of the effects of '1992' seem particularly large. We are looking at a set of policy changes whose precise shape is still to be determined, at induced responses from firms which are speculative, and at induced responses from policy-makers that are inevitably hard to predict. The work that has been surveyed in this chapter gives good grounds for the belief that the potential effects of '1992' are quite large; it remains to be seen whether the potential will be realised.

References

Anderson K (1991) Europe 1992 and the Western Pacific countries. *Economic Journal* **101**(409): 1538–52
Arndt S, Willett T (1991) Europe 1992 from a North American perspective. *Economic Journal* **101**(409): 1567–79
Balassa B, Bauwens L (1988) The determinants of intra-European trade in manufactured goods. *European Economic Review* **32**(4): 1421–37; and Sapir and Jacquemin 1989
Baldwin R (1989) The growth effects of 1992. *Economic Policy* **9**: 247–81
Ben-David D (1991) Equalizing exchange: a study of the effects of trade liberalization. *NBER Working Paper* No 3706, Cambridge, Mass.
Buigues P, Ilzkovitz F (1991) The effects of the removal of non-tariff barriers in the European internal market. Typescript II/94/91-EN, Commission of the European Communities, Directorate-General for Economic and Financial Affairs, Brussels

Corden W M (1972) Economies of scale and customs union theory. *Journal of Political Economy* **80**(3): 465–75; and Sapir and Jacquemin 1989

Davenport M, Page S (1991) *Europe 1992 and the Developing Countries*. Overseas Development Institute, London

Emerson M et al (1989) *The Economics of 1992*. Oxford University Press, Oxford

Gasiorek M, Smith A, Venables A J (1991) Completing the internal market in the EC: factor demands and comparative advantage. In Winters L A and Venables A J (eds) *European Integration: Trade and Industry*. Cambridge University Press

Hufbauer G C (ed) (1990) *Europe 1992: an American Perspective*. Brookings Institute, Washington DC

Jacquemin A, Sapir A (1989) (eds) *The European Internal Market: Trade and Competition*. Oxford University Press

Mayes D G (1978) The effects of economic integration on trade. *Journal of Common Market Studies* **17**(1): 1–25; and Sapir and Jacquemin 1989

Neven D (1990) EEC integration towards 1992: some distributional aspects. *Economic Policy* (10): 13–62

Norman V (1989) EFTA and the internal European market. *Economic Policy* **9**: 424–65

Owen N (1983) *Economies of Scale, Competitiveness and Trade Patterns Within the European Community*. Clarendon Press

Page S (1991) Europe 1992: views of developing countries. *Economic Journal* **101**(409): 1553–66

Pintado X et al (1988) Economic aspects of the European economic space. *EFTA Economic Affairs Department Occasional Paper* No 25, Geneva

Sleuwaegen L, Yamawaki H (1988) The formation of the European common market and changes in market structure and performance. *European Economic Review* **32**(4): 1451–75

Smith A (1990) The market for cars in the enlarged European Community. In Bliss C and Braga de Macedo J (eds) *Unity with Diversity in the European Economy: The Community's Southern Frontier*. Cambridge University Press for CEPR

Smith A, Venables A J (1988) Completing the internal market in the European Community: some industry simulations. *European Economic Review* **32**(4): 1501–25

Williamson J (1971) Trade and economic growth. In Pinder J (ed) *The Economics of Europe: What the Common Market Means for Britain*, Charles Knight

Winters L A (1987) Britain in Europe: a survey of quantitative trade studies. *Journal of Common Market Studies* **25**(4): 315–35; and Sapir and Jacquemin 1989

Winters L A (1992) The welfare and policy implications of the international trade consequences of '1992'. *American Economic Review* papers and proceedings, May

Wonnacott R, Wonnacott P (1967) *Free Trade Between the U.S. and Canada: The Potential Economic Effects*. Harvard University Press, Cambridge, Mass.

CHAPTER 6

Integration under communism and economic relations after communism in Eastern Europe

ALAN H SMITH

Introduction

The economic institutions that contributed to the collapse of communism in Eastern Europe at the end of 1989 and the consequent break-up of the Council for Mutual Economic Assistance (CMEA) were established before that organisation's foundation in 1949. The most important of these were the imposition of the highly centralised (Stalinist) system of economic planning and administration on a national basis (see Dyker, Chapter 12, *The National Economies of Europe*, on the Soviet Union) in each country of the bloc; the imposition of Stalinist heavy industrial priorities in each country of the bloc: and the redirection of the East European countries' pre-war trade patterns away from Western Europe (and Germany in particular) towards the Soviet Union.

This resulted in the creation of an 'artificial' economic system in each country of the bloc together with a network of trade relations that were determined more by political priorities than by the dictates of comparative advantage. Both the domestic planning systems and the system of trade relations, once established, proved highly resistant to piecemeal reforms, while the ageing communist leaderships in the Soviet Union and Eastern Europe lacked the political will, or desire, to introduce more radical economic reforms, such as might have improved economic performance, but which would have threatened their own positions of leadership or party control over the economy.

Consequently an economic system that was inherently sub-optimal was sustained, largley by political force, for over forty years in Eastern Europe (and considerably longer in the Soviet Union), and this resulted in an accumulation of economic problems which ultimately could not be resolved without wholesale economic-systemic change. The costs of sustaining a sub-optimal economic system in Eastern Europe were in part borne by the Soviet Union, which in turn contributed to the deterioration in Soviet economic performance in the 1980s and a widening gap between Soviet and US gross national product (GNP) in the 1980s. The growing reluctance of the Soviet leadership under Gorbachev to continue to bear the costs of its East European empire, combined with political pressures in Eastern Europe (which were, to no small degree, derived from popular frustration at poor economic performance) resulted in the overthrow of the old communist regimes throughout the East European CMEA countries.

In central Eastern Europe, in particular, the new post-communist governments argue that the economic problems confronting them cannot be overcome without radical economic changes to the economic system, which involve the (re)creation of a capitalist market economy in a relatively short period of time. Although the collapse of communist power and the attempt to create market economies in Eastern Europe have made the old institutional structure of the CMEA redundant, the old economic system and the system of trade relations established during the communist period have bequeathed a set of trade dependencies which will make the integration of the East European economies into Western Europe exceedingly difficult, and which has serious implications for their prospects of membership of the European Community (EC) in either the short term or the long term.

An understanding of these features is essential for proper evaluation of the problems which surround the process of recreating a 'single Europe'. This chapter presents an analysis of the problems created by the 'Stalinist' division of Europe; an analysis of attempts to reform the system prior to the collapse of communism; and an assessment of the prospects for reform in the post-communist era in Eastern Europe.

The origins of the CMEA and the isolation of Eastern Europe

The Council for Mutual Economic Assistance (CMEA) was founded in January 1949. The founding members were the USSR, Bulgaria, Czechoslovakia, Hungary, Poland and Romania. Albania joined the following February and the newly established German Democratic Republic became a member in 1950. The essentially political nature of the organisation was reflected by the subsequent extension of membership to three non-European developing socialist economies, Mongolia, Cuba and Vietnam. Mongolia was granted membership of the CMEA in 1962 as a political response to the Sino-Soviet dispute, a conflict which also resulted in Albania leaving the organisation. The accession of Cuba in 1972 coincided with the first expansion of EC membership and was intended to indicate that the CMEA was not a purely European Organisation. The same primacy of political over economic considerations was reflected in the extension of membership to Vietnam in 1978, which was calculated to indicate that that country was now firmly part of the socialist camp following the end of the Vietnam War. Although membership was in each case determined by political factors, the developing countries that became full members of the CMEA have been the major beneficiaries of Soviet and East European economic aid, and have also benefited from preferential prices and terms of trade within the CMEA. The question of the status of, and costs of support for, the non-European members of the CMEA has been a major area of controversy between the USSR on the one hand, and Eastern Europe on the other, and proved in 1990–1 to be a major obstacle to the establishment of a purely formal, advisory organisation to replace the CMEA.

The CMEA fulfilled few economic functions between its creation in 1949 and the death of Stalin in 1953. The major factors contributing to the division of Europe into two separate economic camps had already come into sharp focus in the immediate post-war years, before the organisation's foundation. The East European countries' initial attempts to expand regional trade links (reflected in proposals to form regional customs unions in central Eastern Europe and the Balkans) and to expand trade with Western Europe rather than with the Soviet Union were stymied by Stalin's *de facto* veto on the participation of the East European economies in the Marshall Plan for European Reconstruction. This prevented not just receipt of US capital assistance in the reconstruction and modernisation of industry but also participation in the emerging schemes for economic integration and co-operation that were being formulated in Western Europe. In contrast, Marshall Plan aid to Western Europe, which was directed at the development of industries that could survive without protection, not only assisted economic recovery but also contributed to greater economic integration between the West European states, and to the eventual emergence of the EC.

East European isolation from US capital and technology was compounded by US controls over the export of goods with military and/or strategic significance to communist countries, which were applied to the East European countries following the communist take-over of power. Countries receiving Marshall Aid were also required to accede to the embargo on technology which was enforced by the Co-ordinating Committee on Multilateral Export Controls (CoCom), which still exercises control over the export of militarily useful technology to communist countries in the 1990s.

The imposition of the Soviet system in Eastern Europe

The imposition of the Stalinist system of economic planning and administration in the wake of the communist take-over of power in 1948, followed by the imposition of the Stalinist growth model which incorporated Stalin's preference for the development of heavy industry in each individual East European country, created formidable obstacles to the development of East European trade links with Western Europe and to the establishment of rational trade links between the East European economies themselves.

After 1948 each East European country was required to replicate the Soviet economic system of highly centralised command planning. Consequently each East European country established its own separate national planning hierarchy, incorporating a central planning agency which was responsible for the formulation of detailed central plans for industrial production on its own territory, together with national industrial ministries which covered the administration of an entire sector (or branch) of industry and which were responsible for implementing these plans. Simultaneously each country also developed its own separate national banking and financial system which replicated the Soviet monobank system and retained separate (inconvertible) currencies with arbitrary exchange rates. Separate national agencies were also established to supervise and control domestic wholesale and retail trade and to determine domestic wage rates, wholesale and retail prices (which bore little or no relation to domestic scarcities) on their own territories.

Just as important, each country was forced to replicate the Soviet foreign trade system, which involved creating a separate state monopoly of foreign trade in each East European country, administered by a national ministry for foreign trade which had the sole authority to conduct foreign trade relations (including trade with other socialist countries). This specific, highly centralised model of the state monopoly of foreign trade originally developed as a response to the unique political and economic circumstances of world recession and international hostility in which the Soviet Union had attempted to conduct trade relations with capitalist countries in the 1930s. The system was designed to maximise the strength of the Soviet bargaining position with capitalist states by preventing Soviet producers and purchasers from competing with one another in foreign markets. It was also intended to ensure that scarce hard-currency earning could be concentrated on imports to which the leadership attached the highest priority, namely machinery and equipment for the construction of an industrial base, and not 'squandered' on imports of consumer goods.

This highly centralised system was best suited to large-scale exports of homogeneous unprocessed goods (eg energy, raw materials and precious metals) produced under conditions of increasing marginal costs (where the supplier is large enough to affect world prices, and where a centralised export administration can restrict exports to maximise foreign currency earnings and/or utilise the power of discriminating monopoly), and to the import of machinery and equipment (for which no domestic equivalent exists) associated with large-scale investment and construction projects which have significant spillover effects. Under these circumstances, centralised decision-making permits central planners (at least in theory) to equate the domestic social opportunity cost of the last unit of production to be exported with the marginal social benefit of the last unit to be imported, and to appropriate the ensuing gains from trade (including rental earnings) to the state budget. The advantages of a centralised trade system are maximised when the benefits of a relatively large volume of trade can be estimated accurately at the centre with a relatively small number of calculations. The system is ill-suited to the trade needs of more advanced industrial countries dependent on exports of sophisticated manufactured goods produced under competitive conditions, where detailed information about local production costs and the specific demands of foreign markets is required by the exporter.

The imposition of the Soviet planning system in each individual CMEA country proved to be a highly cumbersome and sub-optimal method of stimulating trade. Individual national planning authorities were effectively required to draw up their own separate five-year and annual plans in ignorance of both the production capabilities and the requirements of the other CMEA economies. Furthermore, as each economy developed its own inflexible price system (which bore no relation to costs or scarcities), it became virtually impossible to plan trade flows according to the principle of comparative advantage.

The CMEA monetary system

A classic feature of the internal operation of centrally planned economies is that central planners determine the flow of inputs and outputs between enterprises. Money is said to be passive in that the holder of money does not have the automatic right to purchase a commodity at the prevailing price, unless the transaction has first been planned and sanctioned by the appropriate authority (commodity inconvertibility). This situation also prevailed in trade between CMEA countries. The mere possession of a CMEA currency did not give the holder the automatic right (legally) to purchase a commodity in that country. The CMEA currencies were also financially inconvertible in that they could not be exchanged into foreign currencies on demand at the prevailing exchange rate. National currencies were therefore effectively of no value as a means of settling intra-CMEA payments, as they failed to give the creditor country command over resources or capital in the debtor country and could not be converted into an external currency which would give command over resources.

The unfitness of national currencies to serve as means of international payment generated a reluctance on the part of the CMEA countries to run surpluses in intra-CMEA trade, and a strong tendency to bilateralism, whereby CMEA members attempted to balance the annual value of trade with each individual CMEA partner. An attempt to overcome this was initiated in 1964 with the establishment of the transferable rouble and the International Bank for Economic Cooperation (IBEC). The CMEA currencies were nominally linked by a fixed exchange rate to the transferable rouble which was in turn linked to convertible currencies by an exchange rate which fluctuated in line with international currency movements subsequent to the demonetisation of gold in 1971. Trade settlements between CMEA countries were denominated in transferable roubles and passed through the IBEC. It was hoped that this would stimulate a form of multilateralism, as surpluses arising in trade with one country were offset against deficits arising in trade with some other country (subject to the proviso that each country maintained an overall balance in its accounts). In practice the system failed to stimulate multilateralism. The transferable rouble functioned purely as a unit of account, not as a means of exchange. It had no physical existence, and like national currencies could neither be converted into hard currencies nor be used to command resources in another country.

The pattern of intra-CMEA trade

The predominant pattern of intra-CMEA trade (known as the 'radial pattern', because trade flows radiated out from the Soviet centre to the East European periphery) was largely determined by Stalin's insistence that each East European country should adopt the Soviet model of extensive industrial growth, which involved giving priority to the construction of a heavy industrial base in each country of the bloc, regardless of the country's natural resource endowment. This pattern of production increased bloc demand for energy and raw materials which were predominantly located in the Soviet Union, and resulted in a relative oversupply of comparatively unsophisticated and increasingly obsolete metallurgical and heavy engineering products. As a result, the East European economies became dependent on Soviet supplies of energy and raw materials and on the Soviet market for their heavy industrial goods, many of which did not meet Western quality standards and consequently could not be sold on Western markets.

At the same time the lower priority attached to the production of consumer goods, and the neglect of food production combined with the rapid transfer of labour from agriculture to industry, resulted in the relative under-supply of these commodities in intra-CMEA trade, and they frequently had to be imported from outside the bloc. Goods which could be traded outside the bloc (and which were in high demand in intra-CMEA trade) became known as hard goods, and CMEA countries were usually willing to export hard goods only if they could receive hard goods of equivalent value in exchange. Similarly an East European countries would import soft goods – unsaleable in the West and not in deficit in the East – only in exchange for exports of its own soft goods.

The CMEA pricing system

The phenomenon of 'commodity bilateralism' resulted principally from the absence of a rational price system in intra-CMEA trade. The construction of an 'ideal' CMEA price system can be examined from two conceptual viewpoints. If the CMEA economies were to be considered open to world trade, then a rational intra-CMEA price system would reflect the prices at which goods that are traded between CMEA members would be traded in world markets. Alternatively, if the CMEA were regarded as a closed economic system (for whatever reason), a rational price system should reflect bloc supply and demand conditions and scarcities.

Hewett (1974) shows that in principle intra-CMEA prices were calculated on the basis of a variant of world market prices which is estimated from an earlier period, and then fixed for a predetermined (plan) period. World market prices were also supposed to be adjusted to remove the effect of 'cyclical, monopolistic and speculative factors' before being used in the CMEA. Until 1974, intra-CMEA prices were normally predetermined for an entire five-year plan period on the basis of an average of estimated world market prices over the preceding five-year plan period. Following the quadrupling of crude oil prices by OPEC in 1974, the formula was altered, first in 1975, so that intra-CMEA prices were based on the preceding three years' world market prices. From 1976 onwards intra-CMEA prices were adjusted annually to reflect an average of the preceding five years' world market prices (the sliding-average world market price system).

In practice prices were determined by bilateral negotiations between trade representatives, who attempted to support their price claims by reference to Western analogues for the goods in question. The resulting estimates of world market prices were then converted into transferable roubles at the prevailing official exchange rate. Estimating world market prices is not a simple process, even for relatively homogeneous products such as fuels and raw materials, where prices differ from time to time and from location to location. The problem is far more complicated in the case of manufactured goods where precise analogues for CMEA products frequently had never (or no longer) existed in world markets. Finally it must be remembered that the CMEA was not a supranational organisation, and that the price rules were only guidelines. Members were free to trade at bilaterally determined prices, and some trade in hard goods was conducted in hard currencies at current world market prices.

The costs of trade: did the Soviet Union subsidise Eastern Europe?

Empirical evidence shows that the system was commercially disadvantageous to the Soviet Union. Prices for manufactured goods traded in the CMEA frequently exceeded world market prices for comparable Western products, although the former often did not meet the quality and performance standards of the latter. This benefited the East European countries, which were net exporters of manufactured goods in their trade with the Soviet Union. Similarly, the marginal cost of Soviet energy and raw materials output is substantially higher than world marginal cost, as additional supplies (especially of oil and gas) have to be extracted from deeper strata in the harsh terrain of Siberia, requiring high expenditures on exploration and extraction, and on transportation across a land-mass to the European sectors of the USSR and then on to Eastern Europe. The use of world market prices for energy and raw materials deliveries meant that the Soviet Union was not compensated for the additional costs of developing Soviet energy and raw materials for CMEA consumption in the 1960s. The use of the sliding-average world market price system after 1975 meant that energy prices, especially crude oil prices (although increasing eightfold between 1974 and 1986) lagged substantially behind world market prices. On the other hand East European agricultural exporters also argue, with some justice, that they were disadvantaged by the use of world market prices for farm products which had been driven down below production costs by the application of government subsidies and agricultural support schemes.

Specialists on the CMEA agree that on balance the Soviet Union forwent substantial economic benefits as a result of its adherence to the system of intra-CMEA trading and pricing. It would have been more profitable for the Soviet Union to divert exports of energy and raw materials from CMEA markets to Western markets in order to obtain hard currency which could then have been used to obtain higher-quality, lower-priced manufactured goods than it obtained from CMEA partners. There is, however, considerable dispute between Western specialists over the size of the benefits forgone by the Soviet Union, and over the reasons why the Soviet Union did not make greater use of its monopolist-monopsonist position within the CMEA to secure more favourable terms of trade.

Somewhat controversial views have been put forward by Marrese and Vanous (1983), who argue that the Soviet Union under Brezhnev deliberately granted an 'implicit subsidy' to East European governments to preserve East European allegiance to the Soviet bloc (and hence the Warsaw Pact), which in turn reduced the level of Soviet defence expenditure required to meet security objectives. They also argue that the size of the subsidies reflected the degree of allegiance shown by the individual countries. Marrese and Vanous (1983) estimate that 'implicit subsidies' totalled $90 billion between 1974 and 1982, reaching $18.6 billion in 1981 alone, with East Germany and Czechoslovakia the principal beneficiaries of Soviet subsidies. Romania, by contrast, actually lost out in its trade with the USSR. These evaluations were reached by re-estimating intra-CMEA trade flows at world market prices, and involved a substantial quality discount on the price of East European exports of manufactured goods to the Soviet Union, in addition to the mark-up resulting from re-estimating Soviet energy supplies at world market prices.

The estimates have been criticised on the grounds that they do not reflect the prices the Soviet Union *would have* obtained if it had diverted intra-CMEA trade to Western markets, where the Soviet Union received less favourable terms of trade than those applying to trade between capitalist countries in general. This is in part because Western manufacturers had to pass the additional costs of dealing with the Soviet Union (including the cost of compliance with CoCom regulations) on to Soviet customers to make such trade profitable. Following this argument, Poznanski (1988) estimates that Soviet forgone gains arose largely from the differences between intra-CMEA and world market prices for oil and gas, and were roughly half the level estimated by Marrese and Vanous in the period from 1974 to 1984, to be eliminated altogether by 1986. It is in any case questionable whether the Soviet Union could have diverted oil and gas exports to Western markets without having an impact on world energy prices (this argument assumes that the East European economies would have been unable, or unwilling, to take an equivalent volume of energy off world markets).

Other critics reject the view that Soviet forgone gains from trade represented a deliberate 'subsidy for security'. Lavigne (1983) and Koves (1983) both argue that the nature of intra-CMEA pricing resulted directly from the *modus operandi* of the CMEA, and cannot be examined in isolation from other factors, including the imposition of heavy industrial priorities on the East European economies. Koves argues that the Soviet Union does (or did) not weigh up the costs and benefits of trade with Eastern Europe with the degree of economic rationality that Marrese and Vanous (1983) suggest, and suggests that 'forgone gains' arose largely because the Soviet Union did not anticipate the second OPEC price increase of 1979, and may even have been outnegotiated by more skilful East European trade representatives. It should also be remembered that the price increases of 1975 were at best inconsistent with CMEA price principles, which predicated that prices should not be affected by monopolistic or cyclical influences on capitalist markets, and that they should in any case have remained fixed until the end of 1975.

My own view (Smith 1991) can be summarised as follows. The increases in world oil prices in 1974 and 1979 resulted in a significant increase in Soviet real wealth, by increasing the value of Soviet oil exports to the West (and by creating at the same time new possibilities for arms exports to the Middle East). The energy and material-intensive East European economies would have been incapable of paying prices based on the new OPEC prices which would have in the first instance resulted in a major reduction in living standards (see van Brabant 1984), and would have created renewed pressure for industrial restructuring and economic reform with far-reaching political consequences. The Soviet leadership under Brezhnev, which attached major import-ance to leadership stability in Eastern Europe and to the cohesion of the Warsaw Pact, and was (correctly) fearful that demand for political reform in Eastern Europe could spread to the Soviet Union, was able to mitigate the effects of world oil price increases on the East European economies by supplying them with energy on more favourable terms of trade than could have been obtained in trade with the West. This was achieved by a combination of instruments and policies, including use of the sliding five-year average price system, continued acceptance of East European soft goods and toleration of Soviet trade surpluses (denominated in transferable roubles) with the East European economies. This reinforced the 'radial' pattern of trade and increased East European dependence on Soviet energy supplies and Soviet markets, and also increased the short-term costs to Eastern Europe of breaking away from the CMEA. (Though as the two major increases in world oil prices were gradually fed into the intra-CMEA price formula, the East European economies did experience a significant deterioration in their terms of trade.) The Soviet Union utilised its growing portfolio of 'claims' on East European resources, against a background of continued preferential trade terms, to press for the implementation of its long-term proposals for East European participation in projects to develop Soviet resources.

Plan and market approaches to integration

The problem of economic integration could be approached from two directions. The first would involve a greater use of market, price and financial levers, and the second a greater use of central plan directives. Logically these approaches lead to two theoretical extremes – one based on the introduction of a free market, implying moves towards full factor and product mobility (which underlies the concept of the EC and is described elsewhere in this volume), and one based on the introduction of a single planning authority and planning mechanism for the entire CMEA region. This latter line of development would have been broadly consistent with the *modus operandi* of the planning system in the USSR itself, and would have involved a supranational centralised planning authority with subsidiary national agencies (whose powers would have been similar to those of a Soviet republican planning authority) responsible for implementing CMEA plan instructions within their own territory. This system would have involved a single banking system for the entire CMEA area (based on a monobank), a single currency and a single ministry of foreign trade responsible for conducting trade relations outside the CMEA. Trade relations between the member states of the CMEA and trade flows related to CMEA investment projects would have resembled those between the constituent republics of the USSR under the traditional Soviet system.

There are many areas where the use of rational price indicators is consistent with improved central planning. Prices that reflected genuine bloc scarcities and opportunity costs would have enabled central planners to make more rational investment decisions, would have facilitated CMEA specialisation along the lines of comparative advantage, and would have provided CMEA countries with a genuine economic incentive to trade with their partners. The creation of a rational CMEA pricing system and a monetary system that functioned as a unit of account and a store of value would have helped to overcome the problems of bilateralism. The critical question, however, was whether price and money levers were to remain at the level of useful adjuncts to central planning, or whether resource flows should be *determined* by the spontaneous reaction of producers and consumers to price and money levers. A critical feature of Soviet command planning was that domestic producers had no choice over the specification of the end users of their output (ie money flows followed rather than determined resource flows in the domestic economy). This was logically reflected in foreign trade relations by the prohibition on domestic producers selling directly to foreign customers (commodity inconvertibility) without the prior approval of the central authorities. If an East European enterprise could have ordered energy or raw materials directly from a

Soviet enterprise without reference to the Soviet Ministry of Foreign Trade, then the Soviet central planners would have lost the right to control the flow of resources on their own territory. Not surprisingly, the supply-constrained Soviet State Planning Commission (Gosplan) proved most reluctant to relinquish this power.

The two alternatives outlined above, and their basic mutual incompatibility, indicate why it proved so difficult to raise the level of economic integration in the CMEA – the full market solution would have greatly weakened the role and the authority of central planning bodies, while the full planning solution would effectively have involved the incorporation of Eastern Europe into the Soviet Union. Although most proposals to improve intra-CMEA relations involved intermediate solutions that either made greater use of market levers or sought less overtly supranational methods of co-ordinating plan levers, the authors of proposed reforms drew their inspiration in the majority of cases from one or other of these totally incompatible paradigms.

Soviet policies towards the CMEA in the 1980s and 1990s

Official Soviet proposals for reform of the CMEA from the death of Stalin up to mid-1987 largely reflected the views of Gosplan, which advocated the supremacy of plan controls over market levers, including a proposal by Khrushchev to establish a common planning organ for the CMEA in 1962. Soviet policy under Kosygin attempted to stimulate greater co-operation between the national planning authorities of the CMEA area by the use of less overtly supranational measures. An additional Soviet concern has been to limit the costs to the Soviet Union of meeting bloc energy demands by attempting to limit East European consumption, and by encouraging East European participation in joint projects to develop Soviet mineral resources for bloc consumption. The largest of these was the Orenburg gas pipeline, which involved each East European participant in supplying pipe and labour for the construction of a fixed length of pipeline for which they were repaid in natural gas.

Soviet policies towards the CMEA and Eastern Europe did not alter drastically in the period following the death of Brezhnev in 1982 up to the middle of 1987, this reflecting continued Soviet preoccupation with attempts to stimulate CMEA independence in science and technology, foodstuffs production and energy and raw materials. The policy was largely motivated by a desire to reduce Soviet vulnerability to Western economic sanctions and embargoes at a time of growing international mistrust in the early and mid-1980s. At the same time the Soviet Union attempted to improve its terms of trade with Eastern Europe by demanding better quality imports of manufactured goods and foodstuffs in exchange for continued energy supplies. Finally, Soviet policies included attempts to harmonise economic reforms among the CMEA countries. These Soviet goals were overtly accepted by the party leaders of the CMEA countries at a specially convened summit in Moscow in June 1984. The communiqué committed the East European leaders, in principle, not only to greater harmonisation of their economic systems and greater use of plan levers in the CMEA, but also to 'reconstruct their industries . . . to supply the Soviet Union with the products it needs [including] foodstuffs, industrial consumer goods . . . and machinery and equipment reaching . . . world technical levels'.

These policies were pursued with greater vigour in the early period of the leadership of Gorbachev, whose initial economic strategy recognised that Soviet and East European economic performance in the 1970s and 1980s had been unsatisfactory, but failed to recognise either the scale or the systemic nature of the problems facing all the centrally planned economies (see Dyker, Chapter 12 in *The National Economies of Europe*, on the Soviet Union). This in turn reflected a greatly misplaced confidence in the capabilities of Soviet and East European science and research and development (R&D). It was hoped that an immediate improvement in Soviet economic performance could be achieved through increased investment in technical modernisation, and that better-quality machinery and equipment imported from the CMEA countries would play a critical role in achieving this. By the middle of 1987 the assumptions on which this policy was based were either discredited or no longer valid. The strategy of 'acceleration' which involved stepping up plan targets exacerbated existing supply shortages and bottlenecks in the USSR and 'accelerated' hidden inflationary pressures as well as the demand for imports of machinery and equipment. Similarly accelerated plan targets in Eastern Europe contributed to growing balance of payments problems and growing hard-currency debt in the majority of East European countries in the second half of the 1980s, following a period of cut-backs in hard-currency imports in the early 1980s which had enabled the East European economies to reduce their hard-currency debt.

These problems, which resulted from a combination of systemic factors and policy mistakes, were aggravated by exogenous factors. Most critically, the collapse in world oil prices in 1986 halved the value of Soviet exports to the West, and greatly reduced the purchasing power and liquidity of importers of Soviet arms in the Middle East. At the same time the Soviet Union was experiencing growing difficulties in maintaining domestic oil and coal production. This was further compounded by the accident at the Chernobyl nuclear power station in April 1986. The safety implications of the accident put an end to CMEA plans for a major expansion of nuclear power to substitute for conventional power generation, which would have released Soviet oil for export to the West. It also revealed critical technical defects in Soviet science policy that could not be overcome in the short term.

The combined effect of the above was that the Soviet authorities could no longer sustain the value of hard-currency exports required to finance the desired level of imports from the West. The shortfall was in part met by reducing Soviet imports of grain and consumer goods, and in part by increasing hard-currency indebtedness. At the same time the Soviet Union increased the volume of oil exports to the West to reduce the impact of price falls on hard-currency revenue targets. According to official Soviet statistics, Soviet oil exports to the industrialised West grew from 78 million tons in 1976 to 95 million tons in 1988 (in a clear example of the phenomenon of the backward bending supply curve), while exports to Eastern Europe fell from 81 million tons in 1986 to 76 million tons in 1989. Although Soviet terms of trade with its CMEA partners deteriorated more slowly than in trade with the West, the Soviet Union was no longer able to offer more favourable terms of trade to Eastern Europe without incurring considerable damage to its own domestic economy.

From 1987 until late 1990 Soviet economic debates and proposals for reform to both the domestic economic system and the foreign trade system became progressively more radical, extending to proposals for the decentralisation of foreign trade and for the gradual introduction of more rational exchange rates and limited forms of internal convertibility. At the same time Soviet proposals for reforming the operation of CMEA moved towards the gradual introduction of market measures. These included a proposal in 1987 for the gradual introduction of convertibility within the CMEA, based on the principle of making domestic currencies freely convertible with the transferable rouble and with one another. This would ultimately result in the establishment of a collective currency which would be convertible with Western currencies. There followed in 1988 an initiative to create 'a unified socialist market in the long term' which would facilitate 'the free movement of goods, services and factors of production'. At the same time the Soviet prime minister, Ryzhkov, expressed growing dissatisfaction with the lack of progress made in improving either the volume or the quality of East European exports to the USSR.

During the period from 1987 until the collapse of communism in Eastern Europe in 1989, Soviet representatives at the CMEA found themselves in an isolated position, striving to hold an untenable middle ground between those leaderships who wished to preserve the old economic and trading systems virtually intact (including Romania, which rejected proposals for a 'unified socialist market'), the GDR, Bulgaria and Czechoslovakia, which accepted with misgivings, and those who wished to introduce market reforms and re-orient trade to the West (Hungary, and to a lesser extent Poland). Practical progress towards the development of a unified socialist market was virtually non-existent, and disagreement was such that it proved impossible even to hold a formal session of the CMEA in 1989. In practice either the Soviet Union would have been required drastically to radicalise and accelerate domestic economic reforms (to include the introduction of market-determined prices, active money and wholesale trade), or the progress towards a socialist market would necessarily have been painfully slow.

Soviet–East European trade relations continued to deteriorate during 1989, with frequent complaints that the Soviet Union was failing to meet contracted energy supplies to Eastern Europe. Although the Soviet leadership attributed this to domestic energy supply problems, including protracted miners' strikes, the suspicion grew in Eastern Europe that the Soviet leadership had placed continued energy supplies to Eastern Europe low on its list of priorities. In December 1989, following the collapse of communism in Poland and Czechoslovakia and the clear evidence that socialism would not survive the elections in the GDR and Hungary, Ryzhkov proposed (to the Soviet Congress of People's Deputies) to base intra-CMEA trade on current world market prices and to conduct payments in convertible currencies from the beginning of 1991. This proposal (with the possibility of a three-year transition period) was adopted by the 1990 CMEA session.

In practice, however, the three-year transitional period was not implemented, and intra-CMEA trade was effectively moved on to a hard-currency basis in January 1991. Trade between Eastern Europe and the Soviet Union collapsed far more quickly than initially anticipated, partly as a result of growing supply problems in the Soviet energy sector and partly as a result of moves to recentralise Soviet trade and payments in response to growing hard-currency pressures. As a result, Soviet enterprises have been prevented from entering into bilateral deals with East European partners, while imports from Eastern Europe do not figure highly in Soviet central priorities. Although the collapse of intra-CMEA trade should accelerate the reorientation of East European trade away from the Soviet Union towards the EC, it will impose significant short-term costs on the East European economies.

Prospects for economic relations between the post-communist East European states

As a result of the collapse of communism in Eastern Europe, each of the East European ex-CMEA economies has entered the stage of transition to an essentially capitalist, full market economy. The speed and sequencing of the transition, and the prospects for success will vary substantially from country to country, in part as a consequence of historic and geographic factors, in part as a reflection of domestic debates concerning the social costs of the transition, including the expected level of unemployment and the effect of the removal of subsidies on the prices for staple goods and its impact on poverty. At one extreme the former GDR no longer exists as a separate country following German reunification. The governments of the other Central East European countries (Hungary, Poland and Czechoslovakia) have rejected any form of compromise between full capitalism and socialism in the form of a 'regulated market economy' in favour of the transition to what can be described as a traditional form of 'European free market economy'. In some cases the rhetoric of government advisers and officials in these countries indicates that they envisage a smaller role for the state in the long term than is the current West European norm.

The final shape of the economic system in the Balkan states may yet depend on internal political factors. Although Western governments harbour some misgivings about the level of commitment of the Romanian president to the principles of the market economy, the Romanian government has, so far, been resolute in its commitment to those principles. In the former Soviet Union, the drama of political events has to a degree masked continued hesitancy on transition to the market.

The process of transition and its implications for economic relations with the EC

The problems confronting the East European economies can largely be attributed to a combination of an artificial, externally imposed, poorly functioning economic system, and poor centralised investment decisions over a period of forty years, which have produced a build-up of low-quality, obsolete industrial capital stock and a neglect of infrastructure, agriculture and services. These problems have been compounded by the bias of investment policies towards 'regional autarky' or import substitution. It is argued, therefore, that domestic reforms are essential to overcome the operational problems of the economy, while foreign direct investment can play a critical role in modernising and replacing the capital stock and creating export-oriented manufacturing industries and services. If these problems can be overcome it is possible that the East European economies could achieve a relatively rapid rate of growth by the end of the

1990s, such as would narrow the gap in living standards between Eastern and Western Europe. Supporters of radical market reforms argue that it is over-optimistic to expect living standards in Eastern Europe to approach those of the richer EC countries, but that the prospects for Eastern Europe can be compared with those of the Mediterranean economies in the EC which have opened themselves up to foreign investment.

The transition to a market economy will require the East European economies to pass through a number of essential stages, with implications for their economic relations with both their trade partners in the former CMEA and with Western Europe. The principal measures can be enumerated as follows (see Hare 1990; Kaser 1990; Lipton and Sachs 1990):

1   The establishment of a legal framework for the operation of a market economy. This involves both the removal of existing legal constraints to the operation of a market economy and the creation (or recreation) of the economic institutions and regulatory infrastructure which are essential for the functioning of a market economy.

2   The relaxation and removal of central controls over retail and wholesale prices and wages, including the relaxation and removal of state subsidies for basic staple goods. This must be accompanied (or preceded) by measures to ensure macroeconomic stabilisation to eliminate excess demand which would otherwise result in hyperinflationary pressures. This will require the creation of a sound monetary system, which will in turn require a tight monetary policy and the removal of subsidies to loss-making industries, with a consequent risk of high levels of unemployment. At the same time the removal of subsidies from basic staples will have the greatest impact on the unemployed and low wage-earners, threatening a major increase in poverty. The establishment of a welfare system and the indexation of pensions is therefore an urgent priority.

3   The creation of a private sector. This will require the relatively rapid creation of a small and medium-scale private sector in both services and production (brought about by the emergence of private activity *ab initio* and the denationalisation of existing small and medium-scale industry). This will in turn require the immediate introduction of wholesale trade, which will be facilitated by decentralised access to imported goods and components to overcome domestic bottlenecks. The creation of a private sector will also involve the eventual privatisation and demonopolisation of existing large-scale industry and the creation of a modern large-scale industrial sector. This will involve the use of Western financial capital both in the form of foreign direct investment through the establishment of wholly-owned subsidiaries in Eastern Europe, and ultimately of exposure to foreign ownership through the international marketing of shares in existing privatised industries.

4   Trade liberalisation is essential to weaken the monopoly powers of domestic enterprises and expose them to foreign competitive pressures. It would also serve both to stimulate domestic efficiency and to moderate pressures for wage and price increases. Furthermore the development of a private sector will require that new entrepreneurs have at least equal access to imported equipment, materials and components as state industry.

Access to scarce hard currency should be largely determined by price (exchange rate policy) rather than by central controls and rationing. The uncompetitive nature of East European products suggests that this will involve a relatively undervalued exchange rate in the short term at least. That will offer some protection to domestic industry, while low domestic labour costs should make Eastern Europe more attractive to foreign investment. Full convertibility at an undervalued exchange rate carries the risk that domestic land and capital will be transferred to foreign ownership too cheaply. In the short term, therefore, convertibility will have to be restricted to current account transactions. This can be achieved either by a liberal system of import licences or by the introduction of residents' convertibility, whereby all residents have the right to purchase foreign currency at the official exchange rate. Limitations on the export of currency could be maintained to prevent speculation. With all this, however, some form of balance of payments assistance will be required to relieve the immediate costs of debt servicing.

The central East European countries, in particular, offer foreign investors a reasonably well-educated and well-trained labour force and possibilities for the establishment of production bases close to the EC market. In the longer term the establishment of capital markets and capital account convertibility in Eastern Europe will allow foreign investors the possibility of buying shares in East European companies. Despite initial enthusiasm, however, Western multinationals have up to now been guarded in their approach to investing in Eastern Europe.

Conclusion

Although the collapse of communism and the transition to a market economy has made the old institutional structure of the CMEA redundant, the legacy of the old economic system and the system of trade relations which has made the East European economies dependent on the safe, undemanding Soviet market for manufactured goods, and on Soviet energy supplies, will complicate the redirection of East European trade flows to the West. The collapse of intra-CMEA trade following the institution of settlements in hard currency in January 1991 and the continued deterioration of Soviet economic performance has added a new urgency to this task.

The East European governments see full membership of the EC as a strategic objective, which would guarantee their status as democratic market economies that are part of a wider reunited Europe, rather than just as an economic objective. However, it is highly doubtful whether any of the East European economies would be capable of withstanding the immediate impact of full membership of the EC. The rapid decline in industrial production and the growth of unemployment in what was East Germany (it is estimated that unemployment and short-time working affected 30 per cent of the East German labour force in 1991), following German monetary union, lends support to the view that large sections of East European industry would not be capable of competing in the EC market in the short term under conditions of free mobility of labour. Even if the problems of product quality and up-to-dateness are ignored, productivity differentials between Eastern and Western Europe are such that East European wage levels would have to be set close to, or below, the level of West European unemployment benefits to equate effective wage costs. Under these circumstances it would be virtually impossible to find a wage level that would both prevent a major exodus of labour from Eastern Europe and make existing East European industry competitive in Western markets.

This suggests that a transitional solution incorporating improved access to EC markets for some, or all, of the East European countries provides the most realistic solution to East European aspirations. This would also help to encourage Western multinationals to establish production bases in Eastern Europe for exporting to the EC. It would provoke some reaction from the outlying countries of the EC, which would find themselves facing increasing competition to attract foreign investment. The Common Agricultural Policy would in any case continue to present a barrier to East European exports of farm products. Ironically, until the problem of full membership is resolved, the East European economies may find that their markets are more open to EC products than the EC is to imports from Eastern Europe.

References

Brabant J M van (1984) The Soviet Union and Socialist economic integration. *Soviet Studies* **36**
Hare P G (1990) From central planning to the market economy: some microeconomic issues. *Economic Journal* **100**
Hewett E A (1974) *Foreign Trade Prices in the CMEA.* Cambridge University Press
Kaser M C (1990) The technology of decontrol: some macroeconomic issues. *Economic Journal* **100**
Koves A (1983) 'Implicit subsidies' and some issues of economic relations within the CMEA. *Acta Oeconomica* **31**
Lavigne M (1983) The Soviet Union inside Comecon. *Soviet Studies* **35**
Lipton D, Sachs J (1990) Creating a market economy in Eastern Europe, *Brookings Papers on Economic Activity.* Brookings Institute, Washington DC
Marrese M, Vanous J (1983) *Soviet Subsidisation of Trade with Eastern Europe: A Soviet Perspective.* University of California Press
Poznanski K (1988) Opportunity costs in Soviet trade with Eastern Europe. *Soviet Studies* **40**
Smith A (1991) Soviet economic relations with Eastern Europe under Gorbachev. In Pravda A (ed) *Soviet Relations with Eastern Europe.* Sage

Part II
The macroeconomic scene

CHAPTER 7

Co-ordinating macroeconomic policy

R K EASTWOOD

Introduction

Recent years have seen intense interest in the ways in which international co-operation over the setting of macroeconomic policies might both improve the functioning of the world economic system and, in the European context, contribute to the evolution of the European Community. At the world level, the breakdown in 1973 of the adjustable-peg exchange rate system that had been set up after the Bretton Woods conference of 1945, and the influence of monetarism towards the end of the 1970s, meant that for a dozen years the international monetary system was better viewed as a non-system; to a greater degree than before or since national policies were determined in an uncoordinated way, and both real and nominal exchange rates were extremely volatile. The 50 per cent real appreciation of the dollar during 1980–5 and the related emergence of an unsustainable US trade deficit, which exceeded 3 per cent of GNP in 1985, were the decisive factors leading to a subsequent period of increased co-operation, but agreement over the appropriate system for the future remains elusive. In the European Community both the logic of the CAP (Common Agricultural Policy: see Howe, Chapter 16 in this volume, on agriculture) and the political commitment to eventual economic union demanded some attempt to achieve exchange rate stability at an earlier stage, and this took the form of the European Monetary System (EMS), founded in 1979. Yet while economists continue to argue about the extent to which the EMS has achieved its objectives, there is acute disagreement at the political level over its future evolution.

The EMS is the subject of Chapter 8; this chapter deals with the arguments for and against co-operation (and the distinction between co-operation and co-ordination), the characteristics of systems of co-ordination, the post-war history of co-ordination among the industrialised countries, and finally prospects for the future.

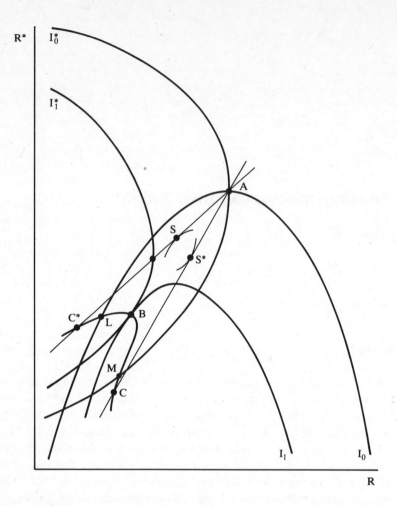

Figure 7.1

Co-ordination: for and against

It is useful to draw a distinction between the broad concept of co-operation, which might mean no more than information exchange, and the more restrictive idea of *co-ordination*, which we will define as joint policymaking. Economic interdependence generally makes co-operation desirable, but it is important to distinguish situations where there is no conflict from situations where there is. The essential ingredient of the no-conflict case is that, while X's best policy *depends* on what Y does (and vice versa), it is either the case that neither country *minds* what the other country chooses to do, or that their wishes happen to coincide. In such cases very weak forms of co-operation suffice; for instance, it is enough for X to decide what to do first, and then to inform Y. Co-ordination is not needed.

Where there is conflict, however, a very different situation arises, illustrated in Figure 7.1. On the axes are R and R^*, the instruments of X and Y respectively. Each country's welfare depends on the choices of both, giving rise to indifference maps for each. In the figure, C is the best possible outcome for X and I_1 and I_0 are two of X's indifference curves, with I_1 preferred to I_0. The starred equivalents are those of country Y. (Only if C and C^* coincide will there be no conflict.) The line passing through A and C, joining up the points at which tangents to the indifference curves of X are horizontal, is X's 'reaction curve'. This indicates X's best choice of R for any given choice of R^* by Y. Similarly, Y's reaction curve is the line passing through A and C^*, joining up the vertical tangency points of Y's indifference curves. The line joining C and C^*, tracing out the common tangency points of X and Y's indifference curves, is the 'contract curve' of Pareto Optimal policy combinations.

What will happen if X and Y decide on policy independently? A clear-cut answer is not possible without more assumptions, the first of which is that X and Y both have all the information contained in the figure. Then, if they move simultaneously, point A is a reasonable candidate as the equilibrium solution: no other point has the property that each country's policy is best given the policy choice of the other. If X has the first move, then the equilibrium is S, since now X can pick its preferred point on Y's reaction curve. Similarly, S^* is the equilibrium if Y goes first.[1] An incentive to co-ordinate arises in all three of these cases, since Pareto improvements on each of the uncoordinated equilibria are possible. For instance, from point A, where there is no incentive for either country to unilaterally alter policy, a co-ordinated move to a point between L and M on the contract curve would make sense for both countries.

To sum up, interdependence and conflict are likely to mean that co-ordination can potentially result in policies being followed that produce better outcomes for all parties.[2] Two important problems that bedevil co-ordination attempts in practice are, however, apparent from the figure. First, while the move on to the contract curve is mutually beneficial, the choice of a point on it involves a direct clash of interests. For instance, a move from A to M gives all the benefits of co-ordination to country X; movement towards L progressively redistributes the benefits towards country Y. Second, since the Pareto Optimal outcomes are on neither reaction curve, each party has an incentive to depart unilaterally from the co-ordinated outcome; in our example, X would be tempted to raise R (and Y to raise R^*) from any point on LM. Effective co-ordination must find ways both of securing agreement over the distribution of the gains and of enforcing the agreement reached.

To illustrate the no-conflict situation, where co-operation but not co-ordination is needed, imagine that X and Y both target GNP by means of fiscal policy and that GNP in each country depends on fiscal policy in both countries. So long as each country can achieve its target whatever policy is adopted abroad, there will be no difficulty in both countries achieving their targets. The same conclusion is reached when, although X and Y cannot reach all of their targets, X's targets are affected by X's and Y's policies *in the same way*. Adding inflation as a target and stipulating that each country has a fixed Phillips curve exemplifies this possibility; each country can neutralise the effects on its targets of a policy change abroad, so a minimal degree of co-operation is all that is needed. (For a detailed account, see Oudiz and Sachs 1984).

A slightly richer model produces both conflict and scope for co-ordination. Imagine that X and Y each target both GNP and inflation, using interest rates, under conditions of floating exchange rates and high international capital mobility. Suppose that the exchange rate depends only on the international interest differential, that output is determined by aggregate demand (absorption plus net exports), and that inflation depends on output and, independently, on the exchange rate: in other words, exchange depreciation has a direct inflationary effect through higher import prices as well as an indirect effect via raised net export demand.

Consider what happens if X and Y set their interest rates independently and simultaneously. At equilibrium, by definition, neither country wishes to cut its rate unilaterally. Such a cut would raise demand and output, but would give a double stimulus to inflation – directly because of demand and indirectly because of import prices. On its own the output increase would be desirable, but the overall inflation cost would (at the margin) just offset the gain. It follows at once that a co-ordinated cut would benefit both countries, since the import price component of the extra inflation would not arise. Uncoordinated behaviour here imparts a deflationary bias to the system as a result of 'competitive appreciation'. The previous analysis using Figure 7.1 fits this case exactly, with R and R^* standing for the two interest rates. Algebraic details are given in the Appendix.

It would be wrong to say that co-ordination makes sense only as a response to the kind of *static externality* discussed above. Even without this, one may be concerned about the dynamic properties of an uncoordinated international economy; the experience of floating rates has convinced many that such a system is intrinsically unstable. Therefore *systemic instability* must be added as a second, independent, ground on which a case for co-ordination can be established. Now, as it happens, economists were on the whole rather optimistic about the stability of freely floating rates before the post-Bretton-Woods period of floating-in-practice. The case was well put by Friedman (1953) who argued that, although speculators might push an exchange rate either towards or away from its long-run equilibrium value, successful speculators would be a force for stability, since they would buy when the currency was cheap and sell when it was expensive. Over time, unsuccessful speculators would be weeded out by natural selection.

Friedman's argument naturally requires some stability in the conduct of national monetary policies; without this, the notion of a long-run equilibrium path for nominal exchange rates loses meaning. Beyond this, the argument may be criticised from two directions. First, natural selection pressures may be strong or weak, depending on – *inter alia* – the degree to which speculators are knowledgeable, liquidity-constrained and risk-averse as well as the underlying entry and exit rates of speculators of different types. There are elements of a vicious circle present, since knowledge of the 'fundamentals' might be less valuable in highly erratic markets than in better-behaved ones. Thus, if an asset market became more erratic for some reason, the knowledgeable speculators on whom Friedman's argument depends might choose to exit.[3] Second, recent research has proved that even if all speculators are risk-neutral, unconstrained and well-informed, 'rational speculative bubbles' can occur. The essential idea is that, during a speculative boom, all holders of the asset may be fully aware that there is a small probability each period of a collapse of the price to its long-run equilibrium value; nevertheless, the extra return made if collapse does not occur just balances the downside risk, so there is no incentive to sell. This view of the world allows markets to be driven by irrelevant variables, since the low-probability event triggering collapse could be anything that each market participant believes that each other participant considers relevant.[4] The importance of rational bubbles is not merely that doubt is cast on the efficiency of freely floating rates, but that the declared intention of central banks to stabilise exchange rates can by itself stabilise them: it is possible to show that a rational bubble cannot begin to inflate if market participants are certain that the rate will not move outside defined limits.

Turning to arguments against co-ordination, five factors deserve mention. These are co-operation costs, enforcement costs, analytical disagreements over the effects of policy, credibility costs and the costs imposed by co-ordination that is only partial (bloc formation). Taking the first two together, it is evidently necessary to weigh the benefits of co-ordinating against the costs of reaching agreement as well as the costs of detecting and punishing defectors.[5] These factors are extremely important, not only in deciding whether co-ordination is appropriate, but also in choosing the form of co-ordination, as will become clear below.

Analytical disagreements over the effects of policies might not seem, in the abstract, to obstruct co-ordination, even if they raise severe problems for any external assessment of the benefits (Frankel and Rockett 1988). Nevertheless, the process of co-ordination is made far easier if the parties both comprehend each other's objectives (even if they are dissimilar) and achieve a measure of agreement about the links between instruments and objectives. If fiscal policy is to be co-ordinated, for example, the choice of how many fiscal variables to co-ordinate, and what they should be, is hard to make unless there is a similarity of view about the effects of fiscal policies on ultimate goal variables.

While it might seem that the credibility of national policies would tend to be enhanced by co-ordination, a counter-example has been given by Rogoff (1985). Suppose that wages are set on the basis of an assessment by workers (or unions) of how accommodating of inflation the central bank will be. If monetary policies are uncoordinated, then all are aware that more accommodation at the margin by one central bank will entail an unwished-for loss of competitiveness: the implication is that central banks will be – and will be expected to be – more accommodating when acting together than independently. In this case co-ordination leads to faster inflation.

Lastly, even if co-ordination does benefit those engaged in it, costs may be imposed upon those excluded. The implications of this from a global standpoint are unclear: the point could be used to support either a multi-level approach to co-ordination (co-ordination between blocs) or a complete disaggregation of policy-making.

Characteristics of systems of co-ordination

There are a number of dimensions of co-ordination which may usefully be distinguished. Taking for granted a given set of macroeconomic instruments and targets – and suppressing the distinction between ultimate and intermediate targets – systems of co-ordination differ according to the *extent* of co-ordination (the number of variables co-ordinated), as to whether co-ordination is *instrument-based* or *target-based*, and as to whether co-ordination is *discretionary* or *rule-based*. Rule-based co-ordination involves the establishment of a set of rules within which individual country policies are freely chosen, while under discretionary co-ordination, agreements are reached on a regular or irregular basis on a set of joint policies. Discretionary co-ordination may also be classified according to the degree to which it is institutionalised. Under *ad hoc discretionary co-ordination*, there is no mechanism to force joint policy-making: failure to agree means a reversion to uncoordinated action. To the extent that such mechanisms are indeed inbuilt, through some combination of an agreed set of principles which are to guide policy-making, voting rules and release of sovereignty to a supranational body such as the International Monetary Fund (IMF), we may refer to discretionary co-ordination as being *institutionalised*.

Some general points can be made concerning the design of co-ordination systems according to each of these dimensions. As far as the *extent* of co-ordination is concerned, it would clearly be desirable on co-ordination cost grounds to establish a separation between policies of internal and external significance, and to limit co-ordination to external policies. Since the most obvious connecting variable between a pair of countries is the exchange rate – and this variable is common in the sense that it is impossible for the two countries to choose different values for it – the case for co-ordination through the exchange rate, and nothing else, clearly warrants examination.

The determination of common variables involves what is known as an '$(N-1)$ problem': once $(N-1)$ bilateral exchange rates have been fixed, there are no more degrees of freedom, so it is logically impossible for each of the N participants to determine their exchange rate independently. The same applies to trade balances. Thus any attempt at co-ordination of exchange rates demands that the $(N-1)$ problem be addressed: in the event of a trade imbalance, who is to adjust policy? Exchange rate systems may be designed to be symmetric, so that reserve gainers and losers both adjust, or hegemonic, so that one country is relieved of the obligation to adjust. Recent history (discussed on pp. 125–7 and in Chapter 8) gives some grounds for believing that symmetric systems may tend to evolve into hegemonic ones.

While co-ordination limited to exchange rates, whether nominal or real, may perhaps dispose of the problem of systemic instability, aspects of the externality problem (in the international fiscal sense), far from being resolved, may actually be intensified. For instance, the more stable a structure of fixed rates is believed to be, the lower will be the tendency for budget imbalances to give rise to international interest differentials. This weakens the market constraint on fiscal indiscipline.

Regarding the choice between *instrument-based* and *target-based* co-ordination, there are general arguments running both ways. Instrument-based co-ordination has the great advantage of transparency, thus lowering the 'detection' component of enforcement costs. When agreed targets are missed, governments can blame events beyond their control. Against this is the consideration that economic shocks arising between co-ordination sessions may make it desirable – not merely in the interest of the country experiencing the shock – for instrument settings to be changed. Suppose, for example, that co-ordination has involved a 'locomotive' – a joint fiscal expansion to allow each country to grow without fear of trade balance deterioration. It would be in the general interest if countries were able to offset any domestic demand shocks that arose during the period of the agreement. Under instrument-based co-ordination further negotiation would be needed, while target-based co-ordination would allow an automatic policy revision.

Turning finally to the choice between *rule-based* and *discretionary* systems, we can identify three general advantages of rule-based systems. First, there is only one round of bargaining, when the rules to be followed are originally defined. Second, there is a clear line of demarcation between national discretion and international obligation, which is important for the conduct of national politics. Third, internationally agreed rules may help governments to achieve domestic credibility. Suppose that there is a hegemonic fixed exchange rate system, in which the anti-inflationary robustness of the leader's central bank is unquestioned (Germany within the EMS, perhaps). Then the difference between unilateral pegging to the pivot currency and formal entry into the system may be in the degree of perceived commitment to the fixed rate. Entry into the system may then reduce inflationary pressure, since wage-setters will be less inclined to count on central bank accommodation. Such hopes clearly underlay the entry of the UK into the exchange rate mechanism of the EMS in October 1990, and the immediate strengthening of sterling (within its band) despite a 1 per cent cut in the short rate of interest, was direct evidence of changed expectations about the future of the exchange rate.

With all the advantages of rules, it cannot be assumed that the optimum degree of flexibility is zero. Hence rule-based systems often embody a discretionary component in the form of a set of procedures for rule changes; the best example is the Bretton Woods system described below. The essential feature making such systems distinct from discretionary systems is that rule changes are not planned as regular events.

Institutionalised discretionary co-ordination will be favoured over rules when flexibility in year-to-year decision-taking is of paramount importance. European Community budgetary decisions are an obvious example. National fiscal policies offer a more interesting case, since the choice of system might depend on which externality was being addressed, and in turn on one's macroeconomic perspective. For instance, if the aim of fiscal co-ordination were international demand management, then discretionary co-ordination of fiscal stances, or impulses, would be indicated. If, however, control of international indebtedness were the issue, rules limiting budget deficits in the medium term might suffice.[6]

Ad hoc discretionary co-ordination will tend to arise in the form either of crisis management or the package deal. For the first of these, the quadrupling of oil prices in 1974 provides a good hypothetical example, since crisis management was certainly called for, but did not materialise. This shock was, in the event, followed by recession in the industrialised countries, due in large measure to unilateral (and self-defeating) attempts to limit trade deficits by, in effect, exporting them; the opportunity to internalise the externality through *ad hoc* discretionary co-ordination was missed. The second case, the package deal, occurs when there is a set of possible reforms which are Pareto-improving in the aggregate, but not individually. The 1978 Bonn summit discussed later is a good example of this type.

Post-1945 co-ordination among the industrialised countries

Bretton Woods: 1945–73

The international monetary system set up at the Bretton Woods conference of 1945 had its roots in the experience of the pre-war decade, during which countries had employed devaluation and trade restrictions in attempts to divert demand from foreign to domestic producers. Since this was impossible in aggregate, the main result was an inappropriate and disruptive reduction in trade flows. Thus the post-war economic order was to be based on the progressive dismantling of trade restrictions and the adoption of a system of fixed exchange rates.[7] The management of the exchange rate system was entrusted to a new international organisation, the International Monetary Fund. Currency values were fixed in terms of gold, and it was the responsibility of individual countries to pursue domestic policies calculated to sustain the fixed parities. Countries made deposits of their own currencies with the IMF, which was authorised to lend to countries experiencing short-term balance of payments difficulties. In the event of a country suffering what was termed a 'fundamental disequilibrium' in its balance of payments, it could devalue with IMF agreement, although this was expected to be – and was – a rare event. The Bretton Woods system, then, involved limited co-ordination in the form of the simplest of exchange rate rules, backed up by a supranational body with the authority to sanction departures from the rule.

Experience with the system highlighted a number of weaknesses. First, it was quite possible that countries would pursue inconsistent balance of payments goals – each aiming for a surplus, for instance. Second, domestic policies could not, in any case, be properly chosen without information about policies abroad – the pure co-operation issue mentioned earlier. Third, it was never clear what was to prevent a country from pursuing policies which would lead to a 'fundamental disequilibrium'. The logic of the system therefore placed considerable weight on both the good faith and the wisdom of the participating governments.

To address these problems, Working Party 3 (WP3) of the Economic Policy Committee of the OECD (Organisation for Economic Co-operation and Development) was set up in 1961. This was a group of senior policy-makers which was to meet approximately quarterly. While it would have been possible in principle to identify inconsistencies (and co-ordinate adjustments) in balance of payments goals, and to exchange information on policies, without discussions of an analytical character, the assessment of policies needed to prevent the emergence of external imbalances demanded an analytical framework. Thus a vital function of the meetings of WP3 was an analysis or 'confrontation' of national policies, with respect both to the governments' own forecasts and those produced by the OECD itself. To the extent that this process led to more accurate assessments of the effects of policies, it must have contributed to the survival of the Bretton Woods system through the 1960s, even if the co-operation involved is judged to have fallen short of formal co-ordination.[8]

Two factors combined to bring about the collapse of the system in 1973. First was the increasing international mobility of capital, which meant that a speculative attack could exhaust a country's foreign exchange reserves more quickly than before. The second was the asymmetrical role of the US dollar. This had developed because the dollar had from the outset been, together with gold, one of the two main forms in which countries other than the USA held foreign exchange reserves. With the post-war expansion of trade, the quantity of gold (its dollar price being fixed, of course) was inadequate to meet the non-US demand for reserves, but this demand could be – and was – met by the non-USA running a collective payments surplus. In US eyes this produced a very satisfactory resolution of the $(N-1)$ problem of payments balances; the USA obtained real resources from the rest of the world in exchange for dollars, and the US deficit could be viewed as reflecting the collective desire of the rest of the world to accumulate dollar reserves. (These were held mainly in the liquid, and hence low-interest-bearing, form of US Treasury Bills.) But the rest of the world resented the seigniorage accruing to the USA, and indeed the likelihood that an eventual devaluation of the dollar (a raising of the dollar price of gold) would impose capital losses, borne disproportionately by those countries which had protected the system by not attempting to convert their dollars into gold.[9] The (now unwanted) US trade deficit was, in turn, blamed on (budget) deficit spending associated with the Vietnam War, introducing a new theme to the international macroeconomic scene which was to recur again and again in the ensuing decades.[10]

In sum, the Bretton Woods system suffered from two structural weaknesses, the first of which was to some extent dealt with as the system evolved, the second of which proved ultimately fatal. The first was that fixing exchange rates did not remove the need to co-ordinate balance of payments aims or to co-operate more generally on macroeconomic policy. The second was that the use of the US dollar as the principal reserve currency gave a dangerous amount of latitude to US policy-makers; when dollar shortage was succeeded by dollar glut, the system proved lacking in an adequate mechanism by which the necessary closing of the US trade deficit could be brought about. (For an account of the collapse of the Bretton Woods system, see Williamson 1977.)

Floating rates, 1973–85

The dozen years after the advent of floating rates were in the main characterised by an intellectual retreat from co-ordination, along with an intensification of co-operation. The growing influence of monetarist ideas meant, at the domestic level, a movement in the direction of simple rules for the conduct of monetary and fiscal policies and greater reliance on market forces to correct disequilibria; the counterpart at the international level was a rejection of interference in foreign exchange markets, and in particular the abolition of foreign exchange controls. (The formation of the EMS in 1979 represented an exception to this trend.)

The adoption of full-scale monetarism by all governments would, by tying down both fiscal and monetary policy, have left no scope for macroeconomic co-ordination beyond the harmonisation of monetary growth rates. In the event, the anti-interventionist rhetoric of even the most committed governments often camouflaged quite different policies: in the UK, unforeseen exchange rate appreciation was clearly influencing the interest rate policy of the Thatcher government as early as the autumn of 1980, while, in the USA, the experiment with monetary targets lasted only from 1979 to 1982. Despite this, institutionalised co-ordination – the EMS aside – was not re-established until 1985. The delay can perhaps be partly explained by the explicitness of the policy U-turn required.

Increased co-operation in the period 1973–85 took the form of annual Economic Summits of the Group of Seven (G-7) countries from 1975 onwards, and the establishment of the G-5 forum in 1982. Finance ministers and the IMF's managing director participate in the G-7 meetings, and are joined by central bank governors in the G-5's. Meetings of the G-n groups are high-profile events, yet real consequences before 1985 are, the 1978 Bonn Summit excepted, hard to discern. In the early years communiqués were rarely issued, and, according to Horne and Masson (1987) the summits 'placed considerable emphasis on the importance of each country "putting its own house in order".' While it is impossible to say what would have happened in the absence of these meetings, the unusual instability of both real exchange rates and current account balances in the period hardly encourages a positive evaluation.

The Bonn Summit of 1978 was notable for the package deal on economic policy achieved by the United States, Japan, and the Federal Republic of Germany. The United States desired expansionary policies abroad for 'locomotive' reasons, while Japan and Germany – as major oil importers – were concerned at the effects of low domestic energy prices in the USA on world oil prices. It was therefore agreed that Germany and Japan would boost public expenditures (by 1 per cent and 1½ per cent respectively) and that consumer prices of energy would be raised by a specified amount in the United States. This episode of co-ordination was undoubtedly a success in its own terms, and – the perceived benefits aside – that success may be attributed to the fact that, unusually, the leaders were in a position to commit themselves personally to carrying the policies through, so that a failure to do so would have involved a clear (and therefore unlikely) breach of trust (Putnam and Henning 1986). This was due to three circumstances. First, co-ordination was instrument-based, making verification easy. Second, the timing of elections in the three countries meant that the leaders would be in office for the duration of the agreement. Third, in each case important domestic constituencies for the policies already existed. In the USA, for example, energy sector reform, long recognised to be necessary, had been impeded by the difficulty of putting together a political coalition that would simultaneously raise consumer prices and tax away the windfall gains to domestic producers that would otherwise accrue. Arguably, the summit agreement provided the impetus needed to overcome this problem, at the same time fulfilling an analogous function in internal debates over how expansionary fiscal policy should be in Germany and Japan.

Floating rates post-1985

The 'Plaza agreement' reached at the September 1985 meeting of the G-5 signalled an official return to the view that some co-ordinated management of exchange rates was desirable. The severe overvaluation of the US dollar which had developed not only was proving undesirable in itself, by virtue of the unsustainable pattern of trade flows which accompanied it, but also had led to increased pressure for protectionist measures in the United States which, if successful, would have threatened a repeat of the 1930s breakdown of the world trading system. The Plaza agreement both promised and delivered co-ordinated, partially unsterilised, intervention by the G-5 central banks, designed to produce an 'orderly depreciation' of the dollar.[11] In the event, the speed of depreciation was dramatic and out of proportion to the policy changes themselves, testifying to the dominant role of expectations in the determination of exchange rates, and the corresponding power of policy announcements to move the markets.

Perhaps partly because of this proof of the sensitivity of financial markets to policy 'news', a salient feature of co-operation since 1985 has been the deliberate element of secrecy involved; this makes it hard to be definite about the amount of co-ordination that has occurred. There has clearly been co-ordination of both relative and absolute interest rates. The spring of 1986 saw co-ordinated interest rate cuts, perhaps best interpreted as a response to a pattern of competitive appreciation, as described earlier in the chapter. The 1987 'Louvre Accord' explicitly involved the establishment of unpublished 'reference ranges' for nominal exchange rates, to be sustained by co-ordinated central bank foreign exchange market intervention and interest rate management.

As far as co-operation is concerned, there are close parallels between the current system and that which operated in the 1960s, with the important difference that nominal exchange rates are no longer treated as prior constraints. This apart, the most visible changes – arguably inessential ones – are that the main forum for co-operation is now the G-7 (rather than WP3) and that the IMF has taken over the supporting functions previously discharged by the OECD. (The institutional details are well described by Crockett 1989; see also Funabashi 1988.)

In sum, the current arrangements, the European Monetary System excepted, take for granted a rejection of rules and represent a weak form of institutionalised co-ordination which emphasises the search for analytical convergence, but stops short of any renunciation of sovereign control over macroeconomic policy. A formal echo of this is to be found in the evolution of the IMF charter. Article IV, which in the Bretton Woods era specified the exchange rate rules, was watered down in 1976 to a mere enjoinment that countries pursue 'stable' domestic policies and avoid exchange rate 'manipulation'. There is no prospect of Article IV being given new teeth.

Proposals for reform

Before looking at some contrasting views on the future of co-ordination, it is important to stress three areas of consensus. First, whatever may happen at the level of the European Community, it is generally assumed that the institutional structure of co-ordination at the world level will not change significantly. Countries will retain sovereignty over the levers of macroeconomic policy, and successful co-ordination will depend, essentially, on the achievement and regular renewal of unanimity among the parties. Second, none of the current proposals envisages any return to a hegemonic system. Third, it is assumed that co-ordination will be limited to a small group of rich countries. It may be noted in passing that from a historical point of view the validity of the first two of these assumptions can be questioned; if the costs of reaching agreements prove too great in relation to the strains placed upon the system, one must expect fresh attempts to simplify matters through a return to rules or hegemony.

Among current proposals, the most extensive scheme is the 'Blueprint' advocated for the G-7 countries by Williamson and Miller (1987). This scheme has three elements:

1 National intermediate targeting of (a) nominal absorption, at a level consistent both with 'acceptable' inflation and an 'agreed' current account balance over the medium term, and (b) the real effective exchange rate, within ± 10 per cent of an agreed estimate of the 'fundamental equilibrium exchange rate' (FEER).[12]
2 Instrument settings as follows: (a) *average* interest rates target world (ie G-7)

nominal demand, (b) *relative* interest rates target real exchange rates, and (c) national fiscal policies target national nominal absorption.

3   The world fiscal/monetary mix in the medium term is aimed at 'maintaining the real interest rate in its historically normal range and avoiding an increasing or excessive ratio of public debt to GNP'.

(Williamson and Miller 1987: 2)

A rather brief discussion of the economic logic of the Blueprint will have to suffice here. The starting-point is the set of national economic objectives, taken to be summarisable in terms of economic growth, employment, inflation and the current account within the balance of payments. Given these, there is an immediate pure co-operation issue: national current account objectives must be reconciled. Once this is done, if there were analytical unanimity, it would be possible to derive an equilibrium set of real exchange rates; in practice there will be inconsistencies that have to be resolved.

Suppose, then, that a consistent set of current account objectives and FEERs have been arrived at, and that it has been agreed on stability grounds that exchange rates are to be managed in a co-ordinated way using relative interest rates. The next question is whether the grid of exchange rate targets is to be expressed in real or nominal terms. In choosing real exchange rate targeting, Williamson and Miller (1987) emphasise the strains that would be placed on a system of nominal exchange rate targeting by national inflation shocks; if the FEERs were constant, then such shocks would cause predictable realignments of the nominal grid, and hence destabilising speculation in the interval before the grid was respecified. Another good reason for real exchange rate targeting is that it locates inflation control primarily at the national rather than the global level.

It might be thought that there would be little reason to go beyond co-ordination of current account objectives and the system of exchange rate management just described, along with a procedure to set the average level of world interest rates as in 2(a) above. However, since Williamson and Miller favour a considerable degree of short-term tolerance of departures from current account targets on feasibility grounds, and in view of the wide margins envisaged for real exchange rates, there is the risk that a country would cheat, if not further constrained, by combining loose fiscal and tight monetary policies. The short-term political attractiveness of this combination is that it allows high absorption without inflation, since real appreciation is used to divert the extra spending to foreign goods – witness the US 'twin deficits' of the early 1980s. Hence, the Blueprint adds a second co-ordinated intermediate target to the real exchange rate in the form of an absorption target, to be managed through fiscal policy. The point about absorption is that it is a demand side variable and, as such, inherently more controllable in the short run than the current account, which is the difference between aggregate supply and demand. A system of current account targets generally acknowledged as hard to hit with any accuracy would encourage cheating: countries would be tempted to adopt unrealistically high output forecasts in order to justify high absorption (especially in election years); the resulting failures to achieve current account targets would be blamed on supply shocks. Explicit absorption targeting would close off this loophole. The Blueprint advocates that absorption targets should be in nominal rather than real terms. The idea is to set up a domestic real absorption/

inflation trade-off; and to exert systemic downward pressure on inflation. Countries that achieve lower inflation than expected would be permitted to absorb more.

In some respects Williamson and Miller's Blueprint resembles what is known (or guessed) about current practice, but it seeks to go further. Once it is accepted on stability grounds that exchange rates are to be managed, there have to be guidelines for the specification of reference ranges as well as for the setting of absolute and relative interest rates. It may make little difference whether reference ranges are specified in real or nominal terms, so long as inflation forecasts over the relevant horizon are not too inaccurate. Since the existing criteria for the setting of reference ranges – and their widths – are not public, it is not possible to compare them with Williamson and Miller's criteria, but it may be that the differences are not of great significance.

More controversial is the proposed assignation of fiscal policy to absorption targets derived from co-ordinated medium-term balance-of-payments targets. The fundamental difficulty is the lack of a consensus that a 'normal' structure for payments balances can be specified.[13] The opposing view would stress the desirability of, for instance, exploiting new investment opportunities in a country through overseas borrowing, rather than by a squeeze on domestic consumption. While that example – by distinguishing borrowing for investment from borrowing for consumption – might suggest planning the path of national wealth creation rather than the trend in net overseas indebtedness, it is also the case that nations quite reasonably save or dissave in aggregate – for demographic reasons, for instance.[14] The real issue is not so much whether the determinants of the equilibrium current balance are subject to change, as whether accurate forecasting of them for planning purposes is possible. The vital disagreement is between the interventionist view that an unplanned structure of net international lending flows will lead to episodes of unsustainable behaviour followed by crises, and the liberal view that places greater faith in market disciplines over such behaviour, while doubting the possibility of rational planning of net lending flows.

There is an intermediate position on the issue which would admit the risk of 'government failure' while insisting on the rationality of private sector behaviour. This would imply replacing medium-term current account targets with medium-term budget deficit targets. The historical evidence gives some support to this idea, since the unsustainable paths followed by the USA, both before the collapse of the Bretton Woods system and again in the early 1980s, were primarily associated with fiscal policy. The trouble is that without medium-term current account targets, FEERs would become impossible to calculate precisely, and the rest of the Blueprint might accordingly have to be discarded.

This view is, however, unduly extreme. It would seem quite possible to retain interest rate co-ordination along the lines envisaged in the Blueprint with reference to necessarily approximate FEERs, while leaving national fiscal policies to be co-ordinated only in the sense that countries would accept the need for fiscal discipline and would accept scrutiny of their policies from this standpoint. As Polak (1989) argues, provided that there had been agreement on what constituted fiscal indiscipline, such scrutiny would not require cumbersome multilateral co-ordination and could therefore be most efficiently handled in the context of bilateral IMF surveillance.

Both the Blueprint and modified versions thereof are founded on the view that interest rates must be co-ordinated to ensure first, that substantial real misalignments are avoided, and second, that an appropriate absolute level of world interest rates is achieved. As we have seen, there are disagreements over whether co-ordination should be extended beyond this and, if so, the precise form that such extensions should take. Alternative proposals start from a more optimistic view of the inherent stability of floating exchange rates given the important proviso that countries follow appropriate domestic policies.

Early floating rate proposals (McKinnon 1984) involved co-ordinated monetary targeting. The case for monetary targets is, of course, essentially based on the proposition that the relationship between the money stock and current or future nominal income are predictable, and the failure of this condition to hold in practice led to an inevitable retreat from such targeting. More recent schemes involve co-ordinated targeting of nominal income or nominal absorption (Frankel 1989). Of these, nominal absorption is clearly preferable for reasons already discussed. Underlying the target would be projected values for real absorption and inflation, thus, first, implicitly projecting real current account balances, and second, setting up a domestic inflation/ spending trade-off for incentive purposes. Like the other possibilities we have discussed, co-ordinated absorption targeting achieves the important objective of freeing governments from the temptation to manipulate absorption via the exchange rate. Governments would be free to manage the composition of absorption, but this is not a matter that calls for co-ordination.[15]

To summarise, rival proposals for future co-ordination differ according to both the extent of co-ordination advocated, and the choice of variables. There is consensus that the system needs to inhibit governments from manipulating the current account, but dispute about whether this is best done by co-ordinating absorption or fiscal deficits. There are two opinions about the inherent stability of exchange rates, with associated views about the desirability of managing them, but in the absence of relevant experience (floating rates combined with stable policies) this dispute is hard to resolve.

Appendix

The deflationary bias example described in the text arises from the following model.

Let Y denote output, Z the rate of inflation, R the interest rate, and a, b, c and d positive constants. A '*' denotes the foreign country. Equation (1) below shows domestic output determined by the interest rate differential (via the exchange rate and thereby net exports) and the interest rate on its own (via absorption).[16] Equation (2) shows inflation dependent on output and additionally on the exchange rate, thus on the interest differential. From equations (1) and (2), three output/inflation trade-offs can be derived. We may hold R fixed and vary R^*, we may do the converse, or we may vary R and R^* together, to show the effect of co-ordinated policy. The slopes of these trade-offs are given in equations (3), (4) and (5).

(1) $Y = -a(R - R^*) - b.R = -(a + b)R + a.R^*$

(2) $Z = c.Y - d(R - R^*) = -\{c(a + b) + d\}R + (c.a + d)R^*$

(3) With R fixed, $\delta Z/\delta Y = (c.a + d)/a = c + d/a$

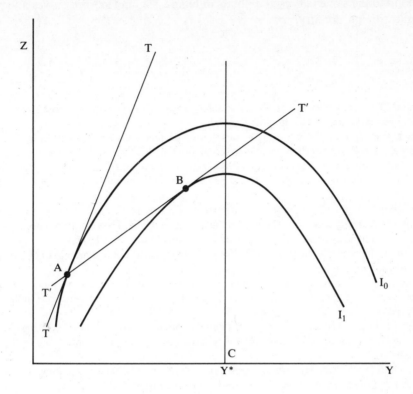

Figure 7.2

(4)   With R^* fixed, $\delta Z/\delta Y = \{c(a + b) + d\}/(a + b) = c + d/(a + b)$

(5)   With $(R - R^*)$ fixed, $\delta Z/\delta Y = c$

Notice that these slopes are in decreasing order of magnitude. For a given output increase, δY, the largest increase in the inflation rate comes if it is the foreign interest rate that is changed (raised): this is because all of the output effect is having to come from exchange depreciation. Less bad is a domestic interest rate cut since the direct increase in absorption means that less depreciation is needed. Best is the co-ordinated cut, since there is no depreciation entailed.

Figure 7.2 illustrates this. I_0 and I_1 are domestic indifference curves; C is the bliss point, with zero inflation and output at its ideal level Y^*. The government acting on its own faces the trade-off TT, whose slope is given in equation (4). It therefore chooses point A. If we suppose that the two countries are identical in terms of indifference maps, then the foreign country is also at point A. A co-ordinated interest rate cut will take both along the trade-off $T'T'$, whose slope is given in equation (5), to the symmetrical Pareto-Optimum at B. Both inflation and output are higher in each country.

This analysis may be taken a little further by employing a diagram with the two interest rates on the respective axes. The result is Figure 7.1 in which I_0, I_1, A, B, and

C correspond to the same curves and points in Figure 7.2, and starred curves and points refer to the foreign country.

Notes

1   A, S, and S^* are, respectively, the Cournot and two Stackelberg solutions, most often encountered in the context of duopoly theory.
2   Likely, but not certain. In 'zero-sum' games there is perfect antagonism: any change that benefits X hurts Y, so that there can be no scope for co-ordination. In a diagram like Figure 7.1 the indifference curves of such a game would be the *same* for the two participants, but ranked in the opposite order. Zero-sum games are common in textbooks, but rare in the real world.
3   While expert opinion was unanimous, and correct, concerning the real overvaluation of the US dollar in the early 1980s, profiting from this judgement would have required both a strong nerve and a deep pocket in the period before the dollar started to fall.
4   The germ of this idea is to be found in Keynes's famous beauty contest metaphor (Keynes 1936: ch. 12, V).
5   The formidable difficulties involved in numerically estimating the costs and benefits of co-ordination are not addressed here. For an attempt at estimating the benefits, see Oudiz and Sachs (1984).
6   Budget deficits are, of course, an imperfect guide to public sector solvency: see Begg (1987).
7   The trade liberalisation component will not be discussed here; for an account, see Little (1982: ch. 4).
8   See Crockett (1989), who stresses the important role of the OECD in establishing a common statistical and analytical framework within which co-operation could flourish.
9   By the time that the USA suspended gold convertibility in 1971, foreign dollar holdings were several times greater in value than US gold stocks.
10   The mechanism may have been as follows: government-driven excess demand in the USA led to a rise in US prices relative to those abroad; as a result, the excess demand was diverted towards foreign goods, so that a trade deficit resulted.
11   Intervention is said to be unsterilised if no attempt is made to offset the automatic effect on the domestic money supply that intervention entails. An example of this would be the sale of dollars for deutschmarks by the Bundesbank *without* a simultaneous purchase of deutschmark-denominated public debt to return the deutschmarks to circulation. While unsterilised intervention will certainly affect exchange rates, sterilised intervention may not do so.
12   The *real effective exchange rate* for any given country is an index of the price of that country's output relative to that of its trading partners. Obtaining this involves first calculating the effective nominal rate, by taking an average of bilateral nominal rates, and then adjusting this to take account of price levels at home and abroad. A set of *fundamental equilibrium exchange rates* (FEERs) for a system of countries is the set of real effective exchange rates which allows each country simultaneously to achieve internal and external balance.
13   Another difficulty is that countries have tended to favour nominal income targets over absorption targets because of the clear unit-elastic trade-off between output and prices that wage-setters are thereby faced with. However, absorption targets would establish a similar trade-off, and one that is not obviously less appropriate, even if it is less simple to specify.
14   For example, high national savings levels in Japan in recent times may partly reflect the large proportion of the population that is of working age: when this 'hump' in the population reaches retirement, we can expect the national savings rate to fall.

15 Note that this proposal *would* allow governments to manipulate aggregate demand via the current account, but only for constant absorption. Arguably, it is appropriate for governments to retain freedom of this kind in order that they should be able to respond to supply shocks.

16 Note that this formulation excludes the direct spillover from foreign output to domestic demand, which arises from the fact that a part of any rise in income abroad will be spent on imported goods; the substance of the argument is not affected by this simplification.

References

Begg D (1987) Fiscal policy. In Dornbusch R, Layard R (eds) *The Performance of the British Economy*. Oxford University Press

Crockett A D (1989) The role of international institutions in surveillance and policy coordination. In Bryant R C, Frankel J A, Goldstein M (eds) *Macroeconomic Policies in an Interdependent World*. Brookings/CEPR/IMF

Dornbusch R (1980) *Open economy macroeconomics*. McGraw-Hill

Frankel J A (1989) An analysis of the proposal for international nominal targeting (INT). In Branson W, Currie D A, Frankel J A, Masson P R, Portes R (eds) *International Policy Coordination and Exchange Rate Fluctuations*. Chicago

Frankel J A, Rockett K E (1988) International macroeconomic policy coordination when policymakers do not agree on the true model. *American Economic Review* **78**

Friedman M (1953) The case for flexible exchange rates. In his *Essays in Positive Economics*. Chicago

Funabashi Y (1988) *Managing the Dollar: from the Plaza to the Louvre*. Institute for International Economics, Washington DC

Horne J P, Masson P R (1987) International economic cooperation and policy coordination. *Finance and Development* **24**(2)

Keynes J M (1936) *The General Theory of Employment Interest and Money*. Macmillan

Little I M D (1982) *Economic Development: Theory, Policy and International Relations*. Basic Books

McKinnon R (1984) An international standard for monetary stabilisation. *Policy Analyses in International Economics* **8**, Institute for International Economics, Washington DC

Oudiz G, Sachs J (1984) Macroeconomic policy coordination among the industrial economies. *Brookings Papers on Economic Activity*. Brookings Institute, Washington DC

Polak J J (1989) Comment. In Bryant R C et al (eds) *Macroeconomic Policies in an Interdependent World*. Brookings/CEPR/IMF

Putnam R D, Henning C R (1986) The Bonn Summit of 1978: how does international economic policy coordination really work? *Brookings Discussion Papers in International Economics* **86**, reprinted in Cooper R N *Can Nations Agree? Issues in International Economic Cooperation*. Brookings Institute, Washington DC

Rogoff K (1985) Can international monetary policy coordination be counterproductive? *Journal of International Economics* **18**: 199–217

Wallich H C (1984) Institutional cooperation in the world economy. In Frankel J A, Mussa M (eds) *The World Economic System: Performance and Prospects*. Dover

Williamson J (1977) *The Failure of World Monetary Reform 1971–74*. Nelson

Williamson J, Miller M H (1987) Targets and indicators: a blueprint for the international coordination of economic policy. *Policy Analyses in International Economics* **22**, Institute for International Economics, Washington DC

CHAPTER 8

European monetary integration

MICHAEL SUMNER

Introduction

In 1978 the EC members agreed to establish the European Monetary System (EMS) and, with the exception of the UK, announced exchange rate parities. Against the background of violently fluctuating exchange rates during the previous five years and the failure of earlier attempts to establish a common currency or even to limit intra-European exchange rate changes, this enterprise aroused considerable scepticism; and the survival of the EMS has caused an equal measure of surprise, sometimes likened to the aeronautical engineer's inability to understand the flight of the bumble-bee. The survival of an organisation, however, is of little interest unless it contributes to the welfare of its members. It is the question of what the EMS has *achieved* that is the central concern of this chapter. As background, the history of earlier co-operative efforts and the institutional features of the EMS are sketched. This leads on to an examination of the effects of the EMS on exchange rates and macroeconomic stability. A comprehensive review of the enormous literature on these issues is well beyond the scope of this chapter. References are selective, and are mainly confined to the most recent contributions. Readers with a larger appetite for further reading will find a full bibliography in the survey by Haldane (1991).

The EMS is neither the beginning nor the end of the story. The EC members are currently negotiating structures which will form the basis for Economic and Monetary Union, a process that will culminate in the adoption of a single currency at some unspecified future date. The final section of the chapter records progress to date on EMU, and discusses the principal economic issues involved. As the story is unfinished, so also is the chapter. Readers are left to write their own conclusion in the light of future developments.

An outline history

Academic discussion of European monetary integration (eg Meade 1957) predates the Treaty of Rome, but for over a decade discussion remained largely academic. As long as the European currencies were pegged to the dollar, the Treaty's recommendation that exchange rate changes should be regarded as matters of common interest was of no practical importance. It remained a dead letter in 1961, when the German mark was revalued, and in 1969, when the mark was revalued again and the French franc devalued. These later changes, symptoms of the general disintegration of the Bretton Woods system, raised the status of intra-EC exchange rates to that of a serious political and economic issue, primarily because currency realignments threatened to dislocate the operation of the Common Agricultural Policy (Giavazzi and Giovannini 1989: 14–15).

The response was the formal adoption of economic and monetary union as a long-term objective at the Hague Summit in December 1969. The Werner Committee was appointed to work out a plan, which it presented in October 1970. The target to be achieved in stages by 1980 was irrevocably fixed exchange rates, which might then be replaced by a common currency – for largely 'psychological and political' reasons. The route to this end required increasingly close policy co-ordination, successively narrower exchange rate bands, liberalisation of capital movements, and institutional innovation, including the establishment of a European Exchange Stabilisation Fund. The report identified the implications of monetary union, including centralised control of monetary policies, but it provided less guidance on the precise sequence of measures to be taken. Serious divergences soon became apparent between German insistence on policy co-ordination as a necessary precondition for narrowing exchange rate bands, and French emphasis on narrower bands, supported by generous borrowing facilities, as a means of inducing policy co-ordination. These contrasting views, dubbed 'economist' and (contrary to conventional usage) 'monetarist' respectively, on how to pursue the agreed objective, have reappeared in all subsequent debates. On this occasion the French view prevailed. The members resolved in February 1971 to narrow exchange rate margins from June; but their inability to agree on a uniform response to the disruption of foreign exchange markets caused by a dramatic weakening of the dollar in May 1971 made implementation impossible.

A second attempt was made in the spring of 1972, after the Smithsonian Agreement had raised hopes of a more durable international monetary system in the form of a package which included wider margins of fluctuation around the dollar. The European plan was to maintain a 'Snake' of narrower intra-European margins within the Smithsonian 'tunnel'. As prospective EC members, the UK and Ireland joined the Snake, but were forced by a sterling crisis to leave within a matter of weeks. Italy and France suffered the same humiliation at later dates, leaving Germany and Benelux as the only stable members of the Snake.

These failed attempts to secure closer monetary integration formed the inauspicious background to the impassioned plea by the President of the EC Commission (Jenkins 1978) for a reassessment of the case for European monetary union and of the means by which it might be achieved. The outcome of the ensuing political process, in which the French president and German chancellor played the initiating roles, was the European Monetary System, established in December 1978 as 'a zone of monetary stability in Europe'.

EMS institutions and practice

The primary institutional component of the EMS is the Exchange Rate Mechanism (ERM). Most participants limit bilateral exchange rate fluctuations to within 2.25 per cent margins around the agreed central parities. Italy moved to these narrow bands from its initial 6 per cent margins in January 1990. Spain and the UK joined the ERM with the wider 6 per cent margins in June 1989 and October 1990 respectively. The central parities are stated in the form of a grid of bilateral rates, or equivalently as a central rate against the ECU, the basket of EMS member currencies with weights based on shares of EC trade and GDP.

When any pair of member currencies reach the limits of their band, the two central banks must intervene to whatever extent is necessary to hold the rates. The central bank of the weaker currency is entitled to draw upon the very short-term financing facility (VSTF) to obtain unlimited quantities of intervention currencies as needed. Since November 1987 the VSTF has also been available to finance intra-marginal intervention (ie where rates remain within the bands), but subject to the consent of the other central bank concerned.

At the intervention point both the central banks concerned supply the stronger currency in exchange for the weaker one, but the process is not symmetrical. The central bank of the weaker currency loses reserves or accumulates external debts which must be repaid; its counterpart accumulates reserves which within much broader limits can be sterilised. This alleged deflationary bias was one of the British government's main objections to the EMS proposals (HMSO 1978, Cmnd 7405). In an effort to meet it, a divergence indicator was established within the EMS with the aim of identifying the currency responsible for straining the system, and of creating a presumption as to which country should bear responsibility for (in the typical case reflationary) corrective action. This divergence indicator is expressed in terms of the ECU, as a basis for comparing each currency's performance with the EMS average.[1] There is a presumption that action will be taken when the indicator reaches its 'threshold', but corrective measures are not mandatory. Moreover, the indicator is subject to several technical limitations, including an asymmetry which makes it less likely that a currency will reach its threshold the larger its weight in the ECU basket. In practice, furthermore, the intervention points are often reached before the divergence threshold, in cases where, of two individual currencies, one appreciates while the other depreciates relative to the others (Vaubel 1980).

The operational ineffectuality of the divergence indicator is not the only evidence of asymmetry in the operation of the ERM. The conduct of foreign exchange market intervention, described by Mastropasqua et al (1988) and Bini-Smaghi and Micossi

(1990) reveals an important difference between Germany and the other participants. Intervention to support intra-ERM rates is predominantly intra-marginal, and hence not obligatory. In practice, out of all the members of the EMS, it is Germany that plays the most negligible role in these operations, with any changes in its reserves being fully sterilised. This description suggests that the '$n-1$' other members target intra-EMS exchange rates while Germany provides the nominal anchor.

Further evidence consistent with German leadership is provided by Giavazzi and Giovannini (1989), among others, who observe that the differential between French and Italian offshore (Euro-currency) and domestic interest rates widens in anticipation of a realignment, whereas German interest rates show little sign of disturbance. During the period in question (up to 1987) domestic interest rates in many member states were insulated by capital controls, now largely dismantled. This may have been the reason why the strongest forms of the German leadership hypothesis do not attract empirical support. For example Fratianni and Von Hagen (1990) propose the following four requirements for German dominance: (a) monetary policy in Germany should be independent of the policies of other members, whereas (b) the latter should depend on German policy but (c) not that of other members or (d) of the countries of the outside world. The only hypothesis which survives their tests is German independence; the sensitivity of their negative results to modifications of some questionable features of their specification would be worth examining.

German independence is, nevertheless, an important result. It answers the fears voiced by an early German critic of the EMS, that substitution of 'collective government discretion over parity changes . . . for automatic monetary rules' implies that 'currency competition is to be suppressed and currency excellence to be punished' (Vaubel 1980: 208). It confirms the asymmetrical operation of the EMS suggested by the pattern of intervention, despite the appearance of symmetry. Germany may not have dominated, but it has led. Other members are faced with a choice between following, though not necessarily within the one-year time horizon assumed by Fratianni and Von Hagen, or relying on capital controls and exchange rate realignments to preserve partial independence. The first of these protective devices has diminished in importance, in a large part as a result of the Capital Liberalisation Directive of 1988. The use of realignments is examined in the next section.

Exchange rates in the EMS

The EMS, or more strictly the ERM, was intended not as a system of rigidly fixed exchange rates, but as a means of implementing the Rome Treaty's aspiration to make exchange rate changes a matter of common concern, with the intention of reducing their disruptive effects by reducing their magnitude and frequency (EC Commission 1979: 79). The reaction of many early analysts (eg Fratianni 1980) was to dismiss it as an adjustable peg system which lacked any objective criterion for adjusting the peg.

The early history of the EMS appeared to confirm this assessment. As Table 8.1

Table 8.1 EMS realignments (percentage changes in central rate)

	Year (month) of realignment											
	1979 (9)	1979 (11)	1981 (3)	1981 (10)	1982 (2)	1982 (6)	1983 (3)	1985 (7)	1986 (4)	1986 (8)	1987 (1)	1990 (1)
Belgian franc	0	0	0	0	8.5	0	1.5	2.0	1.0	0	2.0	0
Danish kroner	−2.9	−4.8	0	0	−3.0	0	2.5	2.0	1.0	0	0	0
German mark	2.0	0	0	5.5	0	4.25	5.5	2.0	3.0	0	3.0	0
French franc	0	0	0	−3.0	0	−5.75	−2.5	2.0	−3.0	0	0	0
Irish punt	0	0	0	0	0	0	−3.5	2.0	0	−3.0	0	0
Italian lira	0	0	−6.0	−3.0	0	−2.75	−2.5	−6.0	0	0	0	−3.7
Dutch guilder	0	0	0	5.5	0	4.25	3.5	2.0	3.0	0	3.0	0

shows, the peg was adjusted no fewer than six times in the first four years; but thereafter the frequency of realignments diminished. Five out of the twelve changes to date have involved the exchange rate of a single currency, though the lira adjustment in 1985 was effected by changing *all* central rates, so that each currency, including the lira, moved 'non-provocatively' within its existing margins. The most striking features of the table are the cumulative appreciation of the mark, usually accompanied by the Dutch guilder, and the trend depreciation of the lira and the French franc.

The success of the EMS in achieving its declared objective has been appraised in a multitude of studies which compare the variability of exchange rates before and after 1979 for the ERM members and a control sample of other countries, typically using the variance or standard deviation of changes in the logarithm of exchange rates as a measure of volatility. Artis and Taylor (1988) question the standard methodology on the grounds that this variable does not appear to be normally distributed, as the standard test implicitly assumes; but their own results, derived on various alternative distributional assumptions, are very similar to the standard findings. On their sample of monthly data from 1973 to 1986, each ERM participant experienced a significant reduction in the volatility of its nominal and real effective (or weighted-average) exchange rate *vis-à-vis* other members; the results for sterling (outside the ERM) and the dollar varied with the distributional assumption, but tended to show increases in volatility, in some cases significant, for both nominal and real effective exchange rates *vis-à-vis* ERM members. Repeating the tests on multilateral effective exchange rates (*vis-à-vis* all other countries) made little difference to the results for sterling and the dollar, but weakened those for the ERM members. There were significant reductions in nominal exchange rate volatility only for the lira and the mark, and for only some of the distributional assumptions employed. The volatility of real rates declined for all members, but the results were strikingly less significant than for their effective ERM rates. Since intra-EC trade dominates external trade for all ERM participants, their multilateral exchange rates assign high weights to other members. The contrast between the results therefore suggests that the stabilising effect of the ERM on intra-System exchange rates has been at least partially offset by more volatile exchange rates with the rest of the world. This outcome is entirely consistent with the founding fathers' ambition to create a zone of monetary stability.

An interesting implication is suggested by Giavazzi and Giovannini (1989), who point out that the correlation coefficient between Germany's multilateral and intra-ERM-area exchange rates fell from 0.9 in the pre-1979 period, when the mark experienced a sustained nominal and real appreciation, to -0.1 in the post-1979 era. They conclude (1989: 58) that 'the EMS might have limited the effect of fluctuations in the dollar/DM rate on Germany's competitiveness'. This effect was anticipated by the German Finance Ministry when the ERM was first under discussion (Healey 1989).

The volatility of exchange rates is significant only indirectly, as a proxy for uncertainty. The effects of the EMS on exchange rate uncertainty have been explored more directly in a number of studies of conditional variability, which examine the variance of the prediction errors from exchange-rate forecasting equations. The findings of these studies, which are based on a variety of prediction schemes, generally reinforce the results for unconditional (or total) variability summarised above. A recent example is the work of Fratianni and Von Hagen (1990), who emphasise that their results set an upper bound on intra-EMS exchange rate uncertainty because they treat realignments as totally unpredictable, despite evidence to the contrary from forward rates and interest differentials. Even on this conservative assumption they report reductions in the uncertainty of intra-EMS rates, both nominal (but only from 1983) and real. In contrast, more uncertainty attaches to extra-EMS rates in the post-1979 period; this increase is larger for the other participants than for Germany.

Forward exchange markets make it possible to hedge risks, though only at a cost. A reduction in uncertainty therefore creates the potential for resource savings in international transactions. The dominance of intra-trade within the total trade of EMS members suggests net benefits from the reduced uncertainty of intra-ERM exchange rates. The interpretation of the increased volatility of extra-ERM rates is less clear, since there are a number of possible sources of shocks. Random disturbances in aggregate demand in the outside world which shift the Hicksian IS curves of all members through their trade effects will have a smaller impact on European prices and output if extra-ERM exchange rates are allowed to act as a shock absorber than if these rates are stabilised. On the other hand, an outside shock which impinges directly on only one member, caused say by a speculative shift from dollars to marks, will have smaller real effects in Germany under the ERM because part of the impact will be absorbed by other members. Fratianni and Von Hagen's results suggest that at least some of the increased volatility of outside rates stems from this second source.

An increased commitment to exchange rate targets weakens a government's ability to influence domestic monetary conditions. This raises the question whether the well-documented reduction in exchange rate volatility has been purchased at the expense of greater interest rate volatility. In point of fact most empirical studies report no significant increase in interest rate variability among ERM paricipants (eg Artis and Taylor 1988). This result is perhaps less surprising than it might appear. Studies of monetary reaction functions confirm the casual impression that monetary authorities adjust interest rates in response to changes in the exchange rate, reserves and overseas interest rates, even in economies which are not pursuing explicit exchange rate targets.

Attempts to identify the real effects of short-term exchange rate volatility have not produced clear evidence that it damages trade. There can be little doubt, however, about the deleterious effects of longer-term departures of the real exchange rate from its equilibrium level. Such misalignments not only distort trade flows, but also cause

Table 8.2   Real exchange rate changes

Period	France	Italy
1979–83	−1.5	17.4
1985–7	7.5	13.7
1987(1)–90(3)	3.0	10.0

Note: Cumulative percentage change in central rate minus change in consumer prices relative to Germany

Sources:
Rows 1 and 2 adapted from EC Commission (1990: 310), row 3 from OECD *Main Economic Indicators*

changes in the location of production, through new investment and scrapping decisions, which are costly to reverse even when the real exchange rate returns to its former level. Hence a sustained departure from the equilibrium level may change the equilibrium itself, as well as generating demands for protection when markets at home and abroad are threatened.

Some instances of misalignment are strikingly clear-cut. It would be difficult, for example, to argue that the almost 50 per cent rise in the US multilateral real exchange rate (measured by relative export price) between 1980 and 1985 reflected a change in the equilibrium rate. It is generally agreed that only a part of sterling's dramatic real appreciation (however measured) to its peak in 1981 can be attributed to the influence of North Sea oil; and that an equal or larger part represented a misalignment caused by monetary contraction. There are no comparable episodes in the experience of the ERM participants; indeed, one of the arguments advanced by early advocates of British entry was that a nominal exchange-rate peg would have prevented the sterling overshoot. But the absence of gross misalignments does not imply the absence of any. Some disturbing evidence is reported by Artis and Nachane (1990), who examine the relationship between mark exchange rates and the ratio of domestic to German prices, for the original EC members and for the UK as a control. Over the EMS period up to late 1986 they find no evidence of co-integration between these series for any country, which means that exchange rates and relative prices (both consumer and producer indices) tended to drift apart. They conclude that any purchasing power parity hypothesis is 'comprehensively rejected'. If there is no tendency for changes in real exchange rates to be reversed, then either misalignments cannot be ruled out, if the equilibrium real rate is constant; or, if it is not, the desirability of monetary union among EMS members is cast into doubt (Vaubel 1988).[2]

The behaviour of real exchange rates among the three largest members of the original ERM (which accounted for practically 85 per cent of the real GDP of the area) is illustrated in Table 8.2. In the early years of the EMS, accordingly, devaluations of the franc more than compensated for relative inflation *vis-à-vis* Germany, so that French competitiveness improved marginally; but thereafter the franc experienced a real appreciation. The same applied to all the smaller members except Ireland: realignments more than offset the inflation differential in 1979–83, but less than half of it in 1985–7. Since the last general realignment in January 1987 the inflation differential between France and Germany has continued the decline which began in 1984, approximating zero in the recent past.

The Italian experience is rather different. The lira entered the EMS at a deliberately undervalued exchange rate, which provided scope for at least some of the real appreciation recorded in 1979–83; but although the inflation differential began falling earlier than in France, the decline in competitiveness has continued at a faster rate. The inflation differential has been reduced to a little over 2 per cent per year in the period since the last lira realignment, which was made to accommodate the adoption of narrower bands; but the cumulative real appreciation amounts to about 40 per cent since the creation of the EMS. Defining real exchange rates in terms of alternative measures of relative prices would, of course, change the story in detail, but not in substance (Giovannini 1990).

While there have never been any explicit rules governing realignments, Giovannini's account suggests a significant change in practice around 1983; according to Padoa-Schioppa (1985) this was also the dividing line between unilateral and genuinely collective decisions about the magnitude of adjustments. After that date the peg was no longer adjusted so as fully to restore the competitiveness of countries which had indulged in relative inflation; why then would such countries choose to remain members of the EMS? The most common answer is that continued participation raised the prospect of indulging in less inflation in the future. The macroeconomic arguments which underly this hypothesis and the evidence bearing on it are considered in the next section.

Macroeconomic effects

The EMS was formed after several years of exceptional divergence between the inflation rates of its members, ranging in 1978 from 2.7 per cent in Germany to 12.1 per cent in Italy. If the zone of monetary stability was to survive, inflation rates would clearly have to converge. In fact they diverged further in the aftermath of the Second Oil Shock, and it was only after 1983 that their (weighted) standard deviation fell below its initial level (Fratianni and Von Hagen 1990, Table 1). Thereafter both the mean and dispersion of ERM inflation rates have trended downwards; but the same is true of OECD countries outside the ERM. Did membership confer any special benefits?

The argument that it did is based on two hypotheses: German leadership, exercised in pursuit of low rates of inflation; and the possibility of non-German members cashing in on Germany's reputation for commitment to price stability by pegging their currencies to the mark. If credibility can be purchased by 'tying one's hands' in this way, then domestic inflation expectations will be reduced directly, and actual inflation can be cut at a lower cost in terms of unemployment than would be possible under a floating-rate regime.

The crucial question, of course, if whether credibility can be acquired merely by announcing an exchange rate peg, especially if the peg is adjustable. An exchange rate commitment is, certainly, totally transparent; announced targets for a range of monetary aggregates can more easily be fudged. The commitment is made to other governments, which share some responsibility under EMS rules for honouring it. A monetary target is not a commitment to institutions of equal status, but a diffused threat to individual wage and price setters whose potential contribution to a lowering of the inflation rate is imperceptible. If the commitment to an exchange rate peg is broken, the political consequences at home and abroad are, to say the least, embarrassing. If failure to hit monetary targets cannot be altogether disguised, a face-saving formula can often be manufactured without incurring political costs.

Counter-arguments include applications of the Rogoff (1985) paradox (discussed by Eastwood, Chapter 7 in this volume) to the effect that international co-ordination may produce higher rates of inflation than floating rates by making central banks more accommodating. The possibility that an initially low-inflation economy might raise its rate of monetary expansion under a fixed-rate regime has aroused more interest among game theorists than among students of Bundesbank behaviour – though arguably the bank's independence was curtailed by the government's responsibility for fixing parities, at least during the early years of the EMS. De Grauwe (1989) observes that participation in the EMS ruled out the 'short sharp shock' of relative monetary contraction and the accompanying overshoot of the nominal exchange rate, and may thereby have delayed the accretion of credibility by members other than Germany.

The frequency of devaluations by the higher-inflation members during the EMS's early years suggests that their enthusiasm for shock treatment would in any case have been limited; but the realignments cast equal doubt on any credibility their exchange rate commitments might initially have had, which in view of the widespread scepticism about the prospects for the EMS at its foundation was probably very low. It seems unlikely, therefore, that Germany's anti-inflationary reputation could have been imported as a free good. More plausibly, credibility was something to be built up by good behaviour as the EMS developed. Good behaviour was manifested in the reduced frequency of realignments after 1983, and encouraged by the undercompensation offered by these realignments for inflation differentials. This latter practice provided discipline, but only at the risk of threatening the long-run viability of the EMS.

The foregoing line of argument suggests that any macroeconomic bonus accruing to the high-inflation members of the ERM would have emerged rather late in its life. There is certainly little evidence of any bonus in the macroeconomic record of the first decade summarised in Table 8.3, which compares the performance of the three largest members, with the UK and USA as controls. Inflation peaked in all countries in 1980–1. Thereafter French and Italian inflation rates converged towards the much lower German rate; but inflation was reduced by similar amounts in the UK and USA. Deflation in France and Italy involved a smaller increase in unemployment than in the UK, but the period of increase was much more protracted. Average growth rates differed little, and were far below earlier norms in Europe.

More sophisticated comparisons have not produced more conclusive results. Artis and Nachane (1990) show that the inflation rates of Germany and each of the other original members (excluding Denmark and Ireland) converge in the post-1979 period, but the same is true of German and UK inflation.[3] This result confirms the common trends suggested by Table 8.3, but does not indicate any specific ERM impact. More

Table 8.3 Macroeconomic performance 1979–89 (percentages)

	France	Germany	Italy	UK	USA
Inflation (CPI)					
Average	7	2.9	10.5	7.1	5.4
Maximum	15.1	6.3	21.2	17.9	13.5
(1980)		(1981)			
Minimum	2.1	0	5.7	3.4	1.8
(1986)			(1988)		
Average growth rate	2.1	1.9	2.4	2.2	2.5
Unemployment					
1979	5.9	3.2	7.6	5.0	5.8
Maximum	10.5	8.0	11.0	12.5	9.5
(1983)	(1987)		(1988)		
1989	9.4	5.6	10.9	6.9	5.2

Note: Extreme values registered in year shown under row heading except where otherwise indicated; unemployment rates are standardised

Source: OECD *Main Economic Indicators*

interesting is Artis and Nachane's finding that, for the other members but not for the UK, an auto-regressive forecast of German inflation, along with a similar domestic forecast, contributes significantly to the prediction of actual inflation. In Italy and France this 'German effect' is confined to the EMS period. For The Netherlands, a member of the pre-1979 Snake, it is significantly stronger after 1979. Only in Belgium, another Snake participant, is there no additional effect in the ERM period. This evidence of a direct impact of forecast inflation in Germany on other participants is consistent with a credibility bonus. Clearly, extending the sample period beyond 1986 so as to be able to detect any changes during the life of the EMS – and examining alternatives to autoregressive forecasts – are obvious candidates for further examination.

More comprehensive studies have been carried out by Giavazzi and Giovannini (1989) and by Barrell (1990b). The essence of their approach is to exploit the 'Lucas (1976) critique', which predicates that a change in policy regime which alters expectations formation will in general cause the breakdown of previously estimated relationships. Giavazzi and Giovannini estimate vector auto-regressions for wage change, inflation and output growth, with controls for monetary policy and international prices. They find no significant parameter changes, but some signs in France and Italy of lower inflation rates than predicted by the model from about 1983. The same is true, however, in the UK: ERM membership is clearly not the only characteristic affecting the stability of estimated relationships in this period. At least one of these authors now takes a sceptical view of this evidence, commenting that 'the "credibility boost" of the EMS has been rather limited, though it should not be wholly dismissed' (Giovannini 1990: 234).

Barrell (1990b) reports briefly on stability tests for models of wholesale and consumer prices, employment and wages in France, Germany, Italy and the UK over a longer data span (ending in 1989) than used in the other studies cited. The absence of adverse shifts in the German price and wage equations may be reassuring to those who feared a relaxation of Germany's anti-inflationary stance. All the Italian equations are unstable. The breakdown of the wage equation in the Italian case is related to the gradual dismantling of indexation agreements, a measure which Barrell suggests saved a large though unquantified number of jobs. In France only pricing behaviour changed, with consequential indirect effects on wages and employment. The breakdown of the British employment and wholesale price equations serves as a further reminder that structural changes can occur for all kinds of reasons, of which the ERM is only one. Apart from the difficulty of identifying their source, structural breaks provide evidence only of qualitative change. The task of quantifying those changes remains to be tackled.

The behaviour of interest differentials provides some evidence on the slow pace of accretion of credibility. Realignments of the Dutch guilder have matched those of the mark with only two exceptions, the last of which was in March 1983. Yet a perceptible differential between Dutch and German long-term interest rates remained until 1988 (EC Commission 1990: Appendix B), despite almost identical inflation rates. Giovannini (1990) documents the persistence of interest rate differentials between Italy, France and Germany since the last general parity change in 1987, and emphasises the profit opportunities they offered. He interprets the interest differentials as a consequence of the 'escape clause' provided by the continued possibility of exchange rate realignments, and concludes that 'lack of credibility is the curse of gradualism' (Giovannini 1990: 263).

In a system of unrestricted capital mobility, belief in the complete fixity of nominal exchange rates would imply equalisation of nominal interest rates irrespective of any inflation differentials. Even though capital mobility is still not totally unrestricted and the escape clause still exists, its general dormancy since 1987 has, indeed, made it more difficult for high-inflation countries to maintain sufficient nominal interest differential to keep their real interest rate in line with those of their low-inflation partners. This so-called 'excess credibility' syndrome weakens domestic counter-inflationary policy and increases the possibility of dynamic instability (Walters 1986) if exchange rate fixity is less credible in labour markets than in financial markets. Accelerated real exchange rate appreciation will impact appropriately on domestic demand, but additional fiscal activism may also be needed to ensure convergence of inflation rates.

What conclusions can be drawn about macroeconomic performance? The first point to notice is that different economists read the same evidence in different ways. Vaubel (1989) provides a telling illustration in contrasting one author's summary of results, to the effect that no differential shift in inflation behaviour was visible, with a cross-reference by another author in the same volume to 'weak evidence', and the editors' inference from the same evidence that 'the EMS has on the whole been remarkably successful'. Part of the difficulty is that the EMS has not operated in a consistent manner throughout its life. There is little evidence of any credibility effect during the early years of frequent and indexed realignments. If there was any advantage to high-inflation members, it was, perhaps, the opportunity

to reduce the electoral cost of the imminent stabilisation recession by shifting the responsibility up to the European level. Thus, just as the IMF is a scapegoat for unpopular corrective policies in developing countries, the EMS served as a bogeyman for the stabilisation crisis in France and Italy.

(Vaubel 1989: 398)

In the second phase, from about 1983, the disciplinary effect of under-indexed realignments makes the credibility hypothesis more plausible. Credibility was not, however, a free good, but required, for example, institutional changes in Italy and a policy reversal in France. The Dutch example (discussed above) suggests that even the best-behaved participants had to demonstrate a satisfactory track record for several years to achieve a Germanic reputation. Even in the final phase, with general realignments in abeyance, the credibility of the ERM remains incomplete, though it is sufficiently developed to create some problems for the least convergent members.

A question which has vexed many analysts, especially those who accord greatest weight to the credibility hypothesis, is the incentive for German membership. Vaubel (1980) saw it as a lever for the German government in its attempts to exercise control over the constitutionally independent Bundesbank – by fixing parities that would preclude politically unpopular deflationary policies, and speculated that monetary stability in Germany might be permanently impaired. Giavazzi and Giovannini (1989) do indeed report underpredictions of German wage and price changes from their vector auto-regressions but, as already noted, neither they nor Barrell (1990b) found significant breaks in these equations. Other candidate explanations for Germany's patience are the gains in competitiveness discussed in the preceding section, and reduced sensitivity to shifts in the attractiveness of the dollar.

Even if, as the credibility hypothesis suggests, inflation convergence proceeded more rapidly within the ERM than it otherwise would have done, the process remains incomplete among the original members, and the more recent adherents have further to go. Forecasts of inflation are typically twice as high for Italy, Spain and the UK as for Germany, France, The Netherlands and Belgium. If the continuing losses in competitiveness that enforce discipline cause future realignments, the deviants may find that credibility is dissipated more rapidly than it can even be built back up.

Prospects: towards EMU

Provisions for the control of capital movements were widespread during the early part of the EMS period. They were particularly important in France and Italy, where, as we have seen, the behaviour of the offshore–onshore interest differential indicates that they were used to restrain speculative flows in anticipation of realignments (Giavazzi and Giovannini 1989). Despite the practice of making 'non-provocative' adjustments, so as to avoid discrete jumps in market exchange rates, and protect the stability of the system as controls began to be dismantled, there was a widespread fear that free trade and free capital movements would prove to be inconsistent with fixed exchange rates and national control of monetary policy (eg Padoa-Schioppa 1988). Progress in 1988 towards the liberalisation of capital flows under the 1992 programme coincided with the commissioning of a study on economic and monetary union from the Delors Committee, which reported in the following year.

The report proposed a gradual process of unification. Stage 1 consists of fully liberalised capital movements (with exceptions for Spain, Greece and Portugal), enlarged ERM membership, and *ex ante* co-ordination of monetary policy by the EC Committee of Central Bank Governors. The latter is replaced in stage 2 by the European System of Central Banks (ESCB), which sets monetary policy, though leaving its execution still in the hands of national central banks; realignments are allowed only under exceptional circumstances. In stage 3 exchange rates are irrevocably fixed, national central banks are replaced by the ESCB, and the process culminates in the adoption of a single currency.

This strategy was approved by eleven of the twelve members in October 1990, with the UK dissenting. Stage 2 should begin on 1 January 1994, and within the following three years the Commission and the ESCB should prepare a report that would enable a decision to be taken on the timing of stage 3.

Giovannini (1990) points out the marked similarities between the Werner and Delors reports. Despite the unfortunate precedent, he takes a guardedly optimistic view of current prospects. The political environment for European integration, he suggests, has been improved by the reduced significance of US links in the wake of the communist collapse, and the elimination of capital controls will enforce closer co-operation to preserve the fixity of parities. Both arguments seem questionable. The political changes in Eastern Europe are creating additional pressures for association and eventual enlargement that will certainly not facilitate closer integration. The freeing of capital movements in advance of full monetary unification may, in fact, precipitate the collapse of fixed parities. Moreover, as Giovannini also observes, the earlier arguments between adherents of the 'monetarist' and 'economist' views are being repeated in successive rounds of discussion, with the added complication that the UK fits into neither camp.

The official British position advocates an evolutionary approach to monetary union in which market decisions determine the pace of change and the eventual outcome. The initial proposal (HMSO 1989) called for the removal of restrictions on the use of national currencies across borders so as to allow competition to enforce convergence. The revised version argued for the creation of a European Monetary Fund in stage 2 to manage the hard ECU, which would never be devalued against any national currency in any future realignments. This hard ECU would circulate in parallel with national currencies, and its success in supplanting them would be a major, though not the only, factor in determining the timing of stage 3.

The parallel currency approach, considered and rejected by the Delors Committee, has been the subject of much academic discussion, most recently by Vaubel (1990). The academic discussion has centred on the question as to whether and how rapidly the attractions of a stable-valued parallel currency would overcome the initial disadvantage of its restricted transactions domain. Clearly a currency can serve as a medium of exchange only if it is generally acceptable, for its acceptance by an individual agent requires the certainty of its acceptance by others.

There are, therefore, serious doubts as to whether the 'discovery procedure' advocated by Vaubel would reach the correct destination. More practical counter-arguments to competitive strategies of indefinite duration are advanced by Gros and Thygesen (1990), who express concern about the potential instability of the transitional phases. Irrespective of academic debate, alternatives to the Delors approach appear to carry little political weight outside the UK.

Leaving aside the unanswerable question of whether the Delors plan will work, what would be the consequences of European monetary union? That question, not addressed in the Delors Report, is the subject of a lengthy study by the EC Commission (1990) which is summarised by Emerson (1990). The most obvious and least contentious benefit of a single currency, the elimination of all exchange-rate-related transactions costs within the union, is one of the least important, amounting to no more than 0.5 per cent of Community GDP, because these costs are large only for cash exchanges. Transparency of prices would reinforce the 1992 programme by eliminating information costs and reducing the scope for discriminatory pricing. The elimination of residual exchange-rate uncertainty would equalise real interest rates, so improving the allocation of investment. More speculatively, dynamic gains would accrue from higher levels of investment induced by this reduced risk premium.

At the macroeconomic level the outstanding question is whether a single currency would be managed in a way which at least matched the best national performance under the EMS, or of some kind of weighted national average. Two requirements for good performance were identified in the Delors Report: a statutory mandate to pursue price stability, and independence of the ESCB in relation to both national governments and Community institutions. Both requirements could in principle be fulfilled at national level, but in practice few governments have been willing to tie their hands to such an extent. It remains to be seen whether they will really be any more willing to do so at the European level when implementation reaches the agenda. The translation of the Delors requirements into concrete proposals is unlikely to be straightforward in either economic or political terms. The former President of the Bundesbank, recalling the conflict between the interests of domestic and external stability in recent German history, regards an explicit statutory priority to domestic price level stability over exchange rate stability as desirable (Pöhl 1990); the Delors Plan envisages intervention in foreign exchange markets as the sole responsibility of the ESCB, but to be exercised in accordance with Community exchange rate policy. On the central political question, Pöhl believes that

> the democratic authorisation for an independent ESCB derives from the fact that the Treaty on which it is based has been negotiated among democratically elected governments and ratified by all the national parliaments of the countries involved.
>
> (Pöhl 1990: 9)

The constitutional issue is unlikely to be resolved as easily as this statement suggests. Moreover, at the practical level the security of tenure required for independence would have to be conditional on satisfactory performance, somehow defined, for declarations of good intentions do not guarantee results (Vaubel 1990).

The major cost of union is the inability to use nominal exchange rate changes to absorb country-specific shocks or, more importantly, asymmetric effects of common shocks such as an oil-price rise. Barrell (1990a) reports some simulations showing large differences in exchange-rate responses of the European economies to common shocks under a regime of floating exchange rates; though the suppression of these differences in responses in a monetary union scenario produces surprisingly small changes in the direct response of output and prices. He notes that the differential responses stem not only from contrasts in factor endowments but also from behavioural differences, especially in the operation of labour markets. The latter are not immutable, but the experience of the 1980s suggests that changes are likely to be slow. Emerson's belief that 'a credible monetary union will affect the behaviour of wage bargainers' (1990: 34) begs the crucial questions of how much and how rapidly.

The elimination of national exchange rates within the union and the control of monetary policy by an independent central bank leave fiscal policy as the only instrument available at national level capable of influencing aggregate demand as a means of adjusting to the differential impacts of shocks. Under the 'binding rules' proposed by the Delors Committee to limit deficit spending and to prevent its monetisation, fiscal policy would also be constrained. Apart from the direct effect of the limitation, Goodhart (1990) argues that the Ricardian implication of these rules, namely that current deficits will require higher future taxes, would reduce the impact of national fiscal policy on aggregate demand and cause counter-productive supply-side repercussions. A federal fiscal system would not suffer from this inefficiency because the higher future taxes would not be localised, and the action to counter the disturbance would in effect spread it across the Community. As Goodhart notes, this point has been appreciated more readily by US commentators than by Europeans.

The veil of ignorance which shrouds the incidence of future relative shocks might make this argument for fiscal federalism seem politically uncontentious, if it were not, arguably, the thin end of a very large wedge. The taxes required to service existing debt would impose smaller welfare costs if they were distributed more evenly, but there are large variations in debt/GDP ratios among Community members; should German tax-payers shoulder some of the burdens incurred by former Belgian governments? The Southern European economies have relied relatively heavily on seigniorage, the profit from currency issue, as a source of government revenue (EC Commission 1990: 122); should Northern tax-payers compensate for the inefficiency of conventional tax collection mechanisms in these economies (see Paci, Chapter 4 in *The National Economies of Europe*, on Italy) when seigniorage is drastically reduced by the combined effects of the 1992 programme and EMU? How would national government expenditure be controlled in a system with a significant federal tax component? How far would redistribution across national frontiers be pursued as an end in itself?

This discussion illustrates the range and complexity of the issues to be decided. If more practical reinforcement to the argument is needed, the German example demonstrates the costs of national unification at an inappropriate exchange rate. Despite the credibility drawbacks of gradualism, therefore, there are strong grounds for pursuing the economist's rather than the monetarist's approach to international economic and monetary union.

Acknowledgements

The constructive comments of David Dyker and Rob Eastwood are gratefully acknowledged.

Notes

1   The divergence indicator is defined as the proportionate deviation of a given currency from its ECU central rate, expressed as a percentage of the largest allowable deviation. This *maximum divergence spread* depends on the currency's weight in the ECU basket, because the value of the basket changes with the value of any of its component currencies. For instance, the maximum divergence of the French franc, which has a weight in the ECU basket of 19 per cent, would be encountered when the franc had fallen 2.25 per cent below its bilateral central rate with the currencies of all other member countries, or $2.25 \times (1 - 0.19)$ = 1.82 per cent below its ECU central rate. The threshold value at which the divergence indicator 'flashes' a warning is set at 75 per cent of the maximum divergence spread.
2   If the equilibrium real exchange rate between two countries is changing while the nominal exchange rate is fixed, then (at least) one member of the union must forgo the benefits of price stability.
3   More precisely, the inflation rates are co-integrated; that is, they exhibit no tendency to drift apart.

References

Artis M J, Nachane D (1990) Wages and prices in Europe: a test of the German leadership thesis. *Weltwirtschaftliches Archiv* **126**: 59–77

Artis M J, Taylor M P (1988) Exchange rates, interest rates, capital controls and the EMS: assessing the track record. In Giavazzi F, Micossi S, Miller M (eds) *The European Monetary System*. Cambridge University Press

Barrell R (1990a) European currency union and the EMS. *National Institute Economic Review* **132**: 59–66

Barrell R (1990b) Has the EMS changed wage and price behaviour in Europe? *National Institute Economic Review* **134**: 64–72

Bini-Smaghi L, Micossi S (1990) Monetary and exchange rate policy in the EMS with free capital movements. In de Grauwe P, Papademos L (eds) *The European Monetary System in the 1990s*. Longman

De Grauwe P (1989) The cost of disinflation and the EMS. Centre for Economic Policy Research Discussion Paper **326**

Delors Committee (1989) *Report on Economic and Monetary Union in the European Community*. Office for Official Publications of the EC, Luxemburg

EC Commission (1979) The European monetary system. *European Economy* **2**

EC Commission (1990) One market, one money. *European Economy* **44**

Emerson M (1990) The economics of EMU. In Dornbusch R, Goodhart C, Layard R (eds) *Britain and EMU*. Centre for Economic Performance

Fratianni M (1980) The EMS: a return to an adjustable peg arrangement. In Brunner K, Meltzer A H (eds) *Monetary Institutions and the Policy Process*. North-Holland, Amsterdam (Carnegie-Rochester Conference Series on Public Policy)

Fratianni M, Von Hagen J (1990) The EMS ten years after. In Meltzer A H (ed) *Unit Roots, Investment Measures and Other Essays*. North-Holland, Amsterdam (Carnegie-Rochester Conference Series on Public Policy)

Giavazzi F, Giovannini A)1989) *Limiting Exchange Rate Flexibility: The EMS*. MIT Press, Cambridge, Mass.

Giovannini A (1990) European monetary reform: progress and prospects. *Brookings Papers on Economic Activity 1990* **2**: 217–91

Goodhart C (1990) Fiscal policy and EMU. In Dornbusch R, Goodhart C, Layard R (eds) *Britain and EMU*. Centre for Economic Performance

Gros D, Thygesen N (1990) The institutional approach to monetary union in Europe. *Economic Journal* **100**: 925–35

Haldane A G (1991) The exchange rate mechanism of the EMS: a review of the literature. *Bank of England Quarterly Bulletin* **31**: 73–82

Healey D (1989) *The Time of My Life*. Michael Joseph

HMSO (1978) *The European Monetary System*. Cmnd 7405. Chancellor of the Exchequer

HMSO (1989) *An Evolutionary Approach to Economic and Monetary Union*. Treasury paper

Jenkins R (1978) Europe's present challenge and future opportunity. *Lloyds Bank Review* **127**: 1–14

Lucas R E Jr (1976) Economic policy evaluation. In Brunner K, Meltzer A H (eds) *The Phillips Curve and the Labour Market*. North Holland, Amsterdam (Carnegie-Rochester Conference Series on Public Policy)

Mastropasqua C, Micossi S, Rinaldi R (1988) Interventions, sterilisation and monetary policy in EMS countries 1979–87. In Giavazzi F, Micossi S, Miller M (eds) *The European Monetary System*. Cambridge University Press

Meade J E (1957) The balance of payments problems of a European free trade area. *Economic Journal* **67**: 379–96

Padoa-Schioppa T (1985) Policy co-operation and the EMS experience. In Buiter W H, Marston R C (eds) *International Economic Policy Co-ordination*. Cambridge University Press

Padoa-Schioppa T (1988) The EMS: a long-term view. In Giavazzi F, Micossi S, Miller M (eds) *The European Monetary System*. Cambridge University Press

Pöhl K O (1990) Prospects of the European monetary union. In Dornbusch R, Goodhart C, Layard R (eds) *Britain and EMU*. Centre for Economic Performance

Rogoff K (1985) Can international monetary co-operation be counter-productive? *Journal of International Economics* **18**: 199–217

Vaubel R (1980) The return to the new EMS: objectives, incentives, perspectives. In Brunner K, Meltzer A H (eds) *Monetary Institutions and the Policy Process*. North-Holland, Amsterdam (Carnegie-Rochester Conference Series on Public Policy)

Vaubel R (1988) Monetary integration theory. In Zis G (ed) *International Economics*. Longman (*Surveys in Economics*)

Vaubel R (1989) Image and reality of the EMS: a review. *Weltwirtschaftliches Archiv* **125**: 397–405

Vaubel R (1990) Currency competition and European monetary integration. *Economic Journal* **100**: 936–46

Walters A A (1986) *Britain's Economic Renaissance*. Oxford University Press

CHAPTER 9

Socio-economic trajectories, European integration and regional development in the EC

MICK DUNFORD

Introduction

Inequalities are very wide in the EC, as the figures for GDP per head by Level II region set out in Figure 9.1 show. Inequalities can be measured in two ways. Measurement in European Currency Units (ECUs) indicates the value of the output of regional economies, and what it can be sold for on international markets. This indicator is an index of the 'quality' of a region's goods and services and of its competitive strength. Measurement in Purchasing Power Standards (PPS) makes allowance for differences in the prices of goods and services in different areas: goods of a given value in ECUs will exchange for relatively more in a low-cost than in a high-cost region. The PPS measure is therefore an index of the volume of goods and services which the outputs of local economies can command or exchange for in their own area, and an indicator of differences in living standards. In 1988 output per head measured in PPS varied from 182 per cent to 40 per cent of the EC average, while in ECUs the extreme values were 215 and 23.

The data on GDP per head provide a relief map of economic development. The variations that the map indicates are a result of several factors: differences in productivity levels, in regional unemployment rates, and, in the case of the ECU measure, in the prices an area's output commands on international and interregional markets (and therefore the inequalities in prices and exchange rates built into regional trade structures).

Half of the ten wealthiest regions in 1985 were in West Germany. In that year West Germany had just under one-fifth of the EC's population, yet accounted for nearly 40 per cent of EC manufacturing output, as it had done for at least fifteen years previously, and had a current account surplus in trade in manufactured goods with every other member state except Ireland (Cutler et al 1989: 78). Most of the other top ten regions were metropolitan economies in a 'greater German' co-prosperity sphere made up of a number of areas that neighbour Germany in Denmark, the Netherlands, Belgium and France. Just beneath these metropolitan areas in terms of GDP per head lay a group of urban and industrial regions clustered around an axis that extends from

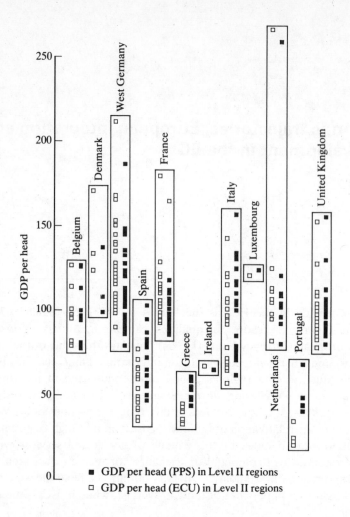

Figure 9.1   European economic development: gross domestic product per head by Level II
region in ECUs and PPS in 1988 (EC average = 100)

Greater London through Belgium and the Netherlands along the Rhine and into the
North of Italy, stretching as far as Emilia-Romagna.

The areas with lower levels of income per head were of two kinds. In Northern
Europe areas affected by the decline of employment in mining, steel, textiles and
shipbuilding had above-average unemployment rates and income per head between 75
and 100 per cent of the Community average. In the underdeveloped South of Europe
there is a broad swathe of regions where the share of income from low-productivity
agricultural sectors was large and unemployment high. In 1984 in these areas, and in
Ireland in the extreme west, per capita incomes were less than 75 per cent of the
Community average (Padoa-Schioppa 1987: 162–3).

In the 1960s and early 1970s the general trend was for regional and national
inequalities of this kind to diminish. However, some fifteen years ago this trend came
to an end and was if anything reversed. In Figure 9.2 indicators of inequalities between

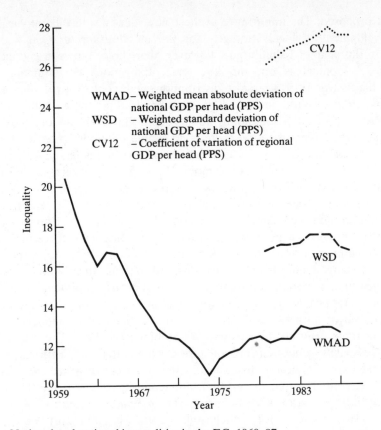

Figure 9.2   National and regional inequalities in the EC, 1960–87

the twelve members of the EC measured in PPS show how convergence gave way to divergence. The regional series covers a shorter period, but the data that do exist for individual countries also show a clear reversal of trends in the early 1970s.

At the root of this reversal is, I shall argue, a change in the model of development. In particular the mid-1970s witnessed a crisis in the development model which we may call Fordism, which was at the root of Western growth in the post-war golden age: rates of growth slowed down, and unemployment increased, as did inflation rates. At this point two of the mechanisms which had underpinned convergence ceased to operate: an earlier wave of production investments in less developed areas came to an end, while the rise in unemployment in developed areas closed off opportunities for emigration.

In the face of this crisis there was, second, a tendency for the state to retreat from intervention in economic life. There was a switch in emphasis to endogenous market-led development strategies, and responsibility for their elaboration and implementation was transferred to the local level. At the same time resource transfers from rich to poor areas diminished, at least for production activities, and regional economies were forced to rely more on their own resources. In these conditions different economies chose divergent development and adjustment strategies.

To justify these changes, the development models of the 1950s and 1960s were criticised, and alternative models of local endogenous development and of development from below proposed. The importance of these new ideas lies in the emphasis they lay on the development of local strategies for the mobilisation of local and regional resources. In this chapter I shall argue, however, that choice between endogenous and exogenous development is not the key issue. Exogenous development strategies addressed the issues of resource redistribution and control over the actions of multiregional firms. With increased internationalisation these issues remain as important as ever. To do something about them, however, action is required at supranational levels. What is more, there is no simple relationship between the speed and quality of development and its endogenous or exogenous character: there is, for example, little to recommend endogenous development processes controlled by political patron–client relations or Mafia entrepreneurs.

The end of Fordism coincided with an increase in the influence of neo-liberalism and an acceleration in the pace of integration among the economies of Europe. In the past processes of economic and political integration have sometimes corresponded with a reduction, sometimes with a stabilisation, and sometimes with an amplification of inequalities in living standards among regions and nations. In relation to the present time, the view that is perhaps most influential is the one embodied in the Cecchini Report, which argues that 'recent developments in trade theory and past experience with the removal of intra-EC tariff barriers indicate that redistributive effects in the wake of freer trade need not be excessive' (Cecchini 1988: 105). There are, however, two sets of reasons for doubting this conclusion. One is that the historical evidence of the last fifteeen years indicates divergence rather than convergence (see Cutler et al 1989: 76–7). The other is that in an important semi-official report entitled *Efficiency, Stability and Equity*, better known as the *Padoa-Schioppa Report*, quite different conclusions were reached. The conclusions of this latter report were far more pessimistic than Cecchini's: 'There are serious risks of aggravated regional imbalance in the course of market liberalisation' (Padoa-Schioppa 1987: 5). To cope with these risks, the Padoa-Schioppa Report envisaged a much more important role for regional policies: 'in a larger and more differentiated Community redistributive functions performed through the budget and the lending instruments of the Community should be considerably developed in size and made more effective in their purpose and design' (Padoa-Schioppa 1987: x).

What I shall suggest is that the model of integration envisaged by the Cecchini Report is one of liberal market integration. In the immediate past this model of integration has widened inequalities. At present there are grounds for thinking that the development of a larger market will favour strong firms located in major metropolitan areas and strong regions. Moves in the direction of monetary union and a permanent fixed exchange rates mechanism could damage the national and regional economies of countries, since enforced monetary adjustment as a means of increasing exports or controlling imports will compel weak economies to select an adjustment path involving greater unemployment, more underused resources and an enforced fall in real wages and incomes.

I shall go on to argue that what happens in Europe will depend on whether this model of liberal market integration gives way to another centred around social and fiscal harmonisation, the assumption of fiscal functions and of responsibilities for the transfer of resources from rich to poor regions at EC level, and interventionist development strategies for less developed areas. Development is, however, a question not only of resources, but also of the ways in which resources are used, and of the ways in which economies and societies are organised. The divergent development of regional economies reflects differences in their pattern of adaptation to the technological and social challenges of a new era. These differences in the degree of 'success' of regional economies offer evidence of the types of adjustment and the institutional structures required for a more cohesive and balanced development of the regions of Europe, and show how essential it is to develop local and regional development programmes.

The implications of the model of development: the Fordist model and its crisis

The model of development of the post-war golden age was centred on Taylorism and mechanisation. The scientific management ideas of F W Taylor rested on two innovations. The first was the separation of the conception and design of work from its execution, and the transfer of mental work to the Organisation and Methods (O&M) Office. The second was the development of time and motion study, so as to split a process of production into a sequence of simplified individual jobs. The 'one best way' and the time required to perform each task was identified, while the simplification of tasks allowed the development of new specialised machines – operated by what the French call specialised (unskilled) workers. With Ford's development of the semi-automatic assembly line the simplification of tasks was accelerated, and the norms set in the O&M office incorporated into the automatic machine system itself: the movement of the machines determined the task that a worker had to do, while the speed of work was determined by the speed of movement of the line.

These developments laid the foundations for rapid productivity growth, which was redistributed to the wage-earning class via collective bargaining and the transfers embodied in the welfare state (Dunford 1990). Growth was led therefore by domestic demand.

All of this occurred against the background of a very specific global configuration of advanced economies. In the first place, domestic production was first and foremost for domestic markets. The volume of manufactured goods traded internationally did, of course, increase. As a share of gross domestic product, however, the industrial exports of EC countries reached a minimum in the 1960s. The second feature was the integration of the more advanced Western half of Europe into a hierarchical order under the leadership of the United States. With the defeat of fascism and as a result of the USA's uncontested economic dominance – at the end of the war the USA accounted on its own for three-quarters of the world's invested capital and two-thirds of its industrial potential (Horowitz 1967: 74) – the United States emerged as the hegemonic world power, and Fordism, or the 'American way', was the technological and social paradigm that other nations in the West adopted and adapted.

The implications for regional development

As far as regional development is concerned, there were two important aspects to the Fordist era. First, mechanisms of redistribution operated in favour of less developed areas: nation-states played a major role in the transfer of resources to less developed

Table 9.1 The regional impact of French taxes and expenditures in 1976 (in French francs per inhabitant)

		Lowest taxes and highest expenditures and transfers		Highest taxes and lowest expenditures and transfers
State budget				
Expenditures[1]	Corse	8,745	Essonne (Paris)	6,335
Taxes	Haute-Loire	5,802	Seine	15,888
Net transfers	Corse	2,938	Seine	−7,710
Social security				
Expenditures	Ile-de-France	5,705	Franche-Comté	4,539
Contributions	Languedoc-Roussillon	3,756	Ile-de-France	7,646
Net transfers	Languedoc-Roussillon	1,792	Ile-de-France	−1,940

[1]Average = 7,070

Source: Davezies, Larrue and Prud'homme 1983: 36–68, 104–18 and 173–94

areas, via regional policies *and* all the other aspects of state expenditure and taxation which have direct and indirect spatial effects. Second, there were attempts to divert investments to less developed areas, while full employment growth in the more developed regions stimulated and presupposed migration from less developed areas and countries.

The redistribution of resources

The nation-state was the locus of a social compromise in all of the mixed economies of the West. An institutional structure was established, as was a set of norms and procedures whose role it was to regulate the actions and interactions of social and economic subjects. Included was a set of mechanisms for revenue generation, the definition and implementation of expenditure programmes, and resource redistribution. These mechanisms resulted in a geographical redistribution of resources that was very important, but seldom treated in an explicit way.

Consider, for example, the French case (see Table 9.1). In 1976 the mechanisms of the French state budget resulted in a net transfer of FF 2,938 per head to the *département* of Corsica and of −FF 7,710 from that of Seine. In Seine the transfers amounted to some 20 per cent of income, and in the two poorest areas to something over 10 per cent; for most *départements*, however, the impact was limited, with the gap between the richest and poorest *départements* reduced from FF 26,400 per head to FF 15,800. The *départements* that financed these transfers remained none the less the richest regions (see Davezies et al 1983: 36–68, especially 66–8).

The social security system, whose annual budget was in 1976 close to that of the state budget proper, reinforced the redistributive impact of the latter (see Davezies et al 1983: 173–94): thus Ile de France made a net contribution of FF 1,940 per inhabitant, while the poorest regions were the largest net recipients of funds, with Languedoc-Roussillon receiving FF 1,792 per head.

The impact of regional planning as such was very limited, compared to that of net budgetary transfers. In 1960–73, for example, the inhabitants of the Pays de la Loire received the highest regional development aids per head. These aids were worth FF 132.12 per inhabitant, or an average of FF 9.44 per inhabitant per year. Yet in 1976 alone the inhabitants of Languedoc received net budget transfers of FF 1,224 per head and social security transfers of FF 1,792. Thus the value of the net transfers under the state budget and the social security system to the most favoured region were 300 times larger than the value of the regional development aid provided to the most favoured region. (The state budget study cited was not comprehensive – the expenditures of the public utilities, whose actions also played a role in the inter-*département* transfer of resources, were not considered. Neither were multiplier effects, as the economic impact of state expenditures spills over from one *département* to another. Consideration of these factors would not, however, alter the basic conclusion.)

It is worth looking also at the identities of the most favoured areas. For the 1960–73 period the rank order of regions on the basis of levels of regional aid and state budget transfer indicators respectively were very similar, but not identical. Some of the areas that were most disadvantaged and that received most aid in the shape of budget transfers (Languedoc, Midi-Pyrénées, and Auvergne) did not do well out of regional development aids, which were directed more towards regions in the west (such as the Pays de la Loire) and north-east (Davezies et al 1983).

State expenditure remains an important component of capital formation and of current expenditure in advanced capitalist societies. At the end of the next section I shall argue that it should be larger, and that it should be used to provide direct services and investments rather than to subsidise private operators. The work of Davezies, Larrue and Prud'homme shows that redistribution is a product of differences in contributions rather than in outlays (see Table 9.1). Levels of expenditure per head are not in general higher in the more underdeveloped areas than in richer areas. The transfers that do occur stem more from the fact that per capita taxes and social security contributions are lower in low-income areas. While, therefore, regional development funds do discriminate in favour of less developed areas, overall expenditure does not. A sensible treatment of spatial imbalances requires that the geographical impact of state expenditures as a whole be given much more explicit attention. Instead of a narrow focus on regional and other explicit spatial policies, a spatial dimension should be added to all state expenditures at national and EC levels.

Inter-regional investment flows

In the era of Fordism there was a significant volume of potential mobile investment that could be diverted to less developed areas in order to help modernise their economic and social structures. (At the same time, it should be noted, the existence of near full employment and high rates of growth in developed areas was at the root of high rates of growth of demand for labour and large-scale movements of people from peripheral to central areas.)

The inter-regional redistribution of investments, public and private, was a major determinant of the map of economic development. It was, moreover, an important goal of most nation-states. To achieve a more equal distribution of development, governments used various instruments. Included were the creation of industrial zones, restrictions on development in strong regions, controls over the location of public investments, and in particular financial incentives. Incentives do not, of course, determine investment decisions: the idea was that the incentives should, first, compensate investors for the higher costs and the absence of external economies in less developed areas, and second, modify the structure of costs and benefits considered in making investment decisions. (Similar results could have been achieved, of course, if firms had been made to pay the higher social costs they created through their location in more developed areas. The choice of most governments was to offer firms incentives to relocate rather than make them compensate host communities in overdeveloped areas if they failed to relocate.)

In many parts of Europe powerful critiques of exogenous (to the less developed region) investment were subsequently advanced. Some of the most striking related to the development of the Italian Mezzogiorno. Of course the evidence of major 'planning disasters' is not hard to find. In Calabria, for example, there are the Saline chemical complex where production of the main product (animal proteins) never started due to health hazards associated with their use, the uncompleted chemical complex at Lamezia Terme, and the Gioia Tauro steelworks. The plain of Gioia Tauro is an area of rich agricultural potential which specialised in the intensive production of citrus fruits and other Mediterranean tree crops. In 1971 it was designated the site for Italsider's fifth integrated steel complex. Agricultural and urban land was expropriated, a village was relocated, and in 1975 work on an immense and expensive port was started, with Mafia entrepreneurs playing a major role as subcontractors in the project.[1] Soon afterwards the plan was dropped. Today an unused port is surrounded by a desert.

While these episodes involved a scandalous waste of resources the answer to the question why they happened is not as simple as the 'planning disaster' label implies. The actors in the drama included not only regional development agencies but also politicians and their clients, criminal organisations, and major public and private groups, while the context of action included political destabilisation, anarchic competition and economic expectations about trends in demand and in profits that proved quite wrong, but that were the foundations of similar decisions by many other firms and governments. (In the French and UK cases major steel and petrochemicals investments were made in less developed areas in the late 1960s and early 1970s. In the case of the French steel industry, for example, the two major private producers planned the expansion of coastal complexes at Dunkirk and Fos-sur-Mer, while the British Steel Corporation's ambitious 1973 Ten-Year Development Programme centred, for example, on major capacity expansion at Llanwern and Port Talbot, Ravenscraig, Scunthorpe and Teesside. With the subsequent fall in demand for steel, the British Development Programme was abandoned *de facto* in 1976 and *de jure* in 1978. In the French case the government had to intervene to save the steel industry in 1978, as levels of indebtedness rose. The incoming socialist administration then nationalised it in 1981. It was subsequently forced, however, to close the Ugine-Aciers plant at Fos-sur-Mer.)

A second criticism of the waves of investment into less developed areas in the late 1950s, 1960s and early 1970s is that they caused an increase in the dependence of those areas on the economies of more advanced areas. In the case of the Mezzogiorno, for example, there was an increase in the degree of dependence of Southern residents on external investment funds, external income transfers, and imported goods. The increase in transfers to residents represented the increase in the difference between the value added generated in the South and the incomes of Southern residents. In their turn, the transfers allowed the Italian South to sustain a trade deficit with the rest of the world, and this was financed in part through public sector deficit spending (see Dunford 1988; Paci, Chapter 4 on Italy, in *The National Economies of Europe*). (Since the early 1950s net imports of goods and services into the Italian Mezzogiorno have consistently been equal on average to over 21 per cent of the South's gross domestic product.)

Dependence is an indicator of some of the inadequacies of the exogenous development model. It does not follow, however, that the situation would have been better in the absence of these investments. Indeed in the subsequent inactive policy period, when external investments into the Italian South decreased, not only did the volume of transfers not fall, but rather current transfers were substituted for capital transfers. As a result, a more pathological type of dependence was created (Graziani 1988). In the active policy period the most important element of the transfers were investments, which increased the productive potential of the South and narrowed productivity differentials. With the increase in investment, incomes increased, which provided finance for the import into the Mezzogiorno of consumer goods. In the inactive period, by contrast, the main effect of the transfers was just to increase the incomes of consumers and the level of aggregate demand. As output in the South fell relative to the rest of Italy, more income was redistributed to Southern residents. The maintenance of local demand did not stimulate endogenous investment, and so relative incomes and levels of productivity fell, so that the dependence of the South was reinforced.

The identification of a relationship between dependence and the development strategies of the Fordist era is related, of course, to the pattern of resource transfers discussed in the last section, and to the measures governments adopted to ensure macroeconomic stabilisation. Within the single economic and monetary spaces of nation-states, inter-regional balance of payments disequilibria have tended to persist. Inter-regional investment flows, fiscal transfers and automatic fiscal stabilisers have, however, permitted the covering of these deficits in a non-deflationary way. Changes in regional adjustment mechanisms in the context of greater economic integration is one of the main factors that differentiate the present from this earlier era.

In evaluating the impact of exogenous investments some authors have argued that at the aggregate level the efficiency of investment was low: in 1963–73 value added per head in the South of Italy grew no faster than in the North, in spite of the higher rate of capital formation (see eg Izzo 1990). But productivity growth was much faster in the capital-intensive exogenous than in the endogenous sector. At the same time there was very little spending on research and development in the South. At the end of the wave of exogenous investment, in the mid-1970s, the South's share of public research spending excluding universities stood at 15 per cent. Without the nuclear sector it stood at 30 per cent. For industrial corporations the South's share stood at 2 cent (Cicciotti 1979). There were, not surprisingly, significant disparities in innovativeness between North and South.

A full explanation for the difference in innovativeness demands consideration of several factors (see Cicciotti 1979).

1 *The type of firms found in the South*   inter-regional firms, which employ more than half of the people working in the South and which are in the sectors that at a national level undertake high levels of research and development spending, place little of it in the South, while local firms are in sectors in which little is spent nationally. Aggregate indicators do, therefore, conceal important differences between inter-regional investments and local investments. In the modern sector disparities in innovativeness, in the rate of diffusion of innovations, and in the pattern of transfer of technologies do exist between North and South, but they are due to the kind of investments extra-regional groups choose to make in the South. The difficulties identified are therefore not arguments against exogenous investment so much as against the division and location of functions within multiregional firms, and the absence of horizontal relationships between research, design, marketing and production within less developed economies or regions.

2 *The skill composition of the work-forces in North and South*   in the North there is a high proportion of managers and a low proportion of independent workers and self-employed people. In the South one finds a high proportion of entrepreneurs and manual workers and a low proportion of managers and clerical workers, this reflecting the branch plant character of Southern industries. Variations in the skill composition of the work-force are a cause and a consequence of the development model.

3 *Urban structures and urban services*   are relatively weak. These weaknesses stem from the fact that large groups have their own internal services or draw on suppliers in the North, while Southern firms make little use of producer services. There is, once again, a supply-side problem *and* a demand-side problem: there is no point in offering producer services if there are no users, and there is no point in requiring firms to use local suppliers if none exists.

It appears, therefore, that the lack of innovativeness has been a result, not of the exogenous character of the investments that non-Southern groups have placed in the South, but of the profile of those investments, and of the absence of strategies aimed at the development of synergies between the exogenous and endogenous sectors.

Finally in this connection, it must be said that the distinction between exogenous and endogenous factors is in itself problematic. In underdeveloped industrial environments exogenous investors do internalise functions – but within industrial establishments. Industrial linkages with the local and regional economies in which externally controlled plants are located are accordingly limited. Important interdependencies between non-local and local enterprises can none the less exist as, for example, Del Monte (1988) showed in some research on the province of Caserta in Campania.

The province of Caserta was industrialised in the 1960s and 1970s through the establishment of branch plants. In 1974–80 2,500 net jobs were created in local firms, while 200 were lost in non-local firms. This evidence led to the identification of a process of endogenous development. In 1980–6, however, the numbers of new local and non-local firms declined, many firms failed, and jobs were lost – 5,000 jobs in non-local and 1,500 in local firms. Del Monte has shown that in Caserta many of the local firms were subcontractors to the non-local establishments. As the non-local firms introduced new technologies and reduced orders for earlier inputs, the local firms that supplied them failed because they were unable to change their output to match the new needs of the exogenous investors. Nor were local firms sufficiently large and independent to compete on extra-regional markets: in the shoe sector, for example, firms in Caserta were small, producing shoes for the cheap end of the market, and producing for large retailers rather than marketing their own brands. The conclusions that Del Monte drew from this study were twofold. First, it is difficult for local firms to grow without exogenous investments. Second, their failure to grow is due more to obstacles to the expansion of existing firms than to limited new firm formation. Initiatives for local economic development should focus, argues Del Monte, on the causes of business failure and obstacles to growth.

In Caserta, therefore, as in other less developed areas, the establishment and growth of local firms was based in part on exogenous investments, and the decline of externally controlled firms had negative effects on the development of local firms. The development prospects of less developed areas do depend, in other words, on extra-regional investments and on the development of linkages between these investments and local initiatives – as well as, of course, on local development strategies aimed at the exploitation of local resources to meet local needs.

The identification of the need for inter-regional investments does not, however, vindicate the instruments of traditional regional policies. Incentives, which alter the structure of costs of a firm, are one of the factors lying behind the general structure of the economies of less developed areas, and in particular of the capital-intensive character of their industrial development. But incentives do not *determine* investment decisions, and incentives have not secured an adequate development of intra-regional linkages. It does, therefore, make sense to invest in infrastructures and services to remove some of the locational disadvantages of less developed areas. Infrastructures and services cannot be justified, however, unless users of these services exist. There must, accordingly, be a parallel development of economic activities and a renewed spatial decentralisation of productive investments from more developed to less developed regions. Instead of grants, state equity capital contributions, controls over the location of major investments, planning agreements with major groups, and state-region plan contracts that include agreements over the decentralisation of major public investments, should be used. (But see Dyker, Chapter 11 on Yugoslavia, in *The National Economies of Europe*, for an account of the dangers of trying to develop the planning agreement approach in an unsuitable political environment.) Where disinvestment by companies in less developed areas effectively writes off substantial public sector infrastructural investment, the companies should be made to pay at at least part of the costs involved.

The crisis of Fordism and the post-Fordist era?

At the end of the 1960s and in the early 1970s the Fordist model broke down (Leborgne and Lipietz 1990). The causes were twofold. In the realm of work organisation, Taylorism prevented the active involvement of the mass of workers in the conduct and improvement of production. The rate of productivity growth that engineers and technicians could secure slowed down, and involved ever higher investment costs. As a result the rate of profit fell, as did investment. The level of unemployment rose. What followed was a crisis of the welfare state which had been developed to cope with low rates of unemployment rather than the mass unemployment of the late 1970s.

To raise productivity, firms sought economies of scale via strategies of internationalisation, and to raise profits they sought out lower-cost suppliers and lower-cost production sites in Third World countries. The 1971 switch to floating exchange rates, and the subsequent reduction in levels of control over international financial movements, opened the way for a dramatic growth of international private banking. This development was given a new impetus after the Oil Shock due to the increase in the supply of petro-dollars. International trade grew faster than domestic markets. The connection between the wages a firm paid and the size of the market it serviced was weakened: wages came to appear more as a cost and less as an element of demand for national output. In these conditions the link between the internal pattern of productivity growth and the national macroeconomic mechanism was weakened. With the rise of monetarism internal demand stagnated. With the internationalisation of the post-Oil Shock recession, so did world demand. In order to reduce its balance of payments deficit each nation sought larger real wage reductions than its rivals, and to improve its capital account each nation introduced ever higher interest rates to attract international deposits. To the earlier supply-side problems were accordingly added the demand-side difficulties of the 'double-sided' crisis of Fordism (Lipietz 1989b).

In these circumstances the operational weakness of state economic intervention intensified. Towards the end of the 1970s significant changes in the organisation, character and goals of national states were set in motion. In almost all countries there was an increase in the importance attached to private initiative, a disengagement of the state from the economic sphere, and a growth in economic initiatives at the local level. What resulted was a paradox: a globalisation of economic activities proceeded alongside a localisation of political strategies (Preteceille 1991). To some the decentralisation and localisation of development strategies was consistent with economic trends. The localisation of welfare action permitted its differentiation. Automatic rights embodied in the Fordist wage–labour relation were dismantled through the establishment of closer (quasi-market) relations between the provision of services and the ability of users to pay. In addition, competition among local authorities increased (Preteceille 1991). With these changes the solidarities that had existed at national level and that had underpinned the distribution and transfers of resources under Fordism were eroded, as individuals came to view themselves as part of a localised community and beyond it of a competitive world. On an ethical front it denoted the substitution of increased competition for co-operation and mutual support.

The implications of these developments for spatial imbalances will be considered in four sub-sections. In the first I shall identify some of the implications of changes in the structure of advanced economies and in the sources of economic growth. Second, I shall discuss some of the divergent models of institutional adaptation to new technologies and their implications for the success of regional economies. In the last two sections I shall discuss the implications of the coexistence of areas at very different levels of development within a single economic space, and consider whether the development programmes envisaged as part of the integration process are sufficient to counteract those processes which may lead to an increase in economic polarisation.

Structural change and spatial development: metropolitan economies and the network-metropolis

In the West the 1970s and 1980s were years of economic crisis and of a new technological revolution. The period showed three key features.

1   Investments made earlier proved unprofitable, whole industries were rationalised, capital was written down, workers were laid off. With the increased internationalisation of capital and the search for cheaper production sites on the one hand, and the concentration of investments in new processes and products in existing establishments on the other, there was a reduction in the volume of (actual rather than potential) mobile investment flows. (In the United Kingdom, for example Hart and Harrison (1990) show how the impetus of industrial movement declined: in 1966–70 there were 568 moves to peripheral regions, in 1971–75 376, and in 1976–80 211. Actual movement was limited due to the decline in aggregate investment and the concentration of what new investment did take place.)

2   There was an acceleration in the development of new technologies, processes and products and, in particular, a rapid development and convergence of electronics, computing and telecommunications. These new technologies are centred on two principles: the principle of integration and real time control, which depends on communication and co-ordination, and the principle of production flexibility. With these developments went major changes in work organisation and the structure and location of economic activities.

3   There was a change in the relationships and allocation of investment funds between industrial, commercial, financial and land and property development activities. In particular, industrial enterprises were subordinated to commercial and marketing functions, producer services and an increasingly independent financial sector.

These developments involved persistent differentials in output and productivity growth rates across sectors. As a consequence, the shares of different industries in output and employment changed. Deindustrialisation went along with the rise of new growth ensembles (high-technology industries, revitalised craft industries, and producer services). In these circumstances the map of economic development was transformed and inequalities reinforced.

In the industrial sector structural changes resulted in a transformation of job patterns. In production, numbers of direct production jobs fell relative to those of maintenance jobs, while in industry as a whole the ratio of 'periproductive' jobs (in marketing, design, sales and distribution) to production jobs increased. The growth of internal industrial sector services (which amount to some two-thirds to three-quarters

Table 9.2   The share of the Paris ZPIU[a] in total national industrial employment, by sectors and functions of production (in percentages) 1986[b]

Sector	Design and research	Sales and marketing	Administration and management	Miscellaneous services	Storage and transport	Manufacture	All functions
T1	54.0	66.0	58.0	48.0	32.0	29.0	44.6
T2	31.0	56.0	37.0	28.0	18.0	14.0	24.0
Vehicles	49.0	66.0	54.0	37.0	32.0	24.0	30.4
Non-'technicien' sectors							
Q1	15.0	38.0	22.0	19.0	11.0	12.0	14.4
Q2	14.0	31.0	20.0	6.0	6.0	5.0	8.0
S1	10.0	34.0	20.0	12.0	10.0	8.0	10.9
S2	13.0	27.0	18.0	16.0	8.0	6.0	8.8
Construction	37.0	28.0	34.0	30.0	15.0	22.0	23.3

Notes:

[a] Zone de peuplement industriel et urbain

[b] The industrial sectors were classified into a number of groups on the basis of the share of very skilled jobs (engineers, executives and technicians) in total employment. The 'T1' industries, with a high proportion of highly skilled 'techniciens', include defence electronics, telecommunications, computers, automation equipment, aerospace, and high power electrical equipment. 'T2' includes base chemicals, parachemicals, machine tools, industrial equipment, precision instruments and equipment, and consumer electronics. The 'Q' activities are those still characterised by the presence of a large complement of skilled manual workers: iron and steel, motor and commercial vehicles, rail equipment, linotype printing, general engineering and metal manufacturing (Q1), and mining and materials (Q2). The 'S' activities have a high proportion of unskilled workers: iron-working, glass and furniture (S1); and food processing, textiles, leather goods and shoes (S2). The construction of private vehicles and vehicle equipment forms a separate class

Source: Beckouche 1991

of the services a firm uses) and of marketed services, the high skill content of these jobs, and the concentration of these activities in major cities where there is a large concentration of professional workers, have been major factors in the polarisation of economic activities.

Consider for example the case of Paris (see Table 9.2). With over 18 per cent of the French population (a population of 10 million people) in 1986, the Paris zone of industrial and urban settlement (ZPIU) accounted for 44.6 per cent of all the 'T1' jobs in France, but just 8.8 per cent of the 'S2' jobs. The Paris ZPIU did not just specialise in sectors with a large share of skilled workers. Within each group of industries it accounted for a high proportion of jobs in research and marketing and much lower proportions of production jobs. The car sector epitomises the contrast: it is, as Beckouche (1991) points out, at one and the same time, a high-technology sector (concentrated in Paris) and a sector that depends for price-competitiveness on the search for shop-floor wage-cost economies in the provinces.

These changes in job structure are a function not only of differential productivities, but also of the increased role of integrative and management functions. Integration is of two kinds.

First, *horizontal integration* occurs between the different research and development, design, production, and commercial functions. The development of horizontal and less hierarchical relations in large organisations creates possibilities for the disaggregation of some headquarters functions and some central services, and the development of small and medium-sized multifunctional units. The decentralisation of these units is, however, dependent on a wider distribution of centres with a critical mass of skilled workers and services, and of networks for the integration of the different units.

Second, integration occurs along *product chains*: silicon ›› semiconductors ›› computers ›› factory control systems ›› machine tools ›› cars. This involves the development of logistic systems that integrate means of telecommunication with means of physical transport and cut across the boundaries of firms. Integration occurs upstream with suppliers and downstream with customers and clients, and involves the development of stable networks of organised relations that require co-ordination and co-operation over methods of production, quality control, stock management and the development of management information systems. The result is a new world in which the boundaries of firms are less clear, in which planning is extended from intra-firm to inter-firm relations, in which values are created along networks, and in which the optimal organisation of the network goes beyond the sum of local optima.

These developments favour locations on computer and telecommunications networks and on major road, rail and air transport infrastructures. This produces a new kind of polarisation which depends on the resources of nodes in networks, their connectivity and connectedness, and the scope for the appropriation of rents. The particular geographical shape of these developments depends on the distribution of major infrastructural investments, as these investments are the precondition for the implantation of such integrated activities. Included are planned investments in means of transport and communication required to run organisations at a distance and allow establishments to interact with one another (a national fibre-optic grid), and in support services and cultural and residential facilities.

These logistic considerations, along with the skill requirements of control functions and high-level service sector jobs on the one hand and the distribution of high-quality research and educational institutions on the other, favour metropolitan areas, as it is in these zones that such advantages are concentrated. The outcome is the establishment of a very close relationship between a world-wide network of global cities and the distribution of the major transnational control functions in large organisations (Smith and Feagin 1987).

In the French case the development of a metropolitan network is at the root of new kinds of spatial polarisation. The opposition between Paris and the 'French desert' has, Veltz (1991) suggests, been superseded by an opposition between the network-metropolis (made up of Paris and a number of second-rank metropolitan zones) and the French desert. Two major cleavages are identified. One is the ever weaker linkage between the development of large cities and that of their hinterlands, due to the weakness of spread effects and the diminished importance of economic activities in the hinterlands for the growth of the metropolitan centres. The other is the ever closer integration of the leading sectors of second-rank centres with the activities in the Parisian pole on which they depend: examples include electronics in Rennes and aerospace in Toulouse. The result is an immense gap between a metropolitan network headed by Paris and the rest of the provinces. With less than 20 per cent of the French population, the Paris region accounts for some 50 per cent of 'abstract' industrial and producer service functions (researchers, designers, engineers, managers and other executives) and over 50 per cent of all the high-tech jobs in France (Beckouche 1991; see also Table 9.2). Jobs in production activities are correspondingly underrepresented. The rest of French design and research jobs are located in the other large metropolises: in particular, a substantial share of design and research jobs in the sophisticated state-controlled sectors of the French economy are located in the large Southern metropolises (Toulouse, Grenoble and Bordeaux).

There are two lessons to be drawn from this evidence. In the first place, the new inequalities are not so much between centres and peripheries as between metropolitan zones well linked to key physical and telecommunications infrastructures on the one hand, and the areas which do not benefit from those linkages on the other. Spatial inequalities are therefore intra-regional *and* inter-regional: there are major inequalities within metropolitan areas where wealth and poverty coexist alongside one another, and there are inequalities between the areas with dominant centres and those without. If development is to be evened out, it is therefore these processes of polarisation of economic activities and functions in metropolitan areas that need to be addressed.

The second conclusion that emerges from studies of global cities is that large firms have internationalised, and are now major determinants of the international division of labour. Internationalisation has, however, allowed them to escape the control of national governments and, as we shall see, to play one state and one area off against another. The emphasis in much of the research work on new industrial spaces on small and medium-sized firms seems therefore misplaced. If large corporations and industrial-financial groups are the dominant actors in the world economic system, more attention must be paid to their actions and attempts made to divert their investments in key control functions towards less developed areas, and to influence the strategies of subcontracting/partnership that they adopt.

Defensive and offensive adaptations to the crisis: the danger of a two-tier Europe

Equally important were the major differences in the pattern of adaptation of regional economies to the development of Fordism, and in particular to the crisis of Fordism (Leborgne and Lipietz 1991; Boyer 1988; Friedman 1977: 48–50). In essence, we can distinguish between areas within countries and whole national economies on the basis of whether they sought to compete through low wages and a competitive environment ('defensive' restructuring) or through high wages, high skills, high productivity and partnership ('offensive' restructuring).[2]

Leborgne and Lipietz identify two sets of relations: *capital–capital relations*, where there are choices between strategies of subcontracting (vertical near-integration) and strategies centred on partnership (horizontal near-integration), and *capital–labour relations*. What Leborgne and Lipietz do not consider are *relations between capital and the state* and the developmental role of the state (Dunford 1991).

Two characteristics (see Figure 9.3) of Fordist industrial relations are identified by Lebourne and Lipietz (Taylorism as a principle of work organisation, and a rigid wage

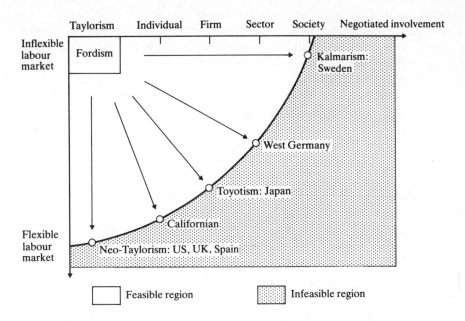

Figure 9.3   From Fordism to . . .? Alternative work and employment relations
Source: adapted from Leborgne and Lipietz 1990

and employment contract) and two ways out of the crisis defined (a neo-liberal path which identifies wage and employment flexibility as a solution for the full-employment profit squeeze, and non-Taylorist strategies of responsible work involvement which are centred around a reunification of mental and manual work and increases in the skill content of jobs, and whose goals are increases in the quality of output, greater productivity, a functionally flexible workforce and improved demand response). On the horizontal axis Leborgne and Lipietz distinguish the level at which the involvement of workers and the concessions of employers are negotiated (if at all), namely not negotiated (Taylorism) individual-, firm-, sector- and societal-level. As the level at which agreements are made rises, more solidaristic, more organised, less hierarchical, less market-oriented and more rigid wage employment and social security arrangements prevail. And as one moves around the arc from bottom left to top right, the proportion of the population that gains from the social compromise increases, and the proportion that comprises the marginalised strata of dual societies diminishes; so too does the extent of income polarisation (Leborgne and Lipietz 1990).

On this basis several alternative models are identified. Neo-Taylorism is Taylorism without the social advantages of Fordism (secure jobs, regular wage increases, wage-related unemployment compensation and a welfare state), while the combination of rigid wage and employment relations with negotiated involvement is named after the Volvo plant at Kalmar in Sweden, the first to dispense with the assembly line. The situation in any given country will be a complex combination of these elements: in the 'Third Italy', for example, there are systems that depend on low wages, multiple job holding, irregular work, the employment of children, and the evasion of taxes and social security contributions, and there are others where a significant proportion of the workers are skilled, well-paid and provided with good collective services (see Paci, Chapter 4 on Italy, in *The National Economies of Europe*).

In the view of Leborgne and Lipietz the regions that have been most successful are the ones that have chosen strategies of offensive restructuring. The fact remains that the variations in productivity and competitiveness are great: areas that chose increased work and employment flexibility and have below-average levels of productivity may not therefore have the extra surplus value to pay for more progressive social compromises, and can perhaps no longer change course. In this case two consequences follow. First, the scope for social harmonisation in the new Europe will be extremely limited unless there are major transfers of resources between regions. Second, in the absence of moves towards a harmonisation of social and employment legislation, the existence of lower levels of social protection in less developed areas will inevitably pose a threat to more advanced areas, as there is always a chance that differentials in wages and wage costs will increase sufficiently to offset the productivity advantage of more developed areas. This threat may lead to the adoption of very cautious economic development strategies in richer regions and countries.

Integration and unequal development

It is these sharp differences in the levels of competitiveness of the regional economies of Europe which, in conjunction with the elimination of tariff barriers, lie at the root of the increase in the extent of regional inequality. As Cutler et al (1989) have shown, the advantages of market integration in the EC have in the past been very unequally divided. In manufactures in particular (SITC categories 5–8) Germany dominates output. In 1985 West Germany, with 19 per cent of the EC population, produced 38.4 per cent of real manufacturing output, while France, Italy and the UK, with 17–18 per cent each of the EC population, produced 23, 16.4 and 12.8 per cent respectively of manufacturing output. In 1987 West Germany accounted for 35.4 per cent of EC exports of manufactures, and exported almost one-half of domestic manufacturing production. Within Europe every country except Ireland had a trade deficit in manufactures with Germany. The fact that some countries' imports exceed their exports implies, of course, that there is a net transfer of sales to the surplus nations. Transfers of sales are also transfers of jobs: in the case of the 1987 German surplus with the rest of Europe (ECU 34 billion), Cutler and colleagues calculate that 1,087 million jobs were transferred (Cutler et al 1989: 17–20).

The existence of these deficits does, of course, impose a constraint on the economic strategies of deficit countries. If deficits on manufactured trade push the current account as a whole into deficit, the nation's economic authorities will choose to deflate in the name of a 'price-effect' (lowering unit labour costs) or a 'volume-effect' (reducing domestic demand). Either way, employment and income growth will slow down. (If the deficit countries were at or near full employment these constraints would not, of course, matter. In practice however there have been substantial underused resources in Europe throughout recent decades.) The result at structural level has been a 'negative-sum game' – a war of competitive recessions (see Eastwood, Chapter 7 in this volume, on co-ordinating macroeconomic policy).

The way to relax the constraint is for surplus nations to recycle their surpluses in the shape of long-term loans to and investments in deficit countries. Over the period 1974–90, however, German surpluses with the rest of the EC were not recycled. German financial institutions provided long-term loans to domestic business, but trade surpluses were translated into increments in foreign exchange reserves and sterilised. At the same time German growth was not sufficient to provide for full employment at home, let alone to create new jobs for inter-regional and international migrants. In these conditions the deficit economies were forced to adopt economic policies leading inevitably to slower growth.

There are reasons to believe that, other things being equal, the removal of non-tariff barriers will exacerbate these problems of unbalanced trade flows, job transfer, and consequent aggregate constraints on trade. What is more, differences in the capabilities of producers in different regions will be equalised only slowly in the absence of inter-regional investment flows. With the removal of non-tariff barriers, however, one of the incentives to relocate investments disappears – the need to relocate production inside protective walls.

In practice, of course, other things are never equal, and short-term or exogenous factors may modify the logic of general mechanisms. In the 1980s, for example, the persistence of EC trade surpluses with the US trading bloc made it easier to absorb endogenous strains. In 1990, after German reunification, the German surplus disappeared, and some of the deficit countries secured significant improvements in export volumes to Germany.

There is, none the less, a fundamental problem in that the internal market programme envisages a model of liberal market integration which will place tighter constraints on national economic authorities without the establishment of the central EC budgets capable of assuming the functions they previously exercised. In the past, nation-states were able to relax the macroeconomic constraints through their fiscal amd monetary policies. In a single market, and *a fortiori* with a single currency, their freedom to act in this manner will diminish. Yet if incomes fall in the weaker areas of Europe, so will demand and investment.

The structural funds: an adequate response?

The standard response to these arguments is that Community financial instruments (such as European Coal and Steel Community grants and loans, European Investment Bank facilities), and in particular the Structural Funds comprising the European Regional Development Fund (ERDF), the European Social Fund (ESF), and the 'guidance' section of the Agricultural Guidance and Guarantee Fund – all financed from the EC Budget) – will be used to offset any increase in regional and spatial imbalance.

The Commission has concentrated Structural Fund resources on infrastructural projects and vocational training. In 1975–86 81.6 per cent of the commitments (funds allocated) under the ERDF were for infrastructural projects. (Industrial projects received a correspondingly small share: 17 per cent in 1985, 12 per cent in 1986, 7 per cent in 1987 and 5 per cent in 1988.) In 1986 over 80 per cent of ESF commitments were for vocational training. There has been no real attempt to use these funds to exert

Table 9.3   EC budget commitments, by category of expenditure, for 1988 and 1992 (projections) (ECU million in 1988 prices)

	1988	1992
Agricultural Guarantee	27,500	29,600
'Structural Funds'	7,790	13,450
Agricultural Guidance	1,201	
ERDF	3,648	
ESF	2,865	
Repayments and administration	5,700	3,550
Other policies	3,213	5,200
Monetary reserve	1,000	1,000
Total	45,303	52,800
Appropriations as a per cent of Community GDP	1.1	1.2

Source: Cutler et al 1989: 90 and 94

direct influence on the location of economic activities. Instead, reliance has been placed on the indirect method of altering the resource endowments of less developed areas. Whether measures of this kind will prove adequate is questionable.[3] Investment in skills, for example, is very likely to reflect the existing profile of jobs within a region rather than the new jobs that are needed in order to close the gap with more developed regions.

In an earlier section I indicated that in assessing the impact of state expenditure on patterns of regional development, we should look at the totality of that expenditure, not just at the elements earmarked for regional projects. The biggest part of the EC budget is, in fact, absorbed by the price support provisions of the CAP, which for the most part transfers resources to farmers in the richer areas of the community (see Howe, Chapter 16, on agriculture). Compared with these expenditures, the resources devoted to the Regional, Social and Agricultural Guidance Funds (less than 20 per cent of the EC budget in 1988), which operate in favour of less developed areas, are quite small. Their impact is further offset by the distribution of the Framework Funds (Eureka, ESPRIT, etc), which go to support research and development and innovation in strong regional economies.

What is more, plans for the expansion of the Community Budget are quite limited: it is intended to increase it from 1.12 to 1.17 per cent of Community GDP 1988–92 (see Table 9.3). The Structural Funds are projected to increase in real terms by 70 per cent, with an increase of ECU 5.7 billion in ERDF expenditure. These projections depend, however, on a planned curtailment of expenditure on agricultural price support whose implementation is far from certain. At the same time it is important to bear in mind that Spain and Portugal, which contain a high proportion of the poorest regions in Europe, only joined in 1986. A major increase would therefore be needed, simply to meet the needs of these two countries. It therefore seems questionable whether the funds envisaged are adequate to deal with existing imbalances and the new disequilibria that the removal of non-tariff barriers will generate.[4]

There is little doubt that moves towards fixed exchange rates or monetary integration would increase these strains: economies and firms with low levels of productivity would collapse, surpluses in strong areas would increase, and incomes in less developed areas would fall due to the loss of employment and the wage reductions required for adjustment. With closer integration, national governments would face tighter constraints, and would have less freedom to transfer resources to deficit regions, while the national economies would themselves become regions of Europe. In these circumstances the use of a method of adjustment which does not depend on competitive recessions presupposes a major expansion of the responsibilities and resources of the EC itself.

Additional competences and resources are a precondition for increased public investments in, and welfare transfers to, less developed areas. To identify this need does not imply acceptance of the principles of the Fordist welfare state, that is the deduction of a part of the direct incomes of the employed to provide a pool out of which money incomes could be paid to those who, for whatever reason, were unable to make a living out of direct wage payments (and who, if in receipt of benefits, were not allowed to do paid work). With the reappearance of high rates of unemployment, the cost of this peculiar kind of solidarity increased, and large sections of the population were denied the self- and social esteem that useful work confers. It is for these reasons that some (see Lipietz 1989a) have suggested the development (as an alternative to the Fordist welfare state) of a third, self-managed sector, dedicated to socially useful work. In less developed areas in particular, the establishment of agencies financed out of welfare transfers, and placed under the democratic control of contractors (local communities, voluntary agencies, environmental protection agencies) would stop the current waste of human resources, allow the development of social services where none exists, facilitate environmental improvements and the creation of a richer cultural life, and contribute to the 'humanisation of economic relations'.

The need for investment decentralisation without incentives competition

The crisis of the welfare state was associated with an increase in the operational weakness of state economic intervention, and at the end of the 1970s significant changes in the organisation, character and goals of nation-states were set in motion. In the field of spatial policies government measures were, for example, scaled down and modified. As Allen, Yuill and Bachtler (1989) show, the objectives, instruments and delivery mechanisms of incentives policies changed in several ways:

1   the extent of eligible areas contracted, spending fell and discretionary policies replaced automatic ones

2   the administration of incentives, decision-making and budgets was decentralised
3   incentives became more closely related to the numbers of jobs created or saved
4   incentives were extended to services.

With these changes in national policy postures went an explosion of local economic development initiatives. The result was, as I indicated earlier, a paradox: a globalisation of economic activities alongside a localisation of political strategies and the identification of a liberal market agenda for collective action (Preteceille 1991).

In all countries there was, however, a category of mobile investments for which regional aid continued to play a significant but variable role. In the 1970s and 1980s major US and Japanese multinationals were anxious to establish production platforms in the EC, in order to get inside the tariff walls that protected European markets. Investments of this kind would, of course, have come to Europe whether there were regional aids or not. Inter-regional and international competition for these investments nevertheless led to a situation in which national, regional and local governments sought to outbid each other in order to influence the decision as to where exactly in Europe these firms would set up: individual governments set the rate of aid at levels required to out-compete other areas, taking into account differences in the attractiveness of different locations for these investors in terms of wages, skill levels, and access to markets. In the case of the United Kingdom, for example, automatic regional aid and discretionary selective assistance played a major role in the attraction of inward investment, and the switch away from automatic towards discretionary incentives not only enabled the government to reduce expenditure and target incentives, but also gave it the discretion required to cap bids from other countries (Dunford 1989). In these circumstances aids were bid up as firms played one area off against another.

The amounts of aid involved are often very large. In one of the few detailed microeconomic studies of incentives available, it was shown, for example, that Ford's £180 million investment in South Wales in the late 1970s received British government subsidies and offsets worth £150 million (cited in Murray 1991: 16). In the more recent case of the Ford–Volkswagen joint venture to make 190,000 minivans per year in Sétubal near Lisbon, escudos 90 billion (£360 million) out of the escudos 450 billion (£1.8 billion) total investment cost were paid by the EC (70 per cent) and the Portuguese government. The Portuguese finance minister was opposed to the deal on the grounds that it created a risk of budgetary deficit, but was overruled. Another escudos 14 billion are needed to develop infrastructures, and the overall public share in the project has been placed at 30–40 per cent.

In the case of a particular area the public funds handed over to large groups may seem warranted as the price of stopping an investment going somewhere else. At a European level, however, government competition for a limited amount of global international investment is wasteful and irrational. At this aggregate level all that results is a transfer of resources from taxpayers to private companies and a reduction in the net tax the firm concerned pays.

What makes the situation worse is that in some cases inward investments are in sectors in which there are already excess capacities in Europe, so that they inevitably have displacement effects. Where, furthermore, strategic industrial objectives exist, decentralised regional incentives can come into conflict with them. Yet the aids given to the new multinational start-ups give them considerable cost advantages over indigenous rivals. In 1989, for example, the European electronics sector recorded a trade deficit of $34 billion. It is a sector which receives substantial state aid on account of its strategic character. At the same time, however, the Italian government paid for more than 50 per cent of the American Texas Instruments' $1 billion Avezzano plant. In the words of Jacques Bouyer, the president of the Groupement des Industries Electroniques, 'no European industrialist has ever received a similar incentive to locate in the United States or in Japan'. (But for a different perspective on EC aid to non-European firms see Hobday, Chapter 14, on the European electronics industry.)

Finally, these investments raise some of the difficulties identified in the past with branch plant economies, but on a larger scale. Competitive strength in the new technologies of the 1990s is rooted not in the existence of production operations, but in the control of key technologies that have multiple applications: making laser printers or photocopiers is less important than involvement in imaging technologies. The alternative course of action involves, therefore, not only agreement and co-operation over incentive levels, but also strategic intervention designed to develop these new technologies independently or in joint ventures. A course of that kind would also require strong measures, and a level of consensus adequate to ensure an equitable distribution of those investments throughout the territories that come together to make the political and economic commitment to implement the project.

Under EC competition policies there has been an attempt to rule out state aids. Along with aid for research and development, regional incentives are viewed as an exception to these rules, yet as 'exceptions' are treated in a strict manner. In relation to national-regional incentives the EC has intervened to set levels of aid, and in the definition of eligible regions. The problem is, however, that no alternative direct method of diverting investments to less developed areas is envisaged. There is clearly a need to control incentives competition. But there is also a need to find new means of leverage over investment location in order to limit the tendencies to uneven development that the neo-liberal programme will create. The alternative is for governments to co-operate and set targets for investment in different areas which are then implemented in planning agreements made with all major European firms and with inward investors (see Holland 1976a; 1976b).

Concluding remarks

In the 1970s and 1980s the unevenness of development in Europe increased, with different regions following different courses in the face of the breakdown of Fordism. In the context of liberal market integration these two realities mutually constrain one another. On the one hand, the need to maintain a trade balance forces the lower productivity areas in the peripheral zones of Europe to grow more slowly so as to limit imports, and to hold down wages so as to increase exports. On the other hand, in the high-wage, high-productivity zones, economic activities are generally more competitive outside of the most labour-intensive sectors. However, the threat posed by competition from low-wage areas limits the extent of redistribution of income and leads to over-cautious approaches to growth. At the level of Europe as a whole the consequence is relative stagnation: eurosclerosis is in fact EC sclerosis, as the superior growth and unemployment records of some non-EC European countries suggests.

The alternative is the selection of another development path. That path would involve an effort to relax the balance of payments constraints on deficit countries, in part via transfers of resources towards less developed areas, the development of a third sector alongside the market and public service sectors, and the transfer to less developed areas of productive activities capable of competing on the basis of high-skill quality production rather than low wages. To achieve this result, a progressive increase in the levels of social protection would be required, to close off the neo-Taylorist path of 'defensive flexibility' and 'defensive restructuring' (Leborgne and Lipietz 1991). The resource endowment of less developed areas would need to be enhanced via infrastructural projects and training programmes. At the same time, however, attempts would have to be made to decentralise high-level functions and the economic activities that use new higher-level skills, through a decentralisation of public investment and the application of leverage over the location of large private groups. In short, it would involve the construction of a real social Europe, and of a more equal Europe, which in the final analysis is the precondition for the expansion of markets on which renewed growth depends.

Notes

1   Two consortia of main contractors were responsible for the construction of the industrial port and the infrastructures for the steelworks: COGITAU and Timperio Spa. As much as 70 per cent of the subcontracts were won by Mafia entrepreneurs, who dominated the construction and haulage sectors, and an 8 per cent levy was imposed on all subcontracts carried out by non-Mafia firms. (Mafia enterprises, it should be said, have several advantages: the *cosche* ('family' links) can discourage competition, wages are held down, and Mafia enterprises have access to immense financial resources flowing from illegal activities.) COGITAU went so far as to make one of the main Mafia entrepreneurs (Gioacchino Piromalli) an official associate (Arlacchi 1988: 93–4).

2   Table 9.4 shows that over the period 1967–80 the share of Western Europe (the EC and EFTA) in world GDP fell significantly in volume, and by a small amount in value. In the case of Japan, volume increased, and value increased even more sharply, while in Latin America an increase in volume was associated with a reduction in value. Two modes of integration can be distinguished here: one which aims at the production of high-quality and high-value output, and one which aims at quantitative increases in the output of goods and services that command low prices on world markets. In relation to these paths Europe finds itself between Japan and Latin America (Leborgne and Lipietz 1990: 5).

The same variations are found within Western Europe. In volume terms all the economies listed, except those of Southern Europe (Spain, Portugal and Greece), lost shares of world output. But just as in the case of Latin America, the economies of Southern Europe increased their share more in volume than in value terms. West Germany and Italy lost in volume but gained in value. What emerges is an image of a Northern Europe that is stagnant overall, but has some zones whose position has strengthened in value terms, and a Southern Europe where growth has been rapid, but where, with the exception of (Northern) Italy, growth has been in the form of increases in the volume of output rather than increases in the value goods and services could command on global markets.

Table 9.4 The shares of different areas in world output

| | The share of world GDP | | | |
| | At purchasing power standards | | At current exchange rates | |
	1967	1986	1967	1986
United States	25.8	21.4	33.8	26.6
Western Europe	26.3	22.9	26.4	26.2
West Germany	5.0	4.2	5.1	5.7
France	3.8	3.4	4.9	4.6
Italy	3.9	3.5	3.6	3.8
Britain	4.8	3.5	4.8	3.6
Southern Europe	3.8	4.2	2.8	2.9
Japan	5.8	7.7	5.2	12.4
Latin America	6.9	7.9	5.1	4.6

Source: CEPII, cited in Leborgne and Lipietz 1990: 19

3   In their study Cutler et al (1989) suggest that the use of the Structural Funds may serve to impose liberal market discipline. The system of matching grants, now slated to play a greater role, requires governments to contribute to the financing of projects the Commission approves. The volume of investment required to make a substantial impact on the gap between rich and poor regions is, however, immense. In the case of Greece, for example, the Padoa-Schioppa programme for upgrading infrastructure would, it was estimated, cost nearly ECU 3 billion a year. In 1989 Greece received ECU 850 million from the Structural Funds, so that a Padoa-Schioppa infrastructural programme would require Greece to invest ECU 2.1 billion a year. That sum is equivalent to 85 per cent of Greek public sector capital formation in 1988. At the same time, however, the Padoa-Schioppa report insisted that Greece and other poor countries should reduce their public sector deficits as a condition for the receipt of structural funds. If revenue did not increase, then, the Greek government would have to reduce its overall level of expenditure while increasing its expenditure on infrastructure. In this way the Commission 'could acquire new powers to determine the direction of public spending in poorer member states' (Cutler et al 1989: 102–4).

4   The initiatives for the reform of the Structural Funds are none the less innovative. The EC measures adopted in 1988 sought a concentration of resources on five priority objectives, rationalisation of methods of assistance, and a doubling of financial resources. Three of the five objectives were regional in character and two were sectoral viz. – (1) to promote the development and structural adjustment of less developed areas with a GDP per head of less than 75 per cent of the EC average; (2) to reconvert regions whose industries are in serious decline; (3) to combat long-term unemployment; (4) to facilitate the occupational integration of young people; and (5) to adjust agricultural structures and promote the development of rural areas. For 1989–93 the Commission allocated ECU 38.3 billion for Objective 1, ECU 7.2 billion for Objective 2, ECU 7.4 billion for Objectives 3 and 4, and ECU 6.2 billion for Objective 5, with ECU 1.2 billion set aside for other measures.

In relation to the regional objectives, the reform involves multi-annual programmed finance (Community Support Frameworks) for agreed regional development programmes, with the possibility of enhanced roles for regional assemblies and direct links between these assemblies and Brussels.

References

Albrechts L, Moulaert F, Roberts P, Swyngedouw E (eds) (1989) *Regional Policy at the Crossroads: European Perspectives*. Jessica Kingsley

Allen K, Yuill D, Bachtler J (1989) Requirements for an effective regional policy. In Albrechts et al (eds) (1989)

Arlacchi P (1988) *Mafia Business: The Mafia Ethic and the Spirit of Capitalism*. Oxford University Press

Beckouche P (1991) French 'high-tech' and space : a double cleavage. In Benko and Dunford (eds) (1991)

Benko G, Dunford M (eds) (1991) *Industrial Change and Regional Development*. Belhaven

Boyer R (ed) (1988) *The Search for Labour Market Flexibility: The European Economies in Transition*. Clarendon Press

Cecchini P, Catinat M, Jacquemin A P (1988) *The European Challenge, 1992: The Benefits of a Single Market: Cecchini Report*. Wildwood House

Cicciotti Enrico (1979) *The Mobilisation of Indigenous Potential in Italy: A Regional Policy Strategy*. Internationales Institut für Management und Verwaltung, Berlin

Coriat B (1991) Technical flexibility and mass production: flexible specialisation and dynamic flexibility. In Benko and Dunford (eds) (1991)

Costello N, Michie J, Milne S (1989) *Beyond the Casino Economy: Planning for the 1990s*. Verso

Cutler T, Haslam C, Williams J, Williams K (1989) *1992 – the Struggle for Europe: A Critical Evaluation of the European Community*. Berg

Davezies L, Larrue C, Prud'homme R (1983) *Les Départements qui Payent pour les Autres: Essai sur la Répartition Spaciale des Fonds Budgétaires*. Institut d'Urbanisme de Paris, Université de Paris – Val de Marne

Del Monte A (1988) Effetti della politica di industrializzazione sulla nascita di nuove imprese. In Giannola A (ed) *L'Economia e il Mezzogiorno*. Milan, Franco Angeli

Dunford M (1986) Integration and unequal development: the case of Southern Italy, 1951–73. In Scott A J, Storper M (eds) *Production, Work, Territory: The Geographical Anatomy of Industrial Capitalism*. Allen & Unwin, Boston, Mass.

Dunford M (1988) *Capital, the State and Regional Development*. Pion

Dunford M (1989) Technopoles, politics and markets: the development of electronics in Grenoble and Silicon Glen. In Sharp M, Holmes P (eds) *Strategies for New Technology*. Philip Allan

Dunford M (1990) Theories of regulation. *Environment and Planning D: Society and Space* **8**: 297–321

Dunford M (1991) Industrial trajectories and social relations in areas of new industrial growth. In Benko and Dunford (eds) (1991)

Friedman A L (1977) *Industry and Labour: Class Struggle at Work and Monopoly Capitalism*. Macmillan

Graziani A (1988) Il Mezzogiorno e l'economia di oggi. In Tamburrino L, Villari M (eds) *Questioni del Mezzogiorno. Le Ipotesi di Sviluppo nel Dibattito Meridionalistico degli Anni Ottanta*. Riuniti, Rome

Hart M, Harrison R T (1990) Inward investment and economic change: the future role of regional development agencies. Paper presented at IBG'90, Glasgow, January

Holland S (1976a) *Capital Versus the Regions*. Macmillan

Holland S (1976b) *The Regional Problem*. Macmillan

Horowitz D (1967) *From Yalta to Vietnam: American Foreign Policy in the Cold War*. Penguin

Izzo L (1990) Un riesame critico della politica di sviluppo del Meridione. Paper presented at the *Forum Internazionale su 'Le Politiche Industriali per il Sud Europa'*, Taormina, 12–13 October

Leborgne D, Lipietz A (1988) L'après-fordisme et son espace. *Les Temps Modernes* **43**(601): 75–114

Leborgne D, Lipietz A (1990) Avoiding two-tiers Europe. *Labour and Society* **15**(2)

Leborgne D, Lipietz A (1991) Two social strategies in the production of new industrial spaces. In Benko and Dunford (eds) (1991)

Lipietz A (1989a) *Choisir l'Audace: Une Alternative pour le XXIème Siècle*. La Découverte

Lipietz A (1989b) The debt problem, European integration and the new phase of the world crisis. *New Left Review* **178**: 37–50

Murray R (1991) *Local Space: Europe and the New Regionalism. Economic Practice and Policies for the 1990s*. Manchester, Council for Local Economic Strategies; Stevenage, South East Economic Development Strategy

Padoa-Schioppa T (1987) *Efficiency, Stability and Equity: A Strategy for the Evolution of the Economic System of the European Community*. Oxford University Press

Preteceille E (1991) Globalisation de l'économie, localisation de la politique. *Espaces et Sociétés* **59**: 5–36

Smith M P, Feagin J R (eds) (1987) *The Capitalist City: Global Restructuring and Community Politics*. Basil Blackwell

Veltz P (1991) New models of production organisation and trends in spatial development. In Benko and Dunford (eds) (1991)

Part III
Europe and the world

CHAPTER 10

The EC, the USA and Japan: the trilateral relationship in world context

PETER HOLMES and ALASDAIR SMITH

Introduction

In this chapter we address the central issue of Europe's economic relations, past and future, with the rest of the world; we concentrate on the trilateral relationship between the EC, the USA and Japan. The formerly communist countries of Eastern and Central Europe (including the 'independent states' which have replaced the old Soviet Union) play a small role in world trade, partly because of their low income levels, partly because the economic system under which they operated until a few years ago discouraged international trade (see Alan Smith; Chapter 6 in this volume). EFTA is small by comparison with the EC, and its trade patterns are in any case very similar to those of the Community. From 1 January 1993, furthermore, the EC and EFTA will be linked together in the 'European Economic Area' (EEA), which formalises and extends the *de facto* free trade regime that has governed trade between the two areas for many years. In using the EC as a proxy for Europe, then, we make a useful and reasonable simplification. The grounds for focusing on the relationships of the EC with the two other industrial giants are obvious: those relationships account for the bulk of the Community's extra-European trade, just as the three sides of the triangle account for the bulk of total world trade. EC trade with the developing world is quantitatively on a fairly small scale. But it is immensely important for a number of reasons, and is treated separately by Christopher Stevens (Chapter 11 in this volume).

The basic facts of Europe's present position in world trade are set out in Tables 10.1–10.3.

Trade between developed countries is largely *intra-industry trade*, in which fairly similar goods are exchanged – a given country exporting cars, electrical appliances and metal products to its partners, and importing cars, electrical appliances and metal products from its partners. By contrast, most trade between developed and developing countries can be explained in terms of differences in factor endowments or conditions of production: labour-rich, low-technology countries trading labour-intensive, low-technology products like clothing and toys for capital-intensive or skill-intensive, higher-technology products like computers and cars from skill-rich and capital-rich

Table 10.1 European Communities (EC6, EC12) third country exports by product group, 1968–88 (per cent)

	1968		1978		1988	
	EC6	EC12	EC6	EC12	EC6	EC12
Chemicals	12.1	11.1	12.1	11.4	13.4	13.6
Other non-electric machinery	15.2	14.4	15.9	15.7	13.7	13.6
Other consumer goods	7.4	7.7	8.1	8.5	10.3	11.2
Automotive products	11.4	11.6	11.0	9.5	12.8	9.3
Other semi-manufacturers	8.7	9.3	9.4	11.0	9.4	9.3
Food	7.4	8.6	7.0	7.6	7.3	7.3
Office machinery and telecommunications	4.5	4.3	4.1	3.8	5.4	5.3
Other transport equipment	3.7	4.5	3.8	4.6	3.6	5.2
Electric machinery and apparatus	4.7	4.6	5.1	4.8	4.7	4.4
Iron and steel	7.3	6.4	7.0	6.7	4.4	4.3
Textiles	5.1	5.2	3.5	3.3	3.6	3.0
Fuels	3.7	2.8	4.2	4.0	1.9	2.8
Residual	0.9	1.2	1.7	2.0	2.3	2.6
Clothing	1.7	1.9	1.5	1.6	2.1	2.2
Power generating machinery	0.6	0.7	2.0	2.3	1.4	2.1
Non-ferrous metals	2.6	2.8	1.6	1.5	1.7	1.6
Raw materials	2.2	2.2	1.4	1.2	1.5	1.5
Ores and minerals	0.8	0.7	0.6	0.5	0.5	0.7
Total merchandise exports	100	100	100	100	100	100

Source: GATT 1991 from UNSO, Comtrade database

advanced countries. It is one of the key features of the trade relationship between Japan and the rest of the industrial world that it involves inter-industry as well as intra-industry trade, and this sheds a lot of light on the tensions that affect that relationship.

Symmetry and asymmetry in the trilateral relationship

Trade between the USA and Japan was notoriously imbalanced throughout the 1980s, with the United States frequently reporting trade deficits in excess of $100 billion, of which over half found a counterpart in the Japanese trade surplus with the United States. At times Japanese imports were about half Japanese exports, and vice versa for the USA. Meanwhile the EC as a whole had a current account surplus of just under 1 per cent of GNP from 1983 to 1990. The overall EC surplus was, of course, composed of a series of sub-totals, with Germany running a consistent surplus while other EC states had deficits totalling less than the German surplus. The EC has, certainly, run a trade deficit with Japan, but the nature of the deficit is quite different from that of the corresponding American one. These deficits have been a fruitful source of controversy and misunderstanding, so it is worth pausing to clarify some important points of principle.

A trade deficit represents an excess of consumption and investment over production, or, to put it another way, an excess of investment over saving; a trade surplus

Table 10.2 European Communities (EC6, EC12) third country imports by product group, 1968–88 (per cent)

	1968		1978		1988	
	EC6	EC12	EC6	EC12	EC6	EC12
Fuels	18.0	17.9	26.5	28.1	12.2	12.8
Office machinery and telecommunications	2.7	2.5	4.5	4.4	10.3	11.4
Food	21.6	22.6	15.8	15.6	11.0	10.0
Other consumer goods	3.4	3.3	5.7	5.5	8.9	9.2
Other semi-manufacturers	6.1	6.8	6.9	7.8	8.1	7.9
Chemicals	5.2	4.7	5.9	4.9	8.1	6.6
Raw materials	11.6	12.4	6.0	6.8	5.0	5.6
Other non-electric machinery	4.9	4.1	4.3	3.9	5.5	5.4
Automotive products	1.7	1.0	3.0	2.2	5.4	4.5
Clothing	1.0	1.0	3.0	2.6	4.6	4.3
Residual	1.6	1.2	2.4	2.1	3.5	3.9
Electric machinery and apparatus	1.9	1.7	1.9	1.6	3.2	3.2
Other transport equipment	2.6	3.3	2.3	3.3	2.3	3.2
Non-ferrous metals	7.1	7.3	2.8	2.7	2.9	2.9
Ores and minerals	6.6	6.1	3.5	3.5	2.6	2.8
Textiles	1.9	2.0	2.5	2.2	2.7	2.6
Iron and steel	1.9	1.9	2.2	1.9	2.4	2.1
Power generating machinery	0.2	0.2	0.8	0.9	1.3	1.6
Total merchandise imports	100	100	100	100	100	100

Source: GATT 1991 from UNSO, Comtrade database

represents precisely the reverse. It is possible on this basis to interpret the US deficit with Japan as the natural outcome of interaction between a low-saving economy and a high-saving one, between a country that wants to spend a lot of money on defence without raising taxes and one that does not want to spend much money on defence at all. The Japanese sell cars to the United States and invest the dollars thus earned in US government bonds. To describe this as a 'natural' outcome of differences in saving behaviour is not to imply that there are no grounds for concern. On the contrary, such a process implies a sustained growth of US debt to Japan, and ultimately a major readjustment or even financial crisis if the Japanese ever decide that they do not want to hold any more American assets. But to see the deficit, as do many American observers and especially many American politicians, simply as the result of 'unfair' Japanese practices or of American uncompetitiveness, is at best to miss a central *macroeconomic* point. We return to this issue later.

The European deficit with Japan is different because it is not an element within a greater deficit. Rather it is a specific deficit matched (in fact more than matched) by a trade surplus with the rest of the world (including a substantial one with the United States). The 'natural' explanation for this pattern would be that Japan is a resource-poor country which has to import natural resources, especially energy from the Middle East, and has to pay for these imports through exports to the EC (and the USA). European politicians and observers are, however, as reluctant as their American

Table 10.3 Leading partners in European Communities (EC12) merchandise trade, 1981–8 (million ECU and per cent)

	Exports				Imports			
Countries	Million ECU 1988	Share in total exports 1988	Compound annual growth rate 81–8	85–8	Countries	Million ECU 1988	Share in total imports 1988	Compound annual growth rate 81–8	85–8
United States	71,795	19.8	9.3	−5.7	United States	68,319	17.6	3.2	−0.3
Switzerland	35,872	9.9	7.1	7.1	Japan	41,565	10.7	13.4	13.3
Austria	22,510	6.2	9.7	7.6	Switzerland	29,428	7.6	8.2	7.5
Sweden	21,120	5.8	7.8	0.5	Sweden	21,943	5.7	8.0	3.8
Japan	17,016	4.7	16.3	17.6	Austria	16,869	4.4	11.8	9.5
Canada	10,122	2.8	11.8	0.7	Soviet Union	12,988	3.4	−1.2	−14.4
Soviet Union	10,113	2.8	2.9	−6.8	South Africa	12,533	3.2	8.0	9.8
Norway	8,510	2.3	4.7	−3.9	Norway	12,498	3.2	2.6	−11.0
Finland	7,762	2.1	9.8	6.3	Brazil	9,329	2.4	7.2	−3.8
Saudi Arabia	7,571	2.1	−5.1	−11.7	Finland	8,993	2.3	8.3	5.9
Hong Kong	6,766	1.9	14.3	14.1	Canada	8,407	2.2	2.8	3.6
Australia	6,365	1.8	6.7	−4.0	Taiwan	8,064	2.1	17.2	26.4
South Africa	6,358	1.8	−1.5	3.8	Korea, Rep. of	7,233	1.9	17.0	29.2
China	5,801	1.6	16.7	−6.9	China	7,004	1.8	16.6	21.2
Yugoslavia	5,713	1.6	3.7	−1.1	Hong Kong	6,316	1.6	6.8	9.4
India	5,637	1.6	7.2	−0.7	Yugoslavia	5,891	1.5	14.9	7.0
Turkey	5,225	1.4	12.5	−1.1	Saudi Arabia	5,470	1.4	−24.9	−14.0
Israel	4,712	1.3	11.2	6.3	Libya	5,223	1.3	−6.4	−24.1
Taiwan	4,459	1.2	21.6	24.9	Australia	4,884	1.3	8.4	−0.5
Korea, Rep. of	4,391	1.2	21.0	16.7	Algeria	4,863	1.3	−4.1	−25.2
Singapore	4,066	1.1	9.8	2.2	Turkey	4,346	1.1	17.1	10.4
Algeria	3,703	1.0	−6.9	−20.5	Poland	3,360	0.9	6.8	−2.0
Egypt	3,675	1.0	−3.1	−17.4	India	3,256	0.8	7.7	2.9
Brazil	3,121	0.9	2.3	5.2	Iran	3,106	0.8	−3.3	−22.7
Iran	2,872	0.8	−6.3	−18.7	Singapore	2,993	0.8	12.1	12.3
Poland	2,756	0 8	2.4	0.3	Thailand	2,966	0.8	10.2	9.1
Libya	2,716	0.7	−15.0	−9.5	Israel	2,885	0.7	7.0	1.7
Morocco	2,609	0.7	3.5	−0.8	Nigeria	2,876	0.7	−10.1	−36.8
Iraq	2,420	0.7	−14.7	−17.6	Iraq	2,786	0.7	−4.3	−26.5
Venezuela	2,403	0.7	0.9	1.6	Malaysia	2,687	0.7	5.1	−1.5
Hungary	2,354	0.6	2.4	−1.8	Agentina	2,623	0.7	3.4	−7.2
Mexico	2,296	0.6	−6.5	−6.5	Mexico	2,456	0.6	−6.1	−21.8
United Arab Emirates	2,288	0.6	−2.6	−11.1	Morocco	2,271	0.6	7.2	2.1
Czechoslovakia	2,170	0.6	6.2	3.3	Romania	2,234	0.6	1.9	−8.4
Nigeria	2,165	0.6	−17.4	−21.5	Czechoslovakia	2,211	0.6	4.7	−0.9
Thailand	2,071	0.6	12.2	8.2	Chile	2,183	0.6	7.7	7.6
Tunisia	2,003	0.6	−0.2	−4.5	Hungary	2,158	0.6	5.5	2.3
Indonesia	1,934	0.5	−1.2	−5.2	Indonesia	2,134	0.6	8.3	3.3
Pakistan	1,605	0.4	5.9	−1.1	Kuwait	2,099	0.5	−6.1	−24.3
Kuwait	1,394	0.4	−5.8	−18.6	Egypt	1,641	0.4	−9.8	−26.6
Total of the above	318,439	87.8	5.1	−1.3	Total of the above	351,091	90.6	3.4	−0.9
Total trade	362,788	100.0	4.6	−1.4	Total trade	387,519	100.0	2.9	−1.6

Source: GATT 1991 from Eurostat, External Trade Statistical Yearbook, 1989

counterparts to accept 'natural' explanations of Japanese success in exporting manufactures, and are subjecting the Japanese phenomenon to ever closer scrutiny.

The real problem which both the USA and the EC face is that Japanese imports, whether they contribute to overall balance of payments problems or not, are concentrated in particular sectors, namely cars and electronics. This brings us back to one of our earlier points. In contrast to the general pattern of trade between advanced economies, Japanese–EC/US trade is to a great extent based on inter-industry rather than intra-industry trade. Competitive pressures in intra-industry trade can be handled by a given enterprise through a relatively painless process of seeking a new niche in the same market. Japanese competition, by contrast, seems to require an all or nothing response, and to threaten the extinction of whole industries and therefore whole lines of technological development (see Chapters 12–15 in this volume). The OECD forecasts that the macroeconomic imbalances will shrink sharply in the 1990s, but that the problem of industrial mix will remain.

Finally in this introductory section, it is increasingly inappropriate to think about world economic relations in terms of trade alone. Investment flows are becoming an increasingly important dimension of the world economy. Investment is harder to trace than trade, so we have a less reliable picture of world investment flows than of flows of imports and exports; but in general terms the pattern of world investment is similar to that of trade, with the biggest flows being among the developed countries rather than from the developed to the developing. Inevitably, given the overall balance of payments trends we have just noted, the outward flow of Japanese investment has been among the most marked, and most controversial, of the features of the 'globalisation of business'.

It is these issues that set the agenda for the succeeding sections of this chapter. First, we look at the institutional context of EC trade policy and assess the real level of protection that policy has afforded. Then we look at the question of how 'common' the policy has in fact been and how it has related to competition policy, devoting a special section to the Common Agricultural Policy. The next two sections come back round to the crucial trilateral issues outlined above, by focusing on two key manufacturing sectors – electronics and cars. In shifting the perspective towards the future we look first at the concept of 'strategic trade policy' and then at the special issues raised by the reform process in Eastern Europe. We end by posing two fundamental and interrelated questions. Will '1992' bring the European Community closer to the rest of the world? And what is the future position of Europe in the international division of labour?

The framework of trade policy

The EC is part of the GATT system. Though it is the member states, not the EC itself, that are the signatories of GATT, the Community (in the future the Union) negotiates as a single entity. The original Rome Treaty specified under Article 113 that by 1969 there should be a true common commercial policy with all trade barriers against third countries unified, while Article 115 provided an escape clause in allowing for the survival of national trade policies as long as the common policy stayed on the drawing-board. In the event, the member states achieved the goal of a common tariff regime, but failed to unify other policies affecting trade, such as technical barriers, administrative restrictions and 'voluntary export restraints'. In 1982 the Commission produced a list of national trade policy measures which it recognised as formal derogations from the common commercial policy. The Commission chose to ignore many other measures in the hope that the reality of a single market would eventually lead to their abandonment.

Common tariff or no, tariff barriers are in practice of very limited significance. As much as 29 per cent of EC imports bear a tariff of 5 per cent or under, and 90 per cent pay under 15 per cent (GATT 1991: 263). What is perhaps more important than the height of tariffs is the fact that they are 'bound' under GATT rules. All GATT members are bound not to raise tariffs on industrial products, and indeed are committed to a series of 'rounds' of tariff cuts.

One of the unspoken aims of the '1992' Plan was to *force* the member states to accept the logic of having a single regime *vis-à-vis* the outside world, and it will in a sense be possible from 1993 to treat the EC as a single trading body. The GATT secretariat has already, in its series of reviews of trade policy by signatories, published a single report on the trade policy of 'the European Communities'. The EC has just joined its first international organisation (the UN Food and Agriculture Organisation) as one entity. But member states are still jealous of their trade policy powers. A complex legal debate is going on about whether the European Commission is authorised to negotiate and the Council of Ministers to agree trade accords on behalf of individual member states, or whether the whole EC can only be bound if each individual state signs given agreements (see Victor 1990). The EC Commission tends to argue that where there is Community competence only Community organs can act. Some member states insist that unless the EC Treaties specifically provide for Community agencies to act, member states must endorse any collective action. This is a minor technicality when all member states are agreed, but there is more than symbolism at issue when, by insisting on the need to sign separately, member states are reaffirming their ultimate right to act independently (see Anne Stevens, Chapter 4, and Peter Holmes, Chapter 3, in this volume). The Uruguay Round of GATT negotiations appears to have led to more formal collective action by the EC-12 than previous rounds, in that the EC Commission is authorised to be the spokesman for the twelve member states. But the pattern of that authorisation makes for a certain rigidity. The EC's negotiators come to the conference table with a negotiating position that has already been hammered out in intra-EC deliberations, and this may make it difficult for them to make concessions. The point has come out with particular clarity in relation to negotiations on agriculture, where the inflexibility of the EC's position is surely linked to the lack of an intra-EC consensus on the right direction to go in. (Contrast this to the position of the US administration, which is given 'fast track' negotiating authority by Congress to get the best deal it can, and then submit it for ratification or rejection as a package.) Thus a final agreement (uncertain at time of writing) will have to have the support of all EC member states. Draft agreements drawn up by the GATT secretariat have provided for a compromise on the legal issue of who should sign, by allowing both the European Communities and all the member states to sign.

The member states of the EC are obliged under EC law to remove all mutual trade barriers. The EC itself bears the GATT obligation to offer 'most favoured nation' (MFN) treatment to all the other signatories of GATT, ie to eschew any kind of discrimination that might lead to suspicion of the formation of trade blocs. In fact it does not do so. The EC is embedded in a web of preferential trade agreements which exploit various exception clauses in the GATT text to offer lower tariffs to its immediate neighbours, and to certain less developed countries with which it wants good diplomatic relations.

Exception clauses or no, doubts have been raised as to the compatibility with GATT of the EC's modes of circumvention of the MFN rules. Even the links with the EFTA zone left a GATT panel 'unable to reach a conclusion' on the question of compatibility with the General Agreement (GATT 1990: 62). However, the EC has, by and large, respected 'tariff binding' – the other pillar of GATT. We argue elsewhere (see Holmes, Chapter 3 in this volume) that the crucial achievement of the EC on the internal plane was the solidity of the pledge that trade barriers inside the EC would never be increased. Forcing them down to zero was a way of signalling this intent with the maximum clarity. The GATT system has set itself the more modest aim of binding tariffs; that is, ensuring that they could only go down, never up. Like other trading powers, the EC has basically stuck to this bargain. Thus tariffs are not an instrument that European politicians can use at their discretion to favour selected interest groups. Both importers and home producers know that the current level of tariff is a ceiling – offering the carrot of free market access to those producers who can be competitive at the given rates and the stick of free competition from outside to those who cannot (see OECD 1987). Agriculture apart (see Howe, Chapter 16 in this volume), this principle holds pretty well. But it leaves quite a lot of room for discretion on matters other than the basic tariff rates. Indeed just as the removal of tariffs caused the relative, sometimes even absolute, prominence of non-tariff barriers to rise *within* the EC, as governments intent on pursuing their own trade policy *vis-à-vis* the non-EC world found it necessary to erect barriers against the 'deflection' of non-EC goods entering the Community through other member countries with different trade policies, so the GATT rules on tariff binding have induced an exploration at the Community's interface with the rest of the world of 'grey area' measures that do not violate GATT openly.

The Rome Treaty laid down that EC commercial policy was to be agreed by Qualified Majority Voting in the Council of Ministers – on proposals from the EC Commission – and then implemented by the Commission. A complex of committees was set up to oversee the activities of the Commission in this connection. There is considerable controversy over the way the Commission uses the powers that have been delegated to it by the Council of Ministers. Some British observers claim that the Commission has resorted to something akin to cunning to get its own way in the face of potential resistance from the Council of Ministers. It must be said, however, that on the whole the Commission has to act within guidelines set by ministers. To the extent that it has room for manoeuvre, it uses it not to thwart any collective vision, but rather to exploit differences between member states and to choose which one of a number of possible compromises should prevail. As we shall see below, there is considerable debate about anti-dumping actions by the Commission, an area where it enjoys delegated executive power, but it seems that even here there is no general dissatisfaction in the Council of Ministers with the way the Commission is exercising its powers. If there were, the Council would, of course, have the power to instruct the Commission to alter its policy.

One of the most sensitive implications of the '1992' Plan is that all goods from third countries will have to be permitted to circulate freely and on equal terms inside the EC, wherever they enter, as Articles 9 and 10 of the Rome Treaty actually lay down; only then will we be able to talk of a truly single market. That means in effect that member countries will no longer be able to maintain national policies sanctioned under Article 115. We can assume, therefore, that from 1993 there will indeed be a common external trade regime. A *second layer of discrimination* exists, however, and the treatment of external imports will continue to differ according to where they come from, even after 31 December 1992.

There is a complex hierarchy of preferential trade agreements affecting less developed countries (see Christopher Stevens, Chapter 11 in this volume). As far as advanced industrial countries are concerned, we can distinguish between intra-European relations and relations with Japan and the USA. As we saw earlier, the EC plus EFTA is effectively a free trade zone; it is also understood that formal non-tariff barriers are not applied between the EC and EFTA, though the EEA agreement does allow the invocation of emergency safeguard measures (see pp. 194–5). In contrast, goods imported from Japan and the USA are subject to the full Common External Tariff and any other measures of trade policy the EC cares to impose.

The actual level of protection

It is a paradox of the present trade policy debate that where special measures such as VERs or anti-dumping duties are not applied, EC trade policy is actually very liberal. Even for Japan and the USA, which do not benefit from any trade concessions beyond the standard GATT obligations, the operational rates of tariff are low. GATT estimated the simple average rate of tariff on industrial products at 6.4 per cent in 1988. There is relatively little deviation around this average. Even for sensitive sectors tariffs are modest: cars bear an average tariff rate of 10 per cent (though some vehicles bear 22 per cent), and textiles and clothing tariffs go from 0 per cent to 17 per cent. Photographic and optical goods carry an average of about 7 per cent. These figures reinforce the view that tariff barriers and their removal are not the most significant element in world trade today.

The standard deviation in 1988 across all EC industrial tariffs was 2.6 per cent. This is important, as it is the differences between tariff rates that determine how much the protective system is altering the direction of economic activity. If some industries have heavy protection and others little, there is an incentive for resources to move into or stay in some sectors rather than others. If, by contrast, all industrial goods were protected equally, then no one industry would benefit relative to others. There are, indeed, some trade restrictions which affect individual sectors very strongly, and without which it is hard to imagine investment taking place within the EC in these sectors, but such measures are usually other than the conventional tariff which figures in the trade textbooks. Non-tariff barriers apart, the most important forms of 'extraordinary' protection are 'safeguard' and 'anti-dumping' tariffs.

Broadly speaking the USA is not subject to trade restrictions other than the regular tariffs in relation to its exports to the EC. The exceptions, and the main bones of contention on trade between the EC and the USA, concern agricultural products and a very limited number of high-tech products. Japanese imports into the EC are in principle treated on the same basis as imports from the USA. The rapid rise of EC imports from Japan in certain very sensitive areas, however, combined with the recession conditions of the 1980s, has led to considerable pressure on the Japanese to 'moderate' their exports to the EC. So far these measures have been negotiated, sometimes tacitly, between the Japanese and individual member states. From 1993 this will no longer be feasible. We take up this point again on pp. 198–203.

Obstacles to a common policy

Let us return to the issue of 'trade deflection' and Article 115. Where a member state has a national barrier to external imports recognised under EC law, and if trade deflection via member states that do not have such barriers is causing 'disruption', the member state in question may at present apply to the EC Commission for permission to impose controls on extra-EC imports as they come in across the intra-EC border. Italy, for example, has exercised the right to stop Japanese cars coming in via France. The most striking use of Article 115 has been in relation to imports of textiles and clothing from less developed and industrialising countries over a period of some thirty years (see Christopher Stevens, Chapter 11 in this volume). Under the rubric of 'Multifibre Arrangements' (MFAs) lasting four to five years each, the main exporting and importing countries sign a series of bilateral voluntary export restraint agreements. These are totally against the principles of GATT, and in order to preserve a façade of legality a special set of exceptional rules have been laid down to govern the quotas.

The cost to consumers in the developed countries is high. The World Bank (1987: 152) cites estimates ranging from $1.4 billion to $6.6 billion for the cost to EC consumers of having to buy textiles and clothing from more expensive sources. Nor is there any evidence that this kind of protection saves jobs. The OECD (1985) notes that in textiles and clothing, as well as in the highly protected iron and steel sector, job losses have continued unabated despite protection. This is partly because restricting imports to keep up prices not only permits the survival of old-fashioned, inefficient firms, but also facilitates the entry of new, more efficient domestic firms. This new entry ultimately drives out the weaklings just as surely as import competition. Peter Holmes (Chapter 3 in this volume, on the integration process) discusses the phenomenon of trade diversion. In the context of the MFA what this means is that inefficient clothing firms in the North of England cannot be protected as long as the UK is part of a customs union, since Italian firms can replace imports from outside the EC. In fact, this is not as high a 'cost' as it seems. The pressure of competition from Italian firms forces UK clothing firms to become more efficient. On the other hand, the higher prices permitted by protection may promote new investment even from local sources, and so induce excess capacity. (The problem is, of course, further intensified when foreign investors from the extra-EC exporting countries can set up plants behind the protective walls too.)

Producers are not easily convinced of the proposition that cutting out one source of competition may simply lead to its replacement by another, so they often plead for the use of intra-EC border measures to segregate national markets against third country competition. The Single European Act did not, in fact, repeal Article 115, and the original White Paper (EC Commission 1985) on the Single Market posited only that Article 115 should not be implementable by the use of intra-EC border controls. Yet the logic of the '1992' Programme is surely its total abolition. What is in practice happening is that the EC Commission is steadily proceeding with its aim of phasing out the use of Article 115 and thus creating a truly common commercial policy. The matter is so sensitive that the Commission is endeavouring to convince the member states of the necessity of *simultaneously* implementing a common external policy and putting an end to the use of Article 115. The directorates of the Commission were at time of writing working on the assumption that the EC will in the future have a totally unified approach to textiles and clothing, with global quotas for products between individual exporters and the entire EC, and with no use of Article 115. However, it is being hinted to exporters that they should not increase their sales to the previously most restricted markets too fast.

The essence of the debate that is going on at the moment is whether the new measures aimed at fashioning a common commercial policy will mark steps towards protectionism or away from it. The external relations directorate of the Commission, in association with the industrial policy divisions, is seeking to 'reassure' business that moving from national to Community policies will not leave them totally at the mercy of Japanese or Korean imports. The reasoning here is entirely political rather than economic, but the economic implications are disturbing. Many writers (eg Hindley 1988) are very concerned about the way that the EC Commission is increasingly invoking anti-dumping duties in areas where national measures were previously in force. Anti-dumping duties were originally developed at the turn of the century to guard against 'predatory pricing', whereby a potential monopolist could undercut newer smaller rivals in order to corner a market. It is widely agreed (Ordover and Saloner 1989) that a special set of rules that go beyond normal anti-trust regulations may be needed for imports. The reason is that it is very expensive for a big firm to engage in predatory price cutting against a small rival, if it is operating in a single geographical territory. The small firm can retaliate against the big firm's home sales base, and the big firm cannot easily confine its price discounts to customers who might be thinking of switching to the new firm. In contrast, where the 'attacking' firm is in a separate country and its home market is protected by tariffs, it is possible to cut prices selectively without suffering either retaliation or loss of home base sales. Thus predatory dumping to capture a world market, and certain other forms of related 'unfair trade practice' often relating to subsidies, are indeed real possibilities (see pp. 203–4 on strategic trade policy). However, most analysts (eg Stegemann 1991) have concluded that there has been widespread abuse of the anti-dumping rules.

GATT permits two forms of contingency measure. Article XIX allows countries suffering a sudden and unforeseen 'surge' of imports to take emergency safeguard measures. But the conditions for doing this are tightly circumscribed, and 'compensation' may have to be offered to injured parties. This puts the country using Article XIX measures in the dock as a violator of GATT, so countries prefer to use Article VI, which permits the use of anti-dumping duties where an exporter is gaining in market share 'unfairly', by selling below his normal price on the home market. The EC Council of Ministers has laid down very complex regulations governing the way the Commission imposes anti-dumping duties. First, sales below 'normal' price must be proved, and then injury must be proved. Even then, the 'Community interest' has to be considered before duties are actually imposed. Considerable discretion exists at each step in the calculation. Critics argue (eg Schuknecht 1991) that it is always exercised in a protectionist way. For example, comparing export prices with 'normal' home prices involves an averaging process. Any home sales below full cost will be treated as abnormal and excluded from the calculation, while any export prices above normal price will be excluded because 'negative dumping' is impossible. The calculation of injury is always dependent on data supplied by the injured party, and the Commission uses informal judgement rather than independent analysis to decided whether loss of intra-EC market share is due to 'unfair' competition. The analysis of Community interest is based on the proposition that the best interests of users and consumers alike are served by the existence of a 'viable community industry', an argument that is, to say the least, controversial.

The Commission has been extremely active in using anti-dumping procedures, particularly in the electronics field (see section on pp. 198–200 and Hobday, Chapter 14 in this volume), and especially against Japan, the NICs and Eastern Europe. Member states have in the past been prepared to use voluntary export restraints as a way of extending the range of restriction on imports from Japan and Korea beyond the coverage of the MFA. However, these risk violating GATT and represent a violation of the Rome Treaty's competition rules as well. The practice has developed among well-organised industries, faced with strong import competition, of seeking government approval for 'industry-to-industry' agreements to limit sales. 'Approval' means that the government may tacitly threaten use of Article XIX measures against the foreign industry, or may just turn a blind eye. Under Japanese law, the Fair Trade Commission can permit limitations on exports if there would otherwise be a threat of trade policy intervention (see GATT 1990). For example the Japanese have agreed with the British car industry to take no more than 11 per cent of the UK market (see pp. 200–3, and Jones, Chapter 13 in this volume). Where agreements like this are made between governments, GATT rules are violated, but the only people who can complain are the other governments – who are not, of course, going to. Where firms or trade associations meet to do deals restricting sales or raising prices, they are in fact forming a cartel. A series of decisions and court cases under Article 85 of the Rome Treaty (see Bourgeois 1989) has made it very clear that such practices are illegal. (The first such case arose when French and Japanese ball-bearing manufacturers agreed to share the French market.)

Anti-dumping actions and VERs carry an importance that goes far beyond their immediate impact. They create disincentives to investment in export success, since they imply that export success may be stymied by European trade barriers; and they create uncertainty for exporters, as they are applied with a high degree of discretion. Outright cartelisation apart, both anti-dumping measures and voluntary export restrictions are likely to have significantly anti-competitive effects. As Patrick Messerlin (1990) has argued, if a price-cutting firm is threatened with anti-dumping action by its less aggressive rivals, there is a clear incentive for all the firms to get together to agree prices that are mutually satisfactory, if less satisfactory for consumers. Export restraints have two kinds of anti-competitive effect: by limiting sales from restrained firms, they reduce the competitive pressure on other firms; and by requiring market-sharing arrangements to be set up by the exporting firms, they make entry of new firms in the exporting country more difficult.

Restrictions on direct imports do, of course, have the perverse effect of attracting inward investment that neutralises the protection. There is, certainly, some disagreement as to how far Japanese inward investments are stimulated by actual or threatened EC protectionism. Thomsen and Nicolaides (1990) argue that globalisation of production is a natural process involving all firms – including the Japanese (see Sharp, Chapter 12 in this volume, on industrial structures). But other writers (eg Belderbos 1991) suggest that EC trade policy *has* been an important factor. In the 1960s many governments were willing to restrict inward investment as well as trade, but considerations of employment and technological conditions make this unrealistic today. Globalisation, whatever its roots, creates a whole new complex of interrelated trade and competition issues, which we treat in the next section.

Trade policy and competition

In an increasingly globalised market it becomes more and more difficult to sustain the view that competition from non-EC-owned firms or non-EC-located production should be regulated differently from wholly indigenous production. The US writer Robert Reich (1990) asks 'Who is "us"?' An increasing proportion of EC-based production is by foreign-owned firms, while EC-owned firms produce more and more abroad. An integrated world market probably brings more technology transfer. And if there are problems of global unfair competition they can be dealt with only by world-wide anti-trust agreements (see Hansen 1991). The internationalisation of business may, in fact, have a major impact on the way the business world on balance views the benefits of protection. Schuknecht (forthcoming) interprets the commitment to an open trade policy within the EC as essentially a triumph of political and economic interests with an export orientation over those more interested in protection against imports. Milner (1988) has shown that multinational firms may well lobby for free trade rather than protection. However, some of the same incentives to take the edge of competition that exist in an national oligopoly situation also exist on a global scale. The European Community, in its most recent statement of principles on industrial and trade policy (EC Commission 1990), has argued that free external competition is an necessary counterpart of a free internal market. However, there are important and difficult issues to face in certain sectors where economies of scale are so large that there may be room only for a very small number of firms in the EC. Merger policy must take trade and technology issues into account. On the whole it seems sensible to argue that we can be more lax about permitting mergers the more open the EC market is. But there does come a point where we must start worrying about global oligopolies, which may form 'strategic alliances', sometimes ostensibly to imitate Japanese *keiretsu* (interlinked) firms. The head of the German Federal cartel office, W. Kartte, has warned that '"strategic alliances" are often tantamount to private market orders, which necessarily lead to distortions of the world economy' (Hansen 1991: 215; see also Holmes 1991). We do therefore need to be vigilant about unfair competition, but not in an oversimplified way that sees all external competition as harmful.

The Common Agricultural Policy

It is certainly the trade effects of the Common Agricultural Policy that have contributed most to the Community's protectionist image. It is fair to add, however, that the Community inherited national traditions of protecting agriculture, traditions found in other developed countries in equal measure, and simply merged them into the CAP.

The CAP attracts particular attention, first because the sheer size of the Community's agricultural trade gives it a major influence on world markets. As the Community limits imports, for example, by imposing levies to bring import prices up to levels at which European farmers can compete, the effect is to depress prices on world markets. Anderson and Tyers (1986) found that the effects of the EC's farm policies on world markets were much bigger in every sector that they studied than the effects of other countries' policies, with the single exception of the rice market, where Japanese import restrictions have indeed a greater impact than the CAP. It is also worth noting that the effects of the CAP are not just on the level of world prices, but also on their variability: guaranteed prices insulate European farmers and consumers from the low prices that obtain in years of plenty, so ensuring that the European market plays no part in absorbing the plenty and implying a bigger price reduction in the rest of the world.

The second feature of the CAP that has brought it into the international spotlight is its 'success' in generating European self-sufficiency through high farm prices. In the early 1960s the Community covered around 90 per cent of its agricultural consumption with own production; by the mid-1980s, according to Anderson and Tyers (1986), it was producing around 105 per cent of its consumption. Keeping up the price of an imported good requires an import tax, whose impact on the level of consumer prices may not be visible to the average citizen, and which contributes positively to budget revenue. Keeping up the price of an exported good requires budgetary expenditure to cover buying the product at the high European price and selling it at the lower world price. As the costs of the CAP have started to appear on the EC budget as well as on consumer budgets, the Community has become more concerned to contain those costs. More important in the present context, as the CAP has constrained the EC to offload its surpluses on to world markets, the costs to farmers outside the Community have become more apparent – and the United States, in particular, has become more militant in its demands for CAP reform.

Although the CAP has ill effects on developing countries, especially in relation to the sugar market (sugar is an unusual product in that it is produced in two quite different ways in temperate and tropical climates), it is other developed countries that (together with European consumers) incur the greatest costs. The CAP has its biggest impact on temperate products, such as beef, lamb, dairy products, sugar beet and grains; it is the interests of exporters of these products in Australia, New Zealand and North America which are most affected.

The extent of the problem that the CAP creates for the world trading system is clearly indicated by the obstacles that it placed in the way of the Uruguay Round of trade negotiations in the period from 1986 to 1992. The Community has been faced with determined pressure from the United States, not itself particularly committed to freer agricultural trade as such but concerned about the increasing competition it faces on world markets from the EC's surpluses, and from the Cairns group of countries, including Australia, whose clear interest as temperate zone agricultural exporters is in freer trade. It continues to defend a policy that imposes great costs on European consumers, increasing costs on the Community budget, and has threatened to scupper a set of trade negotiations in the success of which the Community has a vital interest. Faced with all of these considerations, the EC has been reluctant, to the point of intransigence, to embrace the case for reform. What clearer message do we need about the power of the agricultural lobbies?

Electronics

Many of the points that arose in the discussion of commercial policy can be illustrated by the experience of the electronics industry. The most striking development in this sector is the rise of Japanese firms over the last ten to twenty years. They have moved from being major producers of consumer electronics products in the 1970s to the position of dominant producers in this area and in certain components fields (see Hobday, Chapter 14 in this volume).

EC industry has lobbied intensely for support in this connection. Since the early 1980s the EC has put in place a series of programmes for intra-EC industrial collaboration, but these initiatives have merely served to confirm that here more than anywhere, in the context of a rapidly evolving structure in the industry, trade, competition and technology policy must be integrated.

The Commission has responded to lobbying by embarked on a series of anti-dumping actions in virtually all the areas where Asian producers have been successful – colour TVs, CD players, audio tapes, VCRs. There are strong grounds for querying whether that this kind of protection can work (see Cawson and Holmes 1991). The most obvious one is that since the late 1980s Japanese, Taiwanese and Korean firms (and even one Chinese TV firm) have been investing heavily inside the EC to take advantage of the artificially high prices produced by the anti-dumping duties. The cost to consumers has been considerable, but the gain to EC-owned firms has been minimal. Indeed the latter have almost certainly lost something from the false sense of security arising from the notion that they could afford to delay entry into new product lines. Technological protection through ingenious technical standards does not work either. The new MAC TV standard, for example, is unlikely to be of great benefit for EC industry. Even if it proves to be exactly what EC consumers want, there is no way of ensuring that Asian firms do not simple invest first. If they do, there is no legal way to prevent these firms having access to the entire EC (plus EFTA) market. The EC Commission has tried to impose 'local content requirements' in some cases. This means that electronic products made in foreign-owned factories using imported components may find import restrictions that apply to the relevant finished product being imposed on them as they emerge from the factory. But an EC regulation covering the levying of anti-dumping duties on so-called screwdriver plants making electronics goods has been condemned by GATT. The EC Commission has stated that it will keep this regulation on its books until a new GATT anti-dumping code is agreed, but observers agree that the regulation cannot be used in practice (see EC Commission 1991b: 23).

There is considerable evidence (see Porter 1990, for example) that the success of Japanese consumer electronics may depend as much on fierce internal competition as on any exclusion of foreign firms or 'unfair' trading practice. EC commentators (see EC Commission 1991a) may have more grounds for concern in relation to the electronic components industry. Plausible complaints of dumping have been made with respect to semi-conductors. The Japanese stand accused by the USA and the EC of subsidising production of DRAM memory chips, and thus collectively gaining a near monopoly. This probably represents the most acute challenge there has been to the principle of free trade. Here is a sector where most commentators (see Flamm 1990) accept that Japanese success has been significantly affected by government policies. European firms were never very significant in the sector, but the 1980s saw a retreat by US firms from the memory market, with a 90 per cent share going to Japanese firms according to the EC Commission (1991a). It is no less worrying that in the even more strategic sector of microprocessors two US firms, Intel and Motorola, hold 85 per cent of the world market. It is frankly not at all clear what trade policy can do about this. Selective public procurement led in the past to the promotion of 'national champions' which tended to develop the mentality of defence contractors. There may be a theoretical case for strategic trade policies in such cases (see pp. 203–4). But where the leading EC-based electronics firms are Japanese, there may be more of a case for focusing on the articulation of a binding international code on monopoly and restrictive oligopolistic practices.

Another sector where this kind of problem is likely to arise acutely is telecommunications, where once again globalisation of business means that trade, telecommunications and technology policy issues meet. In the past telecommunications equipment was supplied by 'clubs' of producers to state telecommunications monopolies which could pass on high prices and low quality to captive customers. For better or worse, the utilities are now privatised and on the lookout for the cheapest equipment available. The high R&D costs of telecoms equipment mean that in this industry there is always a temptation to subsidise in order to ensure that exports are offered at (low) marginal cost. The liberalisation and privatisation of intra-EC public procurement raises the question of what will happen if the cheapest supplier is not from another EC state but from the USA or Japan, where huge economies of scale do, indeed, permit sales abroad at lower prices. As with semi-conductors, there is a genuine possibility of unfair competition, and plenty of scope for the interests of users and producers to clash.

In all these policy areas relating to electronics the member states of the EC have pursued rather divergent policies in the past. It is a major challenge to produce a common set of policies that are coherent on all the dimensions involved:

1   across the twelve member states

2   between trade, competition and technology fields
3   across the different elements of the industry (protecting chips production, for example, hurts computer firms).

It would be difficult to overstress the size of the task ahead here.

Cars

The European automotive industry provides a fascinating case-study of European Community trade policy-making. The elimination of non-tariff barriers, as part of the '1992' process, has major implications for external trade policy where different countries have had different external policies. As a result, the Community's institutions face major political and economic difficulties as they confront the implications of the single market programme for the vehicle market.

The car market in Europe shows strong patterns of national preference: the two French producer groups, which have 23 per cent of the EC market, take 60 per cent of the French market and 34 per cent of the Spanish market; Fiat has over 50 per cent of the Italian market, while the UK market is dominated by the US multinationals. The asymmetric pattern of market shares means that some producers are dependent on a limited number of national markets for most of their sales: Fiat makes two-thirds of its Western European car sales in Italy alone, while the two French groups are very dependent on the French and Spanish markets.

Further, a number of EC markets have been subject to restrictions on imports of Japanese cars. In 1977 the Japanese producers agreed a voluntary export restriction with the UK industry, with the connivance and encouragement of the UK government, under which they committed themselves to hold their imports to a share of 11 per cent of the UK market. In France, the Japanese import share is fixed at 3 per cent, by an agreement between the French government and the Japanese producers; while in Italy, Spain and Portugal, Japanese car imports are held to even lower levels through quotas. In the Italian case, a bilateral quota of just 3,000 vehicles was agreed with the Japanese as early as the early 1960s. By contrast, the Japanese market share in the essentially unrestricted German market was 16 per cent in 1990, and averaged 24 per cent in the EC countries other than those specified above in the same year.

Restrictions on imports inevitably impose costs on consumers, because they raise prices. In this case, European producers' market shares are increased, and the combined effect of higher prices and larger shares clearly benefits these producers. Since, however, the principal effect on prices is to raise the prices of Japanese cars, there are benefits to Japanese producers too, to set against their loss of market share. Import restrictions also have subtler effects on the nature of competition in the car market. When Japanese firms face import restrictions, European firms know that an important group of their competitors face limitations on their ability to compete. European firms can therefore set prices that much higher than if they had to worry about their Japanese competitors cutting prices to increase sales. Also, the fact that many of the import restrictions are administered by the Japanese industry acts as a barrier to the entry of new Japanese firms. Thus quantitative restriction on imports is inherently anti-competitive in its implications.

Technically speaking, the planned abolition, after '1992', of Article 115 has limited application to the car market, since the French and UK restrictions on Japanese imports are 'grey area' measures; that is to say, they are not trade restrictions officially recognised by the European Commission as derogations. Their existence has therefore not been dependent on Article 115 support. Nevertheless, national restrictions on Japanese car imports have to be supported by mechanisms which have the same effect as Article 115 border restrictions. A French car-buyer who attempts to circumvent the restrictions on Japanese car imports by buying a car in Germany, for example, will encounter considerable bureaucratic obstacles to registering the car in France. If, however, '1992' abolishes this particular kind of bureaucratic non-tariff barrier to intra-EC trade, by introducing a single European 'type-approval' certificate, for example, then the national restrictions on Japanese car imports will become unsustainable. In the above case, the French restriction on Japanese imports would become ineffective and irrelevant.

The opening up of the French, Spanish and Italian markets to unrestricted Japanese imports would clearly cause great problems for European car-makers, especially for the French and Italian producers who have large shares in these markets. There has been pressure, therefore, on the EC not just to let '1992' destroy national restrictions, but rather to replace them with an EC-wide restriction on Japanese imports.

To add to the difficulties about arriving at a European policy on car imports from Japan, the role of the Japanese firms within the European market is rapidly changing as 'transplant' operations are established. Nissan's plant in England has been functioning since 1988. Toyota and Honda are due to open plants in England in 1992; there are significant Japanese investments in other EC countries, including Spain. The European Commission estimates that the capacity of these transplants will be around 1.2 million cars by the end of 1999, while the UK government is reported to estimate a figure of 2 million (EC vehicle sales . . . 1991). Clearly, if cars produced in Europe by Japanese firms are treated as EC-produced cars – and legally they are entitled to such treatment under Articles 9 and 10 of the Treaty of Rome – then the Japanese transplant operations can ultimately get around *any* European import restrictions.

In the face of all of these difficulties, it is perhaps unsurprising that it took two years of difficult negotiations within the Community, and then between the Community and the Japanese, to arrive at a post-1992 policy. Agreement with the Japanese was reached at the end of July 1991 (Japan, EC . . . 1991). The agreement has four main components:

1 Intra-EC trade will be liberalised by the adoption of an EC-type approval scheme by 1 January 1993, and all national import restrictions will be abolished by the same date.
2 Imports of cars from Japan will be unrestricted after 31 December 1999, and in the intervening period will be limited to the level of 1.23 million (approximately the current level of imports).
3 Cars produced in Japanese-owned plants in the EC will have unrestricted access to the EC market.

4   There is an understanding about the levels of Japanese imports into France, Italy, Spain, Portugal and the UK from which it can be inferred that a deliberate attempt will be made by Japanese firms to reduce adjustment pressures in the markets from which national import restrictions have been removed.

On the face of it, this agreement provides a nice compromise between the competing pressures on the Community – on the one hand to fulfil its promises about '1992', and on the other to safeguard the interests of a key industry. It seems to imply a considerable liberalisation of the market, since the combined effect of imports and transplants should be to double the Japanese share of the EC market in the medium term, and since full liberalisation is promised for the year 2000. There are some unresolved difficulties, however.

Let us begin with the proposed provision for 'restraint' in the five currently restricted markets. If the announced levels of expected imports into these markets are purely forecasts, then it is not clear that they have much real meaning. Assuming that Japanese firms avoid deliberate attempts to exceed the forecast levels of sales, are there going to be measures to discourage French car-buyers, for example, from buying cars in Germany? If so, then we shall effectively be keeping some kind of market-segmenting non-tariff barriers to intra-EC trade, and not fulfilling the promise of 1992 until 2000. The apparent willingness, explicit in the case of the French, to postpone '1992' at least until 1999 is a measure of the perceived importance of the sector under review.

Even more important is the problem raised by the transplants: the European Commission stipulated the import limit of 1.23 million in the expectation that transplant output would reach 1.2 million by the end of 1999. What has been agreed is that transplant output will be treated, in accordance with Article 9 of the Treaty of Rome, as EC goods entitled to free circulation within the Community. However, there is no agreement on what should be done if the estimated transplant output of 1.2 million turns out to be inaccurate (A car sales . . . 1991). In the light of the possibility that the actual level of transplant output might be as high as 2 million, this could be a critical issue.

If transplant output rises faster than the EC expects, then either it will have to accept a still larger Japanese share of the EC market, or it will have to seek to persuade the Japanese to reduce their imports below the agreed level of 1.23 million. The first alternative would be politically and economically uncomfortable, and would make the import restriction irrelevant; while the second would imply that the EC-produced cars are in fact included in an overall sales restriction on Japanese cars, which would imply in turn a very significant departure from a central principle of the Community, namely the free circulation of goods.

A further, possibly minor but none the less interesting, twist is introduced by the existence of Japanese-owned transplants in the United States. Several Japanese producers are now producing in the USA on a very large scale. Honda cars are exported from the USA to Japan, and Honda has repeatedly announced its intention of exporting US-built cars to the EC. There can be no question of the imposition of a restriction on such imports. US-made Hondas are American cars, not Japanese cars, so far as the normal rules of international trade are concerned. The US government would object strongly and successfully to any attempt to impose restraints, direct or indirect, on their export to Europe. Nevertheless, imports from the United States could be influenced by the existence of the import restriction on Japanese-made cars. If the Japanese firms believe that rapid growth of sales from North America will lead to tighter 'monitoring' of imports from Japan, then that belief could itself lead to sales restraint without the need for any explicit statement by the Community.

This leads to the disturbing conclusion that voluntary export restrictions always partake of the character of government-encouraged market-sharing arrangements, whatever their form, whatever the level at which they are imposed. As the European Commission seeks to 'monitor' the sales of 'Japanese' cars in the Community, it has to take account of transplant output if the monitoring is to be effective. The device of 'forecasting' transplant output before arriving at the guidelines for direct imports from Japan helps to make it appear as if transplant output is not subject to any restriction; but in reality Japanese producers are likely to expect that attempts will be made to cut back on their import quotas if their transplant output rises by more than expected. Thus Nissan, Honda, Toyota and all other Japanese producers will receive signals as to what are their respective 'acceptable' shares of the European market. Such market-sharing removes any incentive for them to compete with each other, reduces the competitive pressure on non-Japanese firms, and makes it harder for new entrants to the market. All of these effects run counter to the provisions of Article 85 of the Treaty of Rome.

The ultimate objective of European policy towards the car industry should be to help European producers become more competitive. Comparative studies of car plants in Japan, the USA and Europe have exposed the vast productivity gap between European producers and their competitors. According to Jones et al 1990 (see also Jones, Chapter 13 in this volume), European plants seem to require on average twice the labour input per car that Japanese plants need. In addition, European producers lag far behind Japanese in reliability and consumer satisfaction. Protection has not so far been effective in raising European competitiveness, and this makes it difficult to believe that another seven or eight years of protection will do any better. It is much more plausible to argue that open competition with the Japanese is the incentive that the industry needs to improve its performance. There is evidence from the United States to back up this view: American producers have narrowed the productivity gap with the Japanese as their market has become more and more exposed to Japanese competition. It is high time European producers were subjected to the same discipline.

Strategic trade issues

Much of European trade policy seems concerned with keeping European industry competitive with the Japanese and the Americans, in areas such as consumer electronics, aircraft, cars and computers. Governments often seem to take it as self-evident that special efforts should be made to attain or maintain competitiveness in such sectors. Can this attitude be justified? Or would we do better simply to let the free market determine where we fit in to the world division of labour?

The simplest justification for active trade policy is based on the proposition that the countries and regions which specialise in the production of such high-tech products are better off than those that produce more traditional products. Thus California is richer than Pennsylvania, Japan than China. But this simplistic argument begs the question of what is cause and what effect. Highly skilled and highly educated labour certainly commands much higher rewards in the world market than unskilled and uneducated labour, and is certainly used in high-technology industries. It is equally clear, however, that the artificial fostering of high-technology development is unlikely in itself to create a self-sustaining high-wage economy.

But that is not the end of the story. Paul Krugman (1991) draws our attention to the fact that highly skilled American labour concentrates in California, and on the north-eastern seaboard, even though the American education system is of reasonably uniform quality throughout the country and labour is both free to move and, by European standards, remarkably willing to move across all parts of the country. The concentration of the American microelectronics industry in one particular part of California and one particular part of Massachusetts is strongly suggestive that there are gains to producers from proximity to other producers in the same or related lines of business. Belief in such 'positive externalities' provides one justification for seeking to promote or protect particular activities.

A rather different argument in favour of interventionist policy was presented by Brander and Spencer (1985), who proposed a model in which government assistance to its national champion firm could persuade the champion's rivals to sell less aggressively and thus let the national champion have a disproportionate share of a supposedly profitable market. The simplest illustration of this argument is provided by a story about the aircraft market. Suppose some sector of the market is marginally unprofitable if two producers enter, but very profitable for a single producer. Only one will enter, but which one? A government subsidy to one firm, just large enough so that it is marginally profitable for the firm to enter even in the presence of a rival, will ensure that that firm does, indeed, enter. But then the unsubsidised rival will not, and at a small cost the government has ensured that its champion grabs the profits!

Many observers see in the success of Japanese industrial policy evidence in support of the idea that there are strategic sectors which policy intervention can promote in the national interest. The problem is not so much in accepting that intervention in Japan (and in Korea and Taiwan, also) has been remarkably successful, as in identifying what it is about East Asian industrial policies that has made them so much more successful than industrial interventionism in South Asia or South America. There may well be lessons to be learned by Europe, but it is unfortunately not quite obvious what the lessons are.

The structural impediments initiative

As we saw earlier, both the United States and the European Community are very concerned about competition from Japan, especially in areas such as cars and electronics. There is a strong feeling that Japanese success is the result of 'unfair' features of Japanese policy or of the Japanese economy. Much attention focuses on Japanese trade policy – the presumption being that the present success of the Japanese car industry is the result of past protection. Industrial policy is also seen as playing a role, with the government cooperating with industry in choosing sectors on which to 'target' export efforts. Finally, there are features of the Japanese economy that are not directly related to government policy, such as the high savings rate and the work ethic.

Traditionally, governments have negotiated about each other's trade policies, exchanging 'concessions' in the form of trade barrier reductions. In recent years, the United States has, under the rubric of the 'Structural Impediments Initiative', sought to broaden the agenda of trade negotiations with Japan to encompass a number of aspects of the Japanese economy which are seen as contributing to its 'excessive' trade surplus. While the EC has not been as active as the USA in pursuing this line of action, it has certainly shared the concerns of the USA.

There are considerable difficulties in deciding what are appropriate issues for inter-governmental negotiation. If governments are to negotiate on tariffs and non-tariff barriers which directly affect trade flows, it is hard to argue that industrial or agricultural subsidies which have a strong impact on trade flows should not also be included in the agenda. But there are a number of dimensions to the structural impediments debate which go far beyond the realm of price distortions, however induced, and which introduce some very tricky issues into the discourse. The Japanese market may be hard for Western firms to penetrate because the Japanese language is difficult to learn. But that seems best treated as a fact of life rather than as an unfair Japanese practice requiring a compensating concession from the Japanese. If the Japanese work longer hours than Europeans, is that fair or unfair competition? It is generally accepted that competition from low-wage countries is not unfair; for lower wages may be the only way that these countries can compensate for their relative disadvantages in technology, and/or in capital. But if it is 'fair' to compete by offering lower wage rates, is it equally fair to compete by offering longer working hours, or by accepting unsafer working conditions or a higher degree of environmental pollution? If the structure of Japanese retail trade makes it harder for foreign producers to gain market access, is that a 'natural' feature of the trading world, or an artificial and unfair barrier?

Clearly the wider the agenda for negotiation, the greater the scope for increased friction and tension. The underlying issue is the extent to which the Japanese trade surplus is the natural consequence of a high Japanese rate of saving, or the natural consequence of Japanese efficiency in the manufacturing of products such as cars and CD players, or the 'unnatural' result of unfair policies targeted on particular sectors. Whatever justification can in principle be offered for the Structural Impediments Initiative, its existence is eloquent testimony to the strains imposed on the world trading system by the asymmetries in the trilateral relationship between Europe, Japan and the United States.

The implications of economic reform in Eastern Europe for future trade trends

The evolving pattern of intra-European trade will clearly be an important influence on trade relations between Europe as a whole and the rest of the world. At the same time, the path of economic change in Central and Eastern Europe is unpredictable.

Therefore the effects on international trade of that process of change are equally unpredictable. But the question is so important that is worth having a go. Preliminary answers have been offered by CEPR (1990), Collins and Rodrik (1991) and Hamilton and Winters (1992).

Whether we look at historical patterns of trade, or try to infer from the trade patterns of comparable market economies, the indications are that the countries of Eastern and Central Europe will see dramatic changes in the volume of their trade with the 'West' – the United States and Japan as well as Western Europe. But what structural trends will emerge as this trade expands?

The simplest observations to be made relate to natural resources. Several of the successor states to the Soviet Union are rich in energy, and should increase their energy exports *if* economic reform succeeds in improving the technical efficiency of the energy sector. Most of the countries in the region are well endowed with agricultural resources, though backward in agricultural performance. Agriculture, is, of course, the area in which the most dramatic responses to domestic economic liberalisation may be expected. Here again, then, substantial increases in exports could, *ceteris paribus*, be expected.

More subtle changes might be anticipated in the pattern of manufacturing output and exports. Comparative advantage in industrial products is much influenced by endowments in factors of production. Eastern and Central Europe are certainly short of modern capital, but there is impressive evidence that they are relatively well endowed with well-educated labour. Hamilton and Winters unearth evidence to suggest that the Hungarian education system could be one of the best in the world! In the recent past, much of this educated labour may have been wasted in military and other socially unproductive employments, and there is undoubtedly a desperate shortage of basic commercial skills (in marketing, accountancy, banking, for example). None the less, the labour endowments of Poland, Hungary and Czechoslovakia, and maybe also those of Russia, the Baltic states, Byelorussia and Ukraine, do not suggest that these are countries that will slot into the international division of labour on the same rung as Singapore and Indonesia, or even Greece and Portugal, but rather at the level of Spain, Italy and Ireland, as producers of a wide range of industrial products including some involving quite high technology, and as the hosts of substantial volumes of foreign direct investment.

The path to this happy state will not, however, be a smooth one. From the standpoint of the individual economies of Eastern and East-Central Europe, it is clear from the relevant chapters of *The National Economies of Europe* that restructuring policies, with all their undoubted successes, have still not provided a reliable key to 'unlock' comparative advantage. On the international side, too, there are still plenty of obstacles. The European Community has the central role of overseeing and facilitating the re-entry into the world economy of the Eastern and Central Europeans. The first major step was taken in December 1991, with the signing of association agreements between the Community on the one hand, and Poland, Hungary and Czechoslovakia on the other. These agreements represented a major advance, not least because they seemed to hold out the promise of eventual membership of the Community. But, as ever, the Community is mindful of its own short-term interests as well as its historic mission: the reforming economies continue to face the threat of anti-dumping actions and pressures not to allow too rapid export growth in 'sensitive' product areas, such as steel, textiles, footwear and agricultural products – notwithstanding the fact that such products may offer the best prospects to the Eastern and Central European economies in the short to medium run.

Will 1992 make the EC more protectionist?

The attention of the European Community is now centred on progress towards political and monetary union. But these two developments flow from the '1992' Programme, and it is from the '1992' Programme that we shall learn whether the Community is to be a fortress or a member of a more open world order. Mrs Margaret Thatcher argued in late 1991 that the more integrated the Community becomes, the less open it becomes to the rest of the world. Is this a fair judgement?

The Common Agricultural Policy lies at the root of most of the fears of the rest of the world. As we have seen, the CAP is harmful to European consumers as well as non-EC farmers, and it is not particularly beneficial for many EC farmers. In spite of its economic and budgetary costs, the CAP has proved remarkably resilient, and remains the major obstacle to the completion of the Uruguay Round of trade negotiations. Not only does the EC start off from a point that is unacceptable to its trading partners, but it shows little inclination to move from that point. And this is a *Common* Agricultural Policy – the first genuinely EC-wide economic policy. It is dangerous, however, to assume that a bad EC policy is the result of the process of European integration. Many non-EC countries in Europe, eg Austria, Switzerland and Norway, have agricultural policies that are more irrational and costly than the CAP, so it is not obvious that the CAP is worse than the policies that a non-integrated Western Europe would have adopted.

In Chapter 11, on European relations with the Third World, we see that the EC's position in this area is certainly ambiguous. The Community is generous so long as its own sensitive interests are not threatened, and this sense of conditional generosity is strengthened as we move down the hierarchy of preferences to those trading partners in Asia that have been most consistently subjected to anti-dumping measures and VERs. The EC has been strongly criticised for its misuse of such measures, but again it is not clear that these policies are the result of European integration, or that they will get any worse as integration proceeds.

If we want to obtain a clear perspective on the likely impact of European integration on the world trading system, we need to look more closely at what the '1992' process really means. The essential objective is increased international competition *within* the EC. The emphasis on mutual recognition of standards as the principal means of removing border barriers has in itself a strongly deregulatory effect, as the least demanding national standard will tend to become the European standard. One result will obviously be to open the EC market to non-EC producers. As the German market is opened to French beer, it is opened also to American beer (because the French market is already open to American beer). When European car manufacturers are required to obtain only one set of certification to give their products access to the whole EC market, so Japanese manufacturers will enjoy the same benefit.

At the same time there will be trade diversion, as barriers are reduced in a way that favours intra-EC trade against extra-EC trade. More important, as European producers face the rigours of increased intra-EC competition, they may lobby for increased barriers to extra-EC competition.

The European car market (which we discussed above) provides a nice illustration of the difficulties for the Community. Proponents of open and competitive markets will not applaud the agreement between the EC and the Japanese; but we should observe that national trade restrictions have been replaced by an EC-wide restriction whose effect is not more restrictive than the national restrictions, and which we are promised is to end in 1999; while the effect of Japanese foreign direct investment will be further to weaken the efficacy of protectionist measures. This important example suggests that it is still too early to say whether the '1992' Programme is going to restrict access to EC markets for the rest of the world. The fact is that there are strong forces pulling in both directions.

The future of Europe in the international division of labour

Europe faces an intensification of international competition from a number of different directions. Within the developed world, the United States may be a faltering rival, but Japanese competition becomes more and more formidable. The newly industrialising countries, such as Korea and Taiwan, continue to display rapid export growth, and their success has encouraged other Third World countries to follow the path of export-led growth. The future role of China in the world economy is somewhat dependent on political developments; but in any event, it seems that Europe faces increasing competition in labour-intensive and medium-technology products from that part of the Third World that properly earns the title 'developing'. Some of the competition will come from the Mediterranean periphery – the Maghreb, Israel, Egypt and Turkey.

The kinds of international competition that Europe will face in the future pose considerable policy challenges. The pressure of competition from lower-wage developing countries, and the consequent need for Europe to move up the technological spectrum, will have effects on the distribution of income both between individuals and between regions. The income differential between the more skilled and the less skilled is likely to widen, as the less skilled are subject to stronger competitive pressure on world markets. Those regions, many of them on the European periphery, whose industrial structure is less advanced, may similarly find that international competition widens the gap between them and the more prosperous regions in the core.

Global competition is evident not only in markets for goods, but also in international flows of labour and investment. European firms may come off worst in competition with the Japanese, but those parts of the European economy that succeed in attracting investment by Japanese multinationals will likely do well. The direct competitive pressure on less skilled European workers comes not from the products of Third World workers, but from immigration, and there is a link between the two pressures. Increased protection of European goods markets against the products of the developing world may help to maintain the wage rate of less skilled European workers; but it simultaneously increases the incentive to immigrate into Europe. The development of policy toward migration is one of the major challenges that Europe now faces, to match the challenge of policy-making on capital from outside Europe, as the notion of globalisation develops ever newer layers of meaning.

References

A car sales accord light on consensus (1991) *Financial Times* 23 September: 4
Anderson K, Tyers R (1986) Agricultural policies of industrial countries and their effect on traditional food exporters. *Economic Record* **62**(3): 385–99
Belderbos R (1991) On the advance of Japanese electronics multinationals in the EC. Paper presented at INSEAD Conference, Fontainebleau, October
Bourgeois J (1989) Anti-trust and trade policy: a peaceful co-existence? *International Business Lawyer* **17**(3): 115–21
Brander J A, Spencer B J (1985) Export subsidies and international market share rivalry. *Journal of International Economics* **18**(1/2): 83–100
Cawson A, Holmes P (1991) The new consumer electronics. In Freeman C, Sharp M, Walker W (eds) *Technology and the Future of Europe: Global Competition and the Environment*. Pinter
Cawson A, Morgan K, Holmes P, Stevens A, Webber D (1990) *Hostile Brothers: Competition and Closure in the European Electronics Industry*. OUP
CEPR (1990) *Monitoring European Integration: The Impact of Eastern Europe*. A CEPR annual report. Centre for Economic Policy Research
Collins S M, Rodrik D (1991) *Eastern Europe and the Soviet Union in the World Economy*. Institute for International Economics, Washington DC
EC Commission (1985) *Completing the Internal Market*. White Paper from the EC Commission to the European Council, Luxembourg, June
EC Commission (1990) *Industrial Policy in an Open and Competitive Environment*. Brussels
EC Commission (1991a) *The European Electronics and Information Technology Industry: State of Play, Issues at Stake and Proposals for Action*. Brussels
EC Commission (1991b) *Ninth Annual Report on Anti-Subsidy and Anti-Dumping Activities*. Brussels, May
EC vehicle sales accord with Japan to include light trucks (1991) *Financial Times* 5 August: 4
Flamm K (1990) Semiconductors. In Hufbauer G C *Europe 1992: An American Perspective*. Brookings Institute, Washington DC
GATT (1990) *Trade Policy Review of Japan*. Geneva
GATT (1991) *Trade Policy Review of the EC*. Geneva
Hamilton C, Winters L A (1992) Opening up international trade in Eastern Europe. *Economic Policy* **14**, April
Hansen K (ed) (1991) *International Instruments to Control Restraints of Competition after 1992*. Proceedings of the 1990 Berlin International Cartel Conference. Bundeskartellamt, Berlin
Hindley B (1988) Dumping and the Far East trade of the EC. *World Economy* **11**(4): 445–64
Hine R C (1985) *The Political Economy of EC Trade Policy*. Wheatsheaf
Holmes P (1991) *Trade and Competition Policy: The Consumer Interest*. National Consumer Council, Working Paper 5, London, April
Japan, EC agree on car imports (1991) *Financial Times* 1 August: 6
Julius D (1990) *Global Companies and Public Policy*. RIIA/F. Pinter
Krugman P R (1991) *Geography and Trade*. MIT Press, Cambridge, Mass.
Messerlin P (1990) Anti-dumping regulations or pro-cartel law? The EC chemical cases. *PRE Working Paper Series* no 397, World Bank, Washington, DC
Milner H (1988) *Resisting Protectionism, Global Industries and the Politics of International Trade*. Princeton University Press

O'Clearacain S (1990) Europe 1992 and gaps in the EC's Common Commercial Policy. *Journal of Common Market Studies* **28**(3): 202–17

OECD (1985) *The Costs and Benefits of Protection*. Paris

OECD (1987) *Structural Adjustment and Economic Performance*. Paris

Ordover J, Saloner S (1989) Anti-trust and predation. In Schmalensee R, Willig R (eds) *Handbook of Industrial Organisation* (Vol 1). North Holland Publishing House

Porter M (1990) *The Competitive Advantage of Nations*. Macmillan

Reich R (1990) Who is 'us'? *Harvard Business Review*, April

Schuknecht L (1991) Dumping and anti-dumping in EC-CMEA trade. *Working Paper Series II* no 140. University of Konstanz

Schuknecht L (forthcoming) *The Political Economy of EC Trade Policy*. University of Konstanz

Stegemann K (1991) The international regulation of dumping. *World Economy* **14**(4): 375–406

Thomsen S, Nicolaides P (1990) *Foreign Direct Investment: 1992 and Global Markets*. RIIA

Victor J-L (1990) *The EC Legal Order*. European Perspectives Series. Commission of the European Communities, Luxembourg

Womack J P, Jones D T, Roos D (1990) *The Machine that Changed the World*, Rawson Associates/Macmillan, New York

World Bank (1987) *World Development Report 1987*. OUP

CHAPTER 11

The EC and the Third World

CHRISTOPHER STEVENS

Introduction

As the 'Third World' has become increasingly differentiated as a grouping, so has Europe's relationship with its constituent parts. But there has been a lag, especially in respect to political relations. Consequently, formal policy has diverged increasingly from effective practice. A sharp reorientation is likely to occur in the former as Europe adjusts to the changes required by the completion of the single European market, by the possible move towards greater monetary and political union, by the extension of the 'European space' to include Eastern and Northern Europe, and by the GATT Uruguay Round of trade liberalisation.

There will be winners and losers in the Third World as a result of these changes. The losers are likely to include many of the poorest countries. The main imponderable is the future impact of 'new issues' such as migration, the environment and public health. There is increased awareness that phenomena which originate in developing countries may adversely affect EC welfare. These may require Europe to take a greater interest in the Third World than short-term economic and strategic considerations alone would counsel.

The foundations of EC–Third World relations

Europe and the Third World affect each other in a host of ways, not all of them economic. Many facets of the relationship are still organised primarily on a bilateral, national basis, eg France and Senegal, Britain and India, Germany and Singapore. Purely for reasons of practicality, this chapter focuses largely on the Community-level dimension of the relationship.

Development aid is only one vehicle for Europe's economic influence on the Third World, and not necessarily the most important. European policies on trade, agriculture, industrial subsidies and exchange rates, for example, can all have a much larger impact. The range of such policies is limited by the characteristic of the

European Community (as opposed to its member states) that it does not possess the full array of attributes of a nation-state. It cannot conduct a normal foreign or defence policy; even its responsibilities on debt are limited. Among this limited range of policy instruments there are three principal foundations for Community-level policies affecting the Third World. They are the common commercial policy, the Common Agricultural Policy (CAP), and the partially common aid policy.

Trade policy

The existence of the common external tariff (CET) means that the foundations of Europe's foreign trade regime must be established at Community level. The member states adopt a common position at meetings of the GATT and UNCTAD, and have negotiated at EC level a host of bilateral and multilateral trade agreements with the Third World states.

The CET's purity is reduced in practice inasmuch as member states adopt, to a greater or lesser extent, national policies that influence trade flows. Most important are the growing number of non-tariff barriers (NTBs) to imports. Whereas EC institutions have an unambiguous responsibility for setting tariff policy, their position on NTBs has been less secure (although this will change as part of '1992'). Individual member states have negotiated bilaterally numerous so-called voluntary export restraints (VERs) with developing countries. In addition, there are many national quotas within Community NTBs which restrict the volume of imports that have access to the national markets of particular member states.

The precise number of effective national NTBs is unknown: some are secret, some are not enforced, and some are made on an industry–industry basis and fall outside government scrutiny. But an indication of their extent may be gauged by analysing member states' recourse to Article 115 of the Treaty of Rome. This article, which permits a member to restrict imports from its neighbours of goods originating outside the Community, is a legal linchpin of the national NTB system. Clearly, a French NTB on, say, Taiwanese footwear, would be unsustainable if exporters could evade the restrictions by routing goods indirectly via Germany. During 1988 and the first seven months of 1989, there were sixteen cases of LDC exports being excluded from an EC national market through the use of Article 115, and a similar number of cases in which there was surveillance of imports (Davenport and Page 1991: 43). The import exclusions were imposed in the French, Italian and Spanish markets; the LDCs affected were Brazil, China, Hong Kong, Singapore and Taiwan; and the products involved were footwear, umbrellas, toys, car radios, televisions, silk, handtools, sewing machines, slide fasteners, videos, imitation jewellery and cars.

The Common Agricultural Policy

The CAP is particularly important because of the dominance of agriculture in many developing countries. The transformation of the EC from a major importer of agricultural products to a net exporter of an increasing number of commodities has had profound and complex effects on the Third World. The precise nature of the impact is not easy to identify since it depends upon the commodity composition of each country's imports and exports and also on the time period selected. In broad terms, the impact depends on a given LDC's balance of agricultural trade. The short-term effect on net agricultural exporting states in the Third World has tended to be negative (because the CAP has increased world supply and hence reduced prices), while the impact on food importing states has been positive (for precisely the same reasons). In addition, world price instability for agricultural products may have intensified to the detriment of both agricultural exporters and importers. In the longer term, even food importing LDCs *may* have suffered – for two reasons. First, if low world prices for temperate agricultural products are of a temporary nature, but have encouraged the neglect of an LDC's domestic agriculture, the long-term effect could be to increase the burden of food imports rather than the reverse. Second, if the general equilibrium effects of the CAP have reduced non-agricultural production in Europe, the terms of trade gain of LDC food importers from low world food prices may be offset by the loss incurred on account of higher non-agricultural import prices.

Despite this negative overall verdict, there are some positive aspects of the CAP for some LDCs, at least from a static viewpoint. In addition to the terms of trade effect of food-importing states, a small number of privileged LDCs receive artificially high prices for at least part of their exports because of the CAP. These gains are concentrated on some of the signatories of the Lomé Conventions, together with the non-EC Mediterranean states. Other LDCs have also benefited where the price distortions of the CAP have created a demand for commodities which would not otherwise exist, as in the case of European demand for Thai manioc as an animal feed.

Aid programmes

Unlike trade and agriculture, aid policy is only partially common. There are three main strings to Europe's aid bow: multi-annual Community-level programmes, annual EC programmes, and member state national programmes.

Only a small part of the aid provided by the EC member states is channelled through Community institutions. The greater part is disbursed either through the bilateral programmes of each member state or through other intermediaries, such as the multilateral institutions. The four main contributors to the EC aid budget are Germany, France, UK and Italy which, between them, account for some four-fifths of the total (Table 11.1). The proportion of aid which is channelled through the Community institutions varies widely between the member states. Of the larger EC states, the UK has the highest proportion of its aid going through the EC (at 19 per cent) and France the smallest (at 8 per cent).

The most important element of the Community-level aid programme is the European Development Fund (EDF), which finances the aid provisions of the Lomé Convention. But there are other elements of Community-level aid as well. There are financial protocols to the commercial agreements that the EC has with many of the states of the Mediterranean. Then there is an annually agreed 'non-associates aid programme', which provides financial assistance out of the EC budget in equal proportions to Asia and Latin America. And of particular importance is the food aid programme: cereals food aid is provided from both a Community and a number of bilateral programmes, while dairy product food aid is wholly a Community-level affair.

Table 11.1 Sources of EC aid,* 1989

Member state	Contribution to EC aid	Total aid	Contribution to EC aid as % of total aid	Share of total EC aid (%)
Belgium	111	703	16	4
Denmark	62	937	7	2
France	628	7,450	8	24
Germany	735	4,949	15	28
Ireland	20	49	41	1
Italy	407	3,613	11	16
Netherlands	173	2,094	8	7
United Kingdom	499	2,587	19	19

Notes:
* Oda net disbursements, $ million
Columns may not add up due to rounding
This table includes only those EC states that are members of the OECD DAC (Development Assistance Committee). It excludes, therefore, Greece, Luxembourg, Portugal and Spain. Except in the case of Spain, these are relatively small donors; their 1988 oda was equivalent to under 2% of total disbursement by the other member states

Source: OECD Development Co-operation 1990

In 1989 some 50 per cent of Community-level aid disbursements took the form of funds from the EDF, and a significant part of the remainder that of food aid (although there are question marks over the appropriate valuation for some of the EC food aid commodities, notably dairy products).

Some of the bilateral aid programmes tend to reinforce the geographical and political bias of Community efforts, but with some member states the reverse is true. EC aid has tended to focus on sub-Saharan Africa and, to a lesser extent, the Mediterranean (Middle East and North Africa) (Table 11.2). The share of aid directed towards sub-Saharan Africa has grown slightly over the past fifteen years, while that going to the Mediterranean has declined slightly. Between them, however, these two regions account for around 70 per cent of the total. The principal differences in current geographical orientation between the EC and the bilateral programmes of the large member states are as follows. France, perhaps surprisingly, has a less dramatic concentration on sub-Saharan Africa, even though this remains the most important region for France, and provides a higher proportion of aid than the EC as a whole to Asia and Latin America and the Caribbean. In the case of Germany, the focus on sub-Saharan Africa is much less marked, while a relatively higher proportion of aid is directed to South Asia, Other Asia and the Mediterranean. The most important distinguishing feature with the UK is that its aid programme gives more prominence to South Asia than does that of the EC as a whole.

The 'pyramid of privilege'

On the basis of these three policy instruments the Commission has fashioned a complex set of agreements through which it has conducted a quasi-foreign policy *vis-à-vis* the

Table 11.2 Geographical distribution of EC aid (percentage of gross disbursements)

Countries	Sub-Saharan Africa			South Asia			Other Asia & Oceania			Middle East & North Africa*			Latin America & Caribbean		
	75/76	80/81	88–89	75/76	80/81	88/89	75/76	80/81	88/89	75/76	80/81	88/89	75/76	80/81	88/89
Belgium	66.6	66.0	76.5	5.8	5.0	2.0	8.9	11.9	8.3	12.5	12.2	5.6	6.2	4.9	7.6
Denmark	52.7	51.6	65.4	17.9	31.2	22.1	16.4	8.9	6.0	9.8	6.2	5.0	3.3	2.1	2.9
France	46.5	48.0	52.6	4.2	2.8	3.2	11.1	12.9	15.9	14.6	12.5	9.1	23.6	23.8	19.2
Germany	20.8	29.5	28.5	27.2	20.6	16.0	9.2	9.4	13.7	30.4	28.8	29.0	12.5	11.7	12.7
Ireland	79.8	96.7	95.8	12.5	1.0	3.1	—	0.6	0.3	2.9	0.3	0.3	4.8	1.3	0.5
Italy	24.3	56.1	58.9	18.2	1.7	6.1	6.8	6.6	6.8	45.6	28.1	11.7	5.1	7.5	16.6
Netherlands	19.7	31.2	36.6	24.2	24.9	19.2	14.9	10.6	18.5	4.3	5.4	5.3	36.9	27.9	20.4
United Kingdom	28.4	37.0	52.6	41.0	40.0	25.6	11.6	8.5	10.0	6.5	8.3	4.9	12.5	6.2	6.8
EC	59.6	60.3	63.2	20.8	16.9	10.4	1.9	4.9	6.7	12.4	11.8	8.2	5.4	6.0	11.6

Notes:
* Includes small amounts to southern Europe
Percentages in lines add up to 100% for regional distribution in each two-year period for each individual country/institution

Source: OECD *Development Co-operation 1990*

Third World (Table 11.3). Because of the nature of the instruments, that policy has a high economic content.

Although the Lomé Convention is the EC's most prominent regional preferential arrangements, it is not the only such European accord; nor is it the only North–South package of its kind. The EC has a predisposition to favour formal trade and co-operation agreements, partly because it establishes the legitimacy of Community as opposed to national action. The result has been a series of 'framework agreements' with different parts of the Third World. The Lomé Convention has also spawned imitative action by other countries. In addition to the USA's Caribbean Basin Initiative, the Nordic initiative for a mini-NIEO (New International Economic Order) can also be seen as an attempt to emulate, and improve upon, the regional package approach of Lomé.

The EC's bilateral and multilateral agreements have been described as a 'pyramid of privilege', by virtue of the fact that those at the top provide more favourable treatment than those at the base. The countries at the top have preferences not only over some developed countries, but also over other LDC members of the pyramid. It is therefore a shifting pyramid, since improvements in the terms for states lower down the hierarchy can cut the value of concessions made to those higher up.

Preference agreements can be grouped into three broad categories.

1 At the apex of the pyramid sits the Lomé Convention. Under it the sixty-nine African, Caribbean and Pacific (ACP) states benefit from the most liberal set of non-reciprocal trade preferences that the EC has offered to any group of states. They also receive more EC-level aid than do other LDCs in both absolute and per capita terms. The practical effects of these liberal trade preferences have been limited, however, by the fact that many of them apply to products that the ACP have a very limited capacity to produce (see below).
2 In the middle of the pyramid are the Mediterranean states, which are accorded

Table 11.3 Major EC trade arrangements with the developing countries

Country	Trade agreement
African, Caribbean and Pacific countries	Lomé Convention
Least developed countries	Nine non-Lomé signatories in this category receive special concessions
Northern Mediterranean Cyprus, Malta, Turkey, Yugoslavia	Association agreements, trade and co-operation agreements
Southern Mediterranean Maghreb countries (Algeria, Morocco, Tunisia), Egypt, Jordan, Lebanon, Syria	Preferential trade and co-operation agreements involving free access for industrial exports, specific concessions for some agricultural output, and financial aid and co-operation agreements
Asia India, Pakistan, Sri Lanka, China	Non-preferential commercial co-operation agreements with each country
Association of South-East Asian Nations (Indonesia, Malaysia, Philippines, Singapore, Thailand)	Regional framework agreement
Latin America Argentina, Brazil, Mexico, Uruguay, Andean Pact countries	Non-preferential economic and trade co-operation agreements with each country
Central America	Regional framework agreement
Near East Gulf States (Saudi Arabia, United Arab Emirates, Kuwait, Oman, Qatar, Bahrain)	Gulf Co-operation Agreement
Yemen	Non-preferential agreement covering trade and economic co-operation

Note: Non-preferential agreements involve no preferences in addition to those available via the Generalised System of Preferences

Source: McAleese 1989

trade preferences that are nominally less favourable than those of the ACP but may in practice be the most valuable. The main limitations on these agreements (all of which are bilateral and differ from each other in their details) is that they limit diversification into 'sensitive' product areas, while allowing the states to continue with traditional exports, albeit often under the constraint of quotas.

3   The broad base of the pyramid includes all the remaining LDCs (ASEAN, Latin America, South Asia, etc.). Despite a number of impressive-sounding 'framework agreements', these countries trade only on terms of the Generalised System of Preferences (GSP), and receive Community aid only from the relatively small annual 'non-associates' aid budget and the food aid programme. The GSP is the

lowest common denominator of the EC's trade preferences. It covers most industrial and a few agricultural products and offers tariffs that are generally lower than MFN levels. However, the preference margins are usually lower than those available to the ACP and Mediterranean states through their association agreements with the EC, and are often limited by quotas for sensitive items.

The pattern of trade

Since the mid-1960s the Third World has become relatively less important overall for Europe in terms of trade, finance and military strategy. The share of all third parties in total EC imports and exports has fallen since 1960 as the creation of the Common Market has encouraged members to trade with each other (Figures 11.1 and 11.2). While non-EC developed countries (DCs) were more severely affected by this decline than were LDCs in the period 1960–75, the reverse has been true since then. The LDC share of total EC imports has fallen continuously in the post-Oil Shock period (from 23 per cent in 1975 to only 13 per cent by 1988), while the DC share has stabilised (and was, indeed, slightly higher in 1988, at 26 per cent, than its 1975 level of 23 per cent). In the case of EC exports, the DC share has tended to hold up better than that of the LDCs throughout the period, although, once again, the differentially poor LDC performance was more marked during the second sub-period.

The extent of the decline and the reasons for it have varied between LDC regions. The principal constraint on further deepening of relations with East and South-East Asia is not a lack of European interest, but a lack of European competitiveness *vis-à-vis* Japan and USA. In the case of links with the ACP, there has been a substantial decline in relative importance, first in economic and now, increasingly, in political terms, largely as a result of European withdrawal. By contrast, relations with the Mediterranean and Middle East have remained strong, reflecting substantial European economic and political interests in the region. South Asia and Latin America have retained fairly close links with some member states, but have remained on the periphery for the Community as a whole.

The sharpest fall in trade share has been experienced by the ACP. Their share of EC imports from outside the Community fell from 10 per cent in 1960 to 4 per cent by 1988 (Figure 11.3), and a similar picture applies to EC exports (Figure 11.4). The share of Latin America in both imports and exports also fell sharply, while that of the Mediterranean and ASEAN held broadly stable. The only states to have experienced a steady rise in trade share are the East Asian newly industrialising countries (NICs) – Korea, Taiwan and Hong Kong. Their share of extra-EC imports rose from 1 per cent in 1970 to 6 per cent in 1988, while for exports the rise was somewhat slower – from 1 per cent to 4 per cent.

These changes are related to the commodity composition of trade (Figure 11.5). Over the period as a whole there has been a change in the relative importance of the various sources of European growth, with non-traded services and intra-developed country trade increasing in relative significance. The distortions caused by the CAP have simply accentuated a trend away from the traditional colonial trade pattern of importing raw materials from the South and exporting manufactures to it. In its place, a trade has developed with parts of the South that emphasises a two-way flow of

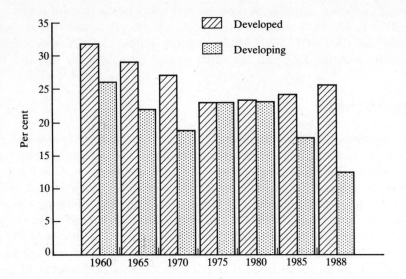

Figure 11.1   EC imports from developed and developing countries as a share of total imports
(intra and extra) 1960–88
Source: Eurostat.

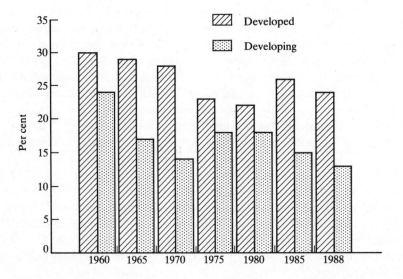

Figure 11.2   EC exports to developed and developing countries as a share of total exports (intra
and extra) 1960–88
Source: Eurostat.

manufactures and services. The leaders of the new pattern of trade have been, on the
European side, the states with relatively weak colonial ties (notably Germany) and, in
the South, the countries of East and South-East Asia. By contrast, formal development

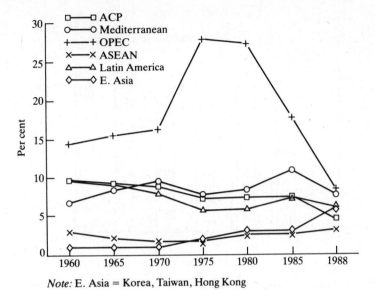

Note: E. Asia = Korea, Taiwan, Hong Kong

Figure 11.3 EC imports from developing countries by region as a share of extra-EC imports, 1960–88
Source: Eurostat.

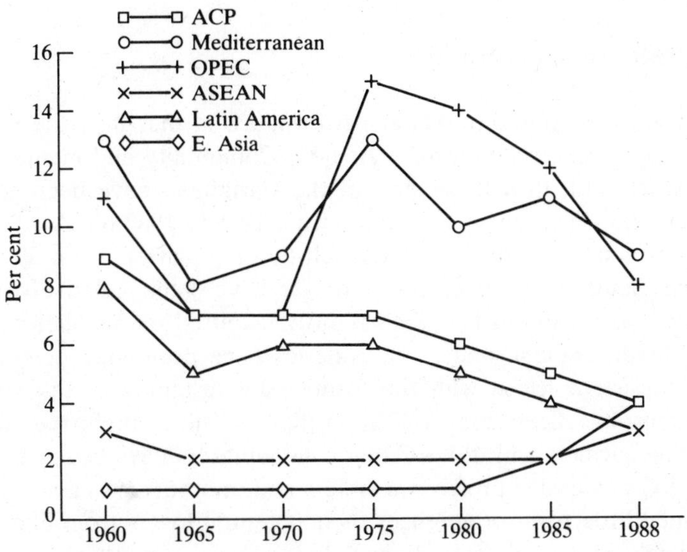

Note: E. Asia = Korea, Taiwan, Hong Kong

Figure 11.4 EC exports to developing countries by region as a share of extra-EC exports 1960–88
Source: Eurostat.

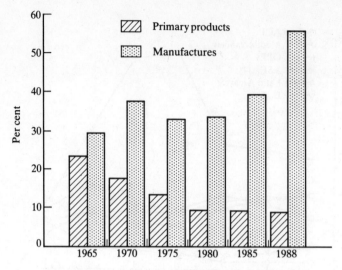

Note: Primary = SITC 0 + 1; Manufactures = SITC 6 + 7 + 8

Figure 11.5   Share of primary products and manufactures in extra-EC imports, 1965–88
            Source: Eurostat.

policy has been fashioned largely by the major ex-colonial states (France and UK), and has focused on their erstwhile colonies.

Have trade preferences worked?

One striking feature of this differential performance is that it is the inverse of the pattern created by formal relationships. At both Community and member state level, sub-Saharan Africa and, to a lesser extent, the Caribbean have been given pride of place in formal policy. Yet during the period from 1975 to 1987 the ACP's share of EC imports from developing countries (LDCs) fell by one-quarter, from 20.5 to 15.1 per cent. East and South-East Asia, by contrast, have been relatively neglected in Community-level policy and at best ambiguously favoured by member states. Only in respect to the Mediterranean and Latin America have pronouncements and practice been broadly consistent: close with the former and distant with the latter.

So incongruous has been the ACP's position as most preferred and yet least successful trading partners with the EC that commentators have begun to question the efficacy of the EC's extensive preference system and, moreover, to assert that since the ACP have gained little from preferences their potential losses from liberalisation will be correspondingly modest (see eg Brown 1988; Davenport 1988).

However, it is too easy to write off the Lomé trade preferences as valueless; much more cautious conclusions are in order. The ACP's poor overall performance reflects two factors: first, the Lomé Convention provides the ACP with either zero or very limited preference over their major competitors for the greater part (by value) of their exports. Second, ACP exports are more heavily concentrated than are those of other

LDCs on commodities for which world demand is growing slowly.

The implication is that while Lomé has been by definition low-powered, ACP trade performance would have been even worse without the Convention. As explained below, there have, indeed, been some positive trade effects of Lomé for the ACP.

The extent of preferences

Despite the apparent liberality of the EC's preferential trade arrangements, it is by no means clear that LDCs are always the beneficiaries of positive discrimination by the EC. In respect to tariffs, for example, the actual rates applying to LDC exports may be higher than those that apply to DC exports. LDCs appear to face lower tariff barriers in the EC market than do DCs only if the analysis is limited to formal tariff rates. In 1983, for example, the average MFN rate applied to total EC imports from DCs was 7.2 per cent; this was much higher than the average GSP rate applied to imports from LDCs. But the average tariff rate *actually imposed* by the EC was lower on imports from DCs than from LDCs (at 4.7 per cent as against 5.3 per cent) (Sampson 1989). There are two reasons for this. First the DCs benefit from a number of EC trade preferences and so do not usually trade on MFN terms. Second, LDC exports to the EC tend to include a higher proportion of 'sensitive' goods than do DC exports.

In the case of NTBs, too, the commodity basket of exports may result in discrimination against LDCs. In 1983, for example, 25 per cent of the EC's imports from LDCs faced NTBs compared with only 19 per cent of its imports from DCs. The impact of NTBs can be especially severe on some of the poorest LDCs: EC imports from India, for example, face significantly more NTBs than do imports from the NICs (Sapir and Stevens 1987: Table 1).

In the case of the Lomé preferences, ACP exports to the EC fall into three broad groups. The largest group is of commodities that enter the Community market duty-free, but would do so even without the Lomé Convention. Hence in this case Lomé provides no preferences *vis-à-vis* exports of the ACP's principal competitors. The second group, accounting for a large part of the remainder, are products which enter duty-free under Lomé but do not do so under the GSP or MFN provisions, and do not compete directly with European production. Hence the ACP states here receive a tariff preference over other third-party exporters to the EC. But the level of GSP or MFN tariffs, and hence the ACP margin of preference, is very low in many cases. In 1987 five commodities accounted for 63 per cent of the total value of ACP exports to the EC. They were crude petroleum, coffee, cocoa, copper and rough wood; the relevant EC MFN tariff rates were 0, 5, 3, 0 and 0 per cent respectively. Moreover, there are no major non-tariff restrictions at either national or Community level on imports into the EC of most traditional ACP exports. Hence, the Lomé regime is unlikely to have significant dynamic effects on ACP exports of these commodities.

The third category is the smallest in terms of ACP export value but is potentially the most significant. It consists of goods that are also produced within Europe and that benefit from substantial EC protection. Preferences on such goods are particularly valuable for three reasons. First, they may facilitate export diversification. Second, ACP exporters, like European producers, are protected against competitive imports from other third-party suppliers. And, not least, ACP export earnings are supplemented by the artificially high prices in the European market brought about by the restriction of supply.

Most notable in this category are products that fall within the CAP, plus clothing and textiles lines that are controlled by the Multifibre Arrangement (MFA), effectively a Community-sponsored VER. In the case of temperate agricultural products, the ACP benefit from a number of openings to the European market, although these are usually restricted by quotas, calendars (that limit preferential access to certain periods of the year) or both. In the case of clothing the ACP are not subject to the MFA, though there have been a number of instances of VER and anti-dumping actions.

The range of CAP products on which the ACP benefit include sugar, rice, beef and horticultural products. Although the mechanisms employed vary between these products, the fundamental nature of the benefit is the same in each case. Because the CAP restricts supply on to the EC market, prices prevailing in Europe are artificially high. The ACP gain at least part of this economic rent for at least part of their exports. The reason for the 'at least part' caveat is that in some cases the EC treasury obtains part of the economic rent through the application of import tariffs, and because ACP access to the EC market is normally limited to a fixed quota which may be less than total exports. If a country is able to sell only a part of its total exports to the EC the effects of high European prices may have to be offset against 'abnormally' low returns in other markets. This would happen if, for example, the CAP pushed world market prices down below what they would otherwise be. Hence the critical factors in determining whether, in the short term, the export revenue of LDC preference holders is higher or lower as a result of the CAP are: the proportion of exports that gain access to the EC market, the level of economic rent received by the exporter, and the price-depressing effects of the CAP in other markets.

Let us now look at the main relevant product categories in turn.

Sugar

The EC–ACP Sugar Protocol is attached to the Lomé Conventions, although it is not part of them. The principal reason for this distinction is that it is of 'unlimited duration', and therefore not subject to periodic renegotiation.

The Protocol provides sixteen ACP states, plus India, with a global quota of 1.3 million tonnes of sugar (white sugar equivalent) for which the EC guarantees to pay similar prices to those offered to European sugar beet producers. These prices are normally well above world levels. The Protocol, which represents a major breach in the CAP system of protection, was negotiated as part of Britain's accession to the Community. The imports are consumed almost exclusively in the UK market.

The share of sugar exports covered by the Protocol varies between the ACP beneficiaries. But all in all, with a possible exception in the case of Zimbabwe, the financial gain of high prices on the EC quota has almost certainly exceeded the financial loss due to the CAP-induced depression of world market prices.

Rice

Most rice imports face a levy calculated to bring the price up to domestic Community levels. But for the ACP 50 per cent of the levy is replaced by an equivalent tax in the exporting state. The preference is volume-constrained. Under Lomé I (1975–80) and

Lomé II (1980–5), the EC was entitled to suspend the preference if total imports from the ACP exceeded the average of the previous three years plus 5 per cent. For Lomé III (1985–90) this threshold was replaced by a fixed quota that was significantly in excess of actual flows during Lomé II. For long-grained husked rice it was set at 122,000 tonnes annually, compared with average annual imports 1982–6 of 95,673 tonnes. However, ACP exports increased rapidly during Lomé III, so that the quota became a binding constraint. For Lomé IV (1990–2000) the quota has been increased to 125,000 tonnes of husked rice equivalent, plus 20,000 tonnes of broken rice.

Beef

Five African states (Botswana, Kenya, Madagascar, Swaziland and Zimbabwe) have a special regime for the export of beef to the EC. They benefit from a 90 per cent reduction in the variable import levy for a quota of beef. The total quota under Lomé IV is 39,100 tonnes annually, but it is subdivided into national quotas with discretionary provisions for a surplus on one state's quota to be transferred to another.

Horticulture

The CAP regime for horticultural products is complex. The basic rule is that the system for supporting European farmers is relatively lightly structured, without the mandatory intervention buying and variable import levies characterising the cereals and meat regimes. For the fresh products of most interest to LDCs the normal regime applying to imports is that the EC levies an *ad valorem* tariff and also establishes a 'reference price'. Countries exporting to the EC are obliged to sell their goods at a 'minimum import price' equal to the reference price plus the tariffs. Failure to comply results in a countervailing levy being imposed to bring the cost of imports up to the required level. Hence it is possible to export fresh fruit and vegetables to the EC, but only if the landed price exceeds the level at which domestic produce is sold.

For the ACP, and some other third-party suppliers (primarily states in the Mediterranean), concessions take the form of full or partial rebates of the *ad valorem* tariff. But there are two provisos. The first is that LDC preference holders must still respect minimum import prices. In other words, they are barred from undercutting domestic European producers, but retain a larger share of the proceeds from any exports they do make, which helps them to compete with other third-party suppliers that have to pay the full tariff.

The second proviso is that these concessions are limited for some products to a fixed quota or specific period of the year (calendar) or both. Such quotas may be very small, eg the quota under Lomé IV for small winter cucumber is 100 tonnes for the whole of the ACP group! Moreover, it does not follow simply from the existence of a preference on paper that all (or any) ACP states can actually exploit that preference within the seasonal restriction imposed. There have been cases in the Mediterranean where the EC has granted a calendar-restricted preference for a product which, for climatic reasons, the 'beneficiary' cannot harvest at that time of the year!

The extent of diversification

The need for the ACP to diversify into new products is particularly pressing, since the central ACP export problem is one of over-reliance on goods facing slow-growing markets. Contrary to the conventional wisdom, the ACP have not performed less satisfactorily than other LDCs on their exports of those tropical products on which they receive modest preferences (Davenport and Stevens 1990). Rather, the problem is that their exports are more heavily concentrated than are those of other LDCs on a product range for which world demand is growing only slowly. The ACP have simply been less successful at diversifying into products with a better market outlook than have other LDCs.

The evidence of the 1980s is that a number of ACP states have begun to break out of this unsatisfactory export product range, and while the EC's trade preferences for the ACP have not had a major effect on trade patterns, there may have been some impact on the margins. They have not prevented the emergence of a trend towards the side-lining of the ACP in EC trade, but there are reasons to believe that this trend would have been more severe in the absence of the Convention.

The number of states within the ACP group that have achieved significant diversification is still a minority, but it is not an insignificant one. The success of Mauritius in developing its clothing exports is well known, but it is by no means unique. In Kenya, for example, horticultural exports have developed very rapidly since the mid-1980s and are now the country's third largest merchandise export to the EC. Some twenty-eight ACP states have emerged as significant exporters of non-traditional products, and, although many still export only a small number of items, one-third export six or more, and five more than fifteen (McQueen and Stevens 1989). Moreover, diversification is not limited to the more advanced African states, such as Kenya, Mauritius, Zimbabwe and Côte d'Ivoire. It also extends to poorer countries at lower levels of economic development, such as Ethiopia, Sudan and Ghana. By 1987 such non-traditional exports accounted for about 8 per cent of total ACP non-fuel exports to the EC, and were also prominent in exports to major non-EC markets, most notably the USA.

The impact of Lomé preferences

How far can the growth of non-traditional exports be attributed to the Lomé preferences? To try to answer the question, studies have been carried out in a selected group of states, the results of which are reported in three working papers: on Jamaica, Kenya and Ethiopia; on Zimbabwe; and on Mauritius (Stevens 1990; Riddell 1990; McQueen 1990). Between them, these five states illustrate the differential importance of the various Lomé trade preferences in relation both to each other, and to those offered by the ACP's other trading partners. They show also the interaction of demand-side constraints (such as the rules of origin) and those on the supply side (notably unsupportive government policies), and the scope for aid to ease the bottlenecks that limit further diversification.

In none of these particular cases do the non-traditional exports 'solve' the problem of stagnant demand for traditional exports. The new markets into which the countries in question have diversified are highly competitive; diversification is a continuing exercise, not a once-for-all shift. But the studies confirm that the ACP are not somehow incapable of diversification. Furthermore, they provide some evidence that the Lomé preferences have made a contribution to diversification.

It has not been possible to draw an unambiguous causal link between the Lomé Convention and the development of non-traditional exports. A host of factors is at work to explain both the success in exporting *these* new products and the failure to export *others* for which Lomé preferences are also substantial. Government policy in the exporting state is clearly a critical factor. In the cases of both Jamaica and Kenya, for example, the move into non-traditional exports has been very recent, partly because of the unsupportive nature of government policies in the earlier period. None the less, there is some degree of circumstantial evidence to suggest that a link exists.

There is also evidence that imperfections in the Convention are a constraint on more rapid diversification. The rules of origin have been a clear impediment, and the quotas that apply to many of the CAP concessions may become a binding constraint in the future. Significantly, EC imports of manufactures from the ACP have risen much more slowly than those of the USA. Although the EC remains the ACP's principal trade partner, it is fast losing this position. ACP exports of clothing to the USA, for example, now exceed sales to the EC. And the ACP export to the USA some manufactured goods, such as electrical machinery, which do not figure in their trade with Europe.

The growth in exports to the USA can be explained partly in terms of buoyant American demand, but there is also an element of EC protectionism in the story. Jamaican exports of clothing, for example, increased by an annual average of 81 per cent (in US dollar value terms) between 1983 and 1988. But almost all of this increase was accounted for by exports to the USA, with nascent exports to the EC emerging only at the end of the period. The dominance of the USA reflects in part the fact that it is very close geographically to Jamaica and has been able to absorb almost everything that Jamaica is capable of producing. However, US trade preferences are superior to those of the EC in a number of respects. In particular, US legislation allows Jamaica to produce woven clothing from Far Eastern material; the Lomé Convention specifically prohibits this. Hence, while Jamaica is able to export both woven clothing (eg shirts) and knitted goods (eg pullovers and T-shirts) to the USA, it is able to export only the latter to the EC.

Emerging trends

A tension has developed between the focus of formal policy towards the South and the focus of the EC's immediate economic interests. In addition to the changes in the pattern of trade already noted, the disparity between formal policy and effective interests has been reinforced by three factors. Firstly, the lack of strong formal links with newly industrialising countries reflects the fact that the EC has very little to offer in terms of non-commercial inducements. The policy instruments available to the EC are designed primarily to assist poor, not-very-competitive states; they are not well suited to the task of reinforcing relations with highly competitive, middle-income states. Attempts to implement more appropriate policies have hit two hurdles: most would be dependent upon private rather than public sector action; and those that are in the public domain (eg on trade policy) often face strong opposing lobbies.

Second, the panoply of Community and member state policies that have fostered relations with Africa may be regarded as a psychological device to ease the process of decolonisation and disengagement for the Europeans. As with the Commonwealth, so francophony and the Lomé Conventions created the appearance that the break between metropole and colony following decolonisation was less than total. This was comforting not only to the Europeans but also to the europhile elites in the new states. As time has passed, however, the European need for such psychological support has diminished.

A third, related, point is that post-colonial agreements gave the appearance and, to some extent, the reality of safeguarding traditional markets for both sides. On the European side, however, this was of interest primarily to France and UK as the most recent colonial powers. These states have become relatively less powerful influences on Euro-South policy and, in addition, have begun to regard traditional commercial links with Africa as an irrelevance or, worse, a distraction.

As formal policy and effective practice have thus diverged, the framework of policies established after independence has come to look increasingly like a hollow shell. The tension has been partially defused up to now by the retention on the part of each EC member state of control over many of the most potent commercial policy instruments. Export credits, investment promotion, debt rescheduling, remain member state responsibilities. Germany, for example, may be inclined to use these to promote its interests in South-East Asia regardless of the Community focus on the ACP. Indeed, it may prefer the Community to concentrate on the ACP so as not to queer its pitch in Asia. But as powers are transferred increasingly from national to Community level, this capacity to run an independent shadow policy withers; the emphasis within Community-level policy acquires a direct importance for national interests.

Recent developments have thus begun to fracture the shell, a process which is likely to intensify in the medium term. The principal agent of change is *trade liberalisation*, externally within the GATT Uruguay Round and internally with the completion of the Single European Market.

The effects of external trade liberalisation

Trade preferences bulk large in Euro-South relations because they are for the south the most tangible of the limited number of instruments available to the Commission. Their value to the beneficiary is related inversely to the level of protectionism (at least if the matter is viewed in a strictly short-term, static perspective). If the level of protection is high, the competitive advantage afforded by preferences may be substantial. By the same token, if the level of protection is low, the opposite is true. Which way is the trend likely to go in the short- to medium-term future? Despite the set-backs on GATT, there is surely a reasonable chance that the 1990s will be a decade of liberalisation.

As a result, the whole edifice built up over the years by the EC is likely to subside gently as its foundations are weakened by liberalisation. Since this is happening at a time when the pace of European integration is quickening, we may expect that a new edifice will be thrown up to replace the old. The Community institutions will acquire a wider range of powers. Among them, no doubt, will be instruments that are of value to the South, and that may be used to construct a new relationship.

The effects of 1992

Why should the new ways not be just as favourable as the old were to the states at the apex of the pyramid of privilege? The answer is that to an extent they may, but that full replacement of old by new is unlikely, for two reasons. The first is that current EC policy reflects the interests of the past; the new policies and practice are more likely to reflect current interests in which the ACP are, at best, less prominent. The second is that parts of the ACP appear to be ill prepared to take advantage of Europe's new methods and instruments.

The impact of 1992 on LDCs may be profound, simply because it brings into play a host of other issues on which an EC decision will be required as circumstances change. It is these *consequential* decisions that may have the most potent effects on Euro-South relations. The removal of border controls as part of '1992', for example, will remove the power of member states to limit imports from their neighbours and, accordingly, their opportunity to police any national NTBs that may be in place. The countries that make most use of national NTBs are France, Ireland and Italy. Those with the fewest restrictions over and above Community-level quotas are Germany and Denmark. Hence, states that export primarily to France, Ireland and Italy have more reason to be worried about possible increased competition from the NICs and other third-party exporters than do countries exporting primarily to Germany/Denmark or having a broad geographical spread. In fact, France tends to be the largest market for the manufactures exports of both the ACP and the Mediterranean.

The impact of the changes in Eastern Europe

A further source of shock to the shell of formal Euro-South relations stems from the EC's need to redefine its policies towards its Eastern neighbours. While it is far too early to judge the speed and success of Eastern Europe's conversion to a free market economy (see Chapters 9, 10, 11 and 12 in *The National Economies of Europe*), it is possible to identify in broad terms the potential consequences for third parties. In the short to medium term, a successful shift to a free market economy in Eastern Europe is likely to be accompanied by increased demand for external capital, and increased supply of exports of basic manufactures and temperate agricultural products. Failure to make the required adjustment successfully, in contrast, could result in an increase in outward migration.

In either case, the tendency would be to increase competition for some LDCs. Eastern Europe could be competitive with the Mediterranean in particular as a host for foreign direct investment and a borrower of commercial and semi-commercial funds; as a supplier of manufactured exports to the Community; and as a source of migrant workers.

By contrast, the ACP would benefit if rising incomes in Eastern Europe result in an increase in world demand for tropical products. Eastern Europe is one of the few areas of the world in which substantial increases in per capita consumption of tropical products could occur in the medium term.

The degree of competition will be greater if, as seems likely, the EC accords preferential treatment to East European countries. Until the revolution in Eastern Europe the region ranked at the bottom of the EC's hierarchy of trade preferences – the 'pyramid of privilege'. Poland, Romania, Czechoslovakia, Hungary and Yugoslavia were, of course, members of GATT, but only Romania and Yugoslavia benefited from the EC's GSP, and all East European countries faced significant non-tariff barriers to the EC market. In the late 1980s negotiations took place on improving the terms of access. Following the revolutions, the pace of transformation has accelerated. For Hungary and Poland, quantitative restrictions on EC imports of industrial products (except textiles and Coal and Steel Community products) were reduced or abolished from 1 January 1990, and the countries integrated into the GSP. By the middle of 1990 similar agreements had been reached with Czechoslovakia and Bulgaria. However, Eastern Europe's more ambitious hopes of an extensive liberalisation of access on products of key importance are making slow progress. In December 1991 the EC agreed with Poland, Czechoslovakia and Hungary a ten-year transition to mutual free trade, with asymmetrically large tariff cuts on imports into the EC during the first five years. But the deal excluded agriculture, steel and textiles, which are the sectors of most importance to Eastern Europe, and the EC approach to Eastern Europe remains cautious, if not illiberal. None the less, the EC cannot avoid taking an increased interest in the East. For all regions of the South, the most potent effect of the East European revolution may be its influence on EC perceptions. It has reinforced the loss of European interest in the South on both political and economic grounds.

The future

Although GATT, 1992 and Eastern Europe are likely to reinforce the trends of the 1960s, 1970s and 1980s, there are also some 'jokers in the pack' which may result in new relationships. Most potently, European interest may be sustained by concern that LDC actions could have undesirable consequences. The two instances that have received most attention concern migration and the environment.

The differential rates of economic and population growth in the EC and the non-EC Mediterranean region have already given rise to substantial inward migration into the Community, and the trend is likely to intensify sharply. This new wave of immigration differs from past flows in two respects, both of which have political implications: the proportion of political as opposed to economic refugees rose strongly during the 1980s to 70 per cent; and two-thirds of immigrants are Muslim.

There is increased awareness that what happens in LDCs may adversely affect EC welfare. Global warming as a result of forest burning, AIDS and drugs are simply the most publicised instances of the ways in which modern technology and more intense global communications have linked North and South on new dimensions.

These new issues present EC policy-makers with a critical problem. They can, to put it crudely, attempt to influence behaviour in the South by 'bribes' or 'threats', but neither is entirely satisfactory. Bribes, in the form of assistance to help an LDC cope with a specific problem (or grow faster to reduce migration) need to be much larger than is likely to be politically acceptable if they are to be effective. Threats, in the form of leverage applied to existing flows, may cause LDC governments to change officially stated policy, but are rarely effective in altering practice on the ground.

If existing instruments are unsuitable for the task, Europe may seek new ones; or it may be forced to tolerate a higher degree of Third World influence on its domestic affairs than it would wish. In either case, the course of Euro-South relations in future may not flow as rapidly towards disengagement as past trends would suggest.

References

Brown D K (1988) Trade preferences for developing countries: a survey of results. *Journal of Development Studies* 24(3)

Davenport M (1988) European Community trade barriers to tropical agricultural products. Overseas Development Institute, *Working Paper 27*

Davenport M, Stevens C (1990) The outlook for tropical products. In Stevens C, Faber D (eds) *The Uruguay Round and Europe 1992: Implications for ACP/EC Cooperation*. European Centre for Development Policy Management, Maastricht

Davenport M, Page S (1991) *Europe: 1992 and the Developing World*. Overseas Development Institute

McAleese D (1989) External trade policy of the EC. Paper presented to the Senior Policy Seminar of the World Bank and HEDCO *Africa and Europe after 1992* Dublin Nov. 27–30

McQueen M (1990) ACP export diversification: the case of Mauritius. Overseas Development Institute, *Working Paper 41*

McQueen M, Stevens C (1989) Trade preferences and Lomé IV: Non-traditional ACP exports to the EC. *Development Policy Review* 7: 239–60

Riddell R (1990) ACP export diversification: the case of Zimbabwe. Overseas Development Institute, *Working Paper 38*

Sampson G P (1989) Trade expansion through the Generalised System of Preferences. In Kiljunen K (ed) *Mini-NIEO: the Potential of Regional North–South Cooperation*. Institute of Development Studies, Helsinki

Sapir A, Stevens C (1987) India's exports of manufactures to the European Community: recent performance and constraints. *Development Policy Review* 5: 379–98

Stevens C (1990) ACP export diversification: Jamaica, Kenya and Ethiopia. Overseas Development Institute, *Working Paper 40*

Part IV
Technology and structural change

CHAPTER 12

Changing industrial structures in Western Europe

MARGARET SHARP

Introduction

The purpose of this chapter is to chart the main changes in Western Europe's industrial structure during the last thirty years, concentrating in particular on the changes that took place in the 1980s. The dominant trend during this period has been the affirmation – or perhaps one should say reaffirmation – of Germany as the dynamo within the Western European economic system. By the mid-1960s (Western) Germany had emerged from the 'economic miracle' of the 1950s as, once again, the strongest industrial economy in Europe. In terms of GDP per head it overtook the UK in the early 1960s and, although shaken by the recessions of the 1970s and 1980s, maintained a surprisingly strong overall position throughout this period, as witness its successful export performance and continuing surplus on the balance of payments. While unification seems likely temporarily to weaken this position – Western Germany in effect assuming the very considerable burden of reconstructing (and cleaning-up) the industrial base of Eastern Germany – it seems probable that the new, reunifed Germany will fairly rapidly emerge as a major force within the European economy (see Flockton, Chapter 3 in *The National Economies of Europe*, on Germany).

In industrial terms, the 1970s and 1980s tend to be viewed as a period of turbulence. They witnessed the two Oil Crises of 1973–4 and 1978–9 which, symbolically, marked an end to the period of fast growth of industries such as bulk chemicals, plastics and artificial fibres, all predicated upon plentiful supplies of cheap oil, and badly shook that other engine of post-war growth – the motor car. As these fast-growth industries of the 1950s and 1960s matured, so they were replaced by new industrial sectors, in particular by electronics and its associated activities – semiconductors, computers, telecommunications and consumer electronics – and by the new, fast-growth chemicals sectors – the high-value-added sectors of speciality chemicals and pharmaceuticals.

As is often the case, the origins of these new activities are to be found in earlier periods – the computer industry, for example, began to emerge in the 1950s – but it takes time for economies of scale and scope to make their mark. The trigger for the 'massification' of the computer industry was the development of the microprocessor (the computer on a chip), which brought costs and size down to levels at which computers became a consumer durable in the home as much as a business machine in the office, and could be incorporated into robots on the production line. The strong links between electronics and defence, with many leading-edge activities seeing their origins in defence requirements, meant that in Europe the early development of these new technologies was often to be found with the big defence spenders, the UK and France, UK firms in particular having close ties with their American counterparts. But defence industries tend to ignore the mass market; as the emphasis switched to civilian application – for example using electronics to monitor and correct the performance of car engines – so the initial advantage of the French and the British receded, and the Germans, the Swiss and the Swedes, with their broad-based capabilities in engineering, moved into positions of dominance, challenged not by the USA, pioneer of these new technologies, but increasingly by the Japanese, who combine broad-based capabilities in engineering with highly efficient production management and a readiness to innovate.

In this chapter we begin by mapping the broad changes in industrial structure and refining these in terms of country and sector. We then turn to trade performance and measures of comparative advantage, linking these to measures of technological performance. In the final section we turn to issues of industrial policy and corporate strategy, noting in particular the increasing role of multinational companies and the problems they pose for policy-makers. In the succeeding chapters, developments in some of these sectors – the car industry, electronics, and chemicals and pharmaceuticals – are explored at greater length.

Broad changes in industrial structure

Table 12.1 shows the changing balance of contributions to value added (GDP) and employment coming from the main sectors of activity for the West European market economies (ie excluding Eastern Europe) for the years 1965 to 1990, with projections through to 2000. The story told is a familiar one – the continuing diminution in the shares of agriculture and mining (although North Sea oil production caused a blip in the latter between 1973 and 1985), and the rise of the service sectors. In terms of value added to total GDP, manufacturing has held its own, and continues to contribute just under 30 per cent to GDP; but in terms of employment, manufacturing had dipped from 30.1 per cent in 1965 to 25.4 per cent of the work-force by 1990, with agriculture falling more dramatically from 16.2 per to 6.8 per cent, mining from 1.5 to 0.7 per cent, and construction from 8.7 per cent to 6.8 per cent. The big gainers in employment have been the service sectors, particularly finance and collective government (ie both central and local) services.

The importance of these changes should not be exaggerated. In value-added terms, perhaps the most notable feature of Table 12.1 is the relative stability of shares, with manufacturing holding its own against services. It is only in terms of employment that we begin to see the 'de-industrialisation' of which there was once so much discussion (Blackaby 1978). Here Europe lags behind the USA, where manufacturing employment by the same Economic Commission for Europe (ECE) calculations now constitutes only 16.5 per cent of total employment.

Table 12.1   European market economies: shares of value added and employment by sector (%)

	Past values				'Base-line' scenario
	1965	*1973*	*1985*	*1990**	*2000*
Value added					
Agriculture	6.6	5.4	5.2	4.8	4.5
Mining and quarrying	2.0	1.4	1.9	1.7	1.5
Manufacturing	28.0	30.6	28.2	28.6	28.8
Electricity, gas and water	2.2	2.8	2.9	3.0	3.0
Construction	9.0	8.0	6.1	6.0	5.9
Trade	13.5	13.5	13.2	13.5	13.8
Transport and communications	6.1	6.4	6.9	7.4	7.8
Finance	12.5	13.4	15.6	15.4	15.6
Collective services	20.1	18.6	19.9	19.6	19.1
Employment					
Agriculture	16.2	10.9	7.6	6.8	5.2
Mining and quarrying	1.5	0.9	0.8	0.7	0.6
Manufacturing	30.1	29.0	26.3	25.4	22.1
Electricity, gas and water	0.9	0.9	0.9	0.9	0.8
Construction	8.7	8.4	7.2	6.8	6.5
Trade	14.3	15.5	17.0	17.8	20.2
Transport and communications	5.7	6.0	5.8	5.6	5.1
Finance	3.5	5.2	7.0	7.6	8.4
Collective services	19.0	23.3	27.3	28.3	31.2

Note: * Estimates

Source: ECE Secretariat database and estimates, Geneva, ECE 1990

There are those who bewail such developments. Manufacturing (making things) is seen somehow to be superior in wealth creation terms to providing services, and the loss of jobs in manufacturing is seen as the thin edge of a thicker wedge of failing to pay one's way in the world. How much truth is there in this? There are a number of points that are worth making.

1   Although there has been substantial growth in international trade in services in the post-war world, trade in manufactured goods still constitutes 90 per cent of total trade; hence, from the point of view of 'paying one's way in the world', manufacturing does matter.
2   However, it is value added – the value of manufactured goods produced – not employment that counts; indeed, producing the same value of goods for a lesser input of effort (employment) should be to everyone's advantage.
3   In any case, many services are what are called 'producer services', closely linked with manufacturing, for example the leasing and maintenance of the computers which control the production line. This means, first, that the buoyancy of that part of the service sector is closely tied to manufacturing activity; and second, that the boundaries between manufacturing and services become increasingly blurred. In a

Table 12.2 The structural composition of output 1980 and 1988

Country	% Contribution to output						% Change in employment 1978–88		
	Agriculture		Industry[a]		Services		Agriculture	Industry	Services
	1980	1988	1980	1988	1980	1988			
UK	1.8	1.4[b]	36.7	31.8[b]	61.5	66.8[b]	−14.6	−21.2	10.9
FRG	2.1	1.5[b]	42.7	40.1[b]	55.2	58.4[b]	−3.5	−0.4	1.9
France	4.2	3.3	33.7	29.3	62.0	67.3	−26.5	−18.0	16.0
Italy	5.8	3.7	39.0	33.4	55.2	62.7	−33.0	−10.4	31.2
Netherlands	3.5	4.0	32.8	30.7	63.7	65.3	1.1	1.2	3.5
Belgium	2.3	2.1	35.9	30.9[b]	61.8	67.1[b]	−15.3	−21.8	14.2
Spain	7.1	5.7[c]	38.6	39.3[c]	54.3	55.0[c]	−31.8	−14.6	23.3
Sweden	3.4	2.7	30.8	30.3	65.8	67.0	−33.1	−4.6	17.2
USA	2.6	2.0[b]	33.6	29.2[b]	63.8	68.8[b]	−6.3	3.6	28.9
Japan	3.7	2.8[b]	41.9	40.6[b]	54.4	56.7[b]	−25.1	8.4	20.9

Notes:
[a] Including mining, utilities and construction
[b] 1987
[c] 1986

Source: *OECD in Figures*, Supplement to *OECD Observer* June/July 1990: 28–9

word, is the computer maintenance engineer part of the manufacturing or the service sector?

Overall, the conclusion has to be that for any individual country it is the total value added of goods and services produced in relation to population that is important: the specific mix between goods and services is irrelevent provided there are buyers for them. However, given the bias of international trade towards manufacturing, it seems unlikely that any country, other than the Monte Carlos of this world, could pay their way entirely on services. In addition, the strength of the bulk of those services will depend on there being somewhere a core of manufacturing. Hence, even if some countries within a broad trading bloc, such as the European Community, specialise in services, there will need to be others that specialise in manufactures. (For a discussion of this point in relation to the USA, see Cohen and Zysman 1987.)

Disaggregation between different European countries (with the USA and Japan brought in to broaden the basis of comparison) does, indeed, reveal somewhat varied patterns of specialisation. Table 12.2 again looks at the broad division between agriculture, industry (here including mining, construction and the utilities) and the service sector in the 1980s, and shows that of the major West European countries only Western Germany and Spain have an industrial sector contributing as much as 40 per cent to GDP (equivalent to its contribution in Japan), whereas the UK, France and Sweden all join the USA in having a services sector that now contributes over two-thirds of GDP. All the countries featured in Table 12.2 saw an increased share of employment in services over the period under consideration. That increase was at its lowest in West Germany and the Netherlands, and highest not, as one might have

Table 12.3 The contribution of the service industries to GDP 1980–8

	Government services		Wholesale and retail trade and hotels		Transport, storage and communications		Finance, insurance and real estate		Community, social and personal	
	1980	1988	1980	1988	1980	1988	1980	1988	1980	1988
UK	13.8	13.1[a]	11.1	11.8	6.2	6.3[a]	16.0	20.3[a]	5.3	6.1[a]
FRG	11.7	11.3[a]	10.7	10.2[a]	5.8	5.7[a]	10.3	11.9[a]	12.9	16.2[a]
France	16.0	16.1	14.1	15.3[a]	5.8	5.9	16.8	20.5	4.3	5.4
Italy	11.0	12.4	18.1	18.8	5.2	6.0	19.2[b]	22.9[b]	0.8[b]	0.9[b]
Netherlands	13.9	11.6	12.9	12.7	6.3	6.9	13.9	17.1	11.5	11.3
Belgium	14.6	13.3	18.4[d]	21.4[d]	7.9	7.8	13.0	16.8	10.2	11.4
Spain	10.3	11.1[c]	18.2	20.7[c]	5.8	5.6[c]	13.2	12.5[c]	8.5	9.6[c]
Sweden	22.3	19.3	10.5	10.8	6.2	5.9	14.2	18.0	4.4	4.7
USA	12.4	12.0[a]	16.9	17.2[a]	6.4	6.1[a]	20.4	25.1[a]	8.3	9.7[a]
Japan	8.5	8.2[a]	15.3	13.3[a]	6.2	6.2[a]	14.6	16.1[a]	13.5	16.7[a]

Notes:
[a] 1987
[b] For Italy Community, etc, services included in Finance, etc
[c] 1986
[d] Includes import duties and excludes hotels (obviously not really comparable with the others)

Source: *OECD in Figures*, Supplement to *OECD Observer* June/July 1990: 36–7

expected, in the UK with its flourishing financial services sector, but in Italy and Spain, with the UK showing a relatively modest increase of 20.9 per cent, exactly the same as that of Japan. (But Japan also saw an 8.4 per cent *increase* in employment in industry, whereas the UK saw a corresponding 21.2 per cent fall over the same period.)

Table 12.3 looks in more detail at growth in the services sector over the 1980s for the same group of countries, focusing on the changing pattern of contribution to GDP rather than employment. The outstanding feature of this table is the growth in the financial services sector, whose contribution to GDP now tops 25 per cent in the USA, and 20 per cent in the UK, France and Italy. It is at its lowest (12 per cent) not, as one might have expected, in Spain, the least developed of the countries featured in Table 12.3, but in West Germany. Other interesting features of this table are the generally falling share of GDP devoted to government services (Italy and Spain being the only countries to buck this trend), and the variation in the share going to retail and wholesale trade and hotels, where the major tourist countries – Italy, Spain and to a lesser extent France – stand out. But there are interesting variations among the other countries, some of which undoubtedly reflect the pattern of relative efficiency of the distribution sector – or perhaps, more significantly, its relative inefficiency in the USA and Japan.

Although the services sector in all these countries now makes a larger contribution to output than manufacturing, much interest still focuses on developments within manufacturing: indeed discussion of changing industrial structures is normally implicitly assumed to centre on manufacturing. Table 12.4 identifies the twenty-eight main (two-digit) branches of manufacturing industry and divides them into three groups: fast-, medium- and slow-growth sectors, ranked by their overall performance for the period

Table 12.4 The structure and growth rates of OECD output ('world demand') by growth sectors and branches

ISIC		% Composition[a]	Growth rates 1963–88		Growth rates 1979/80–8 ('1980s')	
		1980–8 (average)	%pa	rank	%pa	rank
	Fast growth[b]					
356	Plastic products	2.5	7.9	1	41	2
383	Electrical machinery	11.0	6.1	2	7.2	1
351	Industrial chemicals	4.9	5.0	3	2.1	9
352	Other chemicals	5.0	4.7	4	3.6	5
385	Scientific instruments	2.4	4.6	5	3.1	6
382	Non-electrical machinery	11.8	4.2	6	4.0	3
	Medium growth[b]					
341	Paper products	3.5	3.4	7	3.0	7
342	Printing and publishing	5.6	3.4	8	3.8	4
313	Beverages	2.0	3.2	9	1.3	14
362	Glass products	0.9	3.1	10	0.8	17
332	Furniture	1.4	2.8	11	1.2	15
384	Transport equipment	11.0	2.8	12	2.6	8
355	Rubber products	1.2	2.8	13	2.0	10
372	Non-ferrous metals	1.5	2.6	14	1.5	13
311	Food	8.8	2.5	15	1.7	12
381	Fabricated metal products	6.4	2.5	16	0.9	16
	Slow growth[b]					
390	Other manufacturing	1.3	2.2	17	−0.1	20
369	Other non-metallic mineral products	2.7	2.1	18	0.6	18
331	Wood products, exc. furniture	1.8	2.1	19	1.8	11
361	Pottery and china	0.3	1.8	20	0.4	19
353	Petroleum refining	2.4	1.8	21	−2.2	27
314	Tobacco	1.1	1.3	22	−0.3	23
321	Textiles	3.4	1.2	23	−0.2	21
322	Apparel	2.1	0.8	24	−0.8	25
371	Iron and steel	4.0	0.8	25	−0.3	22
354	Coal and petroleum	0.3	0.4	26	−0.8	24
323	Leather products	0.3	−1.0	27	−2.1	26
324	Footwear	0.4	−2.4	28	−3.9	28
300	Total manufacturing	100.0	3.1		2.9	

Notes:
[a] Composition refers to percentage of total manufacturing value-added
[b] For a definition of fast, medium and slow growth, see text

Source: UNIDO Industrial Statistics Database, quoted in Saunders, Matthews and Patel 1991: Table 2.4

1963–88 in the OECD region as a whole. The rank ordering among these twenty-eight branches changed surprisingly little over this twenty-five-year period, despite the substantial decline in overall OECD growth (from 4.5 per cent in the 1960s to 2 per cent in the 1970s, recovering to 2.9 per cent in the 1980s). In general the table shows faster growth in capital goods sectors than in consumer goods (with the exception of

Table 12.5 Manufacturing output growth rates by periods; structural composition and structural change by country and OECD

	UK	FRG	France	Italy	NL	Belgium	Spain	Sweden	OECD Europe average	Japan	USA	OECD average
A Growth rate (%pa) of total manufacturing												
1963–73/4	2.6	4.1	5.0	4.9	3.6	4.1	9.7	4.2	3.6	9.2	4.8	4.6
1973/4–79/80	−1.6	1.4	0.7	2.2	1.3	0.8	1.7	0.7	0.7	2.4	2.2	1.6
1979/80–88	1.6	1.5	0.3	0.6	0.7	0.1	1.6	2.0	1.5	4.7	2.9	2.9
B Composition of manufacturing in 1980–88 (%)												
Fast	36.5	43.4	31.3	35.3	36.4	32.9	25.9	31.8	36.2	41.0	38.9	37.6
Medium	44.2	36.1	43.6	35.7	47.2	45.1	45.3	50.6	41.4	38.6	44.2	42.3
Slow	19.3	20.5	25.4	29.0	16.4	22.0	28.8	17.6	22.7	20.4	16.4	20.1
All manufacturing	100	100	100	100	100	100	100	100	100	100	100	100
C 'Adjustment' changes in composition between 1963–73 and 1980–8 (in % points)												
Fast	3.5	9.1	4.0	2.4	2.2	6.5	3.4	3.5	5.8	5.5	4.5	5.0
Medium	0.5	1.1	5.5	−0.2	3.7	0.1	2.1	3.7	1.5	0.8	0.4	0.0
Slow	−4.0	−11.2	−9.1	−2.3	−6.1	−6.4	−5.2	−7.2	−7.0	−6.2	−5.2	−5.4
Sum of changes	8.0	21.4	18.6	4.9	12.0	13.0	10.7	14.4	14.3	12.5	10.1	10.4

Source: UNIDO Industrial Statistics Database, quoted in Saunders, Matthews and Patel 1991: Table 2.6

consumer electronics, included in electrical machinery), the major changes being the much slower growth of the industrial (commodity) chemicals sector in the 1980s, and the relative rise of the sectors associated with information technology, in broad terms, including paper and printing. (Think how much extra paper the Xerox machine has generated!) Interestingly, transport equipment (mostly motor vehicles), one of the key post-war growth sectors, improved its ranking from twelfth to eighth place over the 1980s, even though its growth rate declined slightly. Table 12.4 also shows how OECD output is dominated by a relatively small number of large sectors. Electrical and non-electrical machinery, instruments and transport equipment, taken together, accounted in the 1980s for 36 per cent of output; the chemicals sectors for another 12 per cent; and food and beverages for 11 per cent. In other words eight of the twenty-eight sectors listed accounted for over 60 per cent of output.

Table 12.5 analyses country by country variations in these three growth categories. As with the broader measures of structure examined in Tables 12.1 and 12.2, the pattern is one of similarity rather than divergence: most countries had a roughly comparable share of manufacturing capabilities in the fast-, medium- and slow-growth categories to the OECD *in toto* (37.6, 42.3 and 20.1 per cent respectively): all experienced faster growth in the fast-growth industries, and slower growth in the slow-growth industries. But there were significant variations. West Germany (43 per cent), Japan (41 per cent) and the USA (39 per cent) were all above the OECD average for shares in fast-growth sectors; Spain at 26 per cent (along with some of the other smaller EC member countries not shown in the table such as Greece and Portugal) falls well below the average.

If these figures were further disaggregated, considerable differences would be highlighted in the weights of individual branches in different countries, indicating a pattern of branch specialisation. For example, within the fast-growth group, Japan's weighting is largely the result of its well-established specialisation in the electronics sectors, while The Netherlands and West Germany are also more specialised than other countries in electrical machinery. (In The Netherlands' case this reflects the importance to its economy of the giant Philips electrical firm.) In chemicals, by contrast, the European countries (especially West Germany, the UK and The Netherlands) are much more strongly represented than Japan. In the slow-growth group, there are some interesting specialisations: Italy in textiles, clothing and footwear; Belgium and Japan in iron and steel; Sweden in wood products, paper and furniture; and Spain in leather goods.

Such exceptions to the pattern of general similarity in national structures (which will reappear in the trade patterns examined in the next section) show that structural change does not necessarily run to a set pattern. While specialisation in some of the older, slower-growing industries might superficially appear as a failure to adapt to world demand, it can in fact mask highly successful development, particularly when success is based upon process innovations (paper and wood products in Sweden), or design and quality innovations (furniture in Sweden and Italy, clothing and footwear in Italy). Correspondingly, of course, retreat from slow-growth industries, a marked feature in most OECD countries, does not necessarily mean poor performance, for it can be offset by growing competitiveness in fast-growth sectors, as has happened *par excellence* in Japan, but not always elsewhere, notably in the UK.

To understand the process of structural change it is therefore preferable to disaggregate by country and by sector, and to examine in detail the different patterns of change in different countries. Crude measures of overall structural change have been developed, one of which – the sum of the *absolute* differences over a given time period, irrespective of sign, in branch shares in total manufacturing – is used in Table 12.6. If the test generates a relatively high figure, this is an indication of a relatively strong impetus to overall structural change, and vice versa. Looking at the OECD as a whole, it would seem that there has been some acceleration in the rate of structural change since the late 1970s, with Japan, the USA, West Germany, the UK and Spain all showing faster change, whereas the structural dynamic in France, Italy, The Netherlands and Belgium (all members of the original EC Six), and Sweden seems to be slowing down compared to the earlier period. The most marked change in position is in fact that of the UK; bottom of the earlier league table (column 1) but second top of the later, after Spain. Given all that has happened to the UK during this period – its reorientation towards Europe as a result of entry into the EC in 1973 and the Thatcher revolution of the 1980s – perhaps this is not so surprising. However, its poor showing in the fast-growth industries (Table 12.5) is, for UK policy-makers, a continuing cause for concern.

Changing patterns of trade

Table 12.7 provides a broad overview of trade flows. The first two columns give the percentage growth of imports and exports over the decade 1978–88 and illustrate

Table 12.6 The magnitude of structural change in manufacturing

Country/area	1963/73–74/79	1974/79–80/88
OECD	5.9	11.1
OECD-Europe	8.7	8.3
EC (12)	8.8	9.3
Japan	9.4	13.9
USA	8.2	7.0
FRG	13.4	19.2
France	15.5	7.5
UK	7.0	16.0
Italy	11.5	10.6
Netherlands	13.8	9.8
Spain	15.7	19.6
Belgium	14.3	12.3
Sweden	13.6	10.4

Note: These magnitudes are given by the sum of absolute differences in branch shares of total value added between given time periods

Source: UNIDO Industrial Statistics Database, quoted in Saunders, Matthews and Patel 1991: Table 2.7

Table 12.7 Overall patterns of trade

Country	% Change volume 1978–88		Export market Shares 1988		Trade coverage ratios 1988			
	Imports	Exports	Manuf. (OECD = 100)	High RDI[a]	High RDI[a]	Med RDI[b] (exports/imports)	Low RDI[c]	
UK	5.2	2.8	7.25	8.47	0.93	0.93	0.67	
FRG	3.3	4.0	18.18	14.95	1.26	2.30	0.93	
France	3.9	3.4	8.43	7.51	0.96	1.05	0.85	
Italy	4.6	2.9	7.43	4.34	0.77	1.18	1.33	
Netherlands	3.2	4.2	5.16	3.74	0.83	1.04	1.19	
Belgium	3.3	4.2	4.76	2.13	0.83	1.06	1.18	
Spain	6.8	5.9	1.97	0.90	0.36	0.73	1.29	
Sweden	4.1	4.2	2.80	2.06	0.89	1.18	1.41	
USA	5.5	6.0	12.81	21.76	0.86	0.52	0.35	
Japan	4.4	6.6	14.71	22.66	5.15	4.23	0.92	

Notes:
RDI = R&D Intensity
[a] High RDI = aerospace, office machinery, computers, electronic components, drugs and medicines, instruments, elect. machinery
[b] Medium RDI = motor vehicles, chemicals, non-electrical machinery, rubber, plastics, non-ferrous metals, other transport equipment
[c] Low RDI = all other industries

Source: *OECD in Figures*, Supplement to *OECD Observer* June/July 1990: 56–7; 60–1

clearly the chronic tendencies of both the UK and Italy to import more than they export, while West Germany and Japan tend to export more than they import. Columns 3 and 4 show that for West Germany this export dominance comes from the general run of manufactures, whereas for Japan it comes especially from high technology (R&D-intensive) categories. The final three columns indicate where West Germany and Japan gain their trading advantage from. Both are well represented in the high and medium R&D intensity (based on R&D/sales ratios) sectors and score modestly in the low R&D sectors.

Table 12.8 assesses each country's trade performance on the basis of the fast-, medium- and slow-growth categories used earlier to analyse industrial production. (The categories are similar to, but not quite the same as, the OECD categories based on R&D intensity used in Table 12.7.) Looking at individual country shares it is notable that West Germany's total export share, at nearly 18 per cent, is more than double that of any other EC country, and exceeds that of both the USA and Japan. Its strong market share is mirrored by its strong presence in the fast and medium-growth categories, particularly in the plastics and chemicals sectors, in transport equipment (predominantly cars), furniture and printing and publishing. By contrast, the UK's average export share for manufactures as a whole is only 7.35 per cent, and its strongest growing sectors are beverages and tobacco, both relatively slow-growing industries. Among high technology industries, the UK has tended to specialise increasingly on those with defence linkages, particularly aerospace (included here within transport equipment) and pharmaceuticals (included within the 'other chemicals' category).

The UK and West Germany both present a fairly even spread of competitiveness, with few cases of outstanding comparative advantage (where particular export shares vastly exceed average shares) or obvious specialisations. The differences in overall trade share between them is, therefore, not explained by differences in industrial structure – for example, Britain tending to specialise in low-growth sectors – but rather by other factors which affect all industries, such as skill levels, investment in new equipment, commitment to R&D, etc. As pointed out in earlier chapters, a central feature of the last few decades has been the vigorous growth of intra-industry trade. Britain and Germany, for example, export both motor cars and car parts to each other in large quantities. This deepening micro-specialisation reflects partly the increasing degree to which multinationals are treating Europe as a single location and shipping parts from one plant to another; partly, the degree of market differentiation – what counts, more and more, in export markets is not price *per se*, but the price-design-reliability package. As we all know, different cars incorporate different combinations of design, engine, features, etc; seemingly small variations in design, for instance, can have a major impact upon sales and trade flows.

Italy is a good example of such a phenomenon: its overall export market share – just over 7.5 per cent – is slightly greater than that of the UK, but its product pattern is much more varied. Italy's strong points (where it has a market share of 12 per cent or more) are in plastics (fast growth), furniture (medium growth – but with a 25 per cent market share Italy is Europe's outstanding exporter in this sector), and five slow-growth branches – pottery, cement, clothing, leather goods and footwear. Italy's weakest points are in the three fast-growing groups (electrical machinery, other

Table 12.8   Shares of total OECD manufacturing exports by product groups: 1984–7

	UK	FRG	France	Italy	NL	EC	Japan	USA
Fast growth								
356 Plastic products	6.73	23.71	9.49	14.72	6.52	68.09	7.34	11.49
383 Electrical machinery	6.23	15.12	6.78	4.42	3.65	39.09	35.10	15.93
351 Industrial chemicals	8.99	21.82	10.37	5.60	10.28	60.93	7.96	17.06
352 Other chemicals	12.92	18.72	14.75	4.87	6.38	63.45	6.89	14.85
385 Scientific instruments	8.58	16.64	6.21	3.32	4.46	42.19	23.51	19.49
382 Non-electrical machinery	8.32	19.97	6.29	8.72	3.00	50.32	17.04	19.76
Medium growth								
341 Paper products	2.95	10.40	5.21	2.85	3.65	28.35	2.67	12.19
313 Beverages	18.36	8.06	36.77	9.68	5.92	88.88	0.99	3.16
342 Printing and publishing	13.99	20.99	9.83	6.52	6.08	64.27	4.47	16.37
362 Glass products	6.42	21.46	17.54	11.15	3.94	66.13	9.88	10.84
332 Furniture	4.41	22.27	7.25	24.98	4.15	72.71	2.68	7.30
384 Transport equipment	5.66	19.57	7.83	3.75	1.37	40.88	24.98	17.51
311 Food	4.97	13.48	11.38	5.06	16.29	65.74	1.63	14.28
355 Rubber products	7.44	17.86	15.78	9.14	3.71	58.82	17.77	9.33
Slow growth								
372 Non-ferrous metals	8.99	17.08	8.43	3.50	4.89	46.84	6.20	9.28
381 Fabricated metal products	7.18	23.31	8.95	11.91	5.12	61.89	11.93	9.08
390 Other manufacturing	14.96	11.42	7.05	17.52	2.11	56.40	16.03	9.72
369 Cement, clay, etc.	4.95	17.86	8.64	22.96	3.61	69.92	9.90	7.72
331 Wood	1.05	7.60	4.06	3.10	1.99	24.17	0.87	12.30
353 Petroleum refining	10.36	6.35	7.21	9.66	27.87	71.37	1.23	11.77
361 Pottery and china	11.13	18.08	6.69	15.85	2.11	61.40	26.41	6.10
314 Tobacco	15.31	14.37	1.93	0.12	20.80	55.67	0.28	6.91
321 Textiles	7.02	19.07	10.00	15.10	5.85	64.02	13.85	6.91
322 Apparel	7.36	15.85	9.93	28.03	4.17	78.69	2.98	3.90
354 Coal and petroleum	7.43	28.21	5.98	4.63	6.25	55.11	10.59	19.13
371 Iron and steel	5.39	20.07	11.73	7.49	3.92	54.32	26.18	2.65
323 Leather products	8.28	14.76	10.19	29.68	3.12	76.24	5.92	7.95
324 Footwear	2.76	7.74	6.90	51.14	1.98	87.78	0.49	3.01
300 Total manufacturing	7.35	17.82	8.64	7.57	5.44	51.97	16.43	14.80

Source: OECD COMPTAP Database, quoted in Saunders, Matthews and Patel 1991: Table 2.9

chemicals, and scientific instruments), and in eight medium or slow-growth markets, including transport equipment and paper products. Yet, despite the fact that its growth industries are out of line with world growth patterns, Italy has succeeded in increasing its overall market share, in part because of its strong showing in the slow-growth markets (see Paci, Chapter 4, on Italy, in *The National Economies of Europe*).

Looking beyond Europe, the USA and Japan have total export shares of 15 and 16.5 per cent respectively (NB less than West Germany). Superficially the USA seems well placed, with above average trade shares in five of the six fast-growing sectors, plus aircraft. But this seemingly advantageous pattern of trade needs to be seen in the light of longer-term trends. The USA was world leader in the introduction of computers,

Table 12.9 Export/import ratios in information technology products: 1965–87

	EC–4*			USA			Japan		
	1965	1979	1987	1965	1979	1987	1965	1979	1987
Typewriters and office machines	1.08	1.33	1.27	2.82	0.48	0.36	0.52	4.54	19.65
Computers and peripherals	1.39	0.83	0.77	4.30	3.48	1.11	0.14	2.20	6.24
Telecommunications equipment	2.15	1.78	1.33	2.84	0.88	0.47	10.18	11.95	15.57
Consumer electronics	1.93	0.59	0.45	0.36	0.17	0.06	86.01	42.01	28.63
Scientific instruments, photographic supplies, watches and clocks	1.55	1.04	0.96	1.94	1.04	0.59	4.38	4.85	6.47
Electrical instruments (measuring and control including medical)	1.24	1.21	1.32	6.42	4.54	1.75	1.04	1.06	2.08

Note: * EC-4 = FRG, France, UK, Italy. Figures *exclude* intra-trade

Source: Anderson ES, Lundvall B-Å and Nielson KV, 1991, Learning, structural change, competitiveness and employment with special respect to IT and EC. EC Conference 17 and 18 October, Report M-BR5, IKE Aalborg Institute of Production

television sets, integrated circuits and many electronic innovations, and at one point dominated world trade in electronic products. The USA's market share in such products did, however, slip markedly in the 1980s. Table 12.9, which details export to import ratios in the main electronics sectors, gives graphic illustration of how, since the 1960s, US dominance in electronics has given way to Japanese. Only in computers do exports continue to exceed imports, and even there the ratio has deteriorated from 4.3 to 1.1.

Table 12.9 also illustrates the strength of Japan's advance in all sectors of electronics, and the broadening of its base from consumer electronics (where its import/ export (X/M) ratio was already 86 in 1965) to other categories. Even in instrumentation, long regarded as an area of strength for European and US firms, Japan's X/M ratio doubled to 2.08 in the period 1965–87, exceeding both the US and European figures. The relative weakness of Europe, even in telecommunications, traditionally seen as its strongest sector in ICT (information and computer technology), is sharply delineated in comparison, especially with the position of Japan.

Looking back over the trends surveyed in the two previous sections, two features stand out. First, the growing convergence of economic and industrial structures: in other words, as countries mature in industrialisation, so both in broad economic structure – the contribution of agriculture, industry and services to output – and in the finer detail of those structures, experience is very similar. The fast-growing industries of Western Europe are the fast-growing industries of Japan and the USA, and although there are of course differences from country to country, these are not vast, and the broad pattern remains one of the convergence, not divergence. The second conclusion follows from the first. If all countries are growing more alike in industrial structure, then increasingly trade is taking place not between sectors, with one country specialising in one industry and another in another, but *within* sectors, with countries trading increasingly specialised products between themselves, as illustrated by the motor vehicle industry referred to earlier.

In spite of this, there do seem to be *national* differences in performance, as measured by market share. The West German performance, for example, seems *always* to be better than that of the UK, whether one is talking about the machinery or the clothing industry. Yet the deutschmark has been consistently stronger than the pound, and on a straight comparison German goods would often seem more expensive. Clearly, however, they are judged more desirable in terms of 'value for money', and in that sense more competitive. It used to be assumed that these differences in competitiveness were related to industrial structures, but the figures we have examined above indicate that this is no longer the case, if it ever was. Only with Japan is there a clear example of structural specialisation (in electronics) which has a knock-on effect on general performance. For other countries and other sectors we have still to provide an explanation for the variable incidence of these non-price factors which can have such an important effect on performance.

Variations in technological performance

One obvious factor that affects performance is technology: not only the growth in output of high technology sectors, which was picked up by the output and trade figures discussed in the previous section, but also the extent to which the general run of goods and services being produced incorporate up-to-date features, and are being manufactured by up-to-date processes. Neither of these features is easy to measure: cars, for example, tend to be classified by engine size, not by whether they have fuel injection systems or electronic ignition; a colour TV is a colour TV irrespective of whether it has remote control or teletext. There are some figures about the use of robotics or computer-aided design and manufacturing (CAD/CAM) systems in different sectors, but they too are patchy and highly unreliable. As a general measure of how far industry in different countries is up-to-date in its use of technology, two sets of figures are generally used; one representing the inputs into technology, namely research and development statistics; the other a measure of technological output, namely patents. Although each has its limitations, both do provide broad measures of technological performance which are comparable over time and between countries.

Table 12.10 shows trends in *industrially financed* R&D as a percentage of GDP. These give some indication of how far *industry itself* is prepared to invest in updating its own products and processes. The final column gives, just for 1988, the total percentage of GDP devoted to R&D in each country, the difference between the two figures indicating the respective government contributions to R&D (which includes support for R&D at universities and research institutes; defence R&D, particularly important for the UK and France; and government support for industrial R&D). A number of interesting features emerge. First, the countries with the best trade performance, West Germany and Japan, also show the best industry-financed R&D performance, whereas the laggards in trade, the UK and Italy, exhibit a rather lack-lustre performance. Second, as one might expect, the more advanced countries have a substantially higher commitment to industrial R&D than countries such as Italy and Spain, important

Table 12.10   Trends in industry-financed R&D as a percentage of GDP: 1967–88

	Industry-financed R&D as percentage of GDP				Gross expenditure on R&D as percentage of GDP 1988
	1967	1975	1985	1988	
UK	1.00	0.80	0.96	1.06	2.29
FRG	0.94	1.12	1.58	1.78	2.85
France	0.61	0.69	0.94	0.96	2.29
Italy	0.35	0.47	0.58	0.54	1.19
Netherlands	1.12	1.02	0.96	1.14	2.33
Belgium	0.59	0.75	1.06	1.13	1.65
Spain	0.08	0.19	0.26	0.32	0.62
Sweden	0.72	0.96	1.71	1.74	3.04
USA	1.01	1.01	1.35	1.38	2.91
Japan	0.83	1.12	1.84	1.95	2.87

Source: OECD, quoted in Patel and Pavitt 1991: Table 3.1

regions of which are still in the process of industrialising. (Note that Italy, whose GDP per capita is now up to that of the UK, has a very low business commitment to R&D; see discussion of the phenomenon by Dunford, Chapter 9 in this volume.) Third, with the exception of the UK, all countries have seen a sizeable increase in the rate of industrially financed R&D over the twenty-one years 1967–88. The performance of two countries in particular stand out – Japan and Sweden. Lastly, the relative contribution of government varies considerably. For the UK, France, the USA, The Netherlands and Italy, government was contributing more than 50 per cent of total R&D in 1988. In the case of the first three, this is explained by high levels of defence R&D. In The Netherlands, it reflects a substantial commitment to basic research; in Italy, it reflects substantial subsidies to the industrial sector. Until the 1980s a high commitment to defence R&D meant that countries such as the UK came close to the top of the league tables in terms of total R&D as a proportion of GDP. The sharp growth of industrial R&D in the 1980s in countries such as West Germany, Sweden and (outside Europe) Japan, mean that even in terms of total R&D the UK and France are now outclassed.

Table 12.11 lists the patent performance (as measured by patents registered in the USA) for the same group of West European countries. (Since the figures are quoted as a percentage of West European patenting as a whole, it is not possible to present comparable figures for the USA and Japan.) The outstanding feature of this table is again the strong performance of (West) Germany, which has not only remained the most active patenter in Western Europe, but actually strengthened its position by seven percentage points between the 1960s and the 1980s. The UK, by contrast, nine percentage points behind West Germany in 1963–8, slipped a further ten points over the same two-decade period, and now faces a gap (between its performance and that of Germany) of over 25 percentage points. Interestingly neither The Netherlands nor Sweden, both strong performers in R&D, shows strong patent performance. Table

Table 12.11   Shares by country of West European patenting in the USA: 1963–88 (per cent)

	1963–8	*1969–73*	*1974–8*	*1979–83*	*1984–8*
UK	24.80	21.56	18.16	15.91	14.67
FRG	33.74	35.62	37.16	40.10	40.91
France	13.42	13.99	14.45	14.29	14.60
Italy	4.27	4.77	4.72	5.37	5.83
Netherlands	4.67	4.36	4.32	4.49	4.62
Belgium	1.63	1.88	1.84	1.64	1.55
Spain	0.42	0.47	0.59	0.47	0.57
Sweden	5.24	5.08	5.65	5.09	4.89

Source: US Department of Commerce, Patent and Trademark Office, quoted in Patel and Pavitt 1991: Table 3.4

12.12 shows areas of technological strength and weakness for the different countries, based on sectors where patenting performance is above or below the *national* average for that country. This reinforces the evidence of the trade and output data cited earlier to give the message that, except in The Netherlands (Philips), Europe's capabilities lie in the chemicals, engineering and defence industries, and not in electronics.

From the statistics, there would seem to be a clear link between trade performance and technological performance. The line taken here in fact follows closely the theories of trade and growth pioneered by Posner (1961) and Vernon (1966) in the 1960s, and subsequently confirmed by the econometric analysis of Soete (1981) and Fagerberg (1988). What it amounts to is this: in seeking to explain differences in industrial performance between countries, the extent to which industry in the different countries use best-practice technology is an important factor. This accords with the earlier analysis of the importance of non-price factors in trade. If design, reliability, etc, matter as much as price in product choice, then products embodying more up-to-date techniques will tend to be seen as more desirable than those embodying technology and design features of previous decades.

Technology, however, does not explain all the differences. For example, a motor car full of the latest electronic gadgetry might well not sell if it were poorly designed or unreliable because of bad workmanship. For that matter, a cheap car which had a reputation for poor reliability (as a result of poor quality control/workmanship) might also prove to be of little market appeal. The quality of workmanship reflects a number of factors, above all the training received either before joining the firm and/or provided within the firm. (In industrialised economies the overall level of education is also relevant: in general, the better educated the work-force the more adaptable and flexible it is. This is particularly important in using new technologies.) Countries such as Germany, Japan and Sweden – all strong industrial performers – are renowned for the thoroughness of their industrial training systems. Since much of this training is done within the firm and rewarded by in-firm promotion, it is not always easy to pick up the contours of the pattern. Nevertheless, Table 12.13 gives some idea of the differences between countries in the level of educational and training qualifications and highlights, in particular, the UK's relatively poor position *vis-à-vis* its main competitors, particularly in relation to the training of technicians and craftsmen. A poorly qualified

Table 12.12 Areas of technological strength and weakness as revealed by patent statistics

	Strength	*Weakness*
UK	Chemicals and pharmaceuticals Defence	Electrical machinery Electronics
FRG	Industrial chemicals Pharmaceuticals Engineering Motor vehicles Defence	Electrical machinery Electronics Materials/raw materials Telecoms
France	Fine chemicals Electrical machinery Telecoms Defence	Motor vehicles Electronics Raw materials
Italy	Fine chemicals Motor vehicles Mechanical engineering	Electrical machinery Electronics Raw-material-based goods
Netherlands	Electrical machinery Electronics Telecoms Raw materials	Fine chemicals Materials Motor vehicles Defence
Belgium	All chemicals	All engineering Electronics Capital goods
Spain	Mechanical engineering Motor vehicles Fine chemicals	Industrial chemicals Electrical engineering Electronics Materials (raw and other)

Source: Derived from Patel and Pavitt 1991: Table 3.5

work-force, combined with low industrial R&D and a poor patenting performance, adds up to what might be called a 'low value-added' profile. The problem for the UK is that within each product group its firms are tending to produce a lower-quality, lower-technology, range of goods and services.

Towards a global market-place

So far, this chapter has considered comparative structural change and industrial performance in terms of countries and industrial sectors. The real 'performers' are, of course, firms, not countries. Within any market, firm performance is constrained, on the one hand, by established institutional arrangements – for example, company law, competition and trade policy, banking practice, education and training practice, regulations and standards – and on the other, by the number, size and behaviour of competitors. By the 1980s the dominant market structure in all the main north European industrialised countries was oligopolistic, with many national markets dominated by two or three large firms, surrounded by a plethora of smaller firms

Table 12.13   Numbers qualifying in engineering and technology, *c.* 1985 (thousands)

	UK	France	FRG
Doctorates	0.7	0.3	1.0
Master's and 'enhanced' degrees	2	6+	4+
Bachelor's degrees	14	15	21
Technicians	29	35	44
Craftspersons	35	92	120

Source: Prais 1988

occupying market niches of one sort of another. There were exceptions. The outstanding strength of the German engineering industry means that small and medium-sized firms remain an important force in that country. Italy, which really moved into industrialisation only in the 1950s, shows an interesting contrast between highly concentrated industries such as cars and domestic appliances, and its dynamically successful small firms in textiles, leather goods and, surprisingly, machine tools (Duchêne and Shepherd 1987, ch. 5; Paci, Chapter 4 in *The National Economies of Europe*, on Italy).

The Treaty of Rome aimed, of course, to change the national focus of production. With the gradual abolition of internal tariffs within the Community, the assumption had been that the national oligopolists of yesteryear would become competitors within the wider Common Market, with concomitant changes in national industrial structures. In fact, until the 1980s, remarkably little regrouping took place. There were one or two cross-country mergers – Dunlop-Pirelli in tyres, Hoesch-Hoogovens in steel – but with little success. Instead, the general economic climate of the 1970s, marked by the the Oil Crises, recession, stagflation and rising unemployment, caused countries to look inwards not outwards, priority being given to preserving markets and employment. As we saw in earlier chapters, a multitude of non-tariff barriers emerged to keep national markets separate, with the larger firms buttressed by subsidies and other special privileges, and particularly by public purchasing contracts. Recession and government-sponsored rationalisation led to a thinning of the ranks, but those who survived became aptly known as 'national champions'.

By the early 1980s, therefore, little had changed: national oligopolies still ruled. However, the writing was on the wall. The crises in the steel and shipbuilding industry had caused the EC Commission to intervene to prevent beggar-my-neighbour subsidies getting out of hand. Even chemicals, a major growth industry of the 1960s, was in trouble, with substantial overcapacity and calls for a crisis cartel to be organised by the EC. (These were turned down, but for a while the Commission turned a blind eye to a 'gentleman's agreement' which enabled a major realignment of capacity to take place: see Sharp and Cook, Chapter 15 in this volume). By this time, however, the focus had begun to switch from declining to growth industries, as governments, with some logic, argued that if industries were to be subsidised, it was best to back those with a future – the sunrise, not the sunset industries.

The failings – or lack of competitive edge – of the European electronics industry were, however, already apparent. The national champion policy had led to a considerable fragmentation of markets at a time when R&D costs were escalating and product life shortening. Increasingly it was apparent that firms such as GEC, Plessey, ICL, Bull, even Philips and Siemens, could no longer afford to develop the next generation of products on their own: their markets, albeit guaranteed, were just too small to justify the up-front R&D and start-up costs. Two events in particular stimulated a 're-think'. The first was the deregulation of AT&T, the giant US telecommunications firm which, until 1983, had held a virtual monopoly of the US market. The *quid pro quo* for its monopoly had been internal regulation and a prohibition on international operations. Deregulation meant the compulsory breaking-up of its monopoly, but it also gave the company, still the largest world manufacturer of telecom equipment, freedom to move into international markets – and Europe was a prime target. The second factor stimulating reassessment was the growing intensity of competition from Japanese firms, not only in consumer electronics where they had established themselves in the 1970s, but also in areas such as semiconductors and computers, previously dominated by US firms. Fearful of future moves towards protection, Japanese firms such as NEC and Toshiba were establishing manufacturing facilities within the European Community itself (see Hobday, Chapter 14 in this volume, on the European electronics industry).

The dilemma for the European electronic firms was real. Years of subsidy and support by national governments had created a fragmented and ineffectual industry, most of whose firms were not operating at the leading edge of the market. Yet the presence of subsidiaries of leading-edge firms (from the USA and Japan) in the European market made trade protection ineffective as the experience in consumer electronics demonstrated so vividly. In the long run, there was no alternative for these firms but to face up directly to competition: yet to achieve this required a reorientation of their focus from being national champions (whose prime markets were national markets) to being global competitors. The first step in this direction was to shift focus from the national to the European market. To help achieve this, and simultaneously to help up-grade technological performance, Vicomte Davignon, at that time Commissioner for Industry and R&D, introduced in 1983 ESPRIT (European Strategic Programme for Information Technology), a programme of pre-competitive collaborative research which brought together firms and research capabilities across the EC (see Chapter 14).

While ESPRIT did not altogether restore competitiveness in the European electronics industry, it did greatly improve it. It acted as a catalyst for bringing the European firms together and creating a European industry in place of a set of fragmented national industries; in so doing, it stimulated a major restructuring of the industry with, in general, two or three firms emerging as dominant European players in each market segment (semiconductors, computers, telecommunications and consumer electronics); it created a model for other EC programmes, based on collaborative research; most important of all, it created a constituency of large firms pressing for the completion of the single market. This latter achievement was particularly significant, for it amounted to a rejection of the implicit economic nationalism which had dominated the national champions era, and a recognition of the logic of the original agenda of the Treaty of Rome. In effect, these large firms came at last to realise that, in fragmenting the European market, they were failing to use one of their main advantages, namely a home market base of 320 million people.

ESPRIT, and other issues of industrial policy, therefore played an important part in stimulating the Single European Act 1986 and the push towards the completion of the single market. The Single European Act itself established what may be called the 'twin track' approach to industrial policy, which continues to prevail in Europe today (Sharp 1990). On the one hand, it legitimises the more interventionist role of the Commission exemplified in ESPRIT and the subsequent R&D support programmes established under the Framework Programme. (For background on these developments see Sharp and Shearman 1987; Sharp 1990.) On the other, the whole ethos of the Single European Act is about deregulation, liberalisation and competition – based on the notion that gains will come from the dynamic economies of scale stimulated by more and more open competition (Cecchini 1988). Community policy is thus, at one and the same time, *both* supportive and interventionist *and* liberal and competitive. The tension between these elements is seen at its most poignant in an area such as tele-communications, where the interventionist arm of the Commission (DG XIII) is currently (1991) promoting the RACE (Research in Advanced Communications in Europe) programme aimed at creating a broadband fibre-optic telecommunications network throughout the whole of the EC (see Chapter 14), whereas the Directorate-General responsible for the Internal Market and Competition (DG IV) is pushing through initiatives which liberalise access to the telecoms network and encourages wholesale competition in the provision, and pricing, of new telematic services (see Sharp 1991; Mansell and Morgan 1991.)

While the tensions (and the underlying politics) are real, there is logic in this twin-track policy. The restructuring of Community industry that took place in the 1980s is the result both of competitive pressures from non-European multinationals *and* of anticipation of 1992. The sharp rise in the incidence of Community mergers and acquisitions has resulted in a substantial concentration of industrial power, which in turn has strengthened the position of existing European multinationals – firms such as Siemens (electronics and electrical engineering), ICI, Hoechst, Bayer (chemicals), Nestlé and Unilever (food manufacturing), and created a series of new European-based multinationals – firms such as Asea-Brown Boveri (heavy electrical), CGE (Telecoms), and Rhône Poulenc (chemicals/pharmaceuticals). The dangers of shifting from a policy of national champions to one of European champions are, however, clear. Inevitably there are pressures for trade protection and limitation of the activities of foreign-based multinationals. Yet firms of the size of these new European giants notoriously elude control; arguably the best control comes from open competition with firms of equivalent size. Hence the need to liberalise the internal market and to adopt a liberal stance on both trade and inward investment by foreign multinationals.

The year 1992 thus represents a watershed for industrial policy. With the Commission (DG IV) taking an increasingly tough line on state aid, the shift of power from national governments to the Commission is continuing; while national (and regional) governments will continue to foster broadly based 'infrastructural' pro-grammes (for example, to promote links between universities and industry), the strategic role will increasingly fall to Brussels. At present, Brussels is attempting to continue the balancing act between the twin tracks of policy – between intervention and competition. But pressures to alter the balance are intense. On the one hand, many firms, particularly in electronics, would like to see a shift towards a more protectionist, interventionist stance, and are, indeed, being supported in this by some governments, particularly the French. On the other, DG IV – and the British and German governments – are anxious to see the Community espouse wholeheartedly the liberal, free trade route. What happens in the end will depend not only on the balance of power within the Commission and the Community, but also, more importantly, on international developments. A major shift by the United States towards protectionism will push the Community firmly towards the more interventionist 'Fortress Europe' position. A successful conclusion to the GATT Uruguay round, and a lessening of the tension between the USA and Japan over trade in technology, would help to maintain the more liberal approach.

Finally, it is worth putting these policy developments into the context of the tendencies in industrial structure and performance documented earlier in the chapter. We began by discussing the degree to which, since the 1960s, the (West) German economy has become the dynamo within the broader West European economic system. Subsequent sections have elaborated on this theme. Time and again the statistics cited have illustrated the fundamental strength of the German system: the dominant export performance, the solid shares of fast- and medium-growth industries, the rising share of industrially financed R&D and the comprehensively trained work-force. It is worth reiterating the word *system*, for it is the mutually reinforcing nature of the German pattern that creates the advantage: the highly skilled work-force, the strong academic base, the interlocking directorships, the links between industry and the banking sector, and the relatively harmonious relationship between unions and management. Earlier case studies have shown that German industry does not respond quickly to change, but moves at a measured pace to assimilate and diffuse the necessary skill base (Sharp 1985). Indeed, in those case studies, the analogy of the hare and tortoise was used to contrast the German response to new technologies with that of Britain and France, and the analogy remains appropriate. The breadth of German strength across industries remains nevertheless impressive, and contrasts with the relatively narrowly based specialisation of the Japanese. But this should not blind us to the other developments documented in this chapter: the growing strength of countries such as Sweden and the Netherlands, who share many elements of the German system; the somewhat quirky showing of the French; the unexploited potential of both Italy and Spain; and the continued relative decline of the British. The year 1992 heralds a new era, associated with the final achievement of a single European market, with the pressing need to shift focus from the European to the global market-place and, not least, with the reunification, not only of Germany, but also of Eastern and Western Europe. How far the next twenty years will repeat the story of the last is impossible at this juncture to predict.

Acknowledgements

This chapter draws on work undertaken for the book published to celebrate the Science Policy Research Unit's 25th Anniversary *Technology and the Future of Europe*, edited by C. Freeman, M. Sharp and W. Walker (1991), and in particular Chapters 2, 3 and 4 of that volume. I am grateful to Pinter Publishers and the authors for permission to use material, particularly tables, from those chapters.

References

Blackaby F (1978) (ed) *De-Industrialisation*. Heinemann Educational

Cecchini P (1988) *The European Challenge: 1992*. Wildwood House for the European Commission

Cohen S S, Zysman J (1987) *Manufacturing Matters: The Myth of the Post-Industrial Economy*. Basic Books

Duchêne F, Shepherd G (eds) (1987) *Managing Industrial Change in Western Europe*. Pinter

Freeman C, Sharp M, Walker W (eds) (1991) *Technology and the Future of Europe: Global Competition and the Environment*. Pinter

Fagerberg J (1988) International competitiveness. *Economic Journal* **98**: 355–74

Mansell R E, Morgan K (1991) Evolving telecommunications structures: organising the new European Community market place. In Freeman et al (eds) (1991)

Patel P, Pavitt K (1991) Europe's technological performance. In Freeman et al (eds) (1991)

Posner M (1961) International trade and technical change. *Oxford Economic Papers* **13**

Prais S (1988) Qualified manpower in engineering: Britain and other industrially advanced countries. *National Institute Economic Review* February: 76–83

Saunders C, Matthews M, Patel P (1991) Structural change and patterns of production and trade. In Freeman et al (1991)

Sharp M (ed) (1985) *Europe and the New Technologies: Six Case Studies in Adjustment and Change*. Pinter

Sharp M (1989) European technology: does 1992 matter? Lecture presented at Imperial College, February 1989, and published as No. **19** in *Papers in Science, Technology and Public Policy*. Obtainable from Publications Office, SPRU, University of Sussex, Falmer, Brighton BN1 9RF

Sharp M (1990) The Single Market and European policies for advanced technologies. Special Supplement in *Political Quarterly* on *The Politics of 1992* October

Sharp M (1991) The Single Market and European technology policies. In Freeman et al (eds) (1991)

Sharp M, Shearman C (1987) *European Technological Collaboration* Chatham House Paper **36**. Routledge & Kegan Paul for the Royal Institute of International Affairs

Soete L (1981) A general test of the technological gap theory. *Weltwirtschaftliches Archiv* **117**

Vernon R (1966) International investment and international trade in the product cycle *Quarterly Journal of Economics* **80**(2): 190–207

Vernon R (ed) (1985) *The Technology Factor in International Trade* NBER/Columbia University Press

CHAPTER 13

The car industry

DANIEL T. JONES

From the 1980s to the 1990s

For the European motor industry the 1980s started with the second Oil Shock and the
recession that followed it, and ended with record levels of demand and preparations for
the Europe without frontiers of 1992. The downturn in demand, forecast some years
ago, finally arrived in 1990, though it is not yet clear how severe it will turn out to be.
Whatever happens, there is now a strong consensus that the European producers face
not only great opportunities with the opening up of Eastern Europe, but also the
greatest challenge yet to their survival from the Japanese producers, now establishing
themselves in Europe.

A great deal did change in the European motor industry during the 1980s. The much
slower recovery after the Second Oil Crisis than after the First (see Table 13.1 and
Figures 13.1 and 13.2) exposed underlying weaknesses in several European auto
producers, triggering off an unprecedented wave of rationalisation. First Rover and
Fiat and later Peugeot and Renault found that overoptimistic investments had left them
with too much capacity, too many workers, and unsustainable levels of overheads (see
Figure 13.3). All the European firms, and their respective governments, were
convinced that adequate scale was essential for survival, and that boosting capacity was
therefore a risk worth taking to ensure a place for their national champion in the auto
oligopoly of the future. Faced with too much capacity chasing too few customers,
however, each in the end faced the need to retrench to survive.

During the first half of the 1980s about one million units of production capacity were
closed down, much of it outdated and inefficient, and the four firms named above
reduced their overheads and break-even levels of output by a total of 1.8 million units.
Many other plants were retooled with lower manning levels, the number of products
offered was rationalised, and a series of highly successful models, such as the Fiat Uno
and Peugeot 205, were introduced. The net effect was that some 420,000 people left the
European motor industry between 1980 and 1986. Because the German producers were
able to achieve higher levels of quality they were able to sell their cars at a premium
throughout Europe and in the USA, and so they survived this period of retrenchment

Table 13.1 Motor vehicle production in the EC, 1973–90 (thousands of units)

	Germany	UK	Spain	Italy	France	Belgium	Neth	Total
1973	3,949	2,164	822	1,958	3,569	299	107	12,868
1978	4,186	1,607	1,144	1,656	3,508	303	85	12,489
1981	3,897	1,184	987	1,434	3,019	237	101	10,859
1982	4,062	1,156	1,070	1,453	3,149	278	109	11,277
1983	4,154	1,289	1,288	1,575	3,336	285	122	12,049
1984	4,045	1,134	1,309	1,601	3,062	249	129	11,529
1985	4,445	1,311	1,418	1,573	3,016	267	128	12,158
1986	4,578	1,203	1,307	1,913	3,195	295	142	12,633
1987	4,634	1,389	1,704	1,913	3,494	352	152	13,637
1988	4,625	1,545	1,866	2,111	3,678	398	149	14,372
1989	4,852	1,626	2,046	2,221	3,920	389	149[1]	15,203
1990	4,661	1,295	1,679	1,875	3,295	313	140[1]	13,258

[1]Estimated

Note: Figures for Total EC are estimated on the basis of national figures. This may involve some elements of double-counting

Source: For all countries except The Netherlands: *Automotive News Market Data Book*, 1991 edition, p. 3; for The Netherlands: Motor Vehicle Manufacturers Association of The United States *World Motor Vehicle Data*, various years

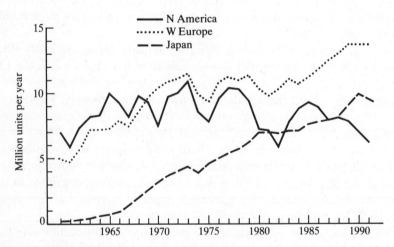

Figure 13.1 Car production
Source: Automotive News

unscathed. Indeed, they hired an extra 46,000 employees during the early 1980s. By the time demand recovered in 1986 the European producers were well placed to turn extra volume into profits (see Figure 13.3). Luckily for them, the boom that started in 1986 was to see them through the rest of the 1980s.

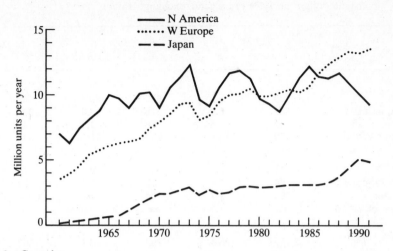

Figure 13.2   Car sales
Source: Automotive News.

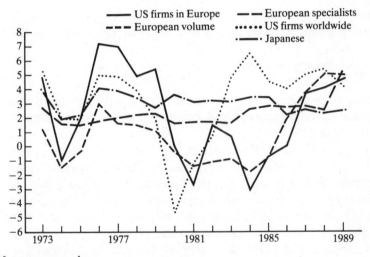

Figure 13.3   Net return on sales
Source: Company accounts, collated by author.

Retrenchment at home was mirrored by retrenchment abroad. Volkswagen closed its assembly plant in the US after a decade of operation and pooled its Brazilian and Argentinian operations with those of Ford, while Renault sold its stake in American Motors after losing a great deal of money and closed its plant in Mexico. As a result, the European mass producers are now the most dependent on their home region of all the large auto manufacturers (see Table 13.2). The European specialist producers, Mercedes, BMW, Porsche, Jaguar, Volvo and Saab, on the other hand, turned their European origin to advantage by selling high-priced luxury cars in large numbers in the USA. For some years they faced no effective competition and exchange rates moved in

Table 13.2 EC trade in motor vehicles (A = thousands of units, B = value in billions of constant dollars at 1989 prices and exchange rates)

	1979		1986		1989	
	A	B	A	B	A	B
Exports						
To EFTA	560	7.2	625	10.4	602	11.0
To N. America	552	6.8	576	14.4	302	9.8
To Japan	39	0.5	58	1.1	142	3.3
To Rest of World	979	11.9	533	10.2	523	11.5
Imports						
From EFTA	83	2.2	82	4.1	71	4.2
From N. America	144	1.5	13	1.4	37	1.5
From Japan	780	2.7	1,104	6.6	1,238	9.9
From Rest of World	na	1.0	na	2.0	na	2.3
Total						
Exports	2,130	26.4	1,792	36.1	1,569	35.6
Imports	1,007[1]	7.4	1,199[1]	14.1	1,346[1]	17.9
Balance	1,123[1]	19.0	593[1]	22.0	223[1]	17.7

[1]Estimates

Note: Figures in column A include vehicles only; the value data given in column B cover vehicles and parts

Source: EC Commission, Directorate for the Internal Market

their favour. More recently, however, sales have slumped, exchange rate changes have eroded profits, and the Japanese have begun to compete in this segment of the market for the first time.

Even the boom in European sales of the late 1980s was not enough to save the industry from a further round of rationalisation. Peugeot was unable to sustain Talbot, acquired from Chrysler in 1978, as a third product range, and Rover, Alfa Romeo and SEAT eventually proved too small to survive on their own. Volkswagen bought SEAT in 1986 and Fiat acquired Alfa Romeo in 1987, while Honda finally took a 20 per cent stake in Rover in 1990. After a string of successful years in the US market, Saab and Jaguar succumbed, and were taken over by General Motors and Ford respectively. Apart from Volkswagen, Fiat, Renault and Peugeot, the only other European firms left are the specialist producers Mercedes Benz, BMW and Porsche, as well as Volvo, which are exploring a collaborative arrangement with Renault.

One important change that resulted from the experiences of the early 1980s was the withdrawal from ownership by national governments and the associated weakening of the concept of national champions (see Chapter 12 by Margaret Sharp in this volume). SEAT and Alfa Romeo were, as we have seen, the first to be sold off, while the German government sold its stake in Volkswagen in 1987, the UK government privatised Jaguar in 1985 and Rover in 1988, and the French government ended the special status of Renault and sold some shares to Volvo in 1990. Volvo is currently negotiating to buy back the Dutch government's stake in Volvo BV. In part this withdrawal from ownership on the part of the state was driven by the escalating costs of sustaining weaker firms in the industry, in part also by the greater vigilance of the EC Commission in vetting state aid and other forms of subsidies that might distort competition.

Although governments have withdrawn from ownership, the industry is still largely organised on a national basis in Europe. Each firm is still highly dependent on its home market, with a relatively much smaller share of the other European markets. The main European firms still assemble the bulk of their cars at home (Fiat 79 per cent, Peugeot 77 per cent, Renault 61 per cent and Volkswagen 56 per cent in 1988) and buy over 80 per cent of their components locally. So far the political climate has not favoured cross-border deals. Cross-border deals that have been struck, for example the FIRE engine collaboration between Fiat and Peugeot, have often come unstuck. It would be fair to say that with many of the formal obstacles now removed, the time might be ripe for a rapid increase in the number of such arrangements. Coalitions of industrial and political forces in France and Italy have, however, continued to resist any attempt by foreign firms to establish assembly facilities.

Towards the end of the decade, as the 1992 programme gathered steam, it became imperative to address the jumble of national limits imposed on Japanese imports a decade or more earlier, in order to achieve a common trading area without internal barriers. At the same time the Japanese auto producers began to invest in production facilities in Europe, which for the first time threatened the protection hitherto enjoyed by many European firms in their home markets. So after a great deal of haggling between member states with very divergent interests, the Commission negotiated in July 1991 a transitional arrangement with the Japanese which will not deliver fully open markets until the year 2000. (See Chapter 10 by Peter Holmes and Alasdair Smith in this volume.)

The European auto producers face three main challenges in the 1990s. The first is to close the performance gap with the Japanese so that they can hold their own against the Japanese firms now locating in Europe. The second is to contribute to the solution of the growing problem of congestion, not just on city streets but also on inter-urban motorways. While growth in individual car ownership remains buoyant, there is growing collective doubt as to whether more and more cars and trucks can be accommodated on European roads, particularly in highly congested areas like The Netherlands. The third is to find ways of reducing emissions from cars. This last challenge goes beyond the dimension of refining petrol and diesel engines to use less fuel and emit less toxic fumes, to a quest for alternative power plants that release less carbon dioxide, emissions of which are thought to be a major contributor to the greenhouse effect problem.

Advancing solutions to congestion and emissions problems depends on the effective mobilisation of R&D resources, and on the ability of the organisations involved to introduce new technologies and successful collaboration with public authorities. We return to these issues later. Our main concern in this chapter, however, is with the question of how European firms can close the gap with the Japanese. As we shall see, this involves more than simply slimming down overheads and investing in some new tooling. It presupposes some fundamental changes in the whole way in which products are conceived, how production is organised, how relations with suppliers are conducted, and how the product is sold to the final customer. How well these changes are implemented will determine how many European auto producers will survive the decade (Womack, Jones & Roos 1990).

Table 13.3   Comparative performance by region

	Japan	America	Europe
Assembly productivity (hours/car)	17	25	36
Quality – defects per 100 cars	60	82	97
Design lead-time (months)	46	60	58
Engineering hours per new car (mn)	1.7	3.1	3.0
Assembler inventories (days)	.2	2.9	2.0
Supplier inventories (days)	1.5	8.1	16.3
Distribution inventories (days)	21	67	67
Parts suppliers per firm	340	1,500	1,500
Dealers per firm*	300	2,000	7,500

* The number of dealer firms required to sell 2 million units, comparing Toyota in Japan with Ford in America and Europe

Source: Womack, Jones & Roos 1990 pp. 92, 118 & 157

The size of the gap

In this section we set out systematically to measure the performance gap in every activity from product development, through component supply to manufacturing and distribution to the customer, between the best Japanese auto firms and European manufacturers. Wherever we look we find at least a two-to-one gap in relation to productivity and quality, and a much more streamlined system involving the direct interaction of far fewer actors on the Japanese side.

Table 13.3 shows that the Japanese take half the human effort to perform the same set of activities to build an identical product with an equivalent level of automation. They also use half the space, run up half the tooling costs, and deliver a product with not much more than half the number of defects. The whole production system, including co-ordination of the supply of components, runs with a tenth the level of inventories and involves only a fifth the number of suppliers.

In addition, the Japanese *design* their cars with half the human effort, and take less than four years to do so, compared with, commonly, five or six years in Europe. They have used this greater design efficiency both continually to expand their product ranges and to redesign their cars more frequently – every four years instead of every eight to twelve years. Now they are developing the capability to design cars specifically for each of the Japanese, American and European markets, giving them an enormous range of volume and niche products to sell across the world.

The Japanese also sell their cars in Japan through a distribution system that is highly concentrated, that offers a higher level of service than is common in Europe, and that is run much more efficiently, delivering customer specified orders within two to three weeks of ordering. This level of service depends on very close contact between dealers and the factory. It has not yet been tried outside Japan.

After the war the Japanese car industry tried to copy mass production manufacturing methods from the Americans, but found it impossible to do so within the constraints of a tiny market, with a labour force that had won job security guarantees from management, and with no money for expensive tooling. So Toyota in particular responded by devising a very different system of making cars that started off pressing all the parts on one press, rather than on lines of 'dedicated' presses. Over time they discovered that their solutions were in fact not less, but more efficient than Detroit's. This is the pre-history of a production revolution which culminated, in the 1870s and 1980s, in the articulation of the philosophy of 'Lean Production'.

What is Lean Production?

What are the secrets of Lean Production? Let us begin with the factory. For a start there are fewer people involved. Those fewer people are organised into teams that take complete responsibility for all the tasks involved, including routine maintenance, quality inspection and making improvements. This responsibility implies a great deal of training, but at the same time fewer layers of supervisors, quality checkers, rectification workers and middle managers.

The whole work process is organised so that at every step waste is removed – wasted effort, wasted time, wasted materials – and so that only what is required *next* is made. Short 'Just-in-Time' production runs eliminate inventory, but – more important – also explicitly expose problems. Classic mass production can only work by isolating each step from the next with mountains of stock, by hiding problems and cushioning inefficiency. Lean Production does the opposite – it seeks to highlight problems and then trace their cause to the ultimate source, so that they can be solved in such a way as never to recur. This is also the route to zero defects. Defects that become immediately apparent at the next work step are eliminated quickly and are not repeated. In this way the system is continually improved and the entire complex operates like one completely integrated flow from beginning to end. The ultimate objective is a near perfect product and an uninterrupted and *lean* production flow.

The Lean Producer also works with far fewer suppliers, who themselves form the peak of a pyramid of several layers of smaller suppliers actually making the parts. A Lean Assembler can have a very different relationship with 340 suppliers than a mass producer with 1500 suppliers. He can develop an individual relationship with each, which will serve as a basis for working together over the long term. Indeed in Lean Production the responsibility for designing the part is devolved to the supplier rather than being done in house. Thus Lean Production does in fact develop a much deeper division of labour than mass production. The difference is that the relationship is not based on an arms length power relationship, but on a genuine shared destiny.

The supplier and assembler typically jointly analyse the costs of designing and making the part to a high degree of detail, always looking for innovations and ways to lower costs. They are encouraged to work together by agreed rules that ensure that each party gets its due share of the profit that results. The suppliers are given every assistance in learning new techniques, but at the same time their performance is continually evaluated and compared with other suppliers, to keep them on the mark and to help them do even better tomorrow.

The principles of Lean Production are summarised in Table 13.4:

Table 13.4 Lean production and mass production compared

Lean production	Mass production
Team-work and upskilling	Endless division of labour
Shared destiny relations, with fewer employees, suppliers and dealers	Short-term, power-based relationships
Growing product variety, shorter product lives, and falling lifetime volume	Standardised products, maximum production volume per product
No safety net	Buffers everywhere
Goal of perfection through continuous improvement	Good enough

Lean production and engineering

Precisely the same principles can be seen at work in design and engineering. Japanese R&D activity is organised around individual projects rather than around traditional functional departments. Each project is led by a very powerful individual, or team leader, who has complete authority over the project and is responsible for gathering round him a team of specialists from each function to work as part of the team for the duration of the project. These team members work together intimately, drawing on specialist services from the different functional departments, making close communication and simultaneous engineering a reality.

The team starts with a top-down approach to analysing the costs of the vehicle, too, working back from a target price and then looking at the precise cost of each part, using value engineering techniques[1] to analyse the trade-offs necessary to meet that target price. Normally, each department likes to start off by designing its ideal component and telling the project coordinator it cannot be made for the price he is asking, after which a process of essentially political bargaining between departments begins, which eventually – perhaps much later on – generates a compromise. By bringing the skills together within a team, and confronting the necessary choices and trade-offs early, an enormous amount of wasted effort and time is saved, and the end product is more coherent and much easier to make. This more than compensates for the time it takes to negotiate the necessary compromises.

Fundamental to an understanding of how Lean Production works in product development is a proper appreciation of what real Team-Work involves. The common image is of a homogeneous Japanese team who all think the same, and invariably accept the superior's viewpoint. This is far from the truth. In fact, Team-Work involves deliberately bringing together people with different skills and confronting the need to meld their different viewpoints together into a final design. Team-Work involves creative conflict, within the context of a strongly shared common goal or vision of the final product.

The project team is, then, more important than the functional department in the Japanese system, and this is reflected in the career structure. There are two very different career paths for engineers within a Japanese firm. The functional career path still exists, but there is an alternative path, along which the worker can develop as a member of successive design teams, gradually playing a more and more significant role, finally ending up as a product team leader. These team leaders – one for each of the the main product lines in the company – are amongst the most important individuals in Japanese firms.

In a flatter, more horizontally organised structure, it is not possible simply to reward good engineers with additional steps up a career ladder. Instead new kinds of reward have to be found – such as increasing the time available for creative engineering as distinct from dealing with the bureaucracy of the organisation. According to exit interviews, the latter is exactly what frustrates engineers most – they actually love doing engineering and seeing the results of their work embodied in products on the market. Lean production liberates the creative capacities of engineers and spares them from being forced to become organisation men and play power games.

Closing the gap

Having outlined the gap facing the European producers, how do we go about closing it? It must be said at the outset that there *is* a growing understanding of the size of the gap in manufacturing practice at the very top of the European firms, even though not yet of the full implications of Lean Production for product development, product strategy, supplier relationships and distribution. Many senior managers now realise that they do, indeed, need to set very ambitious targets, if they are to be ready for head-on competition with the Japanese in Europe. In a word, the European producers will need to double the level of performance in every aspect of their operations by the mid- to late 1990s. Perhaps most important of all, they have to realise that *greater automation is not the way to accomplish this*.

The real problem is how to convince middle management, not only of the need for such changes, but of what is involved in actually implementing them. The demonstration effect of the incoming Japanese plants is essential to the solution of this problem. From that perspective it would, perhaps, have been preferable to have one Japanese plant located in each country, rather than all of them being located in the UK or Spain. As long as Japanese competition comes from across the ocean or even across the English Channel, it is easier to cling to the notion that protection can stave off the evil day when adjustment finally becomes necessary.

The arrival of Japanese assembly and engine plants in Europe, to be followed as in North America by Japanese product development, finally puts to rest any idea that protection against Japanese imports can be effective. In retrospect, the sealing off of the French, Italian and Spanish markets from the Japanese meant that the local manufacturers were never challenged to improve their product quality and productivity. As a result, they lost the top end of each segment of their own markets to the German producers. Now that a deal between the Commission and the Japanese government has been concluded, it should be that much easier to convince middle managers that no one is going to come to their rescue (but note the reservations expressed about the likely real impact of the deal in Chapter 10, on the trilateral relationship). Real progress towards closing the gap can at last begin.

Translating an understanding of Lean Production into actual practice is, however, a difficult task, particularly if the given firm does not have any first-hand experience of running a plant on these lines. So any European firm that wants seriously to address the task must have access to a learning example where their staff can gain hands-on experience. All the US assemblers have had this opportunity through their joint ventures with Japanese producers, Ford through its partial ownership of Mazda, General Motors through its NUMMI joint venture with Toyota and its links with Isuzu and Suzuki, and Chrysler through its Diamond Star joint venture with Mitsubishi. So far the only European firm to be offered such an opportunity is Rover, which as we saw is now 20 per cent owned by Honda.

Some firms have been more successful than others at utilising existing links with Japanese firms. The case of Ford best illustrates the right way to do it. In 1981 Ford was staring bankruptcy in the face, with no cash for investment in the kinds of high-tech solution favoured by General Motors. Luckily for them, they had a minority shareholding in Mazda, acquired several years earlier. Using this as an *entreé*, Ford sent joint management and union teams to Mazda to study their operations in detail. The key lesson they learnt was that their problems were essentially organisational. They then introduced many of the techniques learnt from Mazda in their plants in the United States, even going so far as to video every production step in a Mazda assembly plant to show to the workers back home.

Another lesson they learned was at Hermosillo in Mexico. There they built a new plant based on the layout of a Mazda plant, to build a Mazda-designed product on Mazda principles, to be sold through Ford's dealerships in Canada. Once the plant was up and running the Mazda staff left, and control was turned over to Ford managers. This proved to be another very useful learning situation for Ford, conveniently located away from Detroit and not visibly threatening anyone.

Ford soon learned how to turn round old plants, even though they have not adopted all the principles of Lean Production. They have also rationalised their supplier base so as to achieve cost levels similar to those of Japanese plants in the USA. What they have found more difficult is closing the gap in product development.

So collaboration or a joint venture with a Japanese producer is one way for the European firm to build critical in-house experience of Lean Production, though it does, of course, depend heavily on how well the organisation is structured to learn new techniques. Are there any other ways of becoming Lean? No assembler, European or otherwise, has yet found one, but there may be two possibilities. The first is simply to hire staff with previous transplant or Japanese experience as key manufacturing staff. For the foreseeable future, however, there will not be many of these, and after all the investment in them the Japanese firms are going to make it attractive for them to stay.

The second possibility is to use a plant located near to a Japanese transplant as a guinea pig, particularly if it is located well away from headquarters, where resistance to change is always greatest. An example of this would be for Peugeot, say, to use their UK plant as a model Japanese plant, learning as much as possible from the Japanese transplant down the road. Because of the small size of the existing workforce, no one's job would be threatened if in the process Peugeot learned how to produce twice the number of cars with the same number of employees. Once the plant was working on Lean Principles, it could then be used as a demonstration model for the rest of the group. There are many possible permutations on this theme.

For a component supplier there is one other route to learning Lean Techniques, and that is by becoming a supplier to a Japanese firm – what might be called vertical

Table 13.5 Japanese plans to increase vehicle production capacity in Europe to 1994

Toyota	
Burnaston, UK	200
Lisbon, Portugal	15
Honda	
Swindon, UK	200
Nissan	
Washington, UK	300
Barcelona, Spain	74
Mitsubishi[1]	
Boorn, Netherlands	100
Suzuki	
Linares, Spain	50
Esztergom, Hungary	50
IBC (Isuzu-GM)	
Luton, UK	45

[1]No final announcement of Mitsubishi's plans has yet been made. Negotiations are understood to be held up over the Dutch government's asking price for its ownership stake in Volvo's Dutch subsidiary. Mitsubishi would take this stake to form a joint venture with Volvo to produce and market a Mitsubishi-designed car

Source: Womack & Jones 1991 pp. 11–12; press reports

learning. Ironically, the leading European suppliers may be in a better position to assimilate these techniques than the European assemblers. They have built up a significant scale of operations in North America, and have witnessed the Japanese threat at first hand. Moreover, because of the greater degree to which they have taken responsibility for designing their parts compared to American counterparts, a number of European suppliers have won contracts to supply the US-located transplants. They therefore already have some experience in supplying the Japanese, which they can build on in supplying the Japanese transplants in Europe.

How much time do the European producers have? So far the Japanese producers have committed themselves to building one million plus units of annual assembly capacity and facilities to make nearly half a million engines yearly in Europe, to be fully operative by about 1995 (see Table 13.5). During the second half of the 1990s some of these plants will probably be expanded, and Mazda and Mitsubishi may also decide to establish plants. This could add a further 860,000 units, not counting Rover's capacity of 400,000 which Honda might fully acquire at some point. Quite apart from problems with the European Commission (see Chapter 10 by Peter Holmes and

Alasdair Smith in this volume), does this not court the danger of creating a critical overcapacity situation in Europe in a few years time? The answer to this question is not as straightforward as many have assumed.

We can draw some lessons from what happened in North America. Between 1982 and 1990 the Japanese opened eleven new plants in North America, with a combined capacity of 2.1 million units a year. In 1987–90 imports of built-up vehicles from Japan fell by a million units, leading to an underfulfilment of the voluntary export restraint quota for the three years. Over that period General Motors and Chrysler shut down 9 plants, with a capacity of 2.2 million units, and opened one new plant (Saturn). Ford, which had almost closed the productivity gap with the transplants, did not have to close any plants. The 1992 announcement by General Motors that they intend to close a further 21 plants, including six assembly plants, with a loss of 75,000 jobs, demonstrates that the process is continuing. The net result is that the capacity utilisation level of the entire North American industry has not changed since 1987. There is no overcapacity crisis in North America – rather what we have seen is a steady substitution of poor plants by new, best practice plants. Where this will end will depend on how fast things improve at General Motors and Chrysler.

There is every reason to believe that the situation will be similar in Europe, with Japanese plants driving poorly performing indigenous plants out of business. However the pattern may not be quite as simple in the Old World, since demand will probably continue to grow on a trend basis as Southern and Eastern Europe 'catch up' with West European levels of car ownership. This will absorb some of the new capacity. Nevertheless the full impact of Japanese transplants in Europe will begin to be felt within three or four years.

There is no doubt that the move from mass production to Lean Production will bring with it a significant improvement in productivity, and also living standards. However it is also clear that the transition will not be easy. The real danger is that the process could at some point be frustrated by political moves to freeze Japanese participation in the European market (see Chapter 10, on the trilateral relationship).

A very telling pointer to what could happen in such a situation is contained in an interesting study by Wayne Lewchuk (1987). He demonstrates how difficult the earlier transition from craft to mass production was in the UK. Indeed he shows that the UK motor industry never really adopted full mass production systems until the early 1980s, when craft demarcations and piece-rate pay systems were finally abolished at Rover under Michael Edwardes.

Only for a brief moment (at Trafford Park, Ford's first British assembly plant, in 1915) did British productivity equal that of Detroit. But Ford's British managers, who had less sympathy with and understanding of mass production than their American counterparts, were not able to sustain that achievement, and by 1922 the pattern of production had 'gone native'. If the standard bearer could not sustain mass production methods, it is not surprising that others were not able to either. By the time post-war trade barriers fell in the late 1960s, it was clear that the continental Europeans had been more successful in implementing the mass production system, and the decline of the UK motor industry began in earnest. It took another decade for things to get bad enough for the necessary action to be taken. By that time it was too late to maintain an independent, locally owned motor industry in Great Britain. This, in a word, is what happens to vehicle industries that do not manage to assimilate the leading-edge technology of the given era.

Eastern Europe

Will the opening up of the Eastern European market help European auto producers? There is no question that in the longer term Eastern Europe will offer a significant new growth market for the European industry. It will effectively become the Spain of the 1990s. But it must be remembered that, even though for a long time it absorbed many kits from France and elsewhere, Spain continues to run a large surplus in finished vehicle trade. Eastern Europe, with virtually no hard currency reserves, will need to do the same for many years to come.

Investments in Eastern Europe will certainly give Volkswagen, Fiat and General Motors extra volume, though not for the time being extra profits. However given Eastern Europe's need to export, the right strategy for the European auto producers might be not simply to transfer old models and old, labour-intensive techniques, but rather to use Eastern Europe as their source for entry level products (ie cars for first-time buyers), produced to the highest quality in the most modern and Lean facilities (with adequate, not maximal levels of automation), for the whole of Europe. Indeed there might be a golden opportunity to introduce Lean techniques to these new plants in Eastern Europe right from the start. In return, the West European companies could export limited numbers of up-market cars from the West to the growing elite market in the East.

Globalisation

While volume may well be very important in surviving the 1990s, there is another consideration that cannot be ignored by the European producers. They simply do not have enough footholds in the rest of the world, specifically in the North American and East Asian markets. Contemporary research indicates that it is essential in the long run for large auto firms to be multi-regional producers. This is particularly true as we move away from a bipolar world towards a trilateral world of three macro-regions (Europe, North America including Canada and Mexico, and East Asia), each of which commands the technology and internal market size to go for 'fortress' solutions to inter-regional tensions and frictions if it so desires. Why?

We have shown that Lean Production depends on a great deal of face-to-face interaction at all levels – between design and manufacturing, between design and manufacturing and suppliers, and with the local market-place. It is not surprising in that context that the leading Japanese firms are establishing top to bottom design and manufacturing operations in America and Europe.

It is equally clear that with their more efficient Lean product development process, the Japanese firms can *afford* to develop cars specifically geared to local tastes and market conditions. Moreover, they can then cross-ship these products to other markets as niche products with a very different image. They can consequently offer a larger range of products in each market than a 'world car' producer building only four or five designs worldwide. (The world car has in any case never actually been realised. General Motors and Ford are still struggling with the problem of getting engineers on both sides of the Atlantic to work together.)

The ability to cross-ship products in both directions between regions also makes the firm less vulnerable to trade pressures and exchange rate movements. In addition, it offers greater protection against the cyclicality of some markets. More generally, a presence in each region allows the firm to share in the profitability of each regional market. At present neither the Americans or Europeans can benefit significantly from the profitability of the Japanese market, and Toyota cannot be effectively challenged there. European firms confined to Europe depend heavily on the profitability of their own market, and are vulnerable when it is the turn of the American or Japanese market to boom.

Finally, it is clear that there is also an enormous amount to be gained by having managers and engineers with experience of working in different markets, especially the most challenging markets in terms of tastes and technology. Ford, in particular, has adopted the practice of moving its staff around its global operations and Honda is beginning to do the same, followed by the other Japanese firms. Unless the Europeans are able fully to participate in the North American and East Asian markets (the latter is one of the greatest growth markets, at the moment completely dominated by the Japanese), they will be competing with one hand tied behind their backs.

Building a global presence cannot be done overnight. Indeed the Europeans remember the problems they ran into last time they tried. Although Fiat and Volkswagen are building large East European empires, these will not necessarily be founded on world class facilities. However the expansion of Volkswagen's Mexican plant currently under way, not to mention further ventures in America and East Asia, undoubtedly will. Globalisation is something for the European producers to aim for, after they have made some progress in closing the gap within Europe.

Researching new solutions

How well equipped is the European auto industry to develop new solutions and technologies to meet the twin problems of congestion and emissions? The Japanese auto industry spent more on R&D in 1988 than the whole of Europe put together – $6.9 billion compared with $6.5 billion (and $9.2 billion in the USA). What is more, R&D is far less concentrated in Europe than in either Japan or the USA. The largest European firms, Volkswagen and Mercedes Benz, each spent on R&D in 1988 only the same amount as the third-ranking Japanese firm, Honda; Fiat, Renault and Peugeot each spent only as much as the fourth-ranking Japanese producer, Mazda (Jones 1988). In terms of the number of patents registered in the USA, the comparison is even less flattering.

None of the European assemblers, then, can muster R&D resources on the scale of General Motors, Ford, Toyota and Nissan. It is striking, moreover, that the Americans assemblers register far fewer patents than the Japanese assemblers, even though they are spending considerably more on R&D (Dodwell Consultants 1986; Elm International 1987; PRS 1986). So once the Europeans have caught up in quantitative R&D terms, they may still face a major challenge in terms in terms of effectiveness. It is certainly true that the Europeans, and particularly the Germans, have led the world in building technologically sophisticated cars. But component suppliers have played a key role in sustaining this leadership. Bosch alone registered 236 patents in the USA in 1986, and many of the American and British suppliers, such as ITT (Alfred Teves), Lucas (Girling) and GKN (Unicardan), have significant operations in Germany. The maintenance of German technological strength will depend critically on close working relationships between assemblers and suppliers, and implicitly on the reinforcement of Lean Production elements already present in Europe's leading national car industry. The competitive threat is that the Japanese transplants, encouraged by European local content regulations, will make a *better* job of building relationships with European component suppliers.

Overall, contemporary research suggests that the Japanese make much more efficient use of their R&D activities, in the same way as they develop new cars with far fewer resources than do their competitors in the West (Graves 1987). As we saw, their R&D operations are organised very much in the same way as their product development. This means that they come up with solutions faster and at less cost, and are much better placed to introduce these at the level of production. Not only is their product replacement cycle shorter, but they are well geared up to building smaller volume products that can test new concepts in the market-place. This is a skill the Europeans have lost and need to regain. We are entering a time of growing uncertainty, with multiple competing technological solutions. Firms will have to start off by experimenting with these in small volume products.

The French, Italian and German governments have in the past supported research into more fuel-efficient vehicle technologies, but the results have not had a significant impact on the vehicles produced in those countries. This is in part because European governments have been less ready to force the adoption of such technologies by regulatory measures, as has been done in the USA and Japan, preferring to rely on the high price of fuel in Europe. Now the European Commission and national governments are funding a large-scale research effort focused on 'intelligent' vehicles and 'smart' highways, through the *Drive* and *Prometheus* programmes, which are sub-components of the Eureka programme (see Chapter 14, on electronics).

Prometheus (Programme for European Traffic with Highest Efficiency and Unprecedented Safety) is designed to develop new in-vehicle/highway electronics which will permit more efficient and safer use of European highways while aiding European automotive and electronics firms to gain a larger share of the global automotive electronics market. The idea is to develop communication and navigation capabilities for motor vehicles which will permit them to avoid congestion and accidents, and to move in the direction of automatic operation. The Drive programme complements Prometheus in seeking to develop technologies for roadway management which would permit vehicles to communicate with traffic managers and with each other by means of information networks incorporated in the roadway (Graves 1989).

These developments are enormously exciting. Yet, however important Prometheus and Drive may be for initiating long-term research and developing common standards, the task of developing new, in-vehicle technologies will always depend on the willingness of auto firms to commit themselves to finding 'own solutions' which they think customers will be willing to pay for.

Some of the European volume producers have in the past fought hard against the adoption in Europe of emission standards long accepted in the USA and Japan. They appeared to have little conviction that green technologies could be sold to the public, particularly in Southern Europe, because those technologies would raise the cost of running the small car typical of the Southern European market proportionately more than than that of running the larger car more common in Northern Europe. The French and Italian producers, with their relatively small presence in the more green-conscious markets of Northern Europe, were particularly defensive on environmental issues. Over the last year or so, however, attitudes have changed, and the dominant line among the European producers now seems to be to take the green cause firmly on board, perhaps in the hope that there will ultimately be substantial new funding from the EC for still more radical approaches, for instance the development of electric cars.

That still leaves them with the problem that many of these green technologies will first appear, not in cheap, small, city cars, but in much more expensive cars sold to affluent customers who want to demonstrate both their wealth and their green concern. In the past, new technologies have always trickled down from premium vehicles to the mass market. European volume producers without access to this premium market will be at a further disadvantage. Companies like Honda and Toyota have quite explicitly moved up into these premium markets, and are committed to developing new, environmentally friendly technologies as a competitive weapon. What Europe needs is a similar change of strategy – to one that is proactive rather than defensive in facing the challenges ahead.

An interim conclusion

In early February 1992, European car firms announced labour-force cutbacks totalling more than 5,000, with Ford UK and Vauxhall announcing 2,400 redundancies between them, and BMW unveiling a plan which will reduce manning levels by 3,000 by the end of 1992 (Europe's car makers . . . 1992). While the short-term impact of the recession of the early 1990s was clearly a factor in these developments, the fear of what Japanese competition might do to the European industry after the partial liberalisation of 31 December 1992 was certainly a more important one. If the 1992 job-sheddings are interpreted simply as conclusive proof that the European firms have finally recognised that there is no hiding place from Far Eastern competition, then the news is perhaps on balance good news. But with unemployment in Europe soaring, and the trade unions restless, there is a real danger that domestic political pressures may force national governments in Europe, and the EC, into a more restrictive interpretation of the July 1991 agreement with the Japanese motor industry. If that happens, the prospects of the European car industry closing the productivity gap by the year 2000 will recede, and indeed the impetus of the single market programme as a whole will be seriously jeopardised. At time of writing the future of the European car industry was delicately balanced indeed.

Notes

1   Value engineering and value analysis are techniques for assessing the costs of alternative ways of designing a product or production process.

References

Dodwell Consultants (1986) *The Structure of the Japanese Auto Parts Industry.* Tokyo

Elm International (1987) *The Elm Guide to Automotive Sourcing*, East Lane, Michigan

Graves A (1987) Comparative trends in automotive research and development. IMVP (International Motor Vehicle Project) paper, MIT, Cambridge, Mass

Graves A (1989) Prometheus: a new departure in automobile R&D. IMVP paper, MIT, Cambridge, Mass

The Independent (1992) Europe's car makers slim down, 8 February 1992, p. 1

Jones D T (1988) Measuring technological advantage in the motor vehicle industry, IMVP paper, MIT, Cambridge, Mass.

Lewchuk W (1987) *American Technology and the British Vehicle Industry*, Cambridge University Press

PRS (1986) *The European Automotive Components Industry*, London

Womack J P, Jones D T (1991) European automotive policy: past, present, and future. *Industry, Technology, and Employment Program*, Office of Technology Assessment, Congress of the United States, Final Report, 5 July

Womack J P, Jones D T, Roos D (1990) *The Machine that Changed the World*, Rawson Associates/Macmillan, New York

CHAPTER 14

The European electronics industry

MIKE HOBDAY

Introduction

This chapter analyses the achievements and failures of the European electronics industry. It surveys the rise of the 'national champions' in the post-1960 period and illustrates their collaboration and coalescence into large, integrated, European-based multinationals during the 1980s.

The first section defines the information technology industry as a group of interrelated sectors including telecommunications, defence, consumer electronics, computing, industrial equipment, semiconductors and software. During the post-1960 period, and especially during the 1980s, each of these sectors faced rapid technological change, increased competition and major industrial restructuring, both in Europe and beyond.

The second section identifies the major 'forces for change' in the industry, highlighting world-wide factors as well as Europe-specific factors, including strategies for catching up and building a stronger research base for Europe.

The third section examines the size and growth of the international electronics industry by major equipment sector. The fourth section presents indicators of Europe's weak competitive performance and poor balance of trade in the sector. The fifth section highlights some of the main causes of Europe's industrial and technological weaknesses by looking at the case of semiconductors, and briefly referring to other major sectors. The sixth section presents some of the major European programmes implemented with a view to improving the performance of firms in electronics. The seventh section looks at the response of the large European firms to these programmes and assesses the major restructuring that has taken place since the mid-1980s through acquisitions, mergers and joint ventures across most of the industry. This period witnessed an unprecedented, forward-looking commitment to technological innovation, and a new 'professionalisation' of electronics management. As the eighth section shows, this occurred through the recruitment of high-level managers and directors from US firms which had invested in Europe in the 1960s and 1970s.

The ninth section takes a broad look at the achievements of Europe in electronics, asking whether the European industry is now adequate in terms of scale of enterprise, technological capability and corporate strategy to meet the growing challenge from the USA, Japan and South-East Asia. It assesses the strengths and weaknesses of European policies and suggests that, as we enter the 1990s, we should give more recognition both to the users of electronics equipment and to non-European firms operating within European boundaries.

Finally, an *Appendix* provides a glossary of unavoidable technical terms and commonly used abbreviations.

Definition: electronics as a group of industries

The electronics industry can be defined in general terms as a group of sectors which produce goods and systems based upon semiconductor and software technology. The group comprises five main systems sectors: telecommunications, defence, consumer electronics, computing and electronically controlled industrial equipment. It also includes the semiconductor (or chip) industry, which supplies the basic components for all electronic systems, and the software industry, which is concerned with the design and development of electronic systems.

There is, however, no single, precise definition of electronics that is generally accepted. Some observers include telecommunication and computer services (substantially larger, in value terms, than their associated equipment markets) as well as professional electronics goods such as instrumentation and measurement equipment. Others include parts of 'traditional industries' whose products and manufacturing processes have been transformed by the application of electronics systems (eg automobiles and aerospace).

The electronics (or information technology) sectors relate to each other in various ways. For example, semiconductors, the building blocks of the industry, are produced world-wide by twenty or so large manufacturers, and used by each of the systems producers. Chip makers frequently develop semiconductors in co-operation with systems producers. The systems makers use their skills to combine software and semiconductors to produce various types of equipment.

Each sector within the industrial grouping is further differentiated by major product or system. Since the early 1970s systems firms have produced a seemingly endless variety of products including digital watches, weapons systems, microcomputers, mainframe computers, televisions, telephone exchanges, mobile communication systems and engineering workstations (Table 14.1).

The common technological base (semiconductors and software) of electronics equipment has led observers to speak of 'technological convergence'. In the early 1980s many observers (and firms) believed that the boundaries between the product areas (especially telecommunications and computers) were eroding. Major telecommunications firms, including AT&T (in the USA) and Ericsson (of Sweden) invested heavily in computer technology. On the same pattern computer firms, including IBM (of the USA), invested in telecommunications. More often than not these cross-industry experiments failed commercially. Firms (and analysts) seem to have underestimated the large differences between the sectors in terms of market operations, customers and

Table 14.1 Major product categories in electronics

Industrial sector	Examples of goods and systems
Consumer electronics	Compact disc, high-definition TV, video-cassette players and recorders, stereo systems, camcorders, radios
Telecommunications	Exchanges, telephones, radar, broadcast equipment, mobile and base stations, microwave, fibre-optics, satellite earth stations
Defence	Aircraft, missiles, ships, space, vehicle and testing systems
Computing	Personal, mini and mainframe computers, disk drives, optical disks, laser and other printers, terminals
Industrial	Process control equipment, robot systems, numerical control equipment, motor controls
Semiconductor	Microprocessors, memory devices, diodes and transistors, optoelectronics, standard logic circuits, application-specific integrated circuits, linear devices

basic technologies. In the late 1980s, major firms tended to retreat into core technology areas. Ericsson, for instance, withdrew from office automation equipment after sustaining heavy losses.

Forces for change in the industry

In each of the electronics sectors, industrial and technological change proceeded at an astounding pace during the 1980s. The major forces for change differed according to sector, time period, country, region and, sometimes, individual firm. Table 14.2 highlights some of these forces for change. For the purposes of this chapter it is helpful to differentiate between world-wide industry factors and Europe-specific factors.

World-wide industry factors

Technological advance continued to reduce the costs of semiconductors and electronic systems (measured in terms of cost–performance ratios), expanding the boundaries of what was economically feasible, opening up new market innovations such as the Sony Walkman, the computer engineering workstation, and the high-definition television.

Market growth (see third section, pp. 227–8) continued unabated during the 1980s, despite periods of economic recession, attracting newcomers to the industry and stimulating further investments in technology.

Increased competition resulted from policy measures such as privatisation and market deregulation (in telecommunications) and liberalisation of markets and international investments (in consumer goods and semiconductors), as well as from the entry of newly industrialising countries (eg South Korea and Taiwan).

Internationalisation (or 'globalisation') describes the process whereby large multinational firms extended their marketing, technology and production operations across the major continents of the world. It also refers to the way in which standard, mass-product markets developed on a global basis (eg hi-fi, colour televisions, microcomputers and mobile communications).

Table 14.2 Major forces[a] for change in electronics in the 1980s

World-wide industry factors	European factors
Technological advance	Technological catch-up
Market growth	Influence of EC policy
Increased competition	Preparations for 1992
Internationalisation	Competitive restructuring
Joint ventures	US and Japanese inward investment
Rising investment costs	Professionalisation of management
Market differentiation	
Technological convergence	
The rise of Japan and South-East Asia	

Note: [a] These categories are not mutually exclusive; in a number of cases they overlap with each other

Joint ventures (or 'strategic partnerships') were a common feature of globalisation during the 1980s. In order to gain access to new markets and to develop new technologies, most major electronics firms formed alliances with competitor corporations within and beyond their national boundaries. Government programmes of support for research and development encouraged some firms to form such partnerships on a national or regional basis.

Rising investment costs affected many sectors in areas such as R&D (eg telecommunications exchanges), capital investments (eg semiconductor manufacturing equipment) and global marketing and distribution (eg in consumer electronics), and led to growing entry barriers and increased concentration in some sub-sectors.

Market and technological differentiation proceeded apace in other sub-sectors, resulting in the entry of new innovative firms (eg LSI Logic in semiconductors and Apple Computers in microcomputers, both US firms). The twin forces of, first, rising investment costs/increasing barriers to entry, and second, market differentiation/lowering of barriers, often led to confusing and apparently contradictory industry trends.

Technological convergence, as noted earlier, led firms to invest in closely related electronics fields. Some large Japanese and Korean firms (eg NEC of Japan and Samsung of Korea) allowed the idea of technological convergence to determine global corporate decisions.

The rise of Japan and South-East Asia was swift and impressive. Japan, for instance, displaced the USA in 1986 as the largest supplier of semiconductors on the international market. Korea and Taiwan gained large market shares in consumer electronics, and built up a strong balance of trade surplus with the West (Mody 1987). Some argued that the locus of innovation in electronics was by the mid-1980s rapidly shifting to the South-East Asia region (Gregory 1986).

Europe-specific factors

In addition to the above factors, the strategies of European electronics firms were strongly influenced by important regional considerations.

First, *technological catch-up*: by the early 1980s, European firms lagged behind the

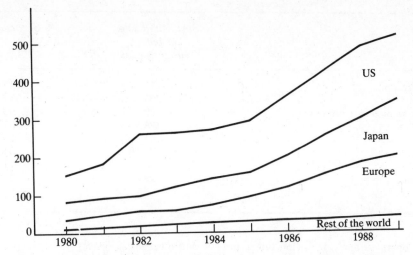

Figure 14.1 Growth of electronic equipment sales in the 1980s ($ billion, current prices)
Source: Electronics, January 1989.

technological leaders in the USA and Japan in several sectors. In particular, a severe weakness in semiconductors led many firms to believe that large programmes of catch-up investment were needed, otherwise European firms would fall further behind in fields such as telecommunications, computing and consumer electronics (Hobday 1989a).

Second, *EC policy* encouraged European firms, research centres and universities to collaborate in large, expensive programmes of R&D in electronics. Key areas included semiconductors, software and high-definition television. EC-subsidised programmes such as ESPRIT aimed to bring about a European competitive recovery in these areas (see pp. 284–7).

Third, *preparations for 1992* led to a substantial restructuring of fragmented European operations, technological improvement and, in some cases, an upgrading of existing management practices.

To sum up, major electronics producers found themselves by the 1980s situated in a rapidly growing industry characterised by deep technological and market uncertainty, high risk and accelerating R&D and investment costs. New innovations continued to generate new products and markets. To survive, firms were often forced to change management direction, to respond to shortening product life cycles, and to invest heavily for the future.

Market size and growth

Figure 14.1 illustrates the rapid growth of the turnover of the world electronic equipment industry (excluding semiconductors), which grew from just over $150 billion in 1980 to an estimated $582 billion in 1990 (*Electronics* January 1990). The components required to produce the equipment represented a market of around $200 billion in 1990, of which approximately $48 billion (24 per cent) were accounted for by

Table 14.3 Major electronics industries: sales in 1990

	Estimated sales ($ billion, current prices)	% of total sales
Computer systems	215	27.5
Components[a]	200	25.6
of which semiconductors	48	6.1
Consumer	128	16.4
Industrial	81	10.4
Communications[b]	77	9.8
Military	58	7.4
Transportation	23	2.9
Total	782	100.0

Notes:
[a] including optoelectronics, television tubes, passive and mechanical devices
[b] including telecommunications, data communications and broadcast equipment

Source: derived from Electronics January 1990

Table 14.4 World electronics market (consumption): Europe vs other regions 1990 ($ billion, current prices)

	Europe	US	Japan	Rest of the world
Equipment	134	214	164	70
(share)	(23%)	(37%)	(28%)	(12%)
Semiconductors	7	17	19	4
(share)	(15%)	(36%)	(40%)	(9%)

Source: derived from Electronics January 1990

semiconductors (*Electronics*, January 1990). Taking components and systems estimates together, the total world electronics market for 1990, measured in 'gross' terms, was of the order of $782 billion.

The sales figures for individual equipment sectors are shown in Table 14.3. The computer systems (or data processing) market is the largest industry, followed by consumer electronics and industrial equipment, although smaller, telecommunications, semiconductors, military applications and transportation also represent significant global industries.

Turning to regional shares (see Table 14.4), Europe accounted for roughly $134 billion or 23 per cent of total equipment sales in 1990, compared with $214 billion (37 per cent) for the USA, and $164 billion (28 per cent) for Japan, with the rest of the world accounting for $70 billion (12 per cent). In semiconductors, Europe accounted for around 15 per cent of world sales in 1990. Most analysts predict continued healthy growth for the European electronics market.

Europe's failure to keep up in electronics

Poor innovation performance

Since the early 1960s, when the rapid growth of sales of semiconductors, computing and consumer electronics began, Europe has failed to keep pace with the investment and innovation dynamic of the USA and Japan. Europe's comparative weakness is demonstrated by trade statistics, indicators of technological performance, and the judgements of industry leaders (see Sharp, Chapter 12 in this volume, on changing industrial structures).

A plethora of sectoral case studies for particular countries and Europe as a whole also testify to the region's weakness in electronics. Hendry (1990) shows how, despite the UK's lead in computing technology in the 1950s, domestic firms failed to commercialise their innovations and were overtaken by US firms. O'Brien (1989) demonstrates the poor performance of European-owned computing firms. Cawson et al (1990) and Sharp (1987b) illustrate how European firms were overwhelmed by Japanese companies in consumer electronics.

In telecommunications, Europe's traditional strengths enabled large firms to remain strong on the international stage, but with signs of weakness in the latter half of the 1980s (Jonquieres 1990; Cawson et al 1990). Hobday (1989a) shows how European firms failed to match the investment and innovative performance of US firms in semiconductor technology. Despite strengths in some sub-sectors of software, Europe's overall performance has been disappointing (Patel and Pavitt 1987; Brady and Quintas 1990).

The worsening balance of trade

As far as the balance of trade in electronics is concerned, Europe's positive balance of 1975 had been transformed into a deficit of approximately $5 billion by 1985. The relatively weak production base, coupled with rapidly growing electronics consumption, continued to exacerbate the deficit, which reached a massive $21.9 billion in 1987 (CEC 1989). The largest components of the deficit were computers (roughly $12 billion) consumer electronics (just over $8 billion) and semiconductor components (nearly $3 billion).

Differences across Europe

There are, of course, significant differences between European economies. West Germany tends to fare relatively well, France less well in most sectors, followed by the UK. The UK's performance is particularly unimpressive, given its initial post-war strengths in radar, computing and telecommunications, semiconductor technology, and continuing strengths in advanced R&D. The Netherlands performs fairly well in consumer electronics due to its large indigenous producer, Philips. Taking into account variations from one country to another, there can be no doubt that, overall, Europe

Table 14.5 European manufacturers' share of the world semiconductor market (%)

1979	16
1980	13
1981	12
1982	12
1983	11
1984	11
1985	12
1986	11
1987	11
1988	10

Source: Dataquest, cited in *Wall Street Journal* 19 June 1989

has failed to match the international competitiveness of the USA and Japan and, increasingly, other countries of South-East Asia such as Korea and Taiwan.

Causes of Europe's weakness in electronics

Europe's problems in electronics cannot realistically be termed a decline. In fields such as consumer electronics, computing, software and semiconductors, Europe had never achieved a strong international position. Europe's weakness in electronics reflects an on-going long-term failure to participate in growing commercial markets, to export overseas, and to make the technological investments necessary to maintain parity or catch up with the world leaders. The case of semiconductors is especially important, as chip technology is crucial for all electronic products.

The case of semiconductors

Poor competitive performance

Europe's competitive performance in chips has been very weak compared with the USA and Japan. As Table 14.5 shows, Europe's share of world sales fell from 16 per cent to 10 per cent between 1980 and 1988. European consumption of chips has been satisfied largely by imports and inward investment from the USA, and more recently Japan.

During the 1980s Philips, the Dutch consumer goods manufacturer, was the only European producer consistently in the top ten list of suppliers. Philips was ranked tenth in the world in 1989, with an annual output of of semiconductors of around $1.7 billion. In 1989 eleven out of the twenty largest producers were Japanese, five were American and only three were European (Philips, SGS-Thomson of France, and Siemens of Germany: *Dataquest*, cited in *Electronic Business* 16 April 1990).

Table 14.6 World market for integrated circuits, 1986 ($ million, current prices)

USA	8,429
Japan	9,852
West Germany	1,102
UK	989
France	684
Italy	390
Total	21,446

Source: Dataquest, Mackintosh, Butler Cox, cited in *Financial Times* 31 March 1987

Inward-looking, nationalistic strategies

Until the mid-1980s most European companies' investment strategies for semiconductors were cautious and limited in scale and scope. European manufacturers concentrated on low-volume, domestic markets. A fairly large proportion of output was in mature, discrete components (eg transistors) rather than integrated circuits. Production was oriented towards in-house customised needs, rather than the large-volume international commodity markets. In 1980, for example, the share of external component sales in total revenue was less than 5 per cent for Philips, Siemens, Thomson, AEG-Telefunken and Plessey (Mackenzie 1985).

In contrast, US multinationals followed aggressive marketing and production strategies within Europe during the 1960s and 1970s. They maintained a constant technological lead and made large investments in new generations of chips such as memories and microprocessors. Tariff barriers erected by Europe encouraged US producers to increase inward investment into France, Germany, The Netherlands, Italy and the UK.

The US lead in manufacturing process technology for standard components (especially memory devices) spilled over to other segments of the chip industry. With each successive wave of chip innovations, technological and financial barriers to entry increased, making it more and more difficult for European producers to recapture lost markets.

European market fragmentation

Compared with the large US and Japanese markets, the European market in the 1980s was fragmented. Table 14.6 shows the home market base in which European chip companies operated. The larger US and Japanese home markets were useful for building up economies of scale in R&D, production and marketing.

But although market fragmentation is one of the reasons most often cited for Europe's lacklustre performance in electronics in general, and in chips in particular, it was never the major cause. Indeed during the 1960s and 1970s the Swedish telecommunications firm Ericsson overcame the drawback of its small home market by exporting, as did Japanese firms. Korean and Taiwanese firms have also demonstrated that a large home market base is not a necessary condition for market success in electronics.

Far more important was the lack of dynamism shown by European firms, and their failure to make heavy forward investments in new technology. Government policies aimed at supporting national champions (see below) conspired to reinforce these difficulties, not only in semiconductors but in other sectors too.

Telecommunications, computing and other electronics sectors

National champion policies

Inward-looking strategies at firm level were encouraged by government policies of procurement and subsidy in telecommunications, computers and defence, as well as in semiconductors. Although the major economies of Europe differed in their approaches to electronics, policies tended to support the national champions strategy. This, in effect, meant giving preferential treatment to locally owned firms, through public purchasing and subsidies for research and development and other activities. The aim was to enable domestic firms to become large enough to champion the high-technology needs of the given countries.

The 'economies of scale' argument, often used to support national champion policies, was always a flawed argument. Recent empirical evidence from Porter (1990) and Pavitt (1990) shows that the number of firms competing within an economy is far more important to international corporate success than the size of individual firms. Indeed, national champion policies led to smaller numbers of larger firms, and in many cases to market 'carve-up', inward-looking monopolistic practices and an unhealthy reliance on the state for subsidies and guaranteed orders – as much as 50 per cent of the output of some electronics segments were effectively removed from international competition (Sharp 1987a).

In the USA by contrast, although similar public support policies were followed, the much larger domestic market allowed for substantial competition between government suppliers of electronic systems and software.

The Japanese initiative in consumer electronics

In consumer electronics, European firms were often passive onlookers in an industry increasingly dominated by Japanese firms. Apart from some exceptions, such as Philips of The Netherlands, European firms could offer little to counter the low-cost competition from Japan in inexpensive pocket radios, taperecorders, hi-fi, and black and white and colour televisions.

In response to market protection and voluntary export restraint agreements concluded with Japan during the 1970s, some Japanese firms set up manufacturing plants within Europe. Others formed joint ventures with European companies. During the early 1980s Pye, the UK television manufacturer, was taken over by Sony. Toshiba and Hitachi formed joint ventures with the UK firms, Rank and GEC respectively. In both cases the joint ventures failed and the British firms withdrew, leaving the field to the Japanese producers. By 1985 there were more than fifty Japanese manufacturing plants in Europe, of which thirty-two were in consumer electronics (Sharp 1987a).

Policies towards Japan in relation to consumer electronics varied across Europe. During the early 1970s the UK was the most liberal, allowing direct foreign investment and encouraging joint ventures. In contrast, France attempted to protect local firms and keep Japanese firms out of the economy. However, after 1984 the French government changed its attitude and started to encourage Japanese firms to step up their investments in France. West Germany tended to be more liberal than France before 1984 but less open than the UK. West Germany was, of course, an attractive site on account of its skilled labour force and the efficiency of component input suppliers (Sharp 1987b; Cawson et al 1990).

On the whole, Europe failed to meet the consumer electronics challenge from Japan in the post-1960 period. Major European plants were shut down, giving Japan the opportunity to strengthen its grip on this large electronics sector.

Relative strengths in telecommunications and defence

In telecommunications and defence, government purchasing preferences were applied in most European countries, encouraging firms to behave opportunistically (Dang Nguyen 1985). Telecommunications administrations formed monopsonistic links with their domestic equipment suppliers, preventing competition from foreign companies. Similarly, national defence contractors were given preference over foreign suppliers.

In both these sectors, the traditional strengths of European suppliers in the post-war period were carried through into the electronics era. Japan was prohibited from competing in military technology and was in any case relatively weak in complex telecommunications switching equipment. Thus for a combination of market-structural and genuinely technological reasons, European firms continued to occupy a strong international position compared with Japan.

The gradual decline in computing technology

The negative impact of government involvement and inward-looking firm strategies was also visible in the computing industry, where a large proportion of European output was sold to domestic governments. Despite the strong initial technological base of some countries, the national champions failed to match the technology investments and marketing aggressiveness of US firms such as IBM, DEC and Hewlett Packard. European firms tended to concentrate on proprietary systems which stood little chance of becoming internationally acceptable, standard products (O'Brien 1989).

The lack of entrepreneurship displayed by some of Europe's larger computer manufacturers was compounded by the low level of development of small, dynamic start-up firms. Such firms populated the US microcomputer (and semiconductor) industries densely, pressurising larger firms to become more competitive (Dorfman 1987); some grew to become large multinationals (eg Apple). This virtuous cycle of innovation was almost non-existent in Europe during the 1960s and 1970s.

Although some firms fared better than others, nationalistic policies encouraged corporate parochialism and generated protected, subsidised markets. By the mid-1980s

Table 14.7   Government technology initiatives,[a] 1982–7

Pan-European programmes	Single country programmes
ESPRIT 1	Alvey, UK
ESPRIT 2	FINPRIT, Finland
RACE[b]	Informationstechnik, W Germany
BRITE[c]	La Filiére Electronique, France
Eureka	National Microelectronics Programme, Sweden

Notes:
[a] Not exhaustive, mostly concerned with information technology
[b] RACE = R&D in Advanced Communications and Electronics
[c] BRITE = Basic Research in Industrial Technologies for Europe

major segments of Europe's computing industry were uncompetitive. The next section describes some of the initiatives taken by the EC to change the fortunes of the Community's electronics industry.

European support programmes for electronics

During the mid-1980s Europe embarked upon a series of electronics initiatives (Table 14.7). Their aim was to strengthen Europe's capabilities in semiconductors, robotics, computers, software telecommunications and other sectors. Several national electronics programmes were also set up to support R&D. France, the UK, Italy, West Germany, Sweden and The Netherlands channelled resources directly to their leading electronics manufacturers.

ESPRIT (the European Strategic Programme of Research in Information Technology)

The rationale for ESPRIT

During 1979 and 1980, leaders of the twelve largest electronics firms were invited by the European Commission to a series of discussions to try and reach agreement on how Europe could reverse its deteriorating balance of trade in electronics and counter the success of Japanese projects in areas such as semiconductors (Sharp 1989). The firms agreed to collaborate in R&D in information technology under the ESPRIT Programme, which began in February 1984.

Objectives of ESPRIT

The main objective of ESPRIT was to co-ordinate European R&D and to promote competitiveness in electronics by focusing on collaborative, so-called pre-competitive R&D in five electronics areas: advanced micro-electronics (ie semiconductor-related

Table 14.8 Share of 'Big Twelve' firms in ESPRIT, *c.* 1986

Company name		No of projects	% ESPRIT budget
Thomson	(France)	37	6.9
Philips	(Netherlands)	34	5.9
Siemens	(W Germany)	27	5.9
STET	(Italy)	36	5.0
Bull	(France)	38	5.0
GEC	(UK)	45	4.8
STC/ICL	(UK)	33	4.3
Olivetti	(Italy)	29	3.8
CGE	(France)	27	3.5
AEG	(W Germany)	25	2.3
Nixdorf	(W Germany)	13	1.8
Plessey	(UK)	15	1.5
Total		165	50.7

Source: Hare et al 1988: 55

technology), software, advanced information processing, office systems and computer-integrated manufacturing.

ESPRIT was set up as a ten-year programme. In the region of ECU 1.5 billion (approximately $1.25 billion) were allocated for the first five-year period. Half of the funding came from the EC, and the other half was shared by industry, academia and non-university research institutes. The shares of the largest twelve firms in ESPRIT's total budget are shown in Table 14.8. The second phase of ESPRIT (ESPRIT 2) was agreed in 1987. This was scheduled to run from 1987 to 1992 at a total cost of ECU 3.2 billion.

Eureka

Eureka, which involved nineteen countries (twelve Community states, six EFTA countries and Turkey), was launched by France in 1985 as a response to the US's Strategic Defense Initiative (Arnold and Guy 1986). The aim of Eureka was to improve productivity and competitiveness in European electronics industries through closer co-operation among enterprises and research institutes (CEC 1986). By 1989 Eureka had accepted over 300 projects, worth around ECU 6.5 billion (Sharp 1990).

Eureka's aim was to complement the EC's programmes, which concentrated mostly on pre-competitive research. The programme provided support for firms in tele-communications, semiconductors, high-definition television, automobiles, robotics, materials, lasers and advanced manufacturing technologies.

There can be little doubt that ESPRIT and the other programmes played a crucial part in changing the structure and strategies of Europe's leading electronics corporations. The programmes encouraged co-operation among European companies, stimulated investment in technology, and provided a platform on the basis of which

Table 14.9 European projects, acquisitions and mergers in semiconductors

Date	Venture	Firms	Cost ($ million)[a]
1983–9	Megaproject	Siemens/Philips	930
1986	Mostek acquisition	Thomson	120
1986	Megaproject 2	SGS/Thomson	655
1987	Merger	SGS/Thomson	
1988–95	JESSI	Siemens/Philips Thomson/SGS/Plessey	3,700
1988	Acquisition	Ferranti Semiconductors by Plessey	
1989	Acquisition	Inmos by SGS/Thomson	
1989	Acquisition	Plessey Semiconductors by GEC and Siemens jointly	

Note: [a] Exchange rate $1.7 = £1.0

companies could jointly decide how to meet the competition from the United States and Japan.

Corporate restructuring in electronics

Partly as a result of the technology programmes, the European electronics industry witnessed during the latter half of the 1980s a series of partnership deals, mergers and acquisitions which led to the emergence of pan-European electronics companies.

Semiconductors

The case of semiconductors is again illustrative. As Table 14.9 shows, various mergers and acquisitions took place, leading to a substantially less fragmented industry. In effect, national champions gave way to European champions, supported by the EC rather than national governments.

The Megaproject, for instance, was a four-year joint R&D venture in commodity chip technology (so-called one-megabit and four-megabit DRAMs). The aim of the $930 million project was to enable Siemens and Philips jointly to develop and market advanced chips. JESSI (the Joint European Sub-Micron Silicon Initiative) was to run from 1988 to 1995 at a cost of nearly $4 billion. This followed on from the Megaproject (which ended in 1989) in developing even more advanced memory chips (eg the sixteen-megabit chip).

Table 14.9 also lists some of the important mergers. The UK defence electronics firm, Ferranti, had its chip interests taken over by Plessey, which was in turn the subject of a successful hostile bid by another large UK firm, GEC. SGS of Italy joined forces with Thomson of France to form a joint company in 1989. The new company then acquired Inmos, the innovative UK microprocessor producer.

Across all areas of electronics a similar restructuring took place during the latter half of the 1980s, enabling firms to rationalise R&D and production operations and to market products on a pan-European basis. There was a dramatic transition from a fragmented market to a highly concentrated industry, with only two or three major firms in most sectors.

Other technology areas

In consumer electronics and defence, Thomson of France emerged as a world force via a series of acquisitions of European and US firms. Among Thomson's major European acquisitions were Telefunken of West Germany and Ferguson, the UK television manufacturer. Thomson also acquired the consumer electronics business of the US firm, RCA. As a result, Thomson became in 1987 the No. 3 world supplier of colour televisions, after Philips of the Netherlands and Matsushita of Japan. In defence electronics, Thomson-CSF reached the No. 2 position in the world, after GM Hughes of the US (*Electronic Business* 27 November 1989). No other European defence firm ranked in the top ten list of world suppliers in 1987.

Philips closed many of its smaller European plants during the 1980s, sold off its defence electronics activities to Thomson-CSF, and attempted to rationalise its operations on a world-wide level. The company successfully lobbied the Dutch, German, French and British governments for support, and received large subsidies from the EC to develop high-definition television and semiconductor technology. Recent severe financial problems (see p. 294) have forced Philips to review its investments in advanced semiconductors. However, the company remains one of the world's largest producers of consumer electronics.

Nokia, the Finnish-owned telecommunications and information systems conglomerate, moved into consumer electronics from 1985 by purchasing Luxor of Sweden and Salora of Finland (both television makers) in 1984. In 1987 Nokia purchased the French television manufacturer Oceanic (from Electrolux of Sweden), SEL (a German consumer electronics producer) and an 80 per cent share of the data systems division of Ericsson (Sweden's largest telecommunications producer).

In telecommunications, Siemens acquired Rolm (a major US firm) as well as GTE's overseas interests. Siemens also gained a foothold in the UK market through its acquisition of Plessey in partnership with GEC in 1989. As noted above, Ericsson of Sweden sold off its data systems interests to Nokia in 1987 and retreated into telecommunications. The French company Alcatel grew rapidly. As a subsidiary of CGE, which had already acquired the telecommunications interests of ITT (a US-owned firm), Alcatel became the second largest telecommunications producer in the world after AT&T in 1989.

These examples illustrate the major strategic reorientations that have occurred within the European electronics industry. Several of the national champions of the 1970s joined forces to become the European champions of the late 1980s, encouraged by the policies of the EC.

The professionalisation of European management

Europe's restructuring in electronics involved the recruitment of top professionals from US multinational companies which had invested in Europe in the 1960s and 1970s.

Table 14.10 Examples of US-trained professionals joining European electronics firms

Company/HQ	Name	Position	US company origin
Thomson (France)	Jacques Noel	President of Components Div	Texas Instruments
Thomson (France)	Carlo Zani	Director	Texas Instruments
SGS (Italy)	Pasquale Pistorio	Chief Executive	Motorola
ICL (UK)	Rob Wilmot (later ES2)	Managing Director	Texas Instruments
ICL (UK)	Peter Bonfield	Chairman	Texas Instruments
ES2 (pan-European)	Robert Heikes	Joint Founder	National Semiconductor and Motorola
ES2 (pan-European)	Rod Attwooll	UK Managing Director	Texas Instruments
Plessey[a] (UK)	Doug Dunn	Head of Semi Division	Motorola
Plessey (UK)	Melvin Larkin	Director	Motorola

Note: [a] Later GEC-Plessey due to a take-over in 1989

Table 14.10 identifies the company origins of some of the directors of the new operations. These individuals were attracted by a new spirit of confidence in Europe and the opportunity to help build up a stronger electronics industry.

Often these well-known individuals were supported by teams of less-well-known US-trained technicians, engineers, managers and directors. The individuals in Table 14.10 represent a growing network of managers, known to each other and having in common a professional US style of management, based on a strategic approach to markets and technologies. (Porter 1985 explains the principles of strategic management.)

Rob Wilmot is an example of a US-trained executive. Recruited from Texas Instruments to ICL in the early 1980s, Wilmot became managing director of the ailing UK computer maker. Through a partnership with Fujitsu the company was successfully restructured. Later Wilmot left ICL, and his former deputy, Peter Bonfield (also from Texas Instruments), took over as ICL's managing director and then chairman. Wilmot went on to form a European semiconductor start-up firm ES2, and recruited more employees from Texas Instruments and other US firms. Some firms did not recruit US managers into top positions. Firms such as Siemens, Philips and GEC continued to follow their tradition of internal recruitment. Throughout the industry, however, three decades or so of US inward investment produced a degree of professionalism among cadres made up of European nationals in areas such as marketing, production, management, engineering and international planning, so as to facilitate technology transfer from the USA to Europe.

Competitive status, prospects and policies for the future

This section attempts to highlight Europe's strengths and weaknesses in electronics in dynamic perspective; it also suggests how changes in EC policy could further improve Europe's industrial performance and balance of trade in electronics.

Scale of European operations

In most electronics sectors, the scale of European operations grew during the 1980s through pan-European and wider mergers and acquisitions. In telecommunications, consumer electronics, defence and semiconductors, the restructured European multinationals are now better placed than in the 1980s to support the large investments needed in R&D, manufacturing and marketing.

Table 14.11 compares the top ten European electronics manufacturers with those of Japan and the USA. Of total output from the thirty firms in 1988 of $400.7 billion, European firms accounted for $94.4 billion, roughly 24 per cent. In comparison the USA accounted for $142.9 billion (36 per cent) and Japan $163.4 billion (41 per cent).

Despite restructuring, European firms are on average smaller than their Japanese and US counterparts. However, the scale of operations of most large European firms is probably sufficient to achieve both the economies of scale, and the investment and R&D thresholds, necessary in areas such as consumer electronics, semiconductors and telecommunications.

Sectoral strengths and weaknesses

Table 14.12 presents sales figures for the leading ten international firms in three core electronics sectors: computers, telecommunications and semiconductors. Although the data exclude consumer electronics, defence and software they provide a rough, if static, indicator of Europe's competitive position in electronics as of the late-1980s.

Overall, the position of European multinationals is weak in relation to Japanese and US firms. Europe supplies $42.67 billion (only 18.6 per cent) of total corporate sales of $229.8 billion as listed in Table 14.12, compared with $61.38 billion (26.7 per cent) for Japan and $121.41 billion (52.8 per cent) for the USA, with Canada accounting for $5.4 billion (2.3 per cent).

At the sectoral level, Europe's main strengths still lie in telecommunications. With five out of the top ten world suppliers, European firms account for just under 50 per cent of the sales of the top ten companies in that sub-sector, more than any other region. In semiconductors, however, Europe accounts for only 5.4 per cent, compared with 67.5 per cent for Japan and 27.0 per cent for the USA. In computers, Europe's share is only 9.5 per cent, with Japan at 21.9 per cent and the USA at 68.6 per cent (IBM alone accounts for $62.7 billion).

If we look at the remaining sectors – consumer electronics, software and defence – the picture for Europe is a mixed one. In defence, the USA accounted for nine out of the top ten firms in 1988 (*Electronic Business* 27 November 1989). As we saw earlier, only one European firm, Thomson-CSF, was in the top ten. However, European firms are strong in various market segments and Japan's neutrality means, of course, that its firms still do not compete in military technology.

Table 14.11 Electronics sales of leading firms: European, Japanese and US comparisons: 1988 ($ billion, current prices)

	Europe			USA		Japan	
Rank	Company	Sales	HQ	Company	Sales	Company	Sales
1	Philips	20.8	Netherlands	IBM	59.9	Matsushita	30.4
2	Siemens	17.4	W Germany	Xerox	16.4	NEC	23.4
3	CGE	12.2	France	Digital Equipment	12.8	Toshibia	20.3
4	Thomson	11.1	France	G M Hughes[a]	10.7	Hitachi	19.4
5	GEC	6.8	UK	Unisys	9.9	Fujitsu	18.1
6	Olivetti	6.4	Italy	Hewlett Packard	9.8	Sony	13.7
7	Robert Bosch	6.3	W Germany	NCR	6.0	Mitsubishi	12.5
8	Groupe Bull	5.2	France	Motorola	8.3	NTT	9.7
9	Ericsson	4.3	Sweden	Texas Instruments[a]	6.3	Canon	8.2
10	STC	3.9	UK	Intel[a]	2.8	Sharp	7.7
Totals		94.4			142.9		163.4

Note: [a] Calculated from capital spending data

Sources: *Electronic Business* 13 November 1989: 58 and 66; 16 April 1990: 77–8

On the software side, some European firms are strong in customised software, but most fail to match the dynamism of US firms. In traded software, Europe appears much stronger than Japan, which is inhibited partly by language and partly by lack of dynamic, small start-up companies. US firms dominate the internationally traded software market, particularly in packaged software (Brady and Quintas 1990).

Despite the improved performance of Thomson, Philips and Nokia, European firms compare badly in consumer electronics with Japanese, Korean and Taiwanese firms. The USA is weaker than Europe in consumer electronics, but hopes to make a comeback with high-definition television in the 1990s. On the whole the East Asian economies dominate the international market and especially exports to the large US market (Mody 1987).

Overall, Europe's position in electronics is still weak in comparison to the USA and Japan. Despite major advances in the 1980s, it seems improbable that Europe will match the performance of Japan and the USA during the 1990s. This is likely to lead to a worsening balance of payments position (see Sharp, Chapter 12 in this volume, on changing industrial structures).

Corporate strategies and management

During the 1980s many large European firms adopted outward-looking global strategies, committed themselves to long-term investments, and made unprecedented efforts to catch up in areas such as semiconductors and consumer electronics. By 1990 Siemens was in a position to join forces with the world's largest computer maker, IBM of the USA, to develop extremely advanced semiconductor technology (the 64-megabit memory). Such a partnership would have been inconceivable during the 1970s or early

Table 14.12   Ten largest manufacturers of computers,
telecommunications and semiconductors
1989, by sales ($ billion)

Company	Country	Sales
Computers		
IBM	USA	62.7
DEC	USA	12.7
Fujitsu	Japan	11.9
Unisys	USA	10.1
NEC	Japan	10.0
Hitachi	Japan	9.8
Hewlett-Packard	USA	8.1
Olivetti	Italy	7.3
Bull	France	6.5
NCR	USA	6.0
Telecommunications		
Alcatel	France	15.6
AT&T	USA	11.5
Siemens	W Germany	6.5
Northern Telecom	Canada	6.1
NEC	Japan	6.0
Ericsson	Sweden	5.8
Motorola	USA	4.8
GPT	UK	3.4
Fujitsu	Japan	3.1
Italtel	Italy	1.7
Semiconductors		
NEC	Japan	5.0
Toshiba	Japan	4.9
Hitachi	Japan	4.0
Motorola	USA	3.3
Fujitsu	Japan	3.0
Texas Instruments	USA	2.8
Mitsubishi	Japan	2.6
Intel	USA	2.4
Matsushita	Japan	1.9
Philips	Netherlands	1.7

Sources: *Computers and Semiconductors, Dataquest,* cited in
Jonquieres (1990); *Telecommunications Research Centre*

1980s. Similarly, Philips and Thomson now stand poised to enter the high-definition
television market, having secured large shares of the USA and European colour
television and video-cassette recorder markets (Cawson and Holmes 1991).

The recruitment of top professional managers on a world-wide basis undoubtedly
strengthened the position of many European-owned firms, and provided a valuable
resource for most companies. By the late 1980s the 'management gap' between Europe

and the USA and Japan had been substantially reduced, as a result of the training of European nationals in US firms.

Protection, subsidisation and competition within Europe

In most European countries the competitive environment became more liberal during the 1980s. There are now greater opportunities for foreign firms to export to Europe, and to invest directly in Europe. However, some countries remain less open than others. Italy, France and Germany, for example, are less exposed to competition in telecommunications and defence than, say, the UK, which has taken the lead in market deregulation.

In terms of subsidisation, the large European-owned companies such as Philips and Thomson still enjoy considerable patronage from domestic governments as well as the EC. Italy tends to oppose Commission efforts to reduce state subsidies and controls. The UK, Germany and The Netherlands tend to support Commission moves to liberalise and foster competition. France seems to 'hover between the two camps' (*Financial Times* 22 October 1990).

One of the main lessons of the 1960s and 1970s is that industrial protection and subsidisation cannot sustain competitiveness in the long term. On the contrary, protection can lead to poor management practices and inward-looking corporate strategies. For the 1990s, therefore, further EC measures are needed to intensify competition and harmonise the differences among EC member states. It may also be wise to reduce EC subsidies, as electronics firms are now clearly large enough to finance their own investments as and how they see fit.

Foreign-owned industry and EC policy

Foreign-owned firms operating within European national boundaries are a central component of Europe's competitive capabilities. If foreign firms contribute to the technological base by developing products, carrying out research, development and training, and exporting beyond Europe, then they should surely be treated as part of Europe's industrial and technological infrastructure for EC policy purposes.

Foreign firms can play a major role in transferring technology to Europe and training professional directors, managers and engineers (as described on pp. 287–8). Increased participation of foreign firms within Europe would also help ameliorate the balance of trade deficit in electronics.

In sectors such as semiconductors, computers and consumer goods, foreign companies already boast very substantial production capabilities in Europe, and will in the future be vital to the overall health of Europe's electronics industry, and to European users of electronics. It is interesting in this connection to note that the argument that a strong European semiconductor industry is vital for Europe's overall competitiveness in electronics was the basis for the heavy focus on semiconductors in inward-directed European programmes such as ESPRIT and Eureka. The fact is, however, that within Europe foreign firms have played an important part in transferring semiconductor technology and producing components. As long as

European users are able to obtain leading-edge semiconductors and are able to *use* semiconductors effectively, the lack of locally *owned* production capacity need not necessarily lead to competitive disadvantage in electronic goods and systems. Indeed, Japan and Korea conquered significant shares in world markets for electronics goods *before* they entered semiconductor production in a big way via backward integration.

In practice, European programmes at governmental and Community levels alike have in the main excluded foreign companies. During the 1980s, the general tendency was for policies to be inward-looking, favouring only European firms. To encourage a greater contribution by foreign firms, policies for the 1990s should embrace foreign companies. Indeed, where policies are directed at encouraging R&D and training, then it may be in the best industrial interest of the EC to distinguish firms on the basis of their commitment to the local economy, rather than their nationality. It is arguable that foreign companies which demonstrate a strong commitment to technology development in Europe should receive more support than domestically owned firms which contribute less to the EC. Such a policy would encourage all firms to develop technology and carry out training in Europe.

There is also good reason for urging more outward-looking policies on the part of the EC. If European firms fail to compete in the leading international markets, whether in Europe, the USA, Japan or the Pacific Basin, then they will lose competitive advantage. Competing in such markets inculcates 'best practice' management, marketing and research behaviour, vital to competitiveness (Porter 1990).

EC policy and users of electronics

The policies of the 1980s restructured the supplier base in electronics. EC measures should now turn their attention to the users and consumers of electronics. If users of electronics goods cannot obtain the lowest-cost and most advanced systems, then they will suffer competitive disadvantage in the market. Users of electronics now span almost every important industrial sector from automobiles to aerospace to agriculture. Together their economic size and significance dwarfs that of the electronics industry.

Policies should therefore attempt further to liberalise markets such as telecommunications, computers and defence, where, in several countries, government policies continue to prevent foreign suppliers from competing. The example of the UK shows how telecommunications deregulation can benefit business users, in this case by enabling them to use advanced communication systems (Hobday 1989b). However, most EC countries lag significantly behind the UK in that respect. Further market liberalisation would enable home consumers, industrial users and many other groups to benefit from advances in electronics.

The market recession of 1990

After the optimism of the late 1980s, prospects for the 1990s are now in some respects less bright. European firms confront a number of very severe problems including first, a market recession in 1990, second, strong competition from Japanese and US firms, and third, the length of time taken to convert large-scale technology investments into profitable production (eg in semiconductors and high-definition television). Market recession, financial difficulties and take-overs led some observers seriously to question the health of the European industry and the impact of EC policy at the end of the 1980s (Jonquieres 1990). For example, in 1990 STC sold its subsidiary, and the UK's largest computer firm, ICL, to Fujitsu of Japan. In the same year, STC was itself taken over by the Canadian firm, Northern Telecom. Around that time Philips, the largest electronics producer in Europe, introduced a plan to cut 15 per cent of its work-force, amounting to some 45,000 employees, as a result of falling profitability and pressure from financial markets (*Financial Times* 26 October 1990). Philips expected a net loss of around $1.1 billion in 1990 (*The European* 16 November 1990).

Philips was not the only firm to sustain losses. Others included Nixdorf of West Germany (taken over by Siemens in 1989) and Norsk Data of Norway (previously one of the most promising computer firms in Europe). Profits were substantially reduced for Olivetti, Italy's microcomputer manufacturer. Bull, the French computer manufacturer, forecast a loss of $578 million in 1990 (*The European* 16 November 1990).

Although it is impossible to predict the outcome of these difficulties, it is important to see current problems in the context of the following considerations.

First, US firms such as IBM and Hewlett Packard also face serious difficulties on account of strong competition and declining profitability. Market downturns confront US and Japanese firms just as starkly as European countries.

Second, European firms are undoubtedly larger and technologically stronger than they otherwise would have been if the restructuring of the late 1980s had not occurred. European firms may therefore be relatively well placed to survive the present short-run difficulties.

Third, if European firms are able to weather the current recession and maintain their newly gained technological capabilities, then they could well recover their profitability during the next market upturn. Indeed, one of the key reasons for the success of Japanese and Korean electronics companies has been their ability to maintain a comparatively high level of technology investment during recessions (Hobday 1988).

Seen in the context of the regular cycles of boom and slump in electronics, the current difficulties are an inevitable test of the financial strength and technological commitment of European electronics firms.

Conclusion

During the 1980s the European electronics industry underwent a major restructuring. The national champions of the 1960s and 1970s gave way to European champions. This chapter has argued that these large electronics multinationals stand a far better chance of surviving US and East Asian competition than did their predecessors.

In response to rapid technological change and increased competition, European firms, backed by the European Commission, made significant efforts to catch up technologically and to restructure their operations within Europe and beyond. The EC initiatives of the 1980s helped improve the competitive position of European-owned firms. The programmes strengthened the technological supply side of the EC, enabling firms such as Siemens and Thomson to build up impressive global corporate strategies. Even so, the EC still has a worsening balance of trade in electronics, and its firms fail to match the competitive performance of the large Japanese and US firms in sectors such as consumer electronics, semiconductors, packaged software and computers.

Against this background, notwithstanding a stronger technological base and a restructured industry, it is time for a change in policy direction. Two aspects of policy in particular have been highlighted: the need to consider the users of electronics, and the need to embrace non-European firms within EC policy.

Further measures are needed to liberalise markets and promote competition in areas such as telecommunications and computing, so that business users and home consumers in Europe may be able to enjoy lowest-cost, top-quality electronics goods and services.

The importance of non-European firms operating within European boundaries should likewise be recognised. Many of these firms are important links in the transfer of technology to Europe. To ignore their role and exclude them from EC initiatives would be shortsighted.

While there may have been some justification for the technology supply-side policies of the 1980s, users and consumers of electronics, as well as the foreign suppliers of European electronics, are entitled to have their voice heard during the 1990s.

Appendix: glossary of technical terms and abbreviations

Application-specific integrated circuits (ASICS)   design-intensive semiconductors which allow the user closely to specify the design of the final circuit. They are quite different from standard devices such as memory devices (eg DRAMS).

Dynamic random access memory (DRAM)   a general-purpose IC used to store large quantities of information in binary code in the form of electrical charges.

Integrated circuit (IC)   any semiconductor component with more than one functioning element. Also known as a chip, a microelectronic device, or a semiconductor component.

Megabit   refers to the number of bits of information which can be stored on one silicon chip (one megabit = approximately 1 million bits).

Memory   a family of semiconductors used to store large quantities of information (see DRAM).

Microprocessor   a complex type of semiconductor used to perform the central functions of microcomputers.

Semiconductor   (chip) the material commonly used in the production of ICs, having special electrical conducting properties.

VLSI (very large scale integration) technology   allows for 1 million (one megabit) or more circuit elements to be condensed on to one tiny chip.

Acknowledgement

This chapter was written with the support of the UK Economic and Social Research Council (ESRC).

References

Arnold E, Guy K (1986) *Parallel Convergence: National Strategies in Information Technology*. Frances Pinter

Brady T, Quintas P (1991) Computer software: the IT constraint? In Freeman C, Sharp M, Walker W (eds) *Technology and the Future of Europe: Global Competition and the Environment in the 1990s*. Pinter

Cawson A, Holmes P (1991) The new consumer electronics. In Freeman C, Sharp M, Walker W (eds) *Technology and the Future of Europe: Global Competition and the Environment in the 1990s*. Pinter

Cawson A, Morgan K, Webber D, Holmes P, Stevens A (1990) *Hostile Brothers: Competition and Closure in the European Electronics Industry*. Clarendon Press

CEC (1986) *Eureka and the European Technology Community*. Communication from the Commission to the Council, Commission of the European Communities, Com (86), Final, Brussels

CEC (1989) *The Review of ESPRIT 1984 to 1988: the Report of the ESPRIT Review Board*. May, Executive Version, Commission of the European Communities, Brussels

Dang Nguyen G (1985) Telecommunications: a challenge to the old order. In Sharp M (ed) *Europe and the New Technologies*. Pinter

Dorfman N S (1987) *Innovation and Market Structure: Lessons from the Computer and Semiconductor Industries*, Ballinger, Cambridge, Mass.

Gregory G (1986) *Japanese Electronics Technology: Enterprise and Innovation*. John Wiley

Hare P, Lauchlan J, Thompson M (1988) *An Assessment of ESPRIT in the UK*. Technological Change Research Centre, Heriot-Watt University, 31–35 Grassmarket, Edinburgh

Hendry J (1990) *Innovating for Failure: Government Policy and the Early British Computer Industry*. MIT Press

Hobday M G (1988) Corporate strategies in the international semiconductor industry. *Research Policy* **18**: 225–38

Hobday M G (1989a) The European semiconductor industry: resurgence and rationalisation. *Journal of Common Market Studies* **28** (2)

Hobday M G (1989b) *UK Telecommunications Policies in the 1980s: from Technology Push to Market Pull* Centre for Information and Communications Technology (CICT) Working Paper No. 7, Science Policy Research Unit, University of Sussex

Jonquieres G (1990) Shadows over the sunrise sector. *Financial Times* 25 July 1990

Mackenzie F W (1985) *Microelectronic Components: the Issues for Europe* Mimeo, Centre for Business Strategy, London Business School

Mody A (1987) *Information Industries: the Changing Role of Newly Industrialising Countries*. Mimeo, AT&T, Bell Labs, New Jersey

O'Brien R (1989) *The European Computer Industry – A Mismatch with Industry Trends*. Commission of the European Communities, DGX111, Brussels, July

Patel P, Pavitt K (1987) Is Europe losing the technological race? *Research Policy* **16**: 59–85

Pavitt K (1990) The nature and determinants of innovation: a major factor in firms' and countries' competitiveness. Paper prepared for the conference *Fundamental Issues in Strategy: a Research Agenda for the 1990s* in Napa, California, 29 November to 1 December; also SPRU mimeo, University of Sussex

Porter M (1985) *Competitive Advantage: Creating and Sustaining Superior Performance*. Free Press, New York

Porter M (1990) *The Competitive Advantage of Nations*. Macmillan

Sharp M (1987a) Europe: collaboration in the high technology sectors. *Oxford Review of Economic Policy* **3**(1): 52–65

Sharp M (1987b) *Inward Investment and National Industrial Competitiveness: a Comparative*

Study for Western Europe. Final Report to the Leverhulme Foundation, Mimeo, Science Policy Research Unit, University of Sussex

Sharp M (1989) *Corporate Strategies and Collaboration – the Case of ESPRIT and European Electronics.* Mimeo, Science Policy Research Unit, University of Sussex

Sharp M (1990) *The Single Market and European Policies for Advanced Technologies.* DRC Discussion Paper No 75, Science Policy Research Unit, University of Sussex

Stevens C (1990) *1992: A European Technology Challenge?* Science, Technology and Industry Directorate of the Organisation for Economic Co-operation and Development (OECD), Paris

CHAPTER 15

Chemicals and pharmaceuticals

MARGARET SHARP and LESLEY COOK

Introduction

The purpose of this chapter is to examine recent developments in the European chemicals industry, and to assess in particular the degree to which its changing shape and structure are influenced by underlying changes in technology. The definition of the chemicals industry adopted here is a broad one, derived from its scientific base – the understanding and manipulation of molecules. It comprehends at one extreme the bulk chemicals in the organic and inorganic sectors, and at the other the speciality products in such areas as dyes and paints, food additives and photography. But it also deals with sectors such as pharmaceuticals and agrochemicals, both of which are undergoing major change as a result of developments in biotechnology. Labels are, of course, to some degree arbitrary – it is not easy, for example, to define precisely where pharmaceuticals ends and fine chemicals begin – and this underlines the complexity and heterogenity of the industry. There is much interdependence, and horizontal and vertical linkages abound.

The organisation of the chapter is as follows. The next section seeks to set out the background to developments in the industry. The third section deals with bulk chemicals – the organic and inorganic sectors, the fourth section looks at developments in speciality chemicals, the fifth section picks up on pharmaceuticals and the impact of biotechnology, and the sixth section looks at some of the main issues arising at European level from the discussion. The final section provides a brief concluding review.

Background

Taking the broad definition, the chemicals industry contributes some 10 per cent to OECD industrial output (see Sharp, Chapter 12, Table 12.4) with total OECD output valued at approximately $1,100 billion in 1989. Western Europe currently contributes

Table 15.1 World chemicals market 1989 ($ billion)

Region	Output	Exports	Imports	Home demand	Net trade
W Europe[a]	340	52	25	313	+27
N America[b]	275	33	22	264	+11
Japan	190	20	15	185	+5
E Europe	170	15	19	174	−4
Central/S America	54	6	15	63	−9
Far East	39	14	32	57	−18
India/Pakistan	25	1	5	29	−4
Africa	15	2	9	22	−7
Middle East	12	5	10	17	−5
Australasia	10	1	5	14	−4
Total	1,130	149	157	1,138	

Notes:
[a] Trade figures exclude Western European intra-trade
[b] Trade figures exclude North American intra-trade

Source: UK Chemical Industries Association, quoted in Allen 1990

$340 billion to this total. As noted in Chapter 12, the chemicals industry is a sector where European performance is strong by comparison with that of either the United States or Japan. Table 15.1 (which excludes intra-trade within Western Europe) shows that the chemicals trade balance of Western Europe was greater and its market larger in 1989 than for any other trading bloc.

As indicated, the chemicals industry spans a wide range of activities. At one extreme are product areas such as salt or titanium dioxide akin to mineral extraction, where selling prices are low; at the other lies the production of highly sophisticated chemicals used as ingredients for pharmaceuticals and agrochemicals, requiring many manufacturing steps and selling for thousands of dollars a gramme. A good part of the industry provides bulk chemicals and intermediates for other parts of the industry, creating a clear distinction between this 'upstream' industry, and the 'downstream' sector making products sold to consumers and/or other industrial sectors. Table 15.2 depicts the breakdown of output and markets for the Western European industry. A broad distinction can be made between the (upstream) 'bulk' or 'commodity' chemicals – petrochemicals, plastics and inorganics – and the (downstream) speciality chemicals, pharmaceuticals and agrochemicals.

Another important feature of the industry is the extent to which it is already a global industry. There are hundreds of firms, but the industry is dominated by some twenty large multinationals, most of which are engaged in a number of different sectors, and all of which are to a significant extent vertically integrated (see Table 15.3). Twelve of these twenty are European. The leaders have in the main held their position: the pre-war giants, BASF, Hoechst, Bayer, Dupont, Dow, ICI, Ciba Geigy, have in the post-war period been joined by a few others, notably by some of the major international oil companies such as Shell, and by a number of government-sponsored firms such as Rhône Poulenc (France) and Norsk Hydro (Norway). The Japanese have only just

Table 15.2 Breakdown of output and markets for the Western European chemicals industry 1988 (by value)

Breakdown of output	(%)	End use markets	(%)
Organics	19	Construction	5.7
Inorganics	8	Services	19.2
Fibres	4	(hospitals, research centres, etc)	
Fertilisers	7	Consumer goods	27.4
Plastics	13	Agriculture	10.3
Pharmaceuticals	15	Food industry	3.1
Dyes	2	Metals industry	6.5
Paints	4	Electrical/electronic	3.8
Detergents	4	Mechanical engineering	3.8
Perfumes and cosmetics	5	Automotive	3.6
Others	19	Textiles	6.6
		Paper/printing	3.0
		Other	7.5
Total	100	Total	100

Source: European Chemical Industry Association, quoted in *Financial Times Supplement on Chemicals* 13 July 1989

begun to make their mark on the industry; as yet, their firms are relatively small in relation to the market leaders.

The chemicals industry is often referred to as the first science-based industry. The development of inorganic chemicals – sulphuric acid and soda lime used for making bleach – was closely tied to the textile industry, but its methods were, like much else in the early Industrial Revolution in Britain, the product of astute minds and tinkering technology. The major breakthroughs in chemistry, and the emergence of the chemicals industry proper, came with the development of organic chemistry in the latter years of the nineteenth century. Although it was a British researcher, Perkin, who made the chance discovery in 1856 of aniline dyes – which marked the beginning of organic chemistry – it was to be in Germany (where chemistry had been recognised as a subject for study at universities since the 1830s), and in the United States, that the major discoveries in organic chemistry were made: first the coal tar derivatives, and then, from the mid-1920s onwards, the important developments in petrochemicals. The fast pace of change throughout this period is strikingly illustrated by Figure 15.1, which identifies the major innovations introduced between the years 1840 and 1960.

Figure 15.1 brings out neatly two important and interrelated characteristics of the chemicals industry: fast technical progress and the importance of international operations. The fast rate of technical change has brought change within large companies and led, via sale and acquisition, to the further internationalisation of activities. Mergers and acquisitions have been an essential part of the scene for the last twenty years. They are taking place in all sectors. Sometimes they involve whole companies, sometimes just parts of companies. Table 15.4 sets out 1988 data on acquisitions and mergers world-wide, and illustrates the continuing importance of Western Europe, with 41 per cent of acquisitions originating *from* firms in Western Europe (whereas only 31 per cent of acquisitions were *in* Western Europe). It also

Table 15.3 The world's largest chemicals companies

	World ranking		Sales revenue ($ million)	
	1984	1988	1984	1988
Europe				
BASF (FRG)	2	2	14,230	24,329
Bayer (FRG)	3	3	13,873	23,011
Hoechst (FRG)	4	4	13,365	22,651
ICI (UK)	5	5	13,240	20,817
Ciba-Geigy (Sw)	10	7	6,835	12,027
Rhône-Poulenc (Fr)	13	8	5,392	10,956
Montedison (It)	8	9	7,080	9,757
Norsk Hydro (Norway)	15	10	4,370	9,202
Akzo (NL)	14	11	4,719	8,388
Solvay (Belgium)	18	16	3,590	6,894
DSM (NL)	9	19	7,050	5,120
Atochem (Fr)	22	21	2,621	4,711
Orkem (Fr)	21	23	2,950	3,616
USA				
Du Pont[a]	1	1	30,560	32,917
Dow Chemical	6	6	10,679	16,682
Union Carbide	7	12	9,150	8,324
Monsanto	12	13	6,691	8,293
W R Grace	11	17	6,730	5,786
American Cyan	17	22	3,857	4,592
Japan				
Asahi Chem.	16	14	4,230	7,672
Sumitomo Chem.	19	15	3,492	7,002

Note: [a] Includes oil: chemical sales in 1988 approximately $17 billion, ranking fifth in world

Source: Anizon 1990

gives some indication of the degree to which West European firms were acquiring firms in North America – an issue which is beginning to concern US industrial experts. The most active firms in terms of acquisitions were all European: Elf Aquitaine, Rhône Poulenc and ICI were each involved in thirteen acquisitions in 1988. As Table 15.4 indicates, the most active sectors were speciality chemicals and pharmaceuticals plus health care. Trends in both sectors will be discussed at greater length in later sections of the chapter.

Bulk chemicals: organics and inorganics

Organic chemicals

Organic chemicals are those obtained from coal, oil, gas, vegetable or animal products. Since the Second World War this sector of the industry has been dominated by

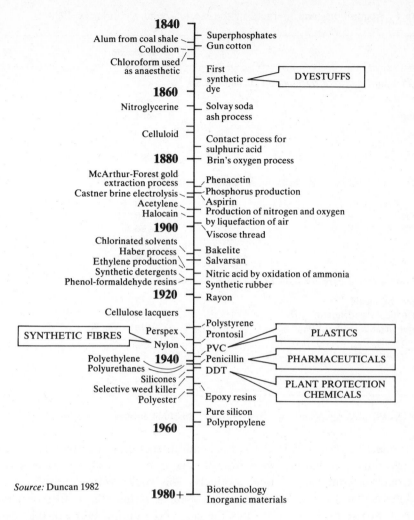

Figure 15.1 Major chemical innovations 1840–1960
Source: Duncan 1982

petrochemicals and the whole range of new products – plastics, artificial fibres, detergents, etc – which have been developed from oil and gas as feedstocks. In this section we concentrate on the bulk 'commodity' petrochemicals. The vast array of downstream, specialised products are discussed in the next section.

The major breakthroughs in hydrocarbon chemistry were made in the 1920s and 1930s. Following on from basic research on macro-molecular structures, innovations came thick and fast: polystyrene, perspex, PVC, polyethylene, synthetic rubbers and nylon and all the artificial fibres. It is notable that all the major innovations were developed in the laboratories of large chemicals companies, and that most of the companies responsible for them still exist today. IG Farben (which was broken up after 1945 into Bayer, Hoechst and BASF), ICI and Du Pont were the most influential, but Union Carbide, Shell, Standard Oil and Dow all made major contributions to the development of petrochemical processes for the new intermediate and final products.

Table 15.4 Acquisitions and mergers in the world chemicals industry 1988

	No. of transactions	% of total
Acquisitions and mergers by location of acquisition		
USA	723	56
W Europe	404	31
Japan	24	2
Other	132	10
Total	1,283	100
Acquisitions and mergers by location of acquirer		
USA	613	48
W Europe	520	41
Japan	56	4
Other	94	7
Total	1,283	100
Acquisitions and mergers by type of business		
Speciality chemicals	217	17
Pharmaceuticals and health care	211	16
Fabricated plastics and rubber	148	12
Bulk chemicals	136	11
Consumer products	80	6
Other	491	38
Total	1,283	100

Source: CHEMTRAK, Kline and Co., Rue Froissart 89, 1040 Brussels, Belgium

The production processes in the petrochemicals sector are complex and interlinked. Figure 15.2 illustrates the pathways from the basic feedstocks – natural gas and crude oil – through intermediate to final products. This shows very clearly how the three major intermediates – ethylene, propylene and benzene – each fosters a family of products downstream. It demonstrates the close relationship between oil-refining and the petrochemicals sector of the industry, and explains why the major entrants into the industry between 1930 and 1950 were all oil refiners. It also illustrates how the chemicals industry is its own best customer – the upstream sector of the industry feeds the downstream sector – and, in turn, why many firms are either wholly or partially vertically integrated. Downstream, where specialist products multiply, many relatively small firms rely for their raw materials on the large producers of the bulk secondary products – broadly speaking the major chemicals and oil companies. Even where they are not vertically integrated, supplier–customer links are strong.

The continuing dominance of these large firms is largely explained by developments in technology. Broad-front technical progress in this industrial sector takes time. Product development is in general followed by process development. That process development may be based upon some significant innovation, but mainly takes the form of incremental change stemming from learning and experience in the application of new technologies. As a result, there has been a very great increase in capital intensity and in the importance of economies of scale. Static economies of scale are

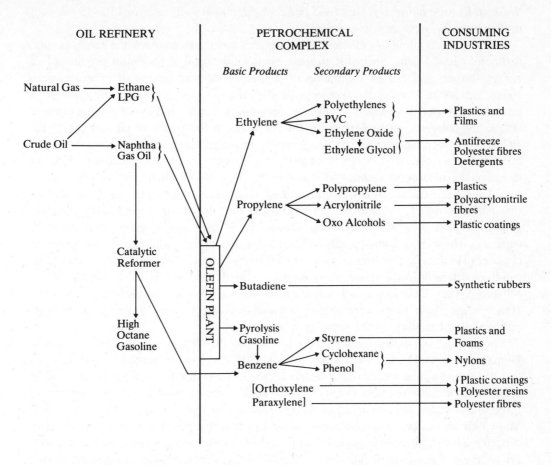

Figure 15.2 Petrochemicals: the production pathway from basic feedstock to final product
Source: OECD 1979: xxvii

moderate (some 10–20 per cent for most leading products): it is technical change which has increased the size of 'efficient' plants. In the early 1950s a 30,000 tons per year ethylene plant was considered large; by the mid-1970s 300,000-ton plants were being built. These vast, capital-intensive plants in turn exerted great influence on the economics of the industry. The costs of shutting down a given plant were such that there was a strong incentive to keep it open in periods of slack demand, even if this meant temporarily selling at well below cost. Equally, once capacity was fully utilised, it was difficult to meet any increase in demand with a marginal increase in output, for that meant building a new (large) plant. Hence the tendency for all firms to plan extra capacity simultaneously when demand is buoyant. As a result, the industry has tended to lurch from famine to glut, with concomitant effects on prices.

The new products which emerged from the petrochemicals discoveries of the inter-war years – new products such as nylon which in turn led to further innovations – resulted in very fast growth of the industry throughout the 1950s and 1960s. At that time the income multiplier – the percentage growth of the industry for every 1 per cent growth in GDP – averaged about three. Against a background of GDP growth rates in

Western Europe in these years of 4–5 per cent, annual growth rates of 12 to 15 per cent in the industry were not uncommon.

With the high minimum efficient size of plant, entry was easy for the large, strong, technology-based firm. Specialist process plant engineering firms could provide plant for any buyer, and the oil companies in particular took advantage of their access to cheap feedstocks to enter the industry. Besides the oil firms, an increasing number of government-based purchasers from the developing world, led by the oil-producing states, also entered, particularly after the increases in the prices of oil and gas of the 1970s. Many were so anxious to get a foothold in the industry that they were willing to take the commercial risk of creating over-capacity and the technical risk of inexperience in process technologies and inadequate R&D capabilities. (It is notable that it has been chemicals companies, not oil companies, which have made almost all the major product innovations.) This raised the threat of considerable capacity expansion at a time when recession and oil price rises had already created excess capacity. There was consequently substantial price cutting and much talk of plant closures. The fact is, however, that most of the new Third World plants were owned or run in co-operation with major multinationals – Shell, Hoechst, ICI, Exxon, Mobil and Mitsubishi Gas, Celanese and Texas Eastern were all involved in such collaborations. Hence while these firms were urging closures in Europe, they were simultaneously involved in expanding world capacity elsewhere.

The problems of excess capacity were to exercise the industry for much of the 1980s. Demand continued to grow but much more slowly: the income multiplier had dropped to 1.4. (Even so, this means that average aggregate growth rates of 2.5 per cent lead to a doubling of capacity every twenty years.) With a gestation period in construction of three to five years, plant ordered in the 1970s was coming on stream in the early 1980s. Many bulk producers sustained major losses as expensive new plants ran at well below capacity. This in turn led to plant closures and the mothballing of new plant, some of it orchestrated by an unofficial cartel organised by the European Commission (see below). But by the mid-1980s the inexorable laws of compound arithmetic meant that demand had once more caught up with supply, prices began to rise, plants were reopened and further capacity expansion planned (see Table 15.5). By 1989 the siren voices were once again warning of over-expansion, prices were softening and profits falling. The recession of the early 1990s merely repeats the pattern seen so often before.

Such price fluctuations, in all their frequency and magnitude, echo, then amplify, the cyclical pattern of expansion in this particular market. Many of the major products, especially the five bulk plastics (polypropylene, polystyrene, PVC, and the high- and low-density polyethylenes) are in effect commodities. Contract prices and spot prices coexist, but prices are sticky, partly because contracts are big and there are close vertical links between buyers and sellers. With high levels of demand these imperfect but highly competitive markets mean relatively stable prices. But when, as in the early 1980s, there is considerable spare capacity, prices fall sharply. What seems to be workable competition in an expanding market can turn into destructive competition when the market stops growing.

The size and importance of many of these petrochemicals investments, and the degree to which they can act as growth points within a regional economy (particularly

Table 15.5 Planned petrochemicals capacity expansion 1988–92

| '000 tons pa | | Projected capacity additions 1988–92 | | | | | | | |
Product	1988 Capacity (world)	Europe	USA	Japan	Rest of world	Total	Increase %	Resultant 1992 capacity (world)	Further possible capacity additions
Ethylene	56,000	2,710	5,630	797	9,397	18,534	33	74,534	26,207
Propylene	27,000	775	420	—	2,244	3,439	13	30,439	5,742
Styrene	12,000	965	720	450	1,766	3,901	33	15,901	6,664
Polyethylene	29,000	1,355	3,000	393	3,548	8,296	29	37,296	10,256
Polypropylene	10,000	1,580	1,759	394	3,101	6,870	69	16,870	4,670
Polystyrene	8,900	225	405	233	854	1,717	19	10,617	1,210
Polyvinyl chloride	18,500	297	930	94	2,378	3,699	20	22,199	2,064

Source: *Financial Times Supplement on Chemicals* 13 July 1989

when they become vast complexes of refineries and chemicals plants as, for example, at Rotterdam[1] or Southampton) means that governments as well as companies inevitably get involved in investment decisions. The British government, not surprisingly, was most anxious to see the joint Shell–Esso plant at Mossmoran developed,[2] the Italian government has in the past given generous subsidies to companies willing to establish plants in the less prosperous Mezzogiorno regions of the country (see Dunford, Chapter 9 in this volume, and Paci, Chapter 4 in *The National Economies of Europe*), and more recently has given tax concessions valued at $600 million to Montedison.[3] The Greek government also has given aid to the construction of plants for synthetic fibres.[4]

State aids of this type are subject to review by the European Commission under the internal market provisions of the Treaty of Rome, and the Commission struggled long and hard through the 1980s to prevent a self-defeating war of subsidies developing between member states. As early as 1978, the producers of Northern Europe were enlisting the help of Vicomte Davignon, at that time Commissioner for Industry, in reining back Italian expansion plans and helping bring about an orderly rationalisation of the industry. Although plans for a crisis cartel along the lines operating at that time in steel were rejected, the Commission turned a blind eye to a 'gentleman's agreement' among the major producers which did result in a substantial rationalisation of capacity. The producers were less lucky in polypropylene, where there were quite elaborate collusive arrangements with monthly meetings and concerted action to raise prices where possible. In 1986 the EC Competition Directorate took the leading polypropylene manufacturers to the European Court, where they were found guilty of price fixing and fined heavily, the largest fines – over £5 million – being imposed on Montedipe (part of Montedison, now Enimont), ICI, Shell and Hoechst (Commission of the EC 1988: 67–8).

Much of the rationalisation that took place in the 1980s was achieved by inter-firm agreements. There are many examples, all of them involving some reduction in the level of competition. In the UK, ICI took over BP's PVC capacity and BP took over ICI's low-density polythene facilities; thus each withdrew from a sector and older capacity was scrapped. In the Netherlands, Shell and Akzo put their PVC and ethylene production into a joint venture. In 1986 ICI and the Italian Enichem also formed a joint venture in PVC. In the latter case the Commission considered that the agreement restricted competition, but elected to exempt it

> for a period limited to five years, primarily because, in the short term, it allows the activities of the two parent companies to be rationalised in the PVC sector, which is part of an industry suffering from serious structural over capacity in the whole of the EEC.
>
> (Commission of the EC 1988: 69)

By the mid-1980s, therefore, a combination of agreements and closures had brought about a significant reduction of capacity. In PVC, the sector which saw the most drastic rationalisation, the number of producers dropped from twenty-eight to eighteen; in low-density polyethylenes the roll fell from twenty-five to nineteen; in high-density polyethylenes from twenty to fifteen (Metz 1984: 874). The result was a major concentration of production within Europe, a trend that continues today. The formation of Enimont, a joint venture between Montedison and the state-owned energy conglomerate ENI and now Italy's largest chemicals company, follows a similar logic. The old problem, however, recurs. It is precisely the firms that are rationalising with one hand that are expanding elsewhere with the other.

The 1980s have also seen the entry of three important new sets of players into the industry, who add to competitive pressures and severely limit opportunities for expansion in Western Europe. The first of these are the Gulf States, whose investments in petrochemicals capacity are now coming on-stream and are likely to build up through the 1990s. They have the advantage of cheap and readily available feedstock supplies, unlike the other new set of players, the newly industrialising countries of South-East Asia, whose fast growing markets have attracted investment from both multinational and domestic sources. In addition, the revolutions of 1989 could mean substantial investment to upgrade Eastern European capacity and exports. Together, these developments augur another period of rapid expansion in world-wide capacity in bulk petrochemicals, and increasing competition for the West European industry.

Collusion and restructuring thus offer only temporary relief from overcapacity and price instability. A third response has been to pursue technological opportunities through innovation, and to increase the degree of specialisation by looking to develop niche markets and exploiting new materials. The main trend now is to develop and produce differentiated products for special uses, often as customised products. The firms willing to rationalise have been getting out of commodity chemicals and expanding into the new, more diversified, specialised markets. Rhône Poulenc, Hoechst, ICI, Dow and Monsanto are examples of firms which have adopted a strategy of deliberate diversification into speciality chemicals, while divesting themselves of capacity in some areas of bulk commodity chemicals production.

Inorganic chemicals

The experience and development of the older inorganic chemicals sector illustrates well the changing pattern of the industry as a whole (Table 15.6). Inorganic chemicals are highly heterogeneous in product specification, process, value, scale of production, rate

Table 15.6 World chemicals output, estimated product group breakdown 1989 ($ billion)

	Western Europe	North America	Japan	World total (including others)
Inorganics	31	19	12	91
Agrochemicals	24	18	10	83
Petrochemicals	119	105	62	414
Artificial fibres	14	15	10	75
Pharmaceuticals	60	44	38	192
Other chemicals*	92	74	58	275
Total	340	275	190	1,130

Note: * Includes specialities and dyestuffs, paints, detergents, cosmetics

Source: UK Chemical Industries Association, quoted in Allen 1990

of growth of output, and so forth. They are not linked (as are organic chemicals) by a common raw material base, or as by-products or joint products. As a result, firms in the sub-branch can and often do produce a limited range of products on a relatively small scale, many exploiting a specific technology related to a particular family of chemicals. The degree of vertical integration thus varies enormously.

The great firms of the years before 1939 – I G Farben (succeeded by Bayer, Hoechst and BASF), ICI, Du Pont, Dow, etc – are still the industry leaders in inorganic as well as organic chemicals. But in inorganics the production lines are more self-contained, and there are more older, medium-sized firms, and more smaller firms also, many of which work closely with their customers. Technical progress has been less dramatic than in the petrochemicals industry. Nevertheless, there is continuing incremental change in process plant technology and consequential increases in both scale and capital intensity. There is also a great deal of development of more sophisticated and specialised products. These changes are leading to very substantial changes in the structure of the industry.

The history of the British firm Laporte illustrates well the sorts of changes that have been taking place in this sector. Laporte was set up in 1888 to manufacture hydrogen peroxide and bleach products. In 1932 it took over National Titanium Pigments, and after the war bought a couple of sulphuric acid companies. By 1970 it was the UK's largest producer of a number of important chemical intermediates with a turnover of some £100 million annually, and was planning expansion both of its titanium oxide business and its more sophisticated fluorine chemicals lines. The problems of the 1970s, however, took their toll, and both developments took longer and proved more expensive than foreseen. By the end of the decade Laporte was reassessing its dependence on capital-intensive production lines. In 1984 it sold off its titanium oxide business to the US SCM Corporation for £80 million, and between 1980 and 1987 spent £134 million on forty acquisitions.[5] In the process it moved itself out of capital-intensive commodity chemicals into speciality chemicals – a metamorphosis paralleled only by Fisons, which moved itself out of fertilisers and into pharmaceuticals.

The restructuring that is taking place is thus largely a matter of companies buying and selling other companies or substantial parts of other companies. The concentration of fertiliser production was brought about in this way. Within the UK, ICI (50 per cent) and Norsk Hydro (which bought Fisons fertiliser business) became dominant, with Fisons and Albright and Wilson withdrawing. Albright and Wilson was bought up by Tenneco, and is now concentrating on its core business in phosphorus chemicals and detergents.[6] More recently, RTZ sold its £568 million chemicals business to Rhône Poulenc: the business consisted 50 per cent of performance chemicals used in textiles, tyres and water processing; 36 per cent of fine chemical intermediates; and 14 per cent of bulk chemicals such as acids. Rhône Poulenc has subsequently sold off a number of enterprises which did not fit well into its own product portfolio.[7]

These examples illustrate the types of change taking place. First, greater concentration comes partly as the result of economies of scale in bulk chemicals processing, and partly because tougher competition leads naturally to a wish to escape dependence on commodity markets. Second, there are also increased economies of scale in a number of semi-bulk products, such as phosphorus, but in these areas firms, unless they are very large indeed, tend to specialise. Third, some firms have moved their technology and capital right out of bulk commodity chemicals and into speciality chemicals where the scope for innovation and establishing a monopolistic position is greater. We examine this sector in the next section.

Speciality chemicals

The term 'speciality chemical' is an awkward but useful term used to describe an enormous range of products. Broadly, it covers products which are 'special' to the producer, that is they are produced in relatively small quantities, are highly differentiated, and are aimed at markets which are imperfect. It includes many fine chemicals with small markets, and products which are to some extent customised, that is specially designed for individual (or small groups of) customers. In other words, it is a sector where producers are attempting to make their products 'more special' and thus carve out monopoly niches. There are many similarities between pharmaceuticals and speciality chemicals, with each market highly differentiated and fragmented into specialist areas (see next section).

A glance back at Table 15.2 indicates that the speciality sector includes such areas as dyes and paints, and specialist products for industries ranging from food manufacturing to textiles, paper and printing to electronics and automobiles. It includes fast-growing areas such as special composites (ie much of the new materials field), but there is no clear line of demarcation between speciality chemicals and other sectors. Erstwhile speciality chemicals become bulk products, as, for example, in the case of carbon fibre; innovative chemicals lose patent protection, with resultant falls in price and expansion of markets.

For many years the speciality chemicals sector has been the preserve of the small or medium-sized firm. Companies such as Cookson or Morgan Crucible have bought as their raw materials the intermediate products of the major companies, added value to them by processing and reworking, and sold them either as final products (for example, Morgan Crucible controls Holts, the car product firm) or as inputs into other final products (eg specialised lubricants for the engineering industry). The large chemicals companies have always had some stake in this market, either directly via wholly owned subsidiaries or indirectly via close linkages with the specialist firms. For their part, too, the speciality firms knit for themselves a web of special relationships which link suppliers and customers. Since their success in the market-place depends upon product differentiation and reaping monopoly rents from customised markets, it is hardly surprising that these linkages – this pattern of quasi-vertical integration – should play so important a part in market structure.

The most marked feature of recent years in this area has been the degree to which the large chemicals firms have integrated forwards into the speciality chemicals area. There are a number of reasons for this.

1 Excess capacity in the bulk petrochemicals sector have squeezed profit margins and led the dominant firms in the sector to search for alternative sources of profit.
2 The threat of substantial Middle East entry into the petrochemicals sector has further reinforced these trends.
3 The large chemicals companies had traditionally made their profits by applying their expertise in the science of chemistry to the discovery and development of new products. As the petrochemicals industry matured, so the locus of innovation shifted from product to process, leaving research departments seeking a new role for their expertise. Given linkages already established with downstream customers or subsidiaries, it was logical for research interests to shift in this direction.[8]

The application of sophisticated chemistry to some of these products has not only made them more R&D intensive, but has also in several cases changed the structure of the sector. *Paints and packaging* are good examples. What had been an old-fashioned, fragmented industry, buying-in raw materials from the major chemicals companies, gradually found itself taken over, and is now a modern, technology-based, concentrated industry. Its product is considerably improved, and highly differentiated. (ICI, for example, has gone to considerable trouble to differentiate its product for different markets, working closely with customers such as automobile manufacturers or off-shore rig constructors.) But, except for highly specialist niche areas, entry is now virtually impossible, because small companies cannot match the breadth of R&D capabilities that the big companies dispose of.

The forward integration of the chemicals majors into these downstream specialist areas has transformed them, with the result that this is now the sector of the industry experiencing the fastest rate of technological change. New composite materials – epoxy glues and resins, special plastics and fibres – all fall into this category. Two examples illustrate the type of developments in hand, and the degree to which they build on close linkage between chemicals company and major users.

The first example concerns the development of *new plastics for automobiles*, where Dow is working closely with General Motors. At its R&D Centre in Zurich, Dow has developed a largely automated plastic moulding process which since 1979 has cut the time taken to make a plastic component by a factor of five. It has also developed processes for volume production of a fibre-reinforced epoxy resin which can be moulded and made suitable for use in panels which are exposed to engine heat, such as car-bonnets.[9] This provides a good illustration of how the development of specialist areas such as plastics requires a high level of co-operation and partnership between supplier and customer. Competitive research and marketing go hand in hand, but while the supplier reaches forward, the customer must also reach back.

The second example is the development of *carbon fibre*, basically an acrylic fibre bound together with epoxy resins to make a light but very tough material. Carbon fibre was developed in the 1960s by the Royal Aircraft Establishment at Farnborough, working in conjunction with Rolls-Royce. Rolls-Royce failed to use it in the development of the RB 211 – its major new engine of the 1970s – which in the end bankrupted it. The new material was offered in 1970 to ICI for further development. ICI turned it down, but it was taken up by Courtaulds who supplied what was then a tiny market. Courtaulds licensed the technology to Hercules, a US chemicals company with interests in defence equipment. By the time the licence expired (in 1979) Hercules had developed multiple uses for carbon fibres and turned to a Japanese producer, Sumitomo, for its supplies of acrylic fibre. This contract gave the Japanese access to the technology, and today they supply 80 per cent of the fast-growing world market in carbon fibre. Ironically, the Pentagon is now worried about over-dependence on Japanese supplies, and has been looking to a US subsidiary of ICI – Fiberite, acquired as part of the 1984 purchase of the Beatrice Group – to supply Hercules with raw materials.[10]

Carbon fibre is a prime example of how Japanese firms, although originally much weaker in chemicals R&D than European or American firms, are seizing opportunities to enter the market for new materials, while also catching up in basic commodity chemicals. The example also illustrates the importance of hands-on experience in developing new materials. Because carbon fibre properties can be varied according to use, the chemist and the engineer must work closely together in the development of the material. Both upstream and downstream relationships are of considerable importance: working upstream with those developing acrylic fibres and epoxy resins, working downstream with the aeronautical and other engineers designing the products. In other words, a major development such as carbon fibre is not a discrete project, but a whole family of interlinked projects – a complex system of developments in which user – producer relationships are critical. Even where overheads are shared, there is no hiding the substantial costs and the major uncertainties incurred in such developments, and it is not surprising to find even large firms, such as ICI, being selective about getting involved.

Advanced materials of many types are being developed in all leading countries, and are recognised as a growth point of great significance. Indeed, advanced materials technology has figured with biotechnology and information technology as one of the three 'generic' technologies which have been the object of special government R&D programmes in almost every major industrial country. Some advanced materials development has been closely related to new developments in information technology, especially in computerisation of design and development and process control technology. Japanese firms in electronics, information technology and the engineering industries (including automobiles and machine tools) are often to be found working in association with strong chemicals firms, especially in the ceramics area. For this reason, if for no other, the European chemicals firms cannot afford to be complacent about Japanese competition in the 1990s. Some European firms have realised this and located new R&D facilities and plant investments in Japan, in order both to facilitate access to this fast-growing market and to be close to the new developments in advanced materials.

The customer–user collaboration found in new materials has become almost routine in some sectors of speciality chemicals. It is often a case of providing a service with products rather than the traditional package of a product with some supporting technical service. This type of innovative 'customised' marketing is growing fast: it is a knowledge-intensive activity, and competitive advantage depends very largely upon scientific expertise and know-how. Just as in engineering contracting, where the sophisticated engineering companies can affect the competitiveness of their customers, so in chemicals, and, in particular, in advanced materials, international innovative and competitive success depends upon access to the most forward-looking and sophisticated customers.

While the entry of the large firms into the downstream specialist areas may have squeezed out many of the small, specialist firms by professionalising the research and development function and putting it beyond the resources of the small specialist firm, by no means all the small firms have been forced out of this sector. Those that remain are in general the ones that have carved out a highly specialist niche for themselves, where narrow expertise commands a high price, and therefore an adequate cash flow. Such firms are often spin-offs from large companies, with the new entrepreneur more often than not coming from either the research or marketing function of the parent firm. But even once established, they do not have the breadth of expertise to shift into new areas, and therefore tend to provide the bread and butter of the acquisitions and mergers figures quoted above in Table 15.4.

The other main impetus to acquisitions and mergers stems from the restructuring activities of the large companies themselves. Hoechst and Rhône Poulenc provide two good examples. The German giant, Hoechst, was concerned as early as 1983 about low profits on commodity petrochemicals, and has since put increasing emphasis on specialities. In 1986 it acquired the Celanese Corporation (USA) for $2.85 billion – a huge step into a strong position in the US market – and the emphasis at Hoechst is now on new high-technology special products for an enormous range of industries and applications.

A massive restructuring of the largely state-owned French chemicals industry has been proceeding along the same lines. Two changes are taking place: first, the industry, encouraged by the government, is becoming more international: associated with this, the lead firms – Rhône Poulenc, Elf Aquitaine and Total CPF – are growing rapidly through acquisition. The important acquisitions are largely in speciality chemicals, although there has also been some rationalisation of bulk chemicals. The policy is explicitly to develop companies large enough to compete in the single EC market of 1992. In January 1989 Rhône Poulenc was less than half the size of the smallest of the three German leaders in the industry, and significantly smaller than ICI, Dow, Du Pont or Ciba Geigy. It had spent some $1.5 billion on major acquisitions in 1986–7 (hence its shift from thirteenth to eighth place in the world league table 1984–8 – see Table

15.3). These included Union Carbide's agrochemicals business ($575 million in 1986), and the basic chemicals operations of Stauffer (disposed of by ICI after the latter had bought Stauffer). In 1989 it went on to spend a further $2 billion-plus on four organic chemicals plants from Monsanto (in USA, Britain and Thailand), Norddeutsche Saserwerke (a German synthetics company), Siliconas Hispanias, ICI's silicon operation in Spain, and Connaught Biosciences (Canada). Then, in early 1990, it acquired GAF-SSC (a US speciality chemicals company – $480 million), RTZ's speciality chemicals business ($839 million) and, subsequently, Rorer (US pharmaceuticals), in a complex deal valued at $3.2 billion.[11] Overall, this had taken Rhône Poulenc, at time of writing, to the position of sixth-largest firm in the industry, on a par with Dow Chemicals, the American multinational.

What we see, therefore, is a major reshuffling of the assets of many medium-to-large chemicals companies. They have taken over firms and disposed of subsidiaries 'not now strategically necessary' (Metz 1984). Overall, this reshuffling has tended to increase concentration in existing activities in the hands of the larger multi-product firms able to exploit innovations quickly and in many markets. When a new product area is identified as having substantial technical and market opportunities, a large firm with strong R&D and finance for product launch can move at a speed and on a scale which no small (or, often, even medium-sized) company can contemplate.

The speciality chemicals sector therefore illustrates graphically the impact of rapid technical change on both the structure of the industry and on the nature of competition. The intense technological activity, the new products, the new applications and refinement of existing products, represent a continuous process. The industry as a whole is changing and growing. There is change in the scale of operation because so much more of the industry is subject to dynamic economies of scale, and these in turn require large-scale R&D and financial and technical resources to open up new opportunities. It is the large firms, on the whole, that are calling the tune. Firms with the corporate, technological and entrepreneurial capacity to innovate are growing; those without these capacities are declining or being acquired. Old-fashioned, smaller firms are simply being squeezed out. But the wider application of more scientific chemistry is also opening up new niches, and there are *new* small firms emerging to exploit these niches.

There is, finally, the paradox of competition, which in many parts of the speciality chemicals business is intense, even though there are also strong monopoly/oligopoly positions. This paradox is a feature of dynamic industries. When the rate of change is fast there are often substantial dynamic economies of scale and scope, including the advantages of a multi-product portfolio to spread risks. But rapid change also offers opportunities to enter markets by innovation rather than by price. This applies to new applications, to new products, to rapidly expanding markets, and to markets where some small differentiation will carve out a new niche. The major firms in the industry are so large and so diversified that they are often seen as monopolists. In the more fragmented speciality sectors, they should more realistically be seen as powerful potential competitors. This is important, since it makes many of these markets contestable – despite patents, close customer–supplier relationships and successful market and product differentiation. Innovation and growth can, in fact, ensure that many apparently strong and highly profitable monopoly positions are but temporary.

Pharmaceuticals

The pharmaceuticals sector began life, like much else in the chemicals industry, in the research-intensive, academically linked chemicals companies which emerged in Germany and Switzerland in the last half of the nineteenth century. Bayer's aspirin, for example, developed in the late nineteenth century, was one of the first drugs to be marketed internationally. With the exception of the German and Swiss companies, the European industry prior to 1945 was highly fragmented. Patent medicines such as Beechams Powders were its mainstay. Dispensing was in the hands of local doctors or pharmacists, who purchased their supplies from specialist wholesalers, who in turn purchased from many different sources including the local distributor of the German chemicals companies.

The modern, research-based drug industry dates from the development of the sulfonomide drugs of the 1930s, which were the first of a new generation of drugs based on a process of screening, testing and modifying a variety of chemical compounds. In the post-war period this was to form the basis of many of the anti-inflammatory and tranquilliser drugs that were developed. The other main source of new drugs were the so-called biologicals – the penicillins, cephalosporins and tetracyclines – derived originally from naturally occurring micro-organisms but, over time, transformed via chemical synthesis and modification into the sophisticated drugs we use today. US firms, taking advantage of the debilitation of the German industry during and after the Second World War, were in the forefront of these new developments, and rapidly expanded to become multinational companies as governments around the world, strapped for dollars, deliberately geared their regulatory frameworks to encourage the establishment of locally based subsidiaries.

By the 1960s the German companies had recovered their pre-eminence, to share with the US and Swiss companies top place in the world pharmaceutical league table. As Table 15.7 shows, while there is constant jockeying for position among the top players in the industry, there is surprisingly little real mobility. Hoechst, Bayer, Ciba Geigy, Sandoz, Hoffmann LaRoche – the top European pharmaceutical manufacturers since the early part of this century – remain top world producers. In the 1950s and 1960s they were joined by the Americans – Merck, Pfizer, Eli Lilley, American Home Products. In the 1980s two new names appeared – Glaxo, the British company, and Takeda of Japan, symbolically representing the two most interesting changes in the industry over the last ten years; first, the rise in importance of British firms, for it is not only Glaxo, but also ICI, Wellcome and Beecham (now merged with Smith Kline to form Smith Kline Beecham) which have emerged as world-class players; and second, the entry of Japanese firms into the world league.

The other European company of significance is Rhône Poulenc, the largest French company, which has been pursuing an active policy of acquisition in pharmaceuticals as well as in chemicals (see pp. 313–14), and as a result boosted its world ranking between 1987 and 1989 from fortieth to twenty-fourth. Its take-over of the middle-ranking US company Rorer in early 1990 has pushed it up further to approximately seventeenth place. However, it is noteworthy that such changes do not mean major increases in market share. Rhône Poulenc's market share increased from 1.2 to 1.7 per cent as a result of the Rorer merger. Merck, the largest company, has only a 4.5 per cent market

Table 15.7 The twenty-five largest pharmaceutical companies 1989

Rank	Company	Country of origin	Pharmaceutical sales[a] ($m)	% of world market
1	Merck	USA	5,485	4.5
2	Bristol Squibb	USA	4,230	3.5
3	Glaxo	UK	4,215	3.5
4	Hoechst	W Germany	3,900	3.3
5	Smith Kline Beecham	UK	3,540	3.0
6	Bayer	W Germany	3,405	2.8
7	Am. Home Products	USA	3,110	2.6
8	Ciba Geigy	Switzerland	2,960	2.5
9	Eli Lilly	USA	2,920	2.4
10	Sandoz	Switzerland	2,705	2.3
11	Pfizer	USA	2,640	2.2
12	Johnson & Johnson	USA	2,625	2.2
13	Takeda	Japan	2,580	2.1
14	ICI	UK	2,295	1.9
15	Eastman Kodak	USA	2,220	1.85
16	Roche[b]	Switzerland	2,163	1.8
17	M. Merrell Dow	USA	2,100	1.75
18	Upjohn	USA	2,050	1.70
19	B. Ingelheim	W Germany	1,870	1.6
20	Schering Ag.	W Germany	1,675	1.4
21	Wellcome	UK	1,640	1.4
22	Sankyo	Japan	1,615	1.35
23	Cyanamid	USA	1,575	1.3
24	Rhône Poulenc[c]	France	1,460	1.2
25	Fuji Sawa	Japan	1,435	1.2

Notes:
[a] Ethical (ie prescription) drug sales only
[b] Does *not* include Genentech (taken over January 1990)
[c] Does *not* include Rorer (taken over in 1990)

Source: Shearson Lehman Hutton 1990

share; Bristol Squibb and Glaxo, the next largest companies, both have 3.5 per cent shares. This is not an industry of national champions: rather, both world-wide and in Europe, it has been marked throughout the post-war period by a relatively stable international oligopoly. Companies tend to specialise in particular product areas and compete intensely with others in that area. Markets are, however, highly fragmented, as a result of widely varying regulatory and price controls, which open the door to product differentiation (by market) and price discrimination.

There are many similarities between pharmaceuticals and speciality chemicals: both feature a market broken up into small specialist areas with intense competition within each area based on claimed product characteristics, not price. Indeed, in a technological sense, pharmaceuticals *are* speciality chemicals. The difference between the two sectors lies in downstream linkages. Many speciality chemicals are produced for specific users to meet special needs, with R&D a joint activity between producer and user. Although the pharmaceutical companies have developed close links with the medical profession – the users of their products – professional ethics prevent doctors from being tied to the use of specific products. The elaborate marketing techniques of the industry represent attempts to create such loyalty on an informal basis, but this also sums up the difference between the two sectors. Because doctors cannot be tied into specific products, there is intense competition for their custom between the main contenders in the market: in the speciality chemicals market, the name of the game is to lock your customer in by making markets bespoke.

The post-war era marked the emergence of the pharmaceuticals industry as a major research-based industry. The tradition established with the sulfonomide drugs – taking a chemical compound with known therapeutic properties, modifying it through chemical synthesis and then testing it for effectiveness – became the accepted route to new drugs. Even the biologicals (pencillin, etc) were synthesised and modified. The process is costly in terms of time: only one in 1,000 of compounds tested remains after the first round of screening; only one in 10,000 survives the full gamut of further testing procedures. What is more, as interest shifted from the early (and effective) anti-infective drugs of the 1950s which helped to eliminate diseases such as tuberculosis, to the chronic diseases of elderly people – heart disease, cancer, arthritis – so the period of testing has had to be extended. In reaction partly to scandals such as that over Thalidomide and, more recently, Opren, partly to the requirements of the medical profession, governments have imposed ever tougher testing requirements. As a result, whereas in 1960 it took on average five years to get from patenting to market launch, by the 1980s this had increased to an average of ten years, stretching frequently to twelve or thirteen years.

The net effect of this lengthening of the period of testing, and of more complicated and demanding test procedures, has been

1   to increase substantially the costs of pharmaceutical R&D
2   to erode the useful (ie post-launch) patent life of a drug during which a substantial premium (monopoly rent) can be charged
3   to put major emphasis, therefore, on rapid world-wide exploitation of any new drug, hence the high-pressure sales techniques
4   to encourage further fragmentation of markets as the industry maximises opportunities for price discrimination. Within Europe, for example, the price charged for the same drug may vary by a factor of as much as three to one.[12] Indeed knowing how to cope with the different regulatory and patent regimes world-wide is a critical asset in the pharmaceuticals industry.

The strategies currently being adopted by the pharmaceuticals industry, and common to European and US multinationals alike, can be seen as a direct response to these trends. They involve, in the first place, a more targeted approach to research. Greater understanding of the body's natural chemistry and immune system has enabled scientists to pinpoint more accurately the size, shape and type of chemical molecule likely to have a therapeutic effect in specific circumstances. This targeted approach to drug discovery underlies two of the 1990s' most successful drugs – Beta blockers (which help with heart attacks) and Tagamet (an anti-ulcer drug), both discovered by the British scientist Sir James Black.

A second route to cheaper drugs has been the development of biotechnology, which initially appeared to offer both a more targeted route to drug discovery and the prospect of 'manufacturing', via genetic engineering and cell culture, the range of therapeutic proteins, such as insulin, growth hormones, the interferons and inter-leukins, which are produced naturally by the body's immune system. In practice, the products of this first generation of 'the new biotechnology' have proved costly and (often) ineffective. But the trial-and-error techniques thus developed have revealed a far more effective route (protein engineering) to targeted drug discovery, which is now being backed by big investments on the part of all the major pharmaceuticals companies (Sharp 1991a).

A third strategy adopted by the drug companies has been to use greater selectivity. The expensive stage in drug development is not the drug discovery (research) stage, but development and launch. The greater the selectivity at the research and/or early de-velopment stage, the lower the costs. Paring down the number of drugs under develop-ment is an obvious economy, and one pursued by a number of successful European companies, among them ICI and Glaxo.

Companies have also sought to hold their own by building across-the-board competence. While greater selectivity may be a logical route to economy, it runs the risk of leaving the company with too few new drugs coming on to the market. A number of companies, for example Hoechst and Bayer, have gone in the other direction, in seeking to broaden their research base. The logic underlying this strategy is that success in drug discovery is like a game of roulette. While the probability of 'success' per $1 invested is always the same, buying more chips (ie spending more on R&D and developing a broader range of drugs) increases any individual's chances of winning.

There has also been a marked increase in collaboration between companies. If development and launch are the expensive stages of new drug discovery, they are also stages which lend themselves to collaboration. For years drug companies have 'shared markets' through exclusive licensing arrangements of one sort or another, and this is an increasingly important trend, though the importance of establishing clear-cut patent rights makes collaboration at the actual research phase difficult. Successful collabora-tion in that phase tends to be vertical – between the large multinationals and the small specialist research companies (eg in biotechnology) or with a university department – rather than horizontal collaboration between two majors.

Finally, there has recently been a notable increase in the number of mergers. Collaboration may help spread development costs and risks, but has to be paid for via shared profits. The year 1989 brought two big mergers: Bristol Myers with Squibb, and Smith Kline with the UK's Beecham. The following year saw Hoffman LaRoche gobble up Genentech, and Rhône Poulenc take over Rorer. There are likely to be many more.

With the development of the Single Market, the European industry already faces the prospect of increased competition and pressure on profits 'from within'. To add to this, there is the probable entry of Japan as a major player in these markets. To date, the Japanese pharmaceuticals industry has not played much part on the global scene; by European standards its companies have been small, tending to concentrate on 'me too' drugs which yield poor profits. Its recent record in innovation, however, has been impressive, and it is likely that on the back of these new drugs, many of them biotechnological in origin, Japanese companies will make a major push into Western markets, either directly or in collaboration with European firms. (For a fuller discussion of these developments see Sharp 1991b.)

The next few years are therefore likely to witness major changes in the pharmaceuticals industry, and what happens in Europe is likely to be mirrored elsewhere in the world. Competition will increase; there will be new players in the industry coming from new countries (Japan) and new technologies (biotechnology). The response will be collaboration and merger, the one often preceding the other. As in other sectors of the chemicals industry, this will bring greater concentration and highlight the issues of control and regulation, with 1992 putting the burden of control firmly on the shoulders of the European Commission. We turn to those issues in the next section.

Chemicals, pharmaceuticals and 1992

Much that has happened in the chemicals industry in the 1970s and 1980s has already anticipated 1992 and the completion of the Single European Market. In the bulk chemicals sectors, most of the firms involved are long-established multinationals which have treated Western Europe as a single market for at least twenty years. It is significant, for example, that it was to the European Commission, not national governments, that these firms looked when over-capacity threatened market stability in the early 1980s. In the speciality chemicals sector, the acquisitions, mergers and reshuffling that have been taking place since the mid-1980s reflect not only the dynamics of the product cycle, but also the need to secure market positions in important product areas across what is, in this case, still a fragmented market. Once again, the large firm, with its corporate planning department and linkages into the banking sector has an advantage over the small: for them the search procedures are easier, cheaper and more efficient. Indeed, the most significant impact of 1992 in bulk, speciality and pharmaceuticals sectors is likely to be in terms of regulation and control, rather than in the creation of the single market *per se*. In this section we therefore concentrate on three main issues: competition policy, the deregulation of the chemicals industry at the national level and its re-regulation at the Community level, and the important question of safety, testing and the environment.

The EC's responsibilities for competition policy embrace, on the one hand, the control of subsidies and state aids, and on the other the control of monopolies and merger. We have already described the endemic tendency towards over-capacity and soft prices in the bulk chemicals sectors. The Commission intervened in the early 1980s to prevent the proliferation of self-defeating state aids. Given the continuing cyclical pattern of the bulk sectors and the tendency to world-wide over-expansion, it seems probable that it will again be called to act as crisis manager. The degree to which national governments are now ready to accept Commission-dictated limits on state aids is significant, and displays an acknowledgement that the problem already goes beyond the jurisdiction of the nation-state. But it could leave the Community vulnerable in a situation where the USA and Japan, operating still as national states, may have a flexibility of action which the Community, operating as it will do by a set of mutually agreed ground rules on such issues as competition and mergers (the level playing field), will lack.

National governments are (and have been for some time) powerless to prevent European or global monopoly/oligopoly patterns emerging among the major multinational chemicals companies, although at the margin they may be able to impose conditions which modify monopoly power. Control, in so far as it can be exercised, has to come now from the European Community, and the fines imposed in the polypropylene case (see p. 307) indicate that neither Commission nor Court will shirk their responsibilities. The new regulations on mergers, which will give the Commission powers to investigate cross-border mergers above a certain size, will help. But it should be remembered that nowhere – not even in the United States – has there been effective control of the large multi-product, multinational companies. Competition among these companies, seemingly very intense, is also very imperfect. The notorious case of Hoffmann LaRoche before the British Monopolies and Mergers Commission is a good example of how competition authorities *can* curb the excesses of monopoly exploitation,[13] and argues for greater co-ordination of action among such authorities, not only within the European Community, but also world-wide, perhaps under the auspices of the GATT.

The main impact of 1992 is likely to be at the level of regulation of the chemicals industry broadly defined. The single European market requires the dismantling of the separate national systems of regulation, and their harmonisation at the European level. Beyond that, there is increasing public awareness and concern about the harmful effects that the widespread (and in many cases unrestricted) use of chemicals is having on the environment in which we live, and considerable pressure for extensive and much stricter control. The new regime of regulation emerging within Europe is likely to represent a sharp change in the level and toughness of controls. This is already reflected in the EC's directives on pollution control, which have sought to limit the use of nitrogenous fertilisers by imposing tough standards on water quality. The major chemicals companies recognise this as merely the tip of the iceberg, and are reckoning on more and tougher controls in the future. Indeed, in the age-old tradition of 'if you can't beat them, join them', the companies, through their European organisation CIFIC, are actively participating in the working groups establishing such standards. From their point of view, of course, restrictions offer both losses and opportunities. Banning the use of chlorofluoro carbons (CFCs) means the loss of one market, but opens up opportunities in the development of alternatives. Similarly, controls on the use of nitrogenous fertilisers may hit the fertiliser market (witness the number of firms quitting this sector of the market) but offers a welcome boost to new, environment-friendly agrochemicals and new seed and plant varieties being developed through plant biotechnology programmes.

The main concern of the major European firms in this respect is that European regulation should not be more onerous than that imposed on their competitors in other markets. An interesting illustration of this problem arises in biotechnology, where the influence of the Greens in (West) Germany has in recent years meant a national regulatory regime on such issues as environmental release which has been much tougher than that prevailing elsewhere.[14] As a result, a number of German chemicals groups, including BASF, are pulling out of biotechnology R&D in Germany and relocating their facilities elsewhere, usually (as with BASF) in the United States. From a Community point of view, the loss is in terms of high-quality research jobs and, ultimately, of retreat from the cutting edge of research work in such new technologies.

The German biotechnology issue illustrates another problem with harmonisation – the problem of individual countries going ahead with *national* regulations before agreement has been reached on Community regulations. Gunter Metz, president of CIFIC, told its annual conference in 1989, 'the process of Europeanisation is not happening fast enough when it comes to national administrations, specifically in the area of environmental regulation'. Conflicting national regulations

> are making it harder, not easier, to tackle environmental problems. At a time when authorities in the EC member states are meant to be moving towards Community level regulations, they are in fact creating chaos in the chemicals sector by burdening us with wildly differing national environmental rules.[15]

In pharmaceuticals the issues are somewhat different. Moves are afoot to harmonise procedures for evaluating the safety, quality and efficacy of new drugs, with special new rules applying to biotechnology drugs with the aim of eventually setting up a European Medicines Evaluation Agency. Given the current extent of fragmentation of markets, however, harmonisation is unlikely to be achieved much before the end of the decade. Right now, the industry is more worried about the prospect of tough restrictions being imposed on their R&D programmes through the influence of the Greens, with moves in some quarters for a five-year moratorium on genetic engineering research. There is also concern as to the probable effects of harmonisation on prices, and some manufacturers fear that there is likely to be a levelling-down of prices towards those of the lower-price countries, Italy and France, to the detriment of companies that have large established sales in the higher-price countries, especially Germany. This, they argue, will in turn squeeze profits and limit the funding of R&D.

Conclusions

What conclusions, then, can be drawn about the prospects for the European chemicals industry? It is a large, amorphous industry which in many respects defies definition. We have attempted to analyse its development by looking separately at the bulk or commodity chemicals sectors, pharmaceuticals and speciality chemicals. But such definitions are artificial and categories merge into each other. It has been, and remains, a highly successful industry, and European firms, many of whose names date back to the early part of the twentieth century, continue to dominate the industry on a world-wide basis. Their success has been built on their ability to harness science and convert it into technology. The chemicals industry was from the start built upon a fast-moving scientific base, which required large R&D departments and continuous mechanisms within the firm for adapting and adjusting to technological change. For this reason, and because the technology itself has created important economies of scale, major parts of the industry have been dominated by large firms. These firms have, since their foundation, operated on an international basis, buying and selling and establishing subsidiaries in all major international markets.

The outstanding characteristic of the industry today is that it has retained the adaptability and the flexibility which marked its initial establishment. In this chapter we have mapped the way in which the locus of innovative activity has shifted from petrochemicals to speciality chemicals and biotechnology. The latter confronts the industry with a major discontinuity whose impact is at present limited to the pharmaceuticals and agrochemicals sectors, but which is likely to have a far wider impact in the future as new methods of chemical catalysis, based on complex 'engineered' molecules, impinge on many of its activities. In the meantime, the advent of the large firm in the speciality chemicals sector has been accompanied by much acquisition and merger activity, which has driven out many of the traditional small and medium-sized firms of this sector and led to a substantial concentration of activity. We identified here an element of the product cycle, for the large firms have professionalised R&D activities in this sector (with a resultant resurgence of innovation), in the process forcing out many of the smaller firms which have been unable to keep up with the changes. In this area, and in biotechnology, the large dominant firm is revealed as having the resources and capability to adapt and colonise new activities, whereas the smaller firm, entering the industry in the vanguard of new activities, is shown in the longer run to be inflexible and to lack the resources for adjustment.

Acknowledgement

The authors are grateful to the Society of Chemical Industry for permission to reproduce Figure 15.1.

Notes

1   Rotterdam is the most famous modern petrochemicals complex. It has five oil refineries, major basic petrochemicals plants (Shell and Gulf naptha crackers, and Esso's aromatics plant) two carbon black plants, and sulphur production facilities. Bulk chemicals require specialised and extensive storage and transhipment facilities, and the particular strength of Rotterdam is that it is both a chemicals complex and a port complex. In 1980 there were in Europe a total of about a dozen large petrochemicals complexes (Molle and Wever 1983).

2   According to Bruce Gardyne (1986: 44), a clause which assisted Shell-Esso was inserted into the Finance Act 1982 after they had threatened to pull out.

3   See Enimont to raise $1 billion. *Financial Times* 26 July 1989.

4   See Commission of the EC (1988).

5   *Economist* 11 July 1989.

6   Albright disposes of its agricultural side to ICI. *Financial Times* 7 November 1983.

7   Graham G 1990 Voracious appetite for acquisitions. *Financial Times* 9 May 1990.

8   It is noteworthy also that the firms that have most successfully moved in this direction are the old-established chemicals firms – Dow, Dupont, Hoechst, Bayer, ICI – whose skills and expertise predate the petrochemicals era.

9   Griffiths J 1989 The plastic car gathers speed. *Financial Times* 18 February 1989.
10 Jackson T 1988 A game for big players. *Financial Times* 15 August 1986.
11 *Financial Times* 20 January and 11 July 1990.
12 See Shearson Lehman Hutton figures quoted in *Financial Times Supplement on Pharmaceuticals* 6 November 1989.
13 On this occasion Hoffman LaRoche, accused of making excess profits by the overpricing of intermediates supplied from within the group, refused to provide any data to refute the allegations, and were effectively damned by their own actions. In the UK they were required to grant licences to other suppliers (thus bringing prices down), but the world-wide publicity attracted by the case was far more damaging. See Monopolies and Mergers Commission (1973) *Cholorodiazepoxide Hc 197* HMSO.
14 In fact the original German proposals, which would have imposed a five-year moritorium on all experiments involving the environmental release of genetically engineered species, have now been dropped in favour of granting permission for such experiments – but only under carefully monitored and controlled conditions. Even for contained (ie inside) experiments the Greens have been reluctant to see genetic manipulation used. Local *Länder* opposition, for example, held up Hoechst's production of genetically engineered insulin for five years.
15 Quoted in *Chemistry and Industry* 19 June 1989: 361.

References

Allen G (1990) Our chemical industry in 2001. Leverhulme Lecture, *Chemistry and Industry* 4 June
Anizon D (1990) Chimie: l'avance des groupes européens. In Crespy G (ed) *Marché unique: marché multiple*. Economica, Paris
Commission of the EC (1988) *Seventeeth Report on Competitive Policy* CEC Publications Office, Luxembourg
Duncan W B (1982) Lessons from the past: challenge and opportunity. In Sharp D H, West T F (eds) *The Chemical Industry*. Ellis Horwood for the Society of Chemical Industry
Gardyne J B (1986) *Ministers and Mandarins: Inside the Whitehall Village*. Sidgwick & Jackson
Metz G (1984) Solving structural problems of the European Chemical Industry. *Chemistry and Industry* 17 December
Molle W, Wever E (1983) *Oil Refineries and Petrochemical Industries in Western Europe: Buoyant Past and Uncertain Future*. Gower
OECD (1979) *The Petrochemical Industry: Trends in Production and Investment*. Paris
OECD (1983) *The Economic Aspects of the International Control of Chemicals*. Paris
Sharp M (1991a) European countries in science based competition: the case of biotechnology. In Hague D C (ed) *The Management of Science*. Macmillan
Sharp M (1991b) Pharmaceuticals and biotechnology: perspectives for the European industry. In Freeman C, Sharp M, Walker W (eds) *Technology and the Future of Europe*. Pinter
Shearson Lehman Hutton (1990) *SLH Universe League Tables*. Shearson Lehman Hutton Securities, New York

CHAPTER 16

The European agricultural industry

KEITH S HOWE

Introduction

The key political development of the immediate post-war period in Europe was the East–West division which, to a large extent, saw the isolation of Eastern Europe and the Soviet Union from the mainstream of European socio-economic intercourse. The political division was paralleled in specifically economic terms by the separation of a western hemisphere of market-oriented economies, at this point totally dominated by the United States, from the socialist economies of the East. The economic strength of the USA was made available for the reconstruction of Western Europe through economic assistance, almost half of which was for food aid (Singer et al 1987: 5), under the European Recovery Programme (Marshall Aid). In marked contrast, the Soviet Union, which had suffered extensively in the war, was still a newly industrialising country (NIC), disposing of abundant natural resources but (largely by its own decision) remaining outside the sphere of Western trade flows and American aid. For the most part, the Soviet Union's new-found allies in Eastern Europe remained backward agrarian societies compared with other more industrially advanced regions in the West. These strongly delineated economic disparities, so sharply correlated with political circumstances, provide a natural line of separation for the discussion of post-war developments in European agriculture up to the end of the 1980s, when new possibilities emerged for the future of Europe as a whole.

Problems of agriculture and farm policy in the European market economies

In the immediate aftermath of war, the recovery of agriculture in Western Europe was essential in terms both of restoring production for domestic consumption and contributing towards improvement in the balance of payments. An array of instruments for policy intervention was already in place, some of which had been introduced before the war to protect farm incomes from the adverse effects of international competition, some created in response to the wartime emergency. Only Denmark, so dependent on agricultural export markets, quickly dismantled wartime controls. A comprehensive discussion of national responses to the new challenges of the immediately post-war period is beyond the scope of this chapter. For this, reference can be made to Tracy (1989) and the series of OEEC/OECD reports on national agricultural policies (eg OEEC 1956; 1958; 1960; OECD 1967; 1975; 1983). However, the main concerns of post-war policy in West European agriculture can be illustrated by focusing on Germany, France and the UK, with supplementary reference to the Mediterranean regions.

Country examples

For *Germany* which after the Second World War was partitioned and became the Federal German Republic (FRG) in the West and the German Democratic Republic (GDR) in the East, the large farms and estates of the main food-producing areas were absorbed into the Soviet-dominated socialist bloc. The Western zone was afflicted by drastic food shortages, and so a policy for rapid production increases was *de rigueur*. Following an established protectionist tradition, import controls made it possible for domestic farm product prices in West Germany to be supported at a level well above that of world prices, and sufficient to cover production costs on marginal farms. Even so, farm incomes failed to keep abreast of upward trends in the non-farm sector, and, from the late 1940s on, demands for income parity from the farm population became increasingly vociferous. In response to the pattern of price support, rye production soon outstripped domestic demand, and pigmeat and butter prices were maintained at high levels only by the virtual exclusion of imports. In sum, the immediate post-war years saw the foundation of a policy of high prices for farm products in the FRG which was later to be continued within the framework of the EEC.

In *France,* priority was given to achieving equilibrium on the balance of payments, to satisfy conditions set out by the OEEC. More interventionist by nature, perhaps, than other Western European governments (but see Holmes, Chapter 2 in *The National Economies of Europe*, on France), the French administration implemented in the immediate post-war period the first of four plans for agriculture covering the period 1947 to 1961. The plans focused on the modernisation of agriculture, with emphasis on mechanisation and increased labour productivity, while at the same time providing price support. In the first (and revised first) plan, the need to export cereals, meat and dairy products was stressed, as was the reduction of oils and fats imports. In the event surpluses developed as early as 1950, resulting in subsidised exports of wheat and sugar, distillation of wine into industrial alcohol, and the destruction of vineyards.

In the *UK*, which alone had steadfastly maintained a *laissez-faire* policy towards agriculture before the outbreak of the Second World War, the wartime emergency saw the government adopt what amounted to a planned farm economy. Farmers acceded to state regulation of markets in return for certain guarantees from the government, notably in the form of provision of price support. So attractive were the benefits of intervention for the industry relative to the condition of inter-war agricultural depression under *laissez-faire*, that the 1947 Agriculture Act can be seen as a natural extension of wartime policies.[1] Based on the idea that consumers should still, in effect, pay for their food at the lowest attainable world prices, farmers would receive deficiency payments for the most important agricultural (not horticultural) products whenever market prices were less than some annually determined guaranteed level. Price support which is achieved by imposition of tariffs and other trade restrictions obliges consumers to pay higher food prices directly; in seeking to keep food prices low, the UK system depended on the willingness of governments (and therefore implicitly taxpayers) to make transfer payments to farmers. The system was inherently progressive since low-income consumers who paid low taxes but spent a relatively high proportion of their disposable income on food were penalised less than proportionately. In addition to a range of so-called production grants and input subsidies aimed at assisting farmers, a state extension service offering them free advice, the National Agricultural Advisory Service (NAAS), was created in 1947, further to facilitate the promotion of technical and economic efficiency in agricultural production.[2]

Industrialisation and agricultural adjustment

The three country examples illustrate the importance attached to price support as a means of stimulating farm production and helping farmers earn satisfactory incomes, while simultaneously increasing the efficiency of farm production. The broad sweep of post-war economic reconstruction was also laying the foundations for a resurgence of economic growth and industrial development in Western Europe, a process which encompassed the rapid industrialisation of agriculture itself. Data for the OEEC countries taken together show that between 1947 and 1960 the number of agricultural tractors increased six-fold, fertiliser use more than doubled, while the farm labour force fell by 15 per cent 1950–60 (Tracy 1989). In other words, machinery purchased from outside the farm sector began to substitute for traditional sources of labour and horse-power, and natural organic manure was increasingly supplemented, if not replaced, by inorganic chemicals from a growing industrial agrochemicals sector. At the same time, growth in the off-farm economy signalled high enough opportunity costs of staying in agriculture to encourage many who in previous generations would have spent their lives as farm workers to seek employment elsewhere.[3] These changes quickly laid to rest the fears expressed in early post-war years that food shortages would continue for some time. By the late 1950s, OEEC agricultural production was half as much again as it had been in 1939 and general overproduction had already become a major issue in some sectors.

It is important to stress, however, that such adjustments in agricultural resource use did not occur uniformly throughout the market economies of Western Europe. For the countries of the Southern European fringe, development progressed more slowly than for their Northern European neighbours. Italy is unusual in exhibiting parallel paths of development, inasmuch as the Italian South remained backward and impoverished while industrialisation progressed impressively in the North. As of the mid-1950s, some 40 per cent of the total working population of Italy was engaged in agriculture – producing just about one quarter of net national income. Broadly comparable proportions also characterised Portugal. In Spain, the half of the total working population occupied in agriculture generated something more than one-third of national income, the same share of total output as Greece (considered to have one of the lowest standards of living in Europe) produced from no less than 60 per cent of the working population.[4] While the specific characteristics of these countries' economies obviously varied, a common underlying concern was the inefficient use of agricultural labour. Underemployment was aggravated by rapidly increasing national populations, and the slow pace of industrialisation provided inadequate opportunities for off-farm employment.

Farm structures

Agricultural adjustment in the sense of the redeployment of agricultural resources is clearly an integral part of economic development. Another dimension critically important in the present context is that of 'structural reform'. This is amply illustrated by reference to any of the series of OEEC/OECD agricultural policy reports cited. Structural reform comprises measures for farm consolidation (exchange of scattered parcels of land), enlargement of farms (including farm amalgamation), and also land reform and provision for land improvement through, for example, land reclamation and irrigation. These measures are properly to be regarded as *assisted agricultural adjustment*. Most importantly, where redeployment or retirement of farmers and their families from agricultural production is accompanied by farm amalgamation, income per head is increased for the remaining family units for any given level of aggregate national farm income. In this way, improved incomes should in principle be attainable without recourse to price supports for farm products, input subsidies and production grants.

The significance of structural improvement can be illustrated with reference to Greece in the 1950s, at which time the average size of farm holdings was 3.6 hectares, with over half the holdings under two hectares. Farming income was too low because agricultural underemployment was a permanent problem, with an estimated 40 per cent of the rural labour force unable to find farm employment on a full-time basis (OEEC 1956: 89). However, the farm structures problem was not confined to Southern Europe. For example, the FRG recognised that in nearly half of its agricultural area improvements in productivity would be dependent on consolidation of scattered farm holdings, often centred on crowded villages with outdated buildings and inadequate road systems (OEEC 1956: 70).[5] Farm fragmentation, in which plots of land belonging to a single holding are geographically dispersed, was a serious problem everywhere except the UK and Scandinavia. But farm amalgamation policies were in place by the early 1960s, most notably in France, Germany, Ireland, the Netherlands, Norway and Sweden (OECD 1964). In the UK, already regarded as having a relatively favourable farm size structure,[6] it was considered that half of all farm holdings accounted for such a small share of total agricultural output that many of them could never be made viable (EFTA 1965: 112), and here too farm amalgamation policies were set in train. British government measures such as the 1959 Small Farmers Scheme were intended to provide assistance for improved productivity and profitability.

Against all this, it was known that some small-scale farmers also earned income from off-farm sources. This was particularly the case in France, where it was estimated for the mid-1950s that supplementary incomes amounted to over 20 per cent of income from farming itself. It is likely that regional disparities in the pattern of supplementary income were as important as those in income from farm production itself. For example, remote mountainous regions of the Pyrenees, the Alps and the Massif Central were particularly disadvantaged as regards alternative employment opportunities, in marked contrast to the large farming areas located on the fertile plains of the developed Paris Basin. France exemplifies the general rule that both within and between countries agriculture typically exhibits a wide range of farm size structures, patterns of agricultural production and farm family incomes.

Consequences of farm policies for production and resource use

The origins of overproduction

By supporting farm product prices in the European market economies, governments sheltered their agricultural sectors from the full impact of market forces. At a time of shortages this might appear harmless enough, since the more speedy the restoration of supplies relative to current demand, the better the opportunity to dampen the potential for food price inflation such as might appear with the derestriction of a war economy. However problems arise once price support starts to generate overproduction. Clearly, the greater the farm productivity gains under price support, the greater the scope for the development of what later came to be called 'structural surpluses', that is a persistent tendency for supply to outstrip demand at administered prices. What would happen if governments stopped intervening in the market? To an extent depending on the relevant elasticities of supply and demand and the rate of growth of population, this would cause market clearing prices to settle below their previous administered minimum levels.

Now it is well known that as economies develop, the income elasticity of demand for food declines, that is as people get better off a progressively smaller proportion of successive increments of income is spent on food. Also, as observed in the developed economies of Europe and North America in particular, population growth rates decline as people become wealthier. Therefore, in the absence of compensating increases in demand for farm products from new markets, the removal of price supports is likely, in the circumstances described, to cause prices and farm incomes to fall, at least in the short run, and to provoke renewed calls for protection. From 1949–50 to 1956 agricultural output in OEEC countries did, in the event, increase at an average rate of 4 per cent per annum, and population by just 1 per cent per annum. Per capita food consumption increased as income increased, though with variations between specific farm products (OEEC 1956: 313). In the aggregate, it increased more slowly than per capita income, in accordance with expectations about the income elasticity of demand.

Approaches to supply restriction

The example of France is illustrative of one possible response to burgeoning surpluses. It was, indeed, recognised as early as the 1950s that surpluses developed at existing levels of support. This led initially to politically unacceptable and therefore largely ineffectual attempts to curtail production increases by reducing administered prices. Methods of intervention then became more elaborate. The idea of selective expansion of production gained prominence. In practice, this meant that increases in output were considered to be tolerable for commodities not in surplus, for example oil crops. In the UK, too, selective expansion became an important feature of policy, in this instance favouring beef and sheepmeat and animal feeds. Animal feed production was also favoured in Belgium, Luxembourg, Norway and Italy. Rapid production growth from domestic and overseas sources soon threatened to undermine the UK government's commitment to assured markets for farm products, at least at acceptable levels of exchequer burden.

Notwithstanding the attractions of novel policies which may help to sidestep a politically sensitive issue, the fact remains that the most obvious way to eliminate surpluses is to allow market prices to fall. This would give the signal for much needed resource reallocation, both within agriculture and between agriculture and the rest of the economy. However, unless in the long run production costs fall in at least the same proportion as product prices, the effect is inevitably a sustained reduction in net farm incomes. Of course, a tradition of agricultural protectionism was established precisely because farm incomes displayed a tendency to remain unacceptably low (Tracy 1989). Against that background, and with the instruments for price support so firmly institutionalised, it would clearly always be difficult to solve any given overproduction problem by politically tolerable policies, especially under electoral systems where governments depended substantially on winning key farm votes.

Resource immobility and market widening

Policies for structural reform ease the pressures on farm incomes if farm consolidation and amalgamation lead to the retirement of farmers, so that fewer producers remain to share a given aggregate income. However, while the hired farm labour force declined rapidly in post-war years, farmers and their families, particularly those more advanced in years, showed reluctance or inability to quit. Farmers' apparent readiness to put up with incomes low relative to non-farm earnings provoked a major international study in the early post-war years (Bellerby 1956). Reasons suggested for tolerance of low incomes included a tendency for farmers themselves to assess their own opportunity cost and that of many of their resources as low. Such observations underpin objections to the opinion widely held in earlier decades that the cause of agricultural depression was to a large extent a problem of marketing of farm products.[7] In fact, it seems rather to have reflected a failure to transfer resources earning low returns out of agricultural production. It can be argued, however, that policies after 1945 reflected that earlier point of view, especially in relation to international trade.

Duchêne et al (1985), for example, discern a common thread in events which extends as far as the successive enlargements of the EEC in the 1980s. Their observations are constructed in relation to the EEC, but the justification of those observations has roots in earlier post-war years. The crux of the argument is that countries consistently pursued a policy of *fuite en avant* which, loosely translated, means attempting to accelerate out of trouble (Duchêne et al 1985: 30). In other words, the need to open up and exploit new market opportunities was seen as a solution to the problem of agricultural overproduction. Since to increase market size indefinitely was impossible within any given domestic economy, access to new export markets became critical. The continuing evolution of post-war European agriculture and agricultural policy within the EC framework can be more effectively understood with this in mind.

The role of the CAP[8]

One fundamental idea associated with the Common Agricultural Policy (CAP) from its inception in 1962 is that it constitutes the only truly common policy in the Community. To what extent that belief is consistent with the evidence is debatable. Nevertheless, the fact that the six original member states had broadly similar traditions in farm policy must surely have eased matters when it came to deciding that the CAP should continue to underpin farm prices by restricting third country access to domestic markets. In addition, the desire to expand export opportunities complemented the political objective of increased national interdependence among the Six. In particular, it was envisaged that French agricultural exports would exchange for FRG industrial exports. This made both political and economic sense, because France needed markets for its abundant farm exports while Germany needed food imports. Similarly, the inclusion of Italy as a Mediterranean producer complemented the otherwise predominantly temperate North European complexion of agricultural production in the Six.[9] This pursuit of complementarity continued after the accession in 1973 of, among others, the UK (another major food importer), and subsequently of Greece, Spain and Portugal, all relatively underdeveloped Mediterranean economies. Not only could these producers meet a growing demand in North European markets for Mediterranean fruit and vegetables, but also their own development would generate rising incomes and an increasing demand for meat and dairy products from Northern Europe. As long as the process of complementary growth in production and consumption remained sustainable, the day when more drastic remedies would be needed to constrain accumulating agricultural surpluses could be put off.

Whatever unifying explanation for the observed general direction of agricultural development and agricultural policy in the post-war European market economies is sought, a number of other issues remain to be explored. Of fundamental importance is the extent to which agricultural and wider societal interests have been accommodated, given the specific directions and emphasis of agricultural policies.

An economic assessment of farm policies in the European market economies

Objectives and outcomes

The specific objectives stated for farm policy in different countries during the early post-war years show a remarkable degree of uniformity. For example, compare the terms of the FRG Agriculture Act 1955 (Tracy 1989: 224) with Article 39 of the Treaty of Rome (Harris et al 1983: 35), or a summary of EFTA farm policies (EFTA 1965: 10). All refer to the provision of a satisfactory standard of living for the agricultural population, and to the need for greater efficiency and market stability and the assurance of adequate supplies to consumers at reasonable prices. As with all such broad-brush statements, the combination of objectives embodied in these documents may in practice not be wholly compatible. In the case of the EC, for example, supplies were indeed guaranteed to consumers. Whether they were guaranteed at 'reasonable' prices is open to question.

The UK Agriculture Act 1947 embodied similar objectives, and on many criteria UK farm policy was a remarkable success. Unlike the approaches widely employed by Britain's continental neighbours, the system of deficiency payments ensured that consumers continued to benefit from cheap food, while at the same time cushioning farmers from international competition. Since the UK imported roughly half of its domestic food requirements, the cost to the exchequer of supporting domestic farmers could be kept within what were considered to be tolerable limits. Nevertheless, UK agriculture was not immune from the impact of technological progress and of the relative slowing of aggregate demand for food as incomes increased and population growth slowed. Agricultural productivity gains were also recorded in the economies from which the UK imported, especially the USA. Thus increasing supply availability and consequent downwards pressure on farm product prices produced a pattern over time which benefited consumers but increased the cost to the taxpayer of UK farm policy,[10] a tendency reinforced by the Agriculture Act 1957 which limited the extent to which the government could reduce aggregate support expenditures on a year-to-year basis. As time progressed, the prospect of transferring the burden of farm support from taxpayers to consumers became more attractive to governments conscious of public expenditure constraints. Membership of the EC and adoption of the CAP therefore became increasingly enticing from an agricultural policy point of view. The UK's eventual accession to the Community in 1973 marked the end of a quarter of a century of an approach to farm policy intervention which matched, for its individuality, the previous century of laissez-faire, and signalled the final synthesis of UK farm policy with the long-established traditions of trade-based intervention of its continental neighbours.

The fundamental reliance of the CAP on minimum import prices to maintain Community prices above world market levels amounted to a continuation of precisely those traditional instruments of policy. The extent to which Community prices have typically exceeded world levels has been the focus of frequent criticism of the intra-Community operation and international effects of the CAP.[11] In EC law agriculture was accorded a unique position, because Community budget expenditures on farm price support were obligatory and, for a long time, effectively open-ended for any products subject to intervention arrangements and offered by farmers for sale at the intervention price.[12] The more intervention stocks accumulated, the stronger were the signals that prices needed to fall to bring supply and demand into market-clearing equilibrium. However, with price support functioning as the main instrument of farm income support as before, and with net farm incomes continuing to lag behind non-farm incomes, public pressure for reductions in administered prices was vigorously resisted by farming interests.

Farm incomes and economic welfare

One crucial question concerns the extent to which net farm incomes were effectively assisted by price support for farm products. The overwhelming bulk of empirical evidence suggests that a constant rate of price support per unit produced is grossly inefficient as a method for increasing farm incomes (see, for example, Johnson 1991: ch. 9; Winters 1987; Harvey 1985). On this procedure financial assistance is directly correlated with volume of output, so that large-scale producers gain most. Yet these same producers are typically the ones best able to exploit any available economies of size. Moreover, it is evident that price support becomes capitalised into fixed asset values, notably land values. This in turn creates an inflationary spiral in land prices as the increased wealth of fortunate landowners is used as equity to secure funds to buy still more land from their less successful neighbours. Going one step further, non-farming landowners may benefit from a similar windfall gain, and oligopolistic industries which supply agriculture with inputs can also capture a share of farm support. Of course, none of these were intended to be the beneficiary of policies directed at helping farmers to improve their incomes. Their success in 'muscling in' on the CAP contributed to a cost–price squeeze in farming as agriculture's overall terms of trade with the rest of the economy declined (see Capstick 1983; Commission of the European Communities 1989: 53, Table G).

As the profit margin per unit of output fell, farmers adopted output-increasing technology in an effort to maintain farm net incomes through extra production.[13] With many innovations (such as the adoption of higher-yielding varieties of crops and livestock developed as a result of public investment) being virtually costless to farmers, productivity growth in agriculture was extremely rapid in the post-war period. For example, from 1970 until the introduction of production quotas in 1984, Community milk production increased by 2.5 per cent per year against a mere 0.5 per cent per year increase in consumption. Thus surpluses are attributable to the effects of both price support and technological progress. Going one step further, these surpluses, already accumulated at substantial budgetary cost, are typically disposed of on world markets with the additional financial assistance of export subsidies ('restitutions' in Community jargon), a practice understandably condemned as unfair trading by other agricultural exporters. Yet the instruments of price support taken by themselves cause distortions in the international trading system, by increasing the price inelasticity of supply of traded farm products for export and of import demand for the same. The result is a general lowering of world prices relative to free market levels, and increased price instability on world markets in the face of supply and demand fluctuations. Even when effects on third-party countries are ignored and the CAP is analysed solely in terms of its impact on the economic welfare of Community citizens, it is persuasively argued that, in aggregate, society incurs significant losses (see eg Buckwell et al 1982; Harvey and Thomson 1985).

Tensions and new directions in farm policy

Taken together, these observations confirm the foresight of the Community's first Agriculture Commissioner, Sicco Mansholt, who in the early stages of the setting-up of the CAP warned against reliance on price support rather than structural reform to assist farm incomes. Political considerations and the entrenched habits of the time no doubt weighed against acceptance of Mansholt's recommendations. Nevertheless, as we have seen, structural issues have remained an ever-present if secondary concern – witness the increased size of the average farm. In the late 1980s, furthermore, structural issues began to assume a new importance. The diversion of resources, especially land, from agricultural production has now come to the fore in the context of programmes addressing the environmental and overproduction problems associated with the industrialisation and intensification of agricultural practices. For example, land 'set-aside' programmes incorporate incentives for afforestation, conservation and rural amenity development. In those respects, structural policies now have a key role to play, as agricultural policy is transformed into a wider policy for rural resources, facilitated by new demands by society on the use of the countryside and a persistent need to constrain agricultural production (see eg Commission of the European Communities 1991a).

It is evident, however, that agricultural policies have often proved in practice contradictory in the structural, as in other contexts. On the one hand, there have been structural initiatives to encourage the reallocation of resources out of agriculture, while, on the other, price support has provided a counter-incentive to retain resources in farm production. The relative strength of these pressures is clearly signalled by the fact that expenditures on price support have never amounted to less than 95 per cent of the total Community farm budget, leaving, therefore, at most 5 per cent available for structural measures.[14] Initially, it was envisaged that *half* of all agricultural expenditures under the CAP would be devoted to structural reform (Duchêne et al 1985: 29).

While normal fluctuations in world economic conditions and the natural variations in the cycle of agricultural production have alternately placed the CAP in a state of financial crisis or respite, the dominant characteristic of the EC agricultural scene since 1960 has been a constant tendency for obligatory agricultural expenditures to inhibit adequate Community resourcing of other economic and social programmes. The CAP has persistently absorbed around two-thirds of all Community budget revenues. This, more than any other issue, has coloured the attitude of public opinion towards appropriate policy for the farm sector. We leave discussion of current prognostications about the future of the CAP to the final section of this chapter.

The socialisation of agriculture in Eastern Europe

At the time of the Second World War, agriculture in Eastern Europe outside the Soviet Union was characterised by the coexistence of very small farms and much larger estates, with a general pattern of highly concentrated land ownership, in what were predominantly agricultural economies. (Bulgaria, with a markedly egalitarian distribution of landholding, was an exception.) The smallest holdings, often the creation of the land reform programmes of the 1920s, were usually too small to offer an adequate family income when farmed full-time. Except for the regions which became the GDR, and for Czechoslovakia, a large proportion of the agricultural labour force was surplus to requirements and therefore potentially available for alternative employment.

Collectivisation

With the consolidation of Soviet hegemony over Eastern Europe after 1945, a transformation of farm ownership and organisation was initiated with the objective of socialising agriculture according to the model implemented in the Soviet Union in the 1930s. Key elements in the process included discrimination against the more wealthy or commercially oriented farmers termed in Stalinist rhetoric 'kulaks' ('fists'), and collectivisation based on modified versions of the Soviet Model Charter of 1935. Wädekin (1982: ch. 5) gives an account of the detailed provisions contained in the legislation of the various countries concerned. In broad summary, collectivisation was completed in Bulgaria by the late 1950s, and in Czechoslovakia, Hungary and Romania by the early 1960s. Albania completed the process in the mid-1960s with collectivisation of farmers in the mountainous areas. In contrast, the process of collectivisation was reversed in Yugoslavia in the early 1950s. In Poland the attempt to collectivise was abandoned after 1956.

In common with the Soviet practice of the early 1930s, collective farms in Eastern Europe could broadly be classified as 'higher type' and 'lower type', according to the extent to which peasants' farm resources and production activities were pooled. For example, the most informal arrangement in 'lower type' collectives involved the sharing of work effort in field cultivation and payment on the basis of labour contribution, with all resources otherwise left in private ownership. In the 'higher type', land and farm capital inputs including working animals were collectivised, while rights to a 'private' plot, its dimensions and permissible stocking, as well as labour obligations to the collective and the terms of wage payments, were all specified in detail.

In addition, state farms on which all resources, including land, were owned by the state were set up parallel to the collectives (which were, of course, technically farming co-operatives). State farm employees received salaries whereas collective farm workers depended to varying extents for their wages on the ability of farms to pay. Numerically, collective farms almost everywhere made up the majority of socialist farms, although typically state farms were substantially larger in terms of land area. Only in the Soviet Union did state farms eventually occupy the greater part of the total agricultural area, accounting for about half the total number of farms, this to a large extent as a result of the Virgin Lands campaign of the mid-1950s, which brought a vast new agricultural area into cultivation for the first time.

Political considerations

Again, while the broad thrust of policy was identical, differences between countries were observable. For example, from 1950 onwards there was only one form of collective – similar to the Soviet *kolkhoz* – in Bulgaria, while Romania maintained two forms until the mid-1950s. The remainder of the region was characterised mainly by the 'higher' and 'lower' types, with one or two transitory types in addition. Wädekin (1982) contrasts the path of collectivisation in the newly socialist countries with the earlier experience of the Soviet Union. While the objectives were ultimately the same, a more cautious policy was initially adopted in the smaller countries of Eastern Europe than had been pursued by Stalin in the late 1920s and early 1930s. For example, the terms 'reorganisation' and 'co-operation' everywhere replaced 'collectivisation', while 'collective farm' gave way to various terms suggestive of a production co-operative based on common work and ownership, save for a subsidiary plot and animals farmed by member households. The approach showed sensitivity to peasant attitudes while remaining geared to the achievement of longer-term political and economic goals. Given the tenuous basis for their political authority, the new socialist regimes could not afford to offend majority peasant populations, particularly in the light of the food shortages of the immediate post-war years. A too aggressive stance by new governments might have provoked a comparable reaction from the agricultural population, increasing still further the disruption to agricultural production which in any event could be expected as an unwelcome by-product of radical reorganisation in farming. Presumably some lessons were learnt from the devastating effects of forced collectivisation in the Soviet Union (see Nove 1969: ch. 7).

Although the Soviet Union alone had nationalised all land outright, the legal distinction between state and voluntarily collectivised land in other countries was in practice ultimately of small significance. While individual peasants technically remained owners of property pooled for collective use, and typically maintained the right to leave a collective if they wished, rights of transfer of property were so constrained that any notion of real private ownership and freedom of action became meaningless. No doubt other subtle pressures were also brought to bear on peasants who showed reluctance to conform. In at least one regard collectivisation across the greater part of Eastern Europe could have been expected to proceed more smoothly than in the Soviet Union – inasmuch as Soviet forces could be used to suppress any civil protest in occupied countries. The eventual abandonment by Yugoslavia and Poland of collectivisation was as much a reflection of changes in political relationships with the Soviet Union in the late 1940s and early–mid-1950s as of any special concern to make concessions to agriculture.

Land reform and economic development

The fact remains, however, that in many respects the objectives of collectivisation in Eastern Europe were closely analogous to those that had been pursued in the Soviet Union. For Eastern Europe, the collectivisation campaign marked a second land reform which was both more effective and enduring than those stemming from legislation introduced after the First World War had been. In the first stage the large estates and larger peasant holdings (the latter typically of between 20 and 50 hectares, but larger in Hungary and parts of Poland) were affected. Some 20 million hectares were redistributed to 65 million small peasant households and landless agricultural workers. Russian peasants had in 1917 expropriated land on the grounds that ownership should rest with those who tilled the soil. Here the same spirit was encouraged by governments. Typically, and Wädekin argues intentionally, the vast majority of the newly created holdings were unviable. Once procurement quotas were imposed for the delivery of farm products to the state, ample scope was provided for imposing intolerable burdens on peasant holdings – particularly those of the 'kulaks' – implicitly exerting pressure in favour of collective farming which, needless to say, benefited from far more favourable treatment.

Similarly, new state and collective farms were given priority in the allocation of scarce machinery, fertiliser, and other input supplies from outside the farm sector. Planned 'material supply' necessarily followed the abolition of markets and the imposition of a price system which had an accounting function but no primary role in guiding resource allocation. The exploitation of agriculture provided a source of much-needed capital for an industrial sector which, with certain exceptions, remained very underdeveloped. But there was no parallel in Eastern Europe to the political dramas of the revolutionary period and the period of collectivisation in the Soviet Union. To a large extent the East European peasantry remained isolated from the political turmoil of the immediate post-1945 period. Moreover, any notion that class conflicts among the peasantry could be exploited through the pitting of impoverished peasants against 'kulaks' was shown to be grounded in a gross oversimplification of reality.

Back to politics

Sokolovsky (1991) considers that the political relationship between the Soviet Union and client states, or rather governments, was a crucial factor in determining the course of collectivisation. Beyond that, however, the special circumstances of each country and region came through strongly. In general terms, the new regimes sought national legitimacy initially on the basis of the loyal support of a relatively small urban working class and intelligentsia. But to cement this it was essential to provide improvements in standards of living, and particularly in food supplies. Collectivisation of the more productive farming areas could logically be seen as the most rapid route to increased food production, even if these areas were not those showing the highest degree of class antagonism. In Poland, especially, the availability of land confiscated from German ownership in the western districts facilitated the creation of collective farms under population resettlement policies. Those who benefited had more reason for loyalty to the government than peasants elsewhere. However, all of the agricultural population suffered in the face of exploitative policies to force the release of resources for industrialisation.[15] Wherever possible, the peasantry retreated into a subsistence-oriented pattern of production despite threats of severe punishment by the state authorities. Thus a community of peasant interests was forged even in areas where different groups within the peasantry might otherwise have been antagonistic to one another.

As food supplies deteriorated, a more liberal attitude was taken towards the peasantry. Poland exemplifies this point, with the almost total retreat from collectivisation in the mid-1950s. In the 1980s some three-quarters of the Polish agricultural area was still in small-scale private peasant ownership (World Bank 1990). Elsewhere, Hungary's economic dependence on agriculture also provoked a move away from collectivisation on the Stalinist model, associated particularly with the 1968 New Economic Mechanism which generally released the economy from the most extreme excesses of central planning (see Hare, Chapter 9 in *The National Economies of Europe* on Hungary; Berend 1990). Bulgaria followed the Soviet approach most closely, invoking the idea of violent class struggle despite having, in practice, one of the most equal rural class structures in all of Eastern Europe. Here, the economy was highly dependent on agriculture, and so control of the sector was effectively synonymous with command over the resource base for industrialisation. In Czechoslovakia, as in Bulgaria and Hungary, collectivisation was initially implemented to a significant extent by force. In other respects Czechoslovakia was markedly different from Bulgaria and Hungary, both because of its already advanced level of industrialisation, and also because the Communist Party had considerable support in the countryside.

In summary, then, the Eastern European countries responded to the Soviet-inspired drive for collectivisation in ways that reflected their individual circumstances. Not least important, amidst all the elements of Stalinist coercion, were domestic political considerations which acknowledged both the circumstances of the moment and the need to have regard for the established values and traditional attitudes of rural people in the countries concerned.

Consequences of socialist policies for farm production and resource use

The framework for decision-making

By contrast with the pattern in the European market economies, active political intervention in the economy was the hallmark of the East European socialist regimes. This meant, in practice, the engagement of the Communist Party apparatus at all levels of decision-making. Formally, the institutions of government (ministries, planning agencies and so on) existed as entities distinct from the Party, but they were nevertheless always permeated by its influence. In the absence of markets, marginalised if not completely abandoned as a system for resource allocation, centralised planning became the rule. In its most developed form, exemplified in the Soviet Union, national objectives for agricultural production were progressively disaggregated down to the level of individual farms. In parallel, decisions were made about the allocation of resources necessary to support production targets. Necessarily, the allocation of inputs to agriculture which originated from outside the farm sector, notably machinery and also fertiliser, involved correspondingly complex decisions about the acquisition and disposition of raw materials and components to the firms manufacturing those inputs. In addition, and particularly during the 1950s, individual farms received detailed instructions about the delivery of output to state agencies, areas to be sown to different crops, herd sizes and composition, and timing and execution of land cultivation and harvesting.

The formidable demands these requirements imposed on data acquisition and information provision at all levels of the administrative hierarchy helped to assure the burgeoning of an extensive and complex bureaucracy, and obviously courted the danger of ineffectual top-heaviness. Yet in some respects the reorganisation of farming and the wider economy into large-scale production units may, indeed, have facilitated the imposition of purposive political and economic control. For example, the majority of the East European countries followed the Soviet example in creating *machine-tractor stations* or their equivalent. At a time of acute capital shortage, the provision of machinery services exclusively through specialist agencies from which farms hired according to need would appear, other things being equal, to have been an efficient approach to allocating scarce resources. The alternative – leaving individual farms to acquire their own machines under conditions of extreme scarcity and lack of funds – might have left some farms with no access to machinery services whatsoever. Similarly, the freedom enjoyed by government to direct resources and production in accordance with specified plans for economic growth and development should, in principle, have assured a more rapid and predictable response than would have market-led adjustments. In any event, markets would have been extremely unlikely to generate a pattern of production and resource allocation consistent with the objectives set by central planners.

Advantages of central planning

There is, indeed, some evidence of the superiority of central planning over the unhindered operation of markets where rapid economic change is a policy objective. For example, under Khrushchev the Soviet Union embarked on an ambitious campaign to improve the availability of livestock products for human consumption. This involved the transfer of large tracts of land previously devoted to cereals production onto the cultivation of maize for livestock feed. Simultaneously, the Virgin Lands campaign launched in 1956 saw the opening up of new productive areas on a scale and at a pace unprecedented in history. The total area sown by Soviet agricultural organisations – 375 million hectares in 1955 – had risen to 522 million hectares by 1965, finally stabilising at around 555 million hectares by the 1980s.[16]

Czechoslovakia presents another example. Almost 90 per cent of the agricultural land of that country had been collectivised by 1961. A largely successful campaign for the industrialisation of agriculture was then launched to cope with farm labour shortages and, it was hoped, lead towards total national self-sufficiency in food production. Agriculture was given priority for investment, especially in relation to grain production, and this included a massive increase in fertiliser use and mechanisation. All this came after five years during which a doubling of agricultural investment had been brought to nought by poor management, low motivation, passive resistance in the work-force, with the consequent waste and inefficiency ensuring that a low positive growth rate in agricultural production had become negative by the turn of the 1960s (Hajda 1979).

A decade of partial reforms

Nevertheless, economic success founded exclusively on the commitment to production of increasing quantities of output through the absorption of ever greater quantities of resources ultimately proved unsustainable. In contrast to the extremely rapid recovery of agricultural production in the advanced European market economies, Eastern Europe found itself at the end of the 1950s and the beginning of the 1960s still affected by shortages of almost all agricultural products. It is against this background that we must seek to assess the wave of agricultural reforms implemented simultaneously in the

Soviet Union and its East European neighbours from *c* 1965 (Wädekin 1982: ch. 11). Substantial organisational rationalisation was sought in what was to remain fundamentally a centrally planned economic system. The role of direct administrative manipulation was diminished, and an enhanced role given to prices, profit, and the payment of various premia (for example, for above-quota output) in the farm economy. In addition, a greater role in decision-taking was granted to collective and state farm workers themselves. The hierarchy of management then in place was typically reorganised and simplified from four levels down to three – central management, brigades or sections, and work groups – with more scope at the grass-roots level for individual and group responsibility in undertaking work tasks of one kind or another. Romania and, to some extent, Bulgaria, it should be said, remained outside this pattern.

Hungary followed the most radical course of reform. The New Economic Mechanism of 1968 introduced some elements of a market economy and set a course for economic policy which from that point on distinguished Hungary sharply from its Soviet bloc neighbours. In agriculture, state and co-operative farms were declared of equal status, and state investment in the co-operatives was increased. Co-operatives were now allowed to decide what to produce and to buy and own machinery, and also to negotiate their own contracts with state enterprises. Prices were deregulated for many products at the same time as specific incentives were introduced to produce output for export. In response, fertiliser use increased by 150 per cent 1968–75, and grain production rose by 80 per cent during the 1970s with wheat yields more than doubling. For the first time since 1945, Hungary became a net exporter of grain, while production and consumption of both meat and vegetables increased simultaneously. Another important feature of this transformation was the attitude adopted towards household plots. These were now recognised as an integral part of the national agricultural economy, interacting with the collective sector which could provide inputs and function as a sales outlet. Important in all the East European countries with collectivised agricultural systems, private plots continued in Hungary to play an absolutely central role in the production of labour-intensive livestock products, fruit and vegetables. For example, in 1976 more than half of Hungary's total output of pork products was produced in the private subsidiary sector (Volgyes 1980).[17]

In the GDR, large-scale, capital-intensive agriculture was developed through the 1960s. Under Soviet influence a system of monoculture was imposed over extensive areas of land. Yet despite achieving relatively favourable yields compared to socialist bloc neighbours, GDR agriculture could never match the success of that of the FRG. In the Soviet Union, finally, notwithstanding steps towards a more rational approach to the pricing of farm products and inputs, inadvisable practices such as the excessive cultivation of grain in semi-arid areas (mainly in the Virgin Lands region) took a heavy toll in the 1960s. The fall of Khrushchev was partly occasioned by his failure to solve the problem of agricultural inefficiency. Then followed the Brezhnev era, now taken to be almost synonomous with general economic stagnation. In fact, the early Brezhnev period, 1965–73, was characterised by sensible policies and impressive growth performance in agriculture. Increasingly, however, as the Brezhnev regime became more and more conservative, solutions to continued problems of production performance were sought in large-scale capital investment rather than in systemic change. From 1965 to the mid-1980s Soviet agriculture's capital stock increased four-fold at the cost of imposing a huge debt burden on the farm sector. Much of the investment was in dubious land-improvement schemes which often did agricultural production more harm than good.

An economic assessment of farm policies in Eastern Europe

Despite the attempts at reform during the 1960s, serious inefficiencies continued to impair performance throughout Eastern European agriculture. Although these are currently being considered in the context of farm policies, it is essential to stress that they are simply one aspect of a drama of attempted systemic reform which touched all aspects of the socialist economy. Because the drama is best exemplified by the case of the Soviet Union, we use material from that country to illustrate how the general economic problems which arise under central planning impinged on agriculture (see also Dyker, Chapter 12 on the Soviet Union in *The National Economies of Europe*).

Soft budget constraints and irrational prices

Enterprises in centrally planned economies typically operate under conditions of what Kornai (1980) has called 'soft budget constraints'. What that means is that there are few, if any, financial penalties associated with excessive expenditures on inputs, because the state simply covers financial losses, *ex post* if not *ex ante*. A corollary of soft budget constraints is that producers regard input prices as tending to zero, which creates excess demand for those inputs and shortages, and consequently stockpiling of durable resources whenever an opportunity arises. Of course, stockpiling further aggravates shortages because it 'locks up' resources which otherwise would be transformed into final products. Poznanski (1988), however, argues that it is not the soft budget constraint in itself which is the critical factor explaining the scale of the inefficiency problem, but rather the absence of a bankruptcy sanction. For example, Cook (1990) notes that in 1988 only 37 state and collective farms (out of more than 25,000) were declared bankrupt in the Russian Republic, in the face of generalised insolvency reflected in the massive accumulated debt burden.

If soft budget constraints lead to 'soft prices', this merely conspires with another serious limitation of the price system as it operated in the East European socialist economies, namely that prices determined by the state tended to be fixed for long periods, and so could not reflect changing supply and demand conditions and relative valuations as they do in a market economy. For example, in the Soviet Union the retail price of bread remained unchanged from 1940 to 1986, that of butter from 1970 to 1986, and of vegetable oils from 1960 to 1986 (Pavlov 1987: 19). For staple food commodities, low fixed retail prices were meant to serve to ensure that supplies in sufficient quantities were within reach of consumers' budgets. But, of course, if administered retail prices are set too low, excess demand is reflected in shortages and in the existence of black markets. The concern about potential famine in the Soviet Union during the winter of 1990–91 flowed as much from suspicions that black marketeers were selling off at high prices supplies diverted from state outlets, as from evidence of absolute shortages. The fact that prices function only as coefficients of account and have no primary role in resource allocation decisions under central planning explains why, in agriculture, it has been possible for farm costs of production to exceed the 'value' of farm output, and for that, in turn, to exceed its equivalent valuation at retail level. But while central planning can tolerate such incongruities, their long-term resource-allocational and budgetary implications are insidious indeed (see Dyker, Chapter 12 on the Soviet Union in *The National Economies of Europe*).

Quality and technological change

The interaction of target planning, soft budget constraints and irrational pricing also ensures that, in the shortage economy which these conditions engender, producers can be sure of selling their output almost irrespective of quality, and that anyone who risks disrupting the pattern of plan fulfilment for the sake of innovation is almost automatically penalised. It is *de rigueur* either to consume what is available or nothing at all, and to continue producing what has always been produced. Some indication of the magnitude of this problem in relation to agricultural inputs can be gained from the case of fertilisers. A four-fold increase in deliveries of chemical fertiliser to Soviet agriculture from the mid-1960s to the mid-1980s made little impact on production trends, despite an application rate per hectare which, by the early 1980s, exceeded US levels by around 10 per cent. Sagers and Shabad (1990) explain part of the poor yield response in terms of poorly balanced supply and application of nitrogen, potassium and phosphates. Such constituents have been produced in extremely rudimentary form, and the ability of the agrochemicals sector to manufacture complex granules is still in the early stages of development in the Soviet Union/CIS. In addition, techniques of fertiliser application have remained crude, and this, together with inadequate storage and transportation facilities, has contributed to extensive input losses. Clearly, evidence of a relatively poor and worsening situation for total factor productivity in Soviet agriculture compared to Western agriculture (see eg Brooks and Johnson 1983; Wong 1986) is explained not only by inefficiencies on Soviet farms, but also by the gross inadequacies of the wider food chain, inadequacies conditioned by the same systemic failures of central planning as those of agriculture itself.

Finally, and by no means least important, it must be borne in mind that since the price mechanism has no allocative function under central planning, that function has had instead to be undertaken by a complex arrangement, periodically rearranged, of planning bureaucracies. Crucially, the more varied and sophisticated an economy becomes, the less possible it is to impose effective co-ordination and control by bureaucratic means. The almost comically disastrous history of Gorbachev's State Agro-Industrial Committee (Gosagroprom), created in 1985 and abolished in 1989, graphically illustrates how an intended instrument of reform can turn into a new, and yet more terrible, monster of bureaucracy. The argument, therefore, that the economic revolution of recent years in the Soviet Union/CIS and Eastern Europe reflects a straightforward failure of attempts to improve economic performance by making adjustments within the framework of central planning is as cogent in relation to agriculture as it is at the more general level. General recognition of the need to return to a system based on private, family farms had at time of writing still not produced a comprehensive reform on the ground in the countries of Eastern Europe in which the collective farm system has been dominant without being efficient. We must expect, however, that the early 1990s will see a rebirth of the family farm over an area stretching from Thuringia to the Urals.

European agriculture since 1945: overview and prospects

Since 1945 European agriculture has been subjected to extensive government intervention in one form or another. In the West, intervention has been largely directed towards assuring food supplies and assisting farm incomes, in the main through the method of farm price support. In the East, by contrast, intervention has been a dimension of the pursuit of wider political and economic objectives under a Soviet-dominated socialist system, in which agriculture has been expected not only to assure food supplies, but also to provide a foundation for much-needed economic development. The tendency for farm incomes to fall relative to non-farm incomes in the market economies is a direct consequence of economic development. Thus agriculture in post-war Europe has followed the path which the sector is conventionally expected to take during the development process. First, it provides the resources on which industrialisation is based; and, second, as development proceeds, it assumes a less and less important position in the national economy. (By 1988 agriculture accounted for just 3 per cent of the aggregate GDP of the EEC 12: Commission of the European Communities 1991b.)

Attempts in Eastern Europe to achieve this transformation through planning and coercion rather than market forces ultimately restricted the contribution agriculture was able to make. The Soviet Union demonstrates this principle in its most extreme form, as agriculture instead became increasingly dependent on capital transfers from the rest of the economy, a complete reversal of the normal development process. Rather than evincing an economic dynamism expressed through capital accumulation, resource redeployment and accelerating technological progress, the Soviet economy epitomised in 1991 the condition of increasing economic paralysis and decay. Only Hungary of the USSR's socialist bloc neighbours had achieved some greater measure of progress, by the skilful inclusion of a quasi-market system within a planned economy. Even in the unique circumstances of Polish agriculture, still dominated by small-scale peasant farmers, reliance by farmers on state monopolies for provision of key purchased inputs and as outlets for products entrapped farmers in an inescapable snare of inefficiency. In summary, therefore, the centralised direction of production and resource allocation, and the concomitant suppression of the market mechanism, ultimately proved unsustainable throughout East European agriculture.

In the European market economies, the predominant contemporary view is that government intervention for agriculture has similarly failed, though for quite different reasons from those operative in Eastern Europe. First, it is generally held that attempts to increase farm incomes by supporting the unit prices of farm products is grossly inefficient. As has been seen, most support goes to those farmers who need it least. To make matters worse, the market system operates to allow owners of fixed assets and oligopolistic suppliers of inputs purchased by farmers to capture a share of the benefits. Consumers suffer economic welfare losses, and extensive empirical evidence points unequivocally to the heavy net burden imposed on society as a whole. The EEC and a number of non-EEC countries, notably the USA, have also grown increasingly aware of the budgetary consequences of farm support. High costs are incurred in buying in surplus farm products. But in addition a further budgetary burden is generated by the competitive subsidisation of the disposal of surpluses on world markets. It is not surprising, then, that the effects of domestic farm policies have become a matter of major international concern.

At time of writing (late 1991) the outcome of the General Agreement on Tariffs and Trade (GATT) Uruguay Round of world trade negotiations rested on the resolution of conflicts of interest focusing on agriculture. There is general agreement now that the instruments of domestic farm policies commonly distort prices, and therefore commodity flows, on international agricultural markets. The political problem for the EC in particular is how to move away from the existing methods of farm support by a route which will introduce market disciplines to constrain overproduction, while protecting vulnerable sections of the farm population at acceptable levels of budgetary expenditure. At long last the European market economies are being forced to realise the full economic costs of pursuing inadvisable farm policies. It must be recognised in this context that prospects for reform are greatly enhanced by the fact that, in Northern Europe at least, agriculture itself has become a relatively small and industrialised component of an advanced industrial (or even post-industrial) economy. Farm policies may conceivably have slowed economic development and agricultural shrinkage, but they have prevented neither.

For the time being at least, security of European food supplies has been achieved, to a large extent as a result of agriculture's exploitation of industrial capital resources and know-how made available through general economic development. European society currently enjoys the benefits of agricultural abundance and no longer regards the countryside environment as the sole preserve of farmers and food production. Recreation, amenity and environmental conservation are relatively new demands on the use of countryside resources. To the extent that farmers contribute to the provision of such public goods by agricultural activities, government assistance may be desirable. However, it is increasingly recognised that such assistance must be in the form of direct income support payments and not, as in the past, tied by a price support formula to the volume of production.

Finally, in so far as agriculture remains a vital activity in less developed areas of the European market economies, current trends must favour the convergence of agricultural and regional development policies. In December 1991 a series of bilateral agreements were signed between the EC and Poland, Czechoslovakia and Hungary, which set out a programme for the achievement of free trade between the Community and each of the three East-Central European countries over a ten-year period, leading eventually to full membership of the Community for the East-Central European Three. The agreements should come into force on a provisional basis in March 1992. Needless to say, they include special protocols on agriculture, and there are no immediate prospects for a total freeing up of agricultural trade between the EC and the Three. But the long-term implication is a huge increase in the relative weight of those less developed parts of the EC such as can only hasten convergence of agricultural and regional policies.

Notes

1 Intervention began, in principle, with the passage of the Import Duties Act and establishment of agricultural producer marketing boards in the 1930s. In practice, imperial preference undermined the effectiveness of these early measures.
2 For information on the development of agricultural extension services in other countries see Penders 1957 and Davies 1963.
3 Agriculture's share in total employment in 1950 and 1988 respectively was: 23.0 and 6.3 in Denmark; 28.3 and 6.8 in France; 24.7 and 4.3 in West Germany; 47 and 15.4 in Ireland; 41 and 9.9 in Italy; 14.1 and 4.8 in the Netherlands; and 6 and 2.2 in the UK.
4 Cf France, with agriculture accounting for 26 per cent of employment and 14 per cent of national income at this time. Corresponding figures for Germany and the UK respectively are 15 per cent and 11 per cent; and 5 per cent and 5 per cent.
5 The progressive fragmentation of farm holdings over successive generations is explained by the post-feudal evolution of cultural and legal attitudes towards rights of inheritance, combined with nineteenth-century French imperial influence in Europe.
6 Average farm size in 1960 was 32 hectares in the UK, compared with 17 hectares in France, 9.3 hectares in Germany, 9.9 hectares in the Netherlands and 17.1 hectares in Ireland. By 1987 these figures had evolved to, respectively, 68.9, 30.7, 17.6, 17.2 and 22.7 hectares. See Commission of the European Communities, *The Agricultural Situation in the Community* (annual), Brussels and Luxembourg, various issues.
7 For definitive statements of those opinions see Venn 1933: 308ff; Cochrane 1979: 120.
8 For a concise review of the impact of the CAP see Commission of the European Communities 1987.
9 Of the original six member countries, the Netherlands was also in search of new export markets – in this case for dairy products.
10 This was not Britain's first experience of such a problem. A guaranteed price system for wheat, oats and potatoes was in operation from 1917 to 1921, at which point it was abandoned because of a rapid escalation in the cost to the exchequer.
11 Especially since 1979, when the EEC graduated to second place after the USA as an exporter of temperate agricultural products.
12 In effect, an intervention price functions as a minimum guaranteed price at which farmers can sell to an agency authorised to hold stocks whenever the balance of supply and demand is such that free market prices would be lower.
13 This behaviour is consistent with Cochrane's concept of the 'agricultural treadmill', or, more accurately in this context, the 'treadmill with cannibalism' (see Cochrane 1979: ch. 19).
14 Following the application of budgetary discipline after 1988 and the provision of additional funds for structural measures, the share of expenditures under the guidance heading in the total expenditure of the European Agricultural Guarantee and Guidance Fund was expected to exceed 5 per cent in 1990. (See Commission of the European Communities 1991b: Table 84.)
15 This involved the use of well-established, Soviet-style procedures such as compulsory delivery quotas, penal taxation, low product prices and high input prices.
16 The increment to the sown area was equal in size to 'the entire cultivated area of Canada, or to that of France, the UK, West Germany, Belgium and Scandinavia taken together' (Hedlund 1989: 6).
17 In the Soviet Union the private subsidiary sector, farmed by both peasants and other

workers, has continued in recent years to contribute around 25 per cent of total agricultural output on the basis of 2 per cent of the agricultural land stock. Of course these plots have been to a large extent dependent on the state/collective sector for provision of inputs. See Wädekin 1973 and Hedlund 1989.

References

Bellerby J R (1956) *Agriculture and Industry Relative Income*. Macmillan

Berend I T (1990) *The Hungarian Economic Reforms, 1953–1988*. Cambridge University Press

Brooks K, Johnson J G (1983) *Prospects for Soviet Agriculture in the 1980s*. Indiana University Press, Bloomington

Buckwell A E, Harvey D R, Thomson K J, Parton K A (1982) *The Costs of the Common Agricultural Policy*. Croom Helm

Capstick C W (1983) Agricultural policy issues and economic analyses. *Journal of Agricultural Economics* **34**(3): 263–77

Cochrane W W (1979) *The Development of American Agriculture: A Historical Analysis*. University of Minnesota Press, Minneapolis

Commission of the European Communities (1987) Twenty years of European agriculture. *Green Europe* (**217**) (reprinted from *The Agricultural Situation in the Community* 1986 report) Brussels/Luxembourg

Commission of the European Communities (1989) *The Agricultural Situation in the Community* 1988 report. Brussels/Luxembourg

Commission of the European Communities (1991a) The development and future of the Common Agricultural Policy: proposals of the Commission. *Green Europe* February: Brussels/Luxembourg

Commission of the European Communities (1991b) *The Agricultural Situation in the Community* 1990 report. Brussels/Luxembourg

Cook E C (1990) Reforming Soviet agriculture: problems with farm finances and equity considerations. In Moskoff W (ed) *Perestroika in the Countryside: Agricultural Reform in the Gorbachev Era*. M.E. Sharpe Inc, White Plains, New York

Czizmadia E, Székely M (1986) *Food Economy in Hungary*. Akadémiai Kiadó, Budapest

Davies A J (1963) Survey of developments in agricultural advisory services in Europe and North America since 1960. In OECD (1963) *Agricultural Advisory Services in Europe and North America*. Paris

Duchêne F, Szczepanik E, Legg W (1985) *New Limits on European Agriculture: Politics and the Common Agricultural Policy*. Rowman and Allenheld for the Atlantic Institute for International Affairs

European Free Trade Association (EFTA) (1965) *Agriculture in EFTA*. Geneva

Hajda J (1979) The politics of agricultural collectivisation and modernisation in Czechoslovakia. In Francisco R A, Laird B A, Laird R D (eds) *The Political Economy of Collectivised Agriculture* Pergamon Press, New York

Harris S, Swinbank A, Wilkinson G (1983) *The Food and Farm Policies of the European Community*. John Wiley

Harvey D R (1985) The CAP: cornerstone or stumbling block? Paper presented to *Agro-Europe Conference*, Reading University

Harvey D R, Thomson K J (1985) Costs, benefits and the future of the Common Agricultural Policy. *Journal of Common Market Studies* Autumn: 1–20

Hedlund S (1989) *Private Agriculture in the Soviet Union*. Routledge

Johnson D G (1991) *World Agriculture in Disarray* 2nd edn. Macmillan for the Trade Policy Research Centre, London

Kornai J (1980) *Economics of Shortage*. North-Holland Publishing Company, Amsterdam, New York and Oxford

Medvedev Z A (1987) *Soviet Agriculture*. W.W. Norton, New York and London

Nove A (1969) *An Economic History of the USSR* 1st edn. Penguin

Nove A (1986) *The Soviet Economic System* 3rd edn. Allen & Unwin

OECD (1964) *Low Incomes in Agriculture: Problems and Policies*. Paris

OECD (1967) *Agricultural Policies in 1966*. Paris

OECD (1975) *Review of Agricultural Policies: General Survey*. Paris

OECD (1983) *Review of Agricultural Policies in OECD Member Countries, 1980–1982*. Paris

OEEC (1956) *Agricultural Policies in Europe and North America* First Report of the Ministerial Committee for Agriculture and Food. Paris

OEEC (1958) *Third Report on the Agricultural Policies in Europe and North America*. Paris

OEEC (1960) *Further Problems in Agricultural Policy*. Paris

Pavlov V (1987) *Overhauling the Entire System of Prices*. Novosti Press Agency Publishing House

Penders J M A (1957) Summary review of developments in agricultural advisory services in Europe. In OEEC (1957) *Agricultural Advisory Services in Europe and North America*. Paris

Poznanski P Z (1988) The CPE aversion to innovations. *Economics of Planning* 22(3): 136–45

Sagers M J, Shabad T (1990) *The Chemical Industry in the USSR: An Economic Geography*. Westview Press, Boulder, Col.

Singer H, Wood J, Jennings T (1987) *Food Aid: The Challenge and the Opportunity*. Clarendon Press

Sokolovsky J (1991) *Peasants and Power: State Autonomy and the Collectivization of Agriculture in Eastern Europe*. Westview Press, Boulder, Col.

Tracy M (1989) *Government and Agriculture in Western Europe, 1880–1988* 3rd edn. Harvester/ Wheatsheaf

Venn J A (1933) *The Foundations of Agricultural Economics*. Cambridge University Press

Volgyes J (1980) Dynamic change: rural transformation, 1945–1975. In Held J (ed) *The Modernization of Agriculture: Rural Transformation in Hungary, 1848–1975*. Columbia University Press, New York

Wädekin K E (1973) *The Private Sector in Soviet Agriculture*. University of California Press, Berkeley

Wädekin K E (1982) *Agrarian Policies in Communist Europe. A Critical Introduction*. Allenheld, Osmin & Martinus Nijhoff, The Hague and London

Winters A (1987) The economic consequences of agricultural support: a survey. *OECD Economic Studies* (9) Autumn

Wong L F (1986) *Agricultural Productivity in the Socialist Countries*. Westview Press, Boulder, Col.

World Bank (1990) *An Agricultural Strategy for Poland*. Report of the Polish/European Community/World Bank Task Force. Washington DC

Index